D1358376

THE ULTIMATE JOB BOOK

DAVID R. EYLER

RANDOM HOUSE
REFERENCE

The Ultimate Job Book
Copyright © 2002 by David R. Eyler

All rights reserved under International and Pan-American Copyright Conventions. No part of this book may be reproduced in any form or by any means, electronic or mechanical, including photocopying, without the written permission of the publisher. All inquiries should be addressed to Random House Reference, Random House, Inc., 1745 Broadway, New York, NY, 10019. Published in the United States by Random House, Inc., New York and simultaneously in Canada by Random House of Canada Limited.

This book is comprised of revised material from *Job Interviews That Mean Business, Third Edition* © 1999, 1996, 1993, 1990 by David R. Eyler, and *Resumes That Mean Business, Third Edition, Edition* © 1999, 1996, 1993, 1990 by David R. Eyler.

Visit the Random House Reference Web site at
www.randomwords.com

Typeset and printed in the United States of America.

Library of Congress Cataloging-in-Publication data:
Eyler, David R.
    The ultimate job book / by David R. Eyler.
        p. cm.
    "This book is comprised of revised material from Job Interviews that mean business, third edition © 1999 . . . and Resumes that mean business, third edition . . . © 1999"—Copyright p.
    Includes bibliographical references and index.
    ISBN 0-375-71988-1 (alk. paper)
    1. Résumés (Employment) 2. Employment interviewing. I. Eyler, David R. Job interviews that means business. II. Eyler, David R. Resumes that means business. III. Title.

    HF5383 .E95 2002
    650.14—dc21   2002068265

0 9 8 7 6 5 4 3 2 1
December 2002

ISBN: 0-375-71988-1

New York   Toronto   London   Sydney   Auckland

CONTENTS

INTRODUCTION

Getting a new job can be a frustrating experience. One of the few certainties in the job market is the enormous volume of human traffic entering and leaving it on a daily basis. The average American worker changes jobs a number of times in the course of a career, and while it was certainly an anomaly, the aftermath of the events of September 11, when hundreds of thousands of people were thrown out of work, demonstrates only too clearly how precarious employment can be. But the rewards of finding the right job, whether measured materially or emotionally, are enormous.

You can have a more successful job search by studying the entire process, understanding the role you play as the hiring sequence unfolds, and preparing effectively. The purpose of this book is to inform—to give you the benefit of many examples and much comparison among candidates experiencing the various situations that may be encountered in the job search process.

Whether you are an entry-level applicant searching for your first job or a mid-career executive looking for a six-figure salary, your chances of successfully applying for a new position depend largely on your power to communicate such vital information as your:

- Ability to do the job
- Appreciation for what the hiring company does
- Aspirations that are compatible with the position
- Awareness of job requirements
- Motivation to succeed

- Potential value to your new employer
- Relevant preparation for the position

All employers want assurance that you can meet these tests. The first opportunity you have to demonstrate your suitability is with your resume. You should be able to establish your credentials on paper clearly, succinctly, and in a convincing manner—preferably in one or two pages. If your resume is successful, you will be asked to attend a job interview. Getting the job, therefore, calls for top-flight resume writing and job interviewing skills and an appreciation for what the hiring official wants to know.

This book is a pragmatic, one-stop guide to the preparation of winning resumes and masterful interviewing, and also to the other elements of the hiring process such as cover letters, networking, research, and legal issues. We have revised and combined two successful books, *Resumes That Mean Business* and *Job Interviews That Mean Business*. The result is a single comprehensive "how to" book, from which you will choose the parts that are the most important and useful to you in your particular situation. Still, most of the information will be helpful to all people.

Eighty actual model resumes give you gut-level insights into what you should emphasize and what you should leave unsaid. Each resume is graphically critiqued to show you ideal resume length, format, and weighting of detail—what is really needed to bring your resume out of the stack. Example after example will show you how to convey meaningful knowledge—of what the employer does, what he or she needs to have done, and why you are the person to do it.

The job interview section follows the sequence of the actual hiring cycle, giving you advice on:

- How to find a job
- How to get an interview
- How to prepare for the interview
- How to arrive and present yourself for the interview
- What to say and not say during the interview
- What to do and not do during the interview
- How to interpret the messages sent by the interviewer
- How to link the entire interview cycle into a smooth and complete presentation of your assets
- How to avoid surprises—and deal with the ones that come anyway
- What kinds of questions to expect from your interviewer

- What to ask your interviewer
- How to enhance the impact of your interview by networking
- How to follow up effectively
- How to negotiate salary and terms of employment

Supporting chapters provide you with essential information on:

- Technology and the Job Search
- Using the Internet
- Working and the Law
- Special Situations
- Accommodating Forced Career Changes

The objective is to guide you through the entire hiring process, providing examples of a wide range of the very best resumes and most useful job interviewing guidance. From the moment you express interest to your acceptance of the job offer, this book will help you take your next step up the career ladder.

In the end it is you, the candidate, who must decide just what combination of substance and methodology makes the best case for your particular talents. The judge who counts most is the interviewer, human resources professional, line manager, or CEO who, after reading your resume and conducting your interview, decides if you are the right person for the job. But *The Ultimate Job Book* is your personal tutor to help you exit the hiring process with the position you want.

David R. Eyler
deyler@att.net
Weyers Cave, Virginia
December 2002

PREPARING A WINNING RESUME

1

RESUME BASICS

Your resume has a purpose. It must impress potential employers sufficiently for them to consider you further in the hiring process. It is the document that—in one or two pages—represents everything you have done to become desirable in the employment marketplace. Salary, security, and career satisfaction all depend on the job you hold. Your resume shows where you have been professionally and where you are qualified to go next.

The preparation and presentation of a resume is part of the standard job application process. It is at once a challenge and a great opportunity to make a favorable impression. Before you have met your potential employers, images and expectations are formed in the minds of those who will judge your worthiness. Your resume makes those first impressions.

Why Your Resume Is Important

The hiring official is probably considering dozens, even hundreds, of applications along with yours. Equal opportunity regulations, modern communications, and highly mobile lifestyles are but a few of the most obvious factors contributing to the large number of applicants for desirable positions.

Serious contenders will know the rules of the resume game and see to it that their resumes receive serious consideration. The hiring process begins on a negative note—reducing the number of candidates to a manageable level. Here are candidates who are not contenders:

1. The sloppy resume senders. Their qualifications might be adequate or they might be outstanding. There are often a few such people in every hiring cycle. They are fine until someone just as good comes out of the stack who took the trouble to make a professional presentation.

2. The resistibles. Here are applicants who have dropped a stitch in the procedural quilt—they missed the "received by" date, failed to include the three references required, a college transcript, or whatever. They have given cause to be eliminated.

3. The underqualified. They lack the required master's degree or some other clearly advertised prerequisite, but thought that would be okay. Objective turndowns.

4. The negative standouts. They sent an unpersonalized cover letter that is a copy of a copy; spilled something on their resume and sent it anyway; crossed out entries from their last try and scribbled in your key words or people; and so on. Subjective turndowns.

5. The poor communicators. Applicants who are apparently qualified, but whose resumes just don't communicate in some important regard. They include too much obvious fluff, they are too long (more than two pages, except in rare cases), they feature sentences and paragraphs that go on and on, and so forth. These individuals just don't come across as being capable of making their point—they are not the ones hired if there are other choices. Largely a subjective judgment.

6. The overqualified candidates. They have held vastly superior positions or salaries, have degrees or work histories that are inconsistent with the position, etc. They fall by the wayside because they haven't read the situation realistically, although they are not apt to be given that reason for the turndown. More than likely they will just find that someone else was judged to be "more appropriate" for the position.

7. The technologically challenged candidate. Applicants today are expected to present at least minimal evidence of comfort with workplace technology. Ineptly sent e-mail, inability to check the company's Web page, a crudely printed resume in an era of high resolution lasers and ink-jets all can flag applicants with unacceptably steep technological learning curves.

Douglas Richardson, an executive in an East Coast human resources firm, writes:

I keep seeing resumes that are little more than buckets into which a lot of data has been dumped in the apparent belief that I will fill in the gaps, synthesize diverse information, connect the dots, and tell you what kind of product you are. I have no incentive to do this, given the number of knights eager to enter the lists. It is not my job to make sense out of your life.

Richardson reflects the plight and the attitude of many potential employers who face large stacks of resumes. It is important to recognize that you have the power to present him with what he considers material worth reading as he cuts the pile down to size.

Resume First Aid

Before we discuss the rules for writing a great resume, let's look at some examples of what can be done. Following are a series of before and after versions of actual resumes that have been improved using the recommendations in this book. Start by just comparing the visual impact of the before and after versions. Then read the point-by-point descriptions of how and why they were changed.

The first aid section contains five resumes not found among the Model Resumes in Part V. If you are later looking for an occupational example, return to this section for the following resumes:

- College Counselor
- English as a Second Language Teacher
- Investment Officer
- Senior Executive Assistant
- Senior Manager

It is also worth noting that these before and after resumes illustrate three of the Special Situations described in Chapter 17:

- A person from another culture adapting to the American job application process is illustrated by the English as a Second Language Teacher example.
- A spouse returning to the job market following the loss of a life partner is illustrated by the Senior Executive Assistant example.
- The transition from a military career to a position in the civilian sector is illustrated by the Senior Manager example.

College Counselor

BEFORE

General Problems

Ms. Brewster's resume shows a profound lack of focus—both visually and substantively. The information is there, but she ignores the fact that resume readers will not take the time to make sense out of her life. She has to do that for them. On resumes, both the format and content must be logically presented to make the information readily understandable to readers.

Specific Points

❶ If the Objective is going to be a simple job title, don't add qualifiers that only say the obvious—"Counselor/advisor in an academic setting" unnecessarily complicates the presentation from the outset.

❷ The chronology hops and skips all over the place. If you cannot present a set of logically connecting dates, don't emphasize the irregularity by using this kind of listing. It is only recommended when one position leads neatly to the next.

❸ Experience needs to be sorted out. Reviewers face an interpretation task that distracts from judging overall strengths. Their job is to evaluate, not organize, your information.

❹ Many of the experiences are very thin, a weakness only made clearer by listing and describing each experience separately.

❺ With little variety in formatting, the different parts of the resume blend together. Even by simply using boldface and underline, it is possible to separate the different sections.

❻ Education is a checkoff item (you have it or you don't) for the kind of job being sought and belongs at the bottom.

❼ Never offer information that might label you as eccentric or different. While there is nothing at all wrong with being a dream interpretation enthusiast, it is not something to feature prominently.

❽ Mention relevant skills, but play down the business aspect for this job.

❾ References are obviously available upon request—no need to say so.

❿ Musician information is harmless, but superfluous—she needs white space more.

BEFORE

Erika M. Brewster
2365 Northwest Avenue, Apartment 38
Washington, DC 20017
202-912-7666

❶ **OBJECTIVE: Counselor/advisor in an academic setting**

EXPERIENCE:

1992 - Present	**Administrative Assistant: Association of Colleges Serving the Military (American Colleges and Universities), Washington, DC** Provide administrative assistance, including revising handbooks and other training materials used internationally.
1991 - 1992	**Conference Coordinator. American Education Association, Washington, DC** Managed logistics of national conference including: registration, travel and on-site arrangements, post-conference follow-up.
1991	**Advisor. Honors Program, The International University, Washington, DC** Advised and counseled students in large honors program; liaison between director and students; planned special cultural events.
1990 - 1991	**Counselor. Internship at The International University, Washington, DC** Led two small groups in addition to one-on-one counseling. Focus on unconscious processes as related to academic and social issues.

❷ **1987 - 1991** — **Project Coordinator. The New Agenda, Projects JKSS, NETWORK, The International University, College of Education, Washington, DC** Managed the daily operations of an educational research office. Research duties included conducting preliminary research searches, report writing and analysis of data. Publicity duties included liaison between national media and project and dissemination of research findings. Managed logistics of training and dissemination conferences. Drafted and wordprocessed correspondence, reports and other materials. Fiscal duties included accounting, procurement and reconciliation. Supervised support staff.

1988 - 1989 **❹** **Housing Director. Shenandoah Musical Academy, Delton, VA** Administered all phases of resident housing. Duties included conflict resolution, informal counseling, supervision of student managers. **❸**

1985 - 1986 — **Secretary. The International University Security Department, Washington, DC** Performed administrative personnel functions for part-time employees, including general payroll tasks, statistics, and projections. Duties included answering telephone calls, wordprocessing, typing and filing.

EDUCATION: **❺** **Master of Science in Education** (Counseling emphasis), The International University, Washington, DC, June 1991.
Bachelor of Science in Business Administration (Personnel), The International University, Washington, DC, June 1986.

❻

PUBLISHED WORKS: Three test-bank chapters in <u>Learning Theory Models</u>, Teachers Guide, Wilson & Wilson, Newhouse Press, 1990.
Articles in <u>The Finder</u>, Winter 1985, Summer and Fall 1987.
❼ <u>Dreaming for Success</u>, Starlight Press, 1988.
"Help from Dreamers," paper presented to the Dreamers Association, Fall 1991.

OTHER: **❽** Owner of Typing, Inc. - a wordprocessing business, contract researcher and wordprocessor for special projects and dissertations; contributing writer/editor for <u>The Finder</u>; freelance musician; dream counselor. **←❼** **❿**

REFERENCES: **❾** Available upon request.

College Counselor

AFTER: FOCUSED RESUME

General Solutions

Ms. Brewster's resume now shows unambiguously what she wants to do and lists, in order of importance, the experiences that will be of interest to the hiring official. Visually, the resume has been given several points of focus, and white space separates one section from another.

Specific Points

❶ The Objective has been simplified to communicate clearly and remove unnecessary wording that might require interpretation.

❷ Since the dates of her jobs were overlapping and left gaps, they have been relegated to secondary status.

❸ Experience has been grouped in its strongest possible clusters—first that which is directly related, next the more generally related, and finally the supporting information.

❹ Since the lack of primary experience in counseling will be apparent to someone in the field, the positions are related positively, but credibly, as student experiences.

❺ Type size and face were changed using a word-processing program. Variety tends to separate the sections more clearly and gives each section greater impact.

❻ Wording of her present position title has been changed just enough to add an academic twist to an otherwise purely administrative job description.

❼ Dream analysis is mentioned, but more matter-of-factly. The comment linking it to counseling was eliminated since the avocation may taint the professionalism of the primary field. The resume is no place to assert rights, stand on principle, or advocate special interests with any potential for raising eyebrows.

❽ Word processing and research are treated more as skills, less as a business.

❾ Reference availability is omitted and nothing lost.

❿ Education is listed to confirm formal qualifications—no elaboration needed.

AFTER: FOCUSED RESUME

Erika M. Brewster
2365 Northwest Avenue, Apartment 38
Washington, DC 20017
202-912-7666

① Objective: COLLEGE COUNSELOR

❸ COUNSELING EXPERIENCE

- <u>Counseling Internship</u>: Completed a supervised practicum that was a part of my master's degree program. Consisted of leading two small groups and additional one-to-one counseling. Emphasis was on academic and social adjustment issues. The International University, Washington, DC, 1990–91. ←————❷

❹
- <u>Honors Program Advisor</u>: Advised and counseled students in a large honors program. Served as liaison between students and the director. Planned cultural events. The International University, Washington, DC, 1991.

- <u>Housing Director</u>: Counseled students as a part of my overall duties administering a college resident housing program. Shenandoah Musical Academy, Delton, VA 1988–89.

❺ GENERAL HIGHER EDUCATION EXPERIENCE **❻**

- <u>Academic Program Administrative Assistant</u>: Provide curriculum database management for college degree programs, including revising handbooks and other training materials used in the advisement of military students internationally. Association of Colleges Serving the Military (American Colleges and Universities), Washington, DC, 1992–present.

- <u>Conference Coordinator</u>: Managed the registration, travel, on-site services, and post-conference follow-up for a major national conference. American Education Association, Washington, DC, 1991–92.

- <u>Educational Research Project Coordinator</u>: Managed operational aspects of an educational research office, including preliminary searches, report writing, analysis of data, liaison between national media and the project, dissemination of findings, logistics of conferences, preparation of publications, fiscal management, and staff supervision. The New Agenda, Projects JKSS, NETWORK, The International University, Washington, DC, 1987–91.

- <u>Secretary</u>: Performed administrative personnel functions including payroll, statistics, and projections, clerical and telephone duties. The International University Security Department, Washington, DC, 1985–86.

OTHER EXPERIENCE

- <u>Writing</u>: Authored three chapters in *Learning Theory Models,* Instructors Guide, Wilson & Wilson, Newhouse Press, 1990. Articles published in *The Finder,* 1985–87. Published *Dreaming for Success,* Starlight Press, 1988, and presented "Help from Dreamers" paper at Dreamers Association, Fall 1991.

❼

❽
- <u>Word Processing and Research</u>: Owner of a private word processing and contract research business.

EDUCATION **❿**

- Master of Science in Education (Counseling Emphasis), The International University, Washington, DC, June 1991.

- Bachelor of Science in Business Administration (Personnel), The International University, Washington, DC, June 1986.

❾

English as a Second Language Teacher

BEFORE

General Problems

Ms. Wang is a foreign student. Most of her experience and education are from China. While her resume does a good job of listing the facts of her situation, it does little to explain what she is trying to accomplish and why that is a plausible goal. Equal formatting strength is given to important and far less important items of information. The reader has to struggle to package her attributes in a way that shows her potential.

Specific Points

❶ Her name would be unfamiliar to most American employers. They need to know at least whether they are addressing a woman or a man, if for no other reason than corresponding with her comfortably.

❷ None of the Work Experience entries describes duties, beyond job titles.

❸ American and foreign experience is combined and, while not difficult to distinguish, the two should be shown more clearly.

❹ Education lists specialized foreign certificates on a par with degrees and offers no explanation of their content or relative value.

❺ Translation experience is useful, but the listing does nothing to enhance it.

❻ The interpreter experience is also useful, but lacks any focus.

❼ Office skills are worth mentioning, but need a professional context.

❽ Typing speed is inappropriate in a resume for a professional position.

❾ Visa status needs further elaboration.

❿ A specific reference would be more helpful in this situation.

BEFORE

LAN WANG ❶
717 Belmont Place, SE. Apartment 4122
Washington, DC 20004
(H) 202-339-1725
(W) 202-667-4612

❷ **Work Experience:**

- **Senior Administrative Assistant, April 1992 - Present, Association of North American Colleges,** 3 Circle of the Associations, Washington, DC 20007
- **Full-Time Graduate Teaching Fellow, 1991-92** (Teaching English to foreign students - TOEFL) English Language Department, Chadwick University, CA

❸
- **Instructor of English, 1985-90,** Foreign Language Department, Shenyi Teachers College, Shenyi, Linhai, China PRC
- **Instructor of English, 1990 Spring Semester,** English Training Program for Managers, Administrative Bureau of New Industry, Shenyi, Linhai, China PRC
- **Instructor of English, Grade 9, 1988 Fall Semester,** Experimental Secondary School of Linhai Province, Shenyi, Linhai, China PRC
- **Video Tape Announcer and Translator, 1985-92,** Audio-Visual Center, Shenyi Teachers College, Shenyi, Linhai, China PRC
- **Mandarin Chinese Radio Announcer, 1977-81,** Town of Mengenh, District of Shenyi, Linhai, China, PRC

Education:

- **M.S.- Education, Curriculum and Instruction, May 1992** (Included extensive work in TESOL and Linguistics) Grade Point Average 3.89 on 4.00 scale. Chadwick University, CA
- **Certificate, Graduate Program in English Linguistics and Literature, 1989,** Shenyi Teachers College, Shenyi, Linhai, China PRC

❹
- **Certificate, English for College Teachers, 1986,** Dayan Institute of Technology, Dayan, Linhai, China PRC
- **B.A.- English Linguistics and Literature, 1985,** Foreign Language Department, Shenyi Teachers College, Shenyi, Linhai, China PRC

❺ **Translation Experience:**

- **"Final Sayings"** - Short Story Journal of Shenyi Teachers College, January 1988.
- <u>History of American Literature</u>**, Section IV, Walt Whitman.**
- <u>Comparative Literature</u>**: Preface to the First Edition.**

❻ **Experience as an Interpreter:**

- **Interpreter for Joann Williams,** Visiting English Teacher, 1988-89, Shenyi Teachers College, Shenyi, Linhai, China PRC

Membership in Professional Organizations:

- Washington Area Teachers of English as a Second Language (WATESOL)
- Association of Foreign Language Translation, PRC
- Association of International Linguistics and Literature, PRC

❼ **Office Skills:**

- Experienced in IBM, Macintosh, and Apple Computers (WordPerfect, Microsoft Word, dBase, Lotus 1-2-3)
- Typing speed - 50 WPM

❽
Visa Status: F-1, Practical Training (9/92 - 7/93)
❾ **Date of Birth: 7/30/59**
References available upon request

❿

English as a Second Language Teacher

AFTER: FOCUSED RESUME

Ms. Wang's resume has been given an introductory statement that prepares the reader for the unique combination of experiences that follows. The list of information has been broken into groups more readily grasped by the reader and brief elaborations are provided at appropriate places.

Specific Points

❶ The Overview lets the reader know that the writer is a woman, and clarifies her situation and what she is trying to accomplish. Gender would normally not be stressed, but when a less familiar name does not convey enough to select a proper term for addressing the applicant, such elaboration is appropriate.

❷ Degrees are singled out for prominence under the education heading and not confused with other training, which is shown later in the resume.

❸ Experience is broken into subheadings, and listed in order of importance.

❹ The most important experience is teaching in America, so it leads the list. A modest job description adds to clarity.

❺ The Chinese teaching experience is separated from other work done there and left to stand on the strength of the job titles.

❻ Interpreter and translator skills that are similar are combined for simplicity.

❼ Current position is listed as professional, but clearly not teaching. A brief statement of duties gives the position as much professional status as possible.

❽ Office skills sound better as something related to her professional skills.

❾ Visa status is explained enough to show an intended progression.

❿ An immediate reference is provided to give the reader an efficient way to clarify anything at issue.

AFTER

LAN WANG
717 Belmont Place, SE. Apartment 4122
Washington, DC 20004

202-339-1725 Residence
202-667-4612 Office

❶ Overview: Chinese woman fluent in English, with recently completed American graduate degree, seeks opportunity to teach English as a second language to students of any language background. Also receptive to other opportunities that would capitalize on language and cultural knowledge.

Education

❷

Master of Science - Education	Bachelor of Arts
Curriculum and Instruction	English Linguistics and Literature
(TESOL/Linguistics Concentration)	Shenyi Teachers College
Chadwick University, CA	Shenyi, Linhai, China PRC
1992	1985

Experience ❸

TEACHING

USA

❹ • *Teacher of English as a Foreign Language,* English Language Institute, Chadwick University, CA, 1991-92. As a full-time graduate teaching fellow, taught English as a second language to foreign students.

CHINA

❺ • *Instructor of English,* Foreign Language Department, Shenyi Teachers College, China, 1985-90.
• *Instructor of English,* English Training Program for Managers, Administrative Bureau of New Industry, Shenyi, China, 1990.
• *Instructor of English,* Grade 9, Experimental Secondary School of Linhai Province, Shenyi, China, 1988.

TRANSLATION ❻

• *Interpreter* in China for visiting American teacher of English, 1988-91.
• *Scholarly translation* of several works from English to Chinese.

OTHER PROFESSIONAL

❼ • *Senior Administrative Assistant,* Association of North American Colleges, Washington, DC, April 1992 - Present. Duties include assisting in the coordination of college level academic programs for members seeking college degrees throughout the world. Various roles aiding in response to user inquiries by telephone and writing. Assist in the preparation of organizational publications.
• *Video Tape Announcer/Translator,* Shenyi Teachers College, 1985-92.
• *Radio Announcer,* Mandarin Chinese language, China, 1977-81.

Related Skills ❽

Experienced in operating IBM and Apple Macintosh personal computers.
Software proficiency: Microsoft Word, WordPerfect, dBase, and Lotus 1-2-3.

Additional Training

Certificate	Certificate
Graduate Program in English Linguistics and Literature	English for College Teachers
Shenyi Teachers College	Dayan Institute of Technology
1989	Dayan, Linhai, China
	1986

Professional Affiliations	**References** ❿
Washington Area Teachers of English as a Second Language (WATESOL)	Dawson Weber, Ph.D.
Association of Foreign Language Translation	Associate Director
Association of International Linguistics and Literature	Association of North American Colleges
	202-667-4612

Personal	
	Immediate reference • Contact freely
	• Others provided upon request.

❾ F-1 Student Visa currently working under the Practical Training provision.
H-1 Work Visa upon attaining permanent professional employment.
Born July 30, 1959

Investment Officer

BEFORE

General Problems

Mr. Ames has smothered perfectly good qualifications in a sea of overstatement, misplaced emphasis, and disorganization. Adding a paragraph that gives some specifics about performance as an investment manager and deleting—or deemphasizing—things no one in his present career field wants to hear about his teaching days can salvage the resume.

Specific Points

1 A telephone number is essential in an age when your first contact from an interested employer is apt to be a call.

2 The Objective leads off with rambling hyperbole that only vaguely relates to managing investments.

3 Claims of being articulate, an excellent communicator, respected leader, etc., are lost in too many words—the paragraph is actually harmful to his image and needs to be removed.

4 Experience is presented too broadly—there needs to be a clear division between what supports the current professional goal and that which is background.

5 Description of the investment duties is fine as far as it goes, but lacks the performance specifics expected in such a readily quantified field.

6 The educator background is largely irrelevant to the objective of getting a better investment management position—set it apart and reduce it in size and detail.

7 Minor speeches, coaching roles, etc., have no place in this resume.

8 The securities examination is a test passed, not education gained—show it as a professional credential under the relevant job description.

9 The Personal information contributes nothing—delete it.

10 Education listings should not be vague about whether a degree has been completed or merely pursued.

BEFORE

BRUCE D. AMES

454 Hermosa Beach Drive Los Angeles, CA 90254

OBJECTIVE
To utilize my repertoire of professional and interpersonal expertise through a dynamic position which requires exceptional communicative skills and extensive contact with the community. Special interests include investments management and marketing.

Recognized as an action-oriented individual who possesses leadership skills and administrative ability integral to the successful implementation of projects. Welcome the challenge of working with new people and changing situations. Articulate . . . communicate proficiently with people at all levels. Respected for unique ability to assess needs, formulate goals and devise strategies to effectively achieve managerial objectives. Demonstrate excellent speaking, writing and research capabilities. Capable of influencing others to perform tasks efficiently.

PROFESSIONAL EXPERIENCE
Since 1992, Assistant Vice President and Trust Investment Officer, The Bank of West Orange County. Establish investment policy, directly supervise investment administration, manage individual and comingled portfolios, evaluate accounts, securities, research and comparative performances. Monitor operations, supervise clerical functions, meet with customers and clients, represent the department.

Co-designed curriculum, taught college preparatory Math (grades 10-12) during tenure as Faculty Member at The Monument School. Developed and co-wrote <u>New Theories in Teaching Mathematics</u> and <u>Mathematics Instruction in the Private Academy</u> (1987). Directed preparation and publication of these textbooks currently used as units of instruction. Presented National 4-H Club speech (1988). As Assistant Volleyball Coach, was responsible for conditioning both boys' and girls' teams. Analyzed performance, instructed team members in game strategies and techniques to prepare for athletic competition.

At Pacific Military and Girls Academy, taught Mathematics, geometry and junior algebra. Participated in faculty and professional meetings, education conferences and teacher training workshops. Cultivated interpersonal skills while a Resident Adviser in a closed dormitory environment. Provided individual and group counseling services relative to problems of personal, social and scholastic nature. Assisted pupils in selecting course of study, counseled students with adjustment and academic problems. Directed dormitory orientation programs, supervised recreational and social activities.

Conducted college-level courses in Basic Mathematics and Arithmetic Theory at the Community College of the North Woods, MN, instructed prospective teachers in teaching mathematics to high school students. As Graduate Teaching Assistant at the University of Minnesota, instructed prospective teachers in Secondary Schools Teaching Methodology. Created and compiled book of formulas, presented classroom orientation lectures.

EDUCATION
Registered Securities Representative, 1992, The Bank of West Orange County.
Post-baccalaureate study (Master of Business Administration), Long Beach College, 1989-92.
Post-baccalaureate study (Master of Education Fellow), University of Minnesota, 1984-88.
Bachelor of Arts in Mathematics (emphasis, Boolean Logic Theory), University of Michigan, 1984.

PERSONAL
Strive to promote highest degree of success in fulfilling potential for self and others. Pleasures include all sports (particularly sailing, cross-country skiing, tennis and swimming) and extensive reading. Interested in developing growth-oriented programs which foster creativity in achieving objectives.

15

Investment Officer

AFTER: FOCUSED RESUME

General Solutions

Mr. Ames's resume has been purged of excessive words. It now defines clearly the primary and secondary information, although the format has remained essentially unchanged. A few more headings and a lot fewer words have transformed a weak effort into a great resume.

Specific Points

❶ Telephone numbers have been added without the addition of a single line.

❷ The Objective is now much shorter and to the point. It includes his interest in people skills and marketing, but is phrased to fit the business environment instead of a graduate school class.

❸ Experience has been divided and reordered to place the emphasis on the business at hand—investment management.

❹ A brief paragraph has been added to describe his actual investment activities and performance, using a recognized standard.

❺ The professional credential has been inserted at a more meaningful point.

❻ Teaching is presented in the context of its current importance—proof that there was a responsible use of his time before coming to the investment world.

❼ For the purposes of this resume, the teaching positions can be treated as generic events that share a common, brief description.

❽ Teaching part-time while a graduate student shows some initiative, but is little more relevant to the investment job; account for the periods of time and move on.

❾ Personal is removed and left for interview small talk—if that.

❿ Education has been clarified to list the bachelor's degree and relegate the others to their proper place as study toward degrees not completed.

AFTER

BRUCE D. AMES

454 Hermosa Beach Drive • Los Angeles, CA 90254 • 213-324-0078 (O), 213-445-0988 (R)

OBJECTIVE

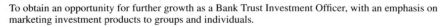

To obtain an opportunity for further growth as a Bank Trust Investment Officer, with an emphasis on marketing investment products to groups and individuals.

EXPERIENCE

Trust Investments

1992 - Present: Assistant Vice President and Trust Investment Officer, The Bank of West Orange County.

- Establish investment policy, directly supervise investment administration, manage individual and comingled portfolios, evaluate accounts, securities, research and comparative performances. Monitor operations, supervise clerical functions, meet with customers and clients, represent the department.

- Perform as an investment generalist working with both fixed and equity funds. Use major outside contract research firm in an advisory capacity. Sit on the Trust Investment Committee. Currently responsible for the management of $150 million of personal and $276 million of institutional funds. Aggregate investment performance according to CDA has been 25th percentile nationally for the past 5 years. Regularly accompany officers from employee benefits and other divisions to assist in developing new business.

- Registered Securities Representative.

Teaching

Prior to beginning my investment career, I served as a teacher at two institutions:

1987 - 1989 The Monument School, Orange, CA.

1990 - 1992 Pacific Military and Girls Academy, Laguna, CA.

In both situations, I taught Mathematics, geometry and junior algebra. Participated in faculty and professional meetings, education conferences and teacher training workshops. Cultivated interpersonal skills while a Resident Adviser in a closed dormitory environment. Provided individual and group counseling services relative to problems of personal, social and scholastic nature. Assisted pupils in selecting courses of study, counseled students with adjustment and academic problems. Directed dormitory orientation programs, supervised recreational and social activities.

Part-time Teaching During Periods of Graduate Study

Conducted college-level courses in Basic Mathematics and Arithmetic Theory at the Community College of the North Woods, MN, instructed prospective teachers in teaching mathematics to high school students. As Graduate Teaching Assistant at the University of Minnesota, instructed prospective teachers in Secondary Schools Teaching Methodology. Created and compiled book of formulas, presented classroom orientation lectures.

EDUCATION
- Bachelor of Arts in Mathematics, University of Michigan, 1984.
- Additional graduate study toward the following degrees:
  Master of Business Administration, Long Beach College, 1989-92.
  Master of Education Fellow, University of Minnesota, 1984-88 (Summers).

Senior Executive Assistant

BEFORE

General Problems

Ms. O'Conner fails to set the context for her experiences. She portrays herself too objectively as an older divorced woman with spotty training and an irregular work history when, in reality, she has done common things in an uncommon setting—as an executive's spouse. Her resume doesn't present her as a woman of multiple talents who can operate comfortably with executives, and that is her greatest asset.

Specific Points

❶ Her actual work experience is not as much of an asset in her job search as is her experience functioning comfortably in management circles.

❷ She unwisely leads her list of accomplishments with an unexplained temporary position.

❸ Since her work history is not a clear progression up a particular career ladder, it should be deemphasized.

❹ The education entries do little to enhance her professional image, so they should be generalized, not featured prominently.

❺ Detailed high school and secretarial school information only draws attention to her nonprofessional education and her age.

❻ Phrased as it is, the college entry emphasizes her lack of a degree.

❼ These sound like things of secondary importance that an executive's spouse might do when, in fact, they can be broken out into valuable competencies.

❽ It is unnecessary to give personal information.

❾ Marital status and family size are not required and should not be volunteered.

❿ The availability of references is a given and should be omitted.

BEFORE

BERNADETTE J. O'CONNER
1455 CORYELL COURT SOUTH
SEATTLE, WA 98112
206-448-0992 RESIDENCE

❶ EXPERIENCE

❷

July 1998-Present: Office temporary, Kelly Personnel Services, Bellview, WA. Typing, filing, receptionist, and as-needed office work as an on-call gal Friday.

September 1985-May 1990: Substitute teacher, Salmon Run Elementary School, King County Public Schools. Taught young children in the absence of their regular teachers.

May 1979-June 1980: Administrative assistant, Bishop Walsh Catholic Church, Renton, WA.

August 1974-January 1977: Secretary, Chief, Computing Services & LAN Branch, Aircraft Manufacturers Association, Washington, DC.

❸ April 1972-November 1973: Receptionist and administrative aide, Inland Aerial Port Authority, Memphis, TN.

❹ EDUCATION

Canton Kansas Senior High School, General Diploma, 1965 ⟵ **❺**

Kathryn Cummings Business School, Kansas City, KS, Certificate in Office Administration, 1969

Kansas City University, 1965-1968, various college courses **❻**

❼ ACTIVITIES

President of the Corporate Officers Wives Club. Organized an informal training program for new spouses to familiarize them with their obligations under the company's social protocols. Sponsored youth activities and initiated the neighborhood crime watch.

❽ PERSONAL

Divorced; 2 adult children **❾**

REFERENCES UPON REQUEST **❿**

Senior Executive Assistant

AFTER: FOCUSED RESUME

General Solutions

Ms. O'Conner's resume was recast to place less emphasis on her actual work experiences and educational accomplishments and more on her ability to function comfortably in the executive environment. Instead of listing specific jobs and educational experiences, her resume was designed to emphasize competencies that would be valued in the job market. Where they were acquired is relegated to a secondary position.

Specific Points

❶ An overview was added to set the context lacking in her original resume. The reader immediately knows he or she is evaluating someone whose professional refinement exceeds her actual credentials.

❷ A list of her competencies is the first thing encountered by an evaluator. Its headings telegraph her strengths, and it isn't necessary to search for them in the understated credits of her original resume.

❸ To get a job at the level she is used to, the key is experience interacting with executive-level people, so that is stressed.

❹ Her resume next establishes that she has tangible workplace skills drawn from both formal work experiences and quasi-personal activities.

❺ Her language capability may be used directly; if not, it denotes refinement, helps her image, and compensates for weak formal education credentials.

❻ Teaching becomes instructional experience—more easily related to needs of the working world outside educational institutions.

❼ A connection is made between her teaching children and applying similar skills in the company environment as her activities are tied into her job competencies.

❽ Work history is honestly presented, but deemphasized.

❾ Education remains a category, but it is generalized and interpreted to mean something in the job market; also, it reflects less formal experiences like using a personal computer and attending company training sessions.

❿ Her incomplete college experience is stated more favorably.

AFTER

BERNADETTE J. O'CONNER
1455 CORYELL COURT SOUTH
SEATTLE, WA 98112

206-448-0992 RESIDENCE

OVERVIEW AND OBJECTIVE

Mature executive career partner with cultivated social and organizational skills wishes to combine that background and personal bearing with tangible professional administrative talents to support achieving the objectives of a challenging organization.

COMPETENCIES

Executive Interpersonal—As the career partner of a senior international corporate officer, became an accomplished participant in, and facilitator of, executive social functions. These strengths were developed in an environment of foreign and domestic, military and civilian, senior professional people.

Organizational, Managerial and Clerical—As the senior person among a professional social hierarchy of other executive career partners, organized and managed a variety of social services related to company families and personnel. As an administrative specialist supporting the secretarial and clerical needs of large organizations, developed an ability to organize and accomplish administrative tasks.

Foreign Language—Written and spoken French

Instructional—As a substitute teacher, managed a classroom and accomplished learning objectives. Similar results were achieved outside the educational setting by imparting the skills of an executive career partner to younger associates.

8 EMPLOYMENT HISTORY

- 1965-1997: Spouse of a senior corporate officer supporting the development of his professional financial management career internationally.
- 1996-1997: Substitute teacher and aide, Salmon Run Elementary School, King County Public Schools. Temporary administrative work for Kelly Personnel Services as a device for re-entering career employment.
- 1964-1992: Various administrative positions including Secretary to the Chief of Computing & the Local Area Network Branch, Aircraft Manufacturers Association, and support positions in such organizations as the Inland Aerial Port Authority, Memphis, TN.

9 EDUCATION

- Liberal arts college preparation ← **10**
- Attended a variety of career partner professional courses associated with such institutions as the International Business Association
- Secretarial and clerical training
- Basic computer literacy

Senior Manager

BEFORE

General Problems

Mr. Woodland's resume is written in the language and format of the military service of which he is no longer a part. His task now is to communicate to the broader world of work what he has done that they might value. This requires evaluating his terminology, determining its relevance in a civilian hiring situation, and making it understood by those not familiar with the military.

Specific Points

❶ Unless the application is directed to someone known to understand and value military rank, remove it from the address. The value of rank should be obvious and, if relevant, it can be integrated into the work history.

❷ He should help the resume reviewer quickly classify him by offering an introductory line suggesting how he fits into the civilian job market.

❸ Move education to the end of the resume. A college education is assumed for the kinds of positions for which he will apply, so it becomes something to verify at the end rather than a leading item.

❹ Listing a series of normal professional development courses is unnecessary. A resume from industry would not likely list comparable ones.

❺ Accomplishments are worded too much like a military personnel evaluation. More natural, less inflated-sounding statements would serve him better, especially if they are related to the civilian workplace.

❻ Career positions show too much detail. Simplify and group them.

❼ Career positions' terminology is stilted, military-oriented, and not apt to be understood. They need to be roughly translated into civilian equivalencies.

❽ The chronology is muddled and too detailed.

❾ Sort the military assignments into clusters that portray a logical work history that accounts for time and shows expected career progression.

❿ For most hiring situations, awards and decorations are best left as unlisted assets. Work history statements can sometimes properly mention combat leadership with honors or service with distinction, but understatement is the rule.

BEFORE

Thomas A. Woodland, Colonel, USA (Retired)
2933 Crepe Myrtle Lane
Gaithersburg, MD 20879
301-562-6403

 Education

 University of Maryland - Bachelor of Science in Business Administration
Park University, Missouri - Master of Arts in Management
Basic Armor Officer's Course, Military Personnel Officer's Course, Adjutant General's Corps
Officers Advanced Course, Armed Forces Staff College, and Command and General Staff
College

Accomplishments

Significant roles in the planning and execution of every Department of the Army program
through Desert Storm. Supervised and led offices of as many as 108 goal oriented team
members. Twenty-eight years of direct office management experience. Recruited, hired, trained,
evaluated, and fired personnel. Coordinated, led, supervised, monitored, and assigned work
within eight major divisions of the Department of the Army.

Career Positions

United States Armor Center at Fort Knox, Kentucky, 1972, Training Battalion Executive Officer;
United States Army Aviation Center & School, Fort Rucker, Alabama, 1970, rotary wing flight
training; 23rd Aviation Brigade, Da Nang, South Vietnam, 1971, Scout Helicopter Platoon
Leader; 81st Aviation Squadron, Fort Knox, Kentucky, 1975, Platoon Leader and Operations
Officer; Personnel Office, Fort Knox, Kentucky, 1972-74, Personnel officer; Hanau, West
Germany, 1975-78, 75th Signal Battalion, Battalion Adjutant, HQ Detachment Commander; Fort
Lewis, Washington, 1978-81, Reserve Component Advisor for the Northwest Army Readiness
Group; Yongsan, South Korea, 1982-85, Plans Officer for the Combined Forces Command; Fort
Sill, Oklahoma, 1986-89, Post Adjutant General; Carlisle Barracks, Pennsylvania, 1993-96,
Chief of Plans & Operations Division, Directorate of Academic Operations, United States Army
Staff College; Fort Jackson, South Carolina, 1997-2000, Senior Army Advisor at the Army
Reserve Complex, Columbia, South Carolina.

Awards and Decorations

Bronze Star, Defense Meritorious Service Medal with one Oak Leaf Cluster, Meritorious Service
Medal with three Oak Leaf Clusters, Army Commendation Medal with one Oak Leaf Cluster,
Vietnam Service Medal with Star, Armed Forces Reserve Medal, Republic of Vietnam Gallantry
Cross with Palm, the Army Aviation Badge, and the Air Assault Badge.

Senior Manager

AFTER: COMPETENCY CLUSTER RESUME

General Solutions

Mr. Woodland's resume is now a competency cluster resume. His market value lies in the specifics of what he did rather than in which organizations he served, so the objective is to reveal his competencies. Work history and education are relegated to the important but secondary roles of verifying assumed levels of performance and training.

Specific Points

❶ Military rank is removed from the address element since in most situations it will no longer be part of his professional identity. Exceptions exist where rank is beneficial, but they are apt to be known at the time of application. An e-mail address conveys technology awareness.

❷ An overview is added to telegraph that a senior manager's credentials are being examined and that his experience includes administrative, personnel, and financial responsibilities.

❸ Competencies are extracted from the maze of military job titles and summarized in ways that give context and scope to the responsibilities.

❹ Civilian occupational parallels are drawn: budget, training, recruitment.

❺ Technical literacy is highlighted, not as a technician but as a senior manager comfortable with modern technology.

❻ Career positions that were formerly a litany of military posts held are brought together into meaningful clusters of functional experience.

❼ His work history highlights and verifies a successful progression from entry-level to senior management.

❽ The job chronology is simple, clear, and accurate. It shows the evaluator what he or she wants most to see—his career progression and no periods unaccounted for.

❾ At the bottom of the work history is a summary that relates military training, combat experience, and a discreet mention of honors.

❿ Education is listed at the end of the resume verifying degrees in business and management. A summary statement covers in-service training.

AFTER

THOMAS A. WOODLAND
2933 Crepe Myrtle Lane
Gaithersburg, MD 20879
301-562-6403
tawoodland@worldnet.att.net

❶

OVERVIEW

❷ After a successful career as a senior officer managing the administrative, personnel, and financial aspects of large, complex organizations in the United States, Asia, and Europe, interested in applying my talents and experience to meeting the challenges of a new organization.

❸ COMPETENCIES

<u>Management</u>—oversaw the operation of offices of more than 100 people serving organizations consisting of thousands of individuals. Experienced and trained in modern management practices. Recruited, trained, evaluated, and mentored people ranging from entry level to senior managers. **❹**

❻ <u>Financial</u>—planned, executed, and was accountable for budgets of tens of millions of dollars.

<u>Training</u>—senior administrative management of major training organizations.

<u>Technology</u>—responsible for the evaluation, acquisition, and use of state-of-the-art computer systems and software. Conversant in the terminology and competent in the use of modern office and instructional technologies.

❺

❼ WORK HISTORY

1997-2000—<u>Senior Management and Technical Consultant at the Army Reserve Complex, Fort Jackson, SC</u>. The active duty army's oversight person for a large organization of civilian reservists relating their civilian and military skills. Policy making, motivation, program quality control, and mentoring.

❽ 1993-96—<u>Chief Academic Planning and Operations Officer, the United States Army Staff College, Carlisle, PA</u>. Planned and implemented a national level program for managers. Duties included budgeting and program development.

1972-92—<u>Middle management positions of increasing responsibility.</u> Duties included personnel, operations, and planning in major units located in Germany, Korea, and the United States.

1969-71—Training as a military officer and aviator, with periods of combat leadership with honors. **❾**

EDUCATION

❿ Park University, Missouri—Master of Arts in Management, 1987
University of Maryland—Bachelor of Science in Business Administration, 1969
A wide range of in-service leadership and management courses.

Communicating Technological Awareness

In an era of rapid change, candidates for most jobs, technical and otherwise, face the challenge of presenting themselves as being a good fit for the employer's technology environment. How they approach it depends on the position for which they are applying and their place on the technology continuum.

If you are a nontechnical person your objective is to come across as someone familiar with workplace technology as a user. Whatever your field, technology surely serves it and you should know the role technology plays, be conversant in the jargon associated with it, and be able to demonstrate at least minimal skills in using it.

As you go up the managerial chain, the ratio of hands-on technological expertise to simple awareness changes. The manager may not be expected to be a programmer, but it could be awkward if he were unable to perform routine operations on spreadsheet and word processing software. It might also raise eyebrows if she couldn't find her way around the Internet or use presentation software. Management candidates have to instill confidence in the hiring committee that they are aware of technology, can function intelligently with it, and know enough about it to hire and manage technical staff.

Technical people applying for positions on predominantly nontechnical staffs have other problems to overcome. They need to come across as communicators who can relate to both worlds. People understand that they have to acquire someone with unique skills, but hiring committees react poorly to people who cannot relate to them on their own terms. They fear the "Data Nazi," the technical staffer who somehow threatens to restrict and control the way they do business.

Your challenge as a technical-expert applicant is to show reasonable understanding of the business in which you will function. Convey an understanding that technology is just one more way to accomplish the overall mission of the organization. Lead with the caveat that you would have to be there awhile before determining how appropriate such ideas might be, but generally relate how you see technology making the organization more productive.

Dos and Don'ts of Resume Writing

There is a large body of wisdom about what you should and should not do in preparing a resume. The following is a collection of the considerations that warrant your attention. They also demand your good judgment—every rule does not apply to all situations and you will have to determine when to depart from the conventional approach enough to give your resume the little something extra that is appropriate in your circumstances.

Use this summary as a checklist when it comes time to plan and critique your resume.

Do	**Don't**
View yourself as a product to be sold to the reader of your resume.	Assume the reader has time to absorb more than the essentials.
Make your resume believable.	Stretch small or incomplete things into more than they will be if scrutinized.
Start with something that the reviewer can identify with and attach value to easily.	Bore the resume's reader.
Use only the words needed to convey your message.	Try to impress anyone with big words or philosophical statements.
Leave white space.	Fill every inch of paper with type.
Lead the reviewer through your points with headings, bullets, bold type, underlining, etc.	Get too carried away with different typefaces or graphic effects that can distract, instead of lead and separate.
Ignore the traditional rules of formatting (other than logical arrangement) if you are submitting a text-only electronic resume.	Waste effort prettying up an electronic resume that you will likely send as plain text.
Include keywords, especially in electronic resumes or those apt to be scanned for electronic evaluation and filing.	Use elaborate explanations at the expense of crucial keywords needed to pass the electronic screening process.
Avoid opening up problem areas that are not required items or clearly to your advantage.	Volunteer a photograph or similar unexpected extras—attractive, average, or too good-looking can all pose problems in the wrong situations.
Limit your resume to a page or two unless there is a compelling reason to make it more.	Use white space and formatting gimmicks to the extent that they make your resume too long.
Keep relevant content at the center of your thinking as you present your information.	Drift into listing more than the reviewer for this particular job wants to know.

(cont'd)

27

Do	Don't
Make your goals and objectives fit the job under consideration.	List your broader life goals and values in your resume.
Show that you know something about the job and the company.	Mention skills or interests that the job would never demand.
Be clear about the level of authority or responsibility both for your objective and in describing past duties.	Leave it to the reviewer to guess where you fit into the organization—theirs or the ones in your past.
Let your achievements speak for themselves—state them clearly, quantify and define where desirable.	Embellish your accomplishments—their substance has to be strong enough to convey their value.
Go easy on the adjectives.	Attempt to show action or importance with modifiers whose purpose is transparently obvious to the reader.
Give specifics where there isn't a compelling reason not to—names and numbers let the reader judge the significance of the things you mention.	Expect the reviewer to attach importance to things that you haven't demonstrated as being significant.
Include a clear qualifications statement in your resume.	Leave it to the reviewer to figure out how your preparation might satisfy his or her requirements.
Use a brief summary statement that embraces your overall qualifications.	Make your summary a second resume.
Determine that the position has the potential to meet your realistic salary requirements before applying.	State a salary requirement in your resume.
Prepare a list of relevant references and make them aware of your job-hunting activity—get their permission to use their names.	List references in your resume or state the obvious—that they are available on request. Don't let an employer surprise a reference by contacting them before you do.
Resist the urge to include personal data not directly relevant to the job.	Tell the reviewer about your hobbies, number of children, excellent health, love of boating, other-than-professional memberships, etc.
Let your accomplishments and preparation speak for themselves.	Appraise your own worth.
List dates even in the modified resumes that are not chronological lists of past positions.	Make the dates the main feature of any resume that deserves a different focus.

Do	Don't
Avoid qualifying statements such as "had exposure to."	Stretch your experience beyond that which can be directly claimed as yours.
State an honest reason for leaving if other than just looking for a better opportunity.	Make negative statements about the job or people you are leaving behind.
Show evidence of hard work and dedication.	Merely state that you are hardworking and dedicated—if it has to be separately claimed, you didn't communicate it substantively.
Prepare your resume professionally— that doesn't necessarily mean go out and hire someone. It does mean, at the very least, using a good word processor, printer, and business-quality paper.	Settle for a mechanically weak resume that looks like a first draft out of a beginning keyboarding class.
Eliminate unnecessarily long words, sentences, and paragraphs.	Overstate your case.
Say enough to market fairly what you have to offer.	Be so sparse as to show lack of interest or less substance than you actually have.
Proofread carefully. If you have one, use a word-processing program that checks spelling, perhaps grammar too. Then proofread it again. Spellcheckers can't cope with every nuance of language.	Commit to final copy without aging your early drafts for a few days and subjecting them to some editing.
Use a good quality paper and an interesting type style that suits your circumstances.	Choose an unusual size or color of paper—same for ink, typeface, etc.
Determine who should receive your resume and address it accordingly.	Send your resume to some broad entity like the personnel department unless specifically directed to do so.
Provide telephone numbers that will respond with a businesslike answer.	List a telephone number that elicits a "she no longer works here" response, is disconnected, or otherwise fails to leave a favorable impression.
List your most recent job first.	Give the same attention to old jobs as to those of recent years—condense them if necessary and make a collective statement.

(cont'd)

Do	Don't
List military service if it represents important employment or training—and emphasize those aspects.	Dwell on past military experience, honors, etc., unless they relate to the job at hand.
Mention civic clubs and community service only if such activity is an expectation for the job—college president, for example.	Fill the end of the resume with a summary of everything you ever belonged to or achieved privately—Eagle Scout, pilot's license, etc.

2

RESUME PROTOTYPES

The resumes in this book serve as illustrations of how a resume can sell the talents of a job applicant. They should be used to stimulate ideas rather than as specific models to copy. The resumes have been labeled as belonging to one of three general types. In some you will clearly see the qualities of the other two—a Work History chronology may be the perfect way to end a Competency Cluster Resume, for example. The Work History Resume may be most effective if the individual job descriptions become miniature Focused or Competency Cluster Resumes. You are advised to see the broad potential and select the most powerful combination with which to portray your unique talents.

The Work History Resume

The Work History Resume sometimes referred to as a Chronological Resume because jobs and personal data are listed in the order they occurred. It is the traditional resume and the one most commonly used when pursuing a regular career progression that has one position logically and continuously leading to the next.

Strengths	Weaknesses
Shows ideal job progression.	Exposes spotty career pattern.
Showcases strong employers and positions held.	Highlights inconsistencies in levels and types of employment.

(cont'd)

Strengths	Weaknesses
Sets the stage for next most logical growth move in your career.	Fails to support your aspirations if the building blocks are not there in terms of the right positions previously held. Not a career-changer's resume.
Stresses impressive job titles.	Reveals insignificant positions.
Everything easily accounted for.	Reveals *everything*.
Sets the stage for presenting strong references from prior positions.	Risks inviting reference checks where you would just as soon not have them.
Looks like a "real" resume—straightforward and traditional in both content and presentation.	Not particularly imaginative—relies on excellent content to give it value.
Clearly links dates of employment and verifies continuity.	Indicates breaks in employment as well as brief tenure in jobs.
Shows long experience.	Makes your age obvious; suggests you may have been stalled in a job too long; reveals periods of unemployment.

Work History Resume Template

> Name
> Address
> Telephone Number(s)
> Personal e-mail

Overview or Summary, Goal or Objective. An appropriately brief and relevant statement of your main qualifications and goal. This is optional and can be omitted if it simply states the obvious.

Employment—A chronological list of the jobs you have held. Format can vary, but respect these rules:

- Most recent position is listed first.
- List dates continuously and consistently by month and year—or year only.
- Account for gaps in the sequence.
- Avoid showing each new position with the same employer as a new job. (Use a subheading approach to avoid repeating the same information.)
- State your job title. (Give some brief indication of what that means in the organization—the title of the person to whom you reported, for example.)
- Describe your duties and responsibilities in terms that mean something. (Number of people supervised and their status.) (Volume of business generated.) (Amount of change in indicators that measure what you do.)
- Mention several believable, verifiable accomplishments. (Things that would be valued by the employers you are now seeking to impress.)
- Consolidate older and less relevant experience at the bottom of the resume.
- Respect the one-page limit. Use two at the most and only if justified.

Education—List your most important degree or certificate of training first in the section which, itself, will go either at the beginning or end of the resume, depending on the relative importance of your work and education. Provide name of school or college, major (if it adds to the value for the job in question), year of graduation, and state (possibly city) where college is located, depending on how well known it is.

Comments, professional affiliations, or other concluding statements can be added if kept brief and if they contribute to, rather than detract from, the main resume.

Examples of Work History Resumes

William K. Akrin
56 Tura Road
Bennington, CT 48009
860-222-9988 (Office)
860-333-9075 (Residence)
wmakrin@att.net

Overview

Technical Writer with formal training and experience in computer technology and technical writing seeks editorial opportunity with mass market user's magazine.

Experience

January 1998 - Present: Technical Writer
Brainware Computer Products, Inc., Bennington, CT.

Assist in the preparation of technical manuals that support the use of software products created at Brainware. Experience includes interviewing programmers and systems engineers to identify program features. Convey features and step-by-step instructions for use in lay language. Attend national workshops to receive feedback on manuals and products. Full range of mass market software including desktop publishing, graphic arts, and business packages featuring word processing, databases, spreadsheets, etc.

September 1995 - December 1998
Full-time study for bachelor's degree.

June 1988 - August 1990: Customer Service Technician
Matson Software, Ltd., Norwich, CT.

Telephone contact for users of Matson Software products including their complete line of word processing, spreadsheet, graphic presentation, and database programs. Assisted users in isolating their problems and guiding them to solutions. Maintained records on nature of questions addressed and assisted technical writing staff in the revision of manuals.

Education

Associate in Arts (AA)
Computer Studies
Asnuntuck Junior College, CT, 1993

Bachelor of Technology (BT)
Technical Writing
West Connecticut College, CT, 2000

Darlene W. Robinette

96 Galveston Lane
Houston, TX 77271
281-222-9988 (Office)
281-333-9075 (Residence)
robie96@aol.com

Education

Bachelor of Science	Master of Business Administration
Business Administration	Finance
Smith University, 1973	University of Texas, 1984

Chartered Financial Analyst (CFA)
1989

Experience

April 1991 - Present: **Vice President & Trust Investment Officer, National Bank & Trust of Eastern Texas, Houston, TX ($1.5 billion trust department).** Senior portfolio manager in a group of six; managing both fixed and equity in collective and other funds (personal, pension, and endowment). Responsible for all fixed income funds (approx. $300 million personal/$100 million employee benefits); responsible for most equity funds (approx. $400 million personal/$20 million employee benefits); foundations and charities account for an additional $75 million. Involved in business development activities, including presentations to support new business and existing accounts—also cooperative development projects with other elements of the trust department. Handled installation of IBM-AT dedicated to investment function; computer literate and proficient with DOS, LOTUS, asset allocation programs, Microscan, LOTUS Financial, Norton Utilities, communications, and disk maintenance.

June 1990 - March 1991: **Vice President & Trust Investment Officer, United Bankshares Trust, Fort Worth, TX ($580 million trust department).** Chaired the investment committee. Lowered transaction costs 32 percent. Implemented standard investment procedures. Established a research capability and client newsletter. Brief tenure due to inability to adapt to the culture and lifestyle of the area.

July 1987 - May 1990: **Assistant Vice President and Trust Investment Officer, Chicago Retail Trust Bank, Chicago, IL ($250 million trust department).** Senior investment officer responsible for setting overall investment posture; conceived and implemented a new common trust fund, revised others. Organized and conducted investment conference for 200 members of the local professional community. Implemented formal procedures to control commission use and allocation. Established investment management goals, including performance measurement techniques. Wrote monthly economic/investment commentary for distribution to 300 regional bankers, government officials, corporate officers and selected clients.

Eight previous years: **Retail stock broker,** Scott & Delmonico, Inc., Milwaukee, WI.

Comments: Reason for leaving relates to the declining economy of the region where oil, gas, and space programs show little promise in the near future. Investment performance for the past five years: 14th percentile equities; 23rd percentile fixed income; 19th percentile combined.

The Focused Resume

The Focused Resume is often discussed as a Targeted Resume because it presents capabilities and achievements in a manner that caters to a particular kind of job. The Focused Resume is somewhat like the Competency Cluster Resume and shares a number of its advantages and disadvantages. The emphasis in both is on extracting and highlighting selected characteristics of your work history, rather than listing it in a traditional way. The difference is that the Focused Resume aims at a particular job and is arranged in blocks of abilities and achievements, whereas the Competency Cluster Resume is more general and is centered around a series of functional areas under which your talents are grouped.

Strengths	Weaknesses
Makes a strong case for a specific type of job.	Is relatively narrow and can leave out some things that might have been valued by the reviewer.
Showcases abilities in a single light.	May have less impact than your overall experience.
Demonstrates that you know what is important to this particular employer.	You may misjudge what the emphasis should be.
Can be customized with a different focus for each of several situations.	Selectively limits your presentation.
Tends to deemphasize your employers and positions held—a strength if you are not strong in these areas.	Tends to deemphasize your employers and positions held—a weakness if it obscures outstanding entries in these categories.
Useful when you are applying for a job that does not logically flow from your last position or general work history.	Unnecessarily vague if you are building on a clear career ladder.
Useful for people with beginning or interrupted work histories—focuses on current skills, not prior jobs.	Fails to take advantage of job progression record, if it exists.
Useful where work history is scattered or has not moved at the expected pace.	Unclear for the employer who is interested in linking every statement you make to a past job.

Focused Resume Template

> Name
> Address
> Telephone Number(s)
> Personal e-mail

Overview or Summary, Goal or Objective. An appropriately brief and relevant statement of your main qualifications *and goal*—the focus of your resume must be developed clearly at this point.

Abilities or Strengths or Assets.
- A series of short (a line or two) bulleted statements that tell the employer exactly *what you can do* for his or her company. (It requires that you know what is vital in the job.)
- Your statements reflect on your past training and experience—in the form of current abilities.
- Your statements reflect on your awareness of what the employer needs— and how you can supply it.

Achievements or Accomplishments.
- A series of short (a line or two) bulleted statements that show *what you have accomplished.*
- The more related to the job you have in mind, the better.
- Quantify the magnitude of your achievements.
- Put them into a context that is easily evaluated by this particular employer.

Work History—List your jobs in the order held, most recent first. Dates should be given, but how you do that will depend on how much emphasis you want to place on them. Just listing the years is acceptable. If there are breaks and you want to de-emphasize them, list the dates on the ragged right of the paragraph showing your employment history and make the reader look for them.

Education—List your most important degree or certificate of training first in the section which, itself, will go either at the beginning or at the end of the resume, depending on the relative importance of your work and education. Provide name of school or college, major (if it adds to the value for the job in question), year of graduation, and state (possibly city) where college is located, depending on how well known it is.

Comments, professional affiliations, or other concluding statements can be added if kept brief and if they contribute to, rather than detract from, the main resume.

Examples of Focused Resumes

Margaret A. Arnold

89 University Drive
Santa Marina, CA 93455
805-886-1903 (Office)
805-876-3921 (Residence)
maa@mymail.com

Overview

Award winning Television Support Technician with national experience in multiple aspects of professional news, talk show, and drama productions seeks network or national cable opportunity.

Professional Abilities

- SET MANAGEMENT — six years of experience in the management of set activities supporting news, talk show, and dramatic television productions.

- LIGHTING — four years as associate lighting director for a producer of nationally syndicated television musical productions. Accomplished user of Kludge and special effects lighting in television applications.

- SET DESIGN — three years professional and five years amateur set design. Professional years included assistant background construction director for the Emmy Award–winning docudrama *War and Space.*

Achievements

- Union cards held in the areas of television stage management, lighting, and set design.

- On the staff of seven production companies that received national industry recognition for excellence during my tenure.

- 1998 Audience Appreciation Award winner for set design in the live audience participation *Minnie Walker Talk Show* series.

Experience

June 1996 - Present: Set Manager, Gordon Boxwood Studios, Hollywood, CA.

June 1995 - May 1996: Set Design Specialist, KNBB Santa Clarita, CA.

July 1992 - May 1995: Lighting Technician, Samuel Whitworth Production Company, Los Angeles, CA.

Education

Associate in Science (AS)
Electronics Technology

Allan Whetstone Junior College, CA 1992

Wadsworth T. Sandsome

35 North Island Drive
Haleiwa, HI 96740
808-675-8345 (Office)
808-776-9078 (Residence)
wadsworth2@aol.com

Position Sought

Director of Counseling Services

Abilities

- State Certified School Guidance Counselor.
- Specialized training in the recognition and treatment of adolescent substance abuse.
- In-depth familiarity with the use of computer databases designed to aid students in the selection of appropriate colleges and majors.
- Experienced group counseling leader.
- Knowledge of private as well as public sources of college bound student financial aid.
- Extensive work with private sector community work-study arrangements.

Achievements

- 80 percent of counselees admitted to college of their choice for the past five years.
- Awarded Parents' Club Award for Excellence 2001 in appreciation for efforts to establish private sector linkage between North Shore School and the burgeoning hospitality industry.
- Founder of Island Helpers Teen Substance Abuse Hotline that serves 3500 callers weekly.
- Summer Consulting Fellow to College Boardroom, a non-profit organization that designs career planning software for students.

Experience

June 2000 - Present: Guidance Counselor, North Shore High School, Kawela Bay, HI.
June 1996 - May 2000: Counselor, Kanehoe Intermediate School, Kanehoe, HI.
July 1992 - May 1996: History Teacher, Pearl Harbor High, Pearl City, HI.

Education

Bachelor of Science (BS)
Social Studies Education
University of Maryland, 1990

Master of Education (MEd)
Guidance and Counseling
University of Hawaii, 1996

The Competency Cluster Resume

The Competency Cluster Resume is also known as a Functional Resume because it groups skills and qualities under headings that constitute important functions in a particular kind of job. The Competency Cluster Resume is somewhat like the Focused Resume and shares a number of its advantages and disadvantages. The emphasis in both is on extracting and highlighting selected characteristics of your work history, rather than listing it in a traditional way. The difference is that the Competency Cluster Resume is more general and is centered around a series of functional areas under which your talents are grouped, whereas the Focused Resume aims at a particular job and is arranged in blocks of abilities and achievements.

Strengths	Weaknesses
Good for showing skills not apparent in recent job descriptions.	Unclear as to just which skills relate to which jobs.
Can place the emphasis on families of expertise not represented in your past work history.	Fails to support with specific sources the expertise presented.
Blurs the progress of your career in favor of concentrating on selected skills you choose to emphasize.	Represents no clear career path.
Makes the best of disjointed work experiences.	May not connect logically constructed career-building steps.
Shows a series of different skill areas.	Makes it obvious if you have only a few areas of expertise.
Can be arranged to stress current objectives rather than past history.	Lacks the support of past employment history related to current goals.
Highlights selected abilities rather than past job titles and employers.	Provides minimal support in the way of working experience in your current specialty.
Does not repeat similar job events.	Deemphasizes work experience.
Good for beginning or changing career directions.	May underemphasize the value of past positions held.
Able to show non-job-related abilities such as those gained in hobbies or nonpaid employment.	You may have to explain at the interview that this experience has no base in paid employment.
An out-of-date, irregular, or irrelevant work history can be subordinated to skills you actually possess.	Expect to explain the nontraditional work history when asked.

The Competency Cluster Resume Template

Name
Address
Telephone Number(s)
Personal e-mail

Overview or Summary, Goal or Objective. An appropriately brief and relevant statement of your main qualifications and goal—optional if it is obvious and adds nothing to the resume.

Competency Headings.
- Select several headings under which you can group the most valuable things you do.
- List these headings in order of importance.
- Develop under each heading a series of short statements that make it apparent you can perform in that area of specialization.
- Use specific examples.
- Give measures of the magnitude of the skill—quantify the number of people involved, the amount of growth achieved, dollars saved, etc.
- Use names, company names, project designator, or anything that aids the reader in judging the significance of your claims.

Work History—List your jobs in the order held, most recent first. Dates should be given, but how you do that will depend on how much emphasis you want to place on them. Just listing the years is acceptable. If there are breaks and you want to deemphasize them, list the dates on the ragged right of the paragraph showing your employment history and make the reader look for them.

Education—List your most important degree or certificate of training first in this section, which will go either at the beginning or end of the resume, depending on the relative importance of your work and education. Provide name of school or college, major (if it adds to the value for the job in question), year of graduation, and state (possibly city) where college is located, depending on how well known it is.

Comments, professional affiliations, or other concluding statements can be added if kept brief and if they contribute to, rather than detract from, the main resume.

Examples of Competency Cluster Resumes

Lynn J. Andersen
973 Albacort Circle
Savannah, GA 31407
912-929-6479 (Office)
912-938-7783 (Residence)
lynnja@msn.com

Overview and Objective

Professional Secretary with six years of advanced office services experience seeks Executive Secretary position with potential for assuming an administrative management role.

Education

Associate in Science (AS)
Secretarial Science
Metropolitan Community College, GA, 1996

Professional Skills

OFFICE MANAGEMENT
- Coordination of office clerical routine.
- Schedule management.
- Vendor liaison with suppliers of services.

DOCUMENT PREPARATION
- 60 WPM using electronic typewriter or word processing equipment.
- Advanced user of principal word processing software packages.

EQUIPMENT OPERATION
- Personal computers and associated peripheral equipment.
- Fax and modems.

DICTATION/TRANSCRIPTION
- 60 WPM vocal dictation.
- Accomplished transcriber.

PERSONNEL
- Preparation and placement of advertising.
- Applicant response, appointment arrangements, EEO record keeping.

EXECUTIVE ASSISTING
- Planning of meetings and conferences, locally and at remote sites.
- Arranging business travel.
- Screening and appointment management.

Experience

November 2000 - Present: Secretary to the Director of Marketing, Rockaway Manufacturing Company, Ltd., Savannah, GA.

May 1996 - October 2000: Secretary, Jensen & Jensen Management Consultants, Tyron, GA.

Patricia D. Lyle
51-C Mount Pleasant Drive
Providence, RI 02906
401-222-9988 (Office)
401-333-9075 (Residence)
lyledp@interland.net

◦ Competencies ◦

Computer Graphics
Color and B&W graphics capabilities using Aldus Freehand on the Macintosh II computer system. Experienced in using both text and graphic scanners. Preparation of products at 300 dpi and full professional quality formats. Expert at trace modification art and logo design.

Desktop Publishing
Oversized Radius screen used for layout of single illustration and multipage publications with desktop publishing software, principally PageMaker. Experienced in brochure, tabloid, magazine, and newspaper layout—expert integration of graphics, including photography.

Drawing Board Artist
Nine years of combined college and commercial experience. Began as illustrator and paste-up person for university publications. Followed by three years of newspaper and two years of national magazine advertising and story art.

◦ Awards ◦

- *Computer Monthly Magazine,* 2001 First Place Award for Commercial Graphics
- The New England Gazette Syndicate, 1998 Award for Excellence in Advertising Graphics
- Numerous collegiate graphic arts and journalism awards

◦ Employment ◦

2000 - Date: Senior Graphic Artist, *Rhode Island Weekends Magazine,* Providence, RI
1998 - 2000: Paste-up and Insertion Technician, *The Providence Daily,* Providence, RI
1996 - 1998: Freelance Artist/Photographer

◦ Education ◦

Bachelor of Arts
Commercial Design
Rhode Island College of Design, 1996

◦ Comments ◦

Interested in taking combined artistic, journalistic, and commercial experience and applying them in a computer-equipped graphic arts studio.

3 MODEL RESUMES

The resumes in Part V are representative of how the standard formats can be applied effectively to a wide variety of situations. Do not be alarmed if your job title is not on the list. They are illustrations of suggested methods and styles and should not be viewed as the perfect format for a given kind of job. Page through them all and let the cumulative impact of a lot of good ideas work for you.

While the model resumes are based on real-life situations, names of people, organizations, professional terminology, numbers, and the data in general are pure fiction. They have been deliberately altered to avoid any chance of conflict with personal or proprietary information. You will be able to look at the samples and determine what real-life substitutions should be made to reflect your circumstances most appropriately.

With the first two chapters as background, you should tap the rich lode of resume technique that fills Part V. To ease your way through what might appear to be an overwhelming array of material, use the index below as a starting point.

All resumes from Resume First Aid and Model Resumes are indexed below. They are listed alphabetically by job title under the following categories:

- Administrative Resumes
- Artistic Resumes
- Education and Institutional Resumes
- Financial Resumes
- Health Care Resumes

- Information Technology Resumes
- Law Enforcement and Security Resumes
- Marketing and Sales Resumes
- Scientific and Technical Resumes

Index by Job Category and Title

ADMINISTRATIVE RESUMES

Job Title	Resume Type	Page
Administrative Assistant	Work History	296
Apartment Manager	Focused	304
Customer Service Representative	Focused	340
Editor	Work History	346
Employment Counselor	Competency Cluster	352
Hotel Manager	Work History	368
Legal Assistant	Competency Cluster	378
Library Technician	Competency Cluster	380
Newspaper Reporter	Competency Cluster	390
Personnel Specialist	Competency Cluster	394
Public Relations Specialist	Focused	404
Purchasing Agent	Competency Cluster	406
Receptionist	Competency Cluster	410
Secretary	Competency Cluster	422
Senior Executive Assistant*	Focused	20
Senior Manager*	Competency Cluster	24

Note: Resumes marked * are found in Resume First Aid, Chapter 1.

ARTISTIC RESUMES

Job Title	Resume Type	Page
Graphic Designer	Competency Cluster	362
Interior Designer	Focused	372
Landscape Architect	Work History	376
Television Support Technician	Focused	436

EDUCATION AND INSTITUTIONAL RESUMES

Job Title	Resume Type	Page
Child Care Worker	Focused	320
College Counselor*	Focused	08
College Professor	Work History	324
English as a Second Language Teacher*	Focused	12
Minister	Focused	386
School Administrator	Competency Cluster	418
School Guidance Counselor	Focused	420
Teacher Aide	Competency Cluster	430
Training and Development Specialist	Work History	438

FINANCIAL RESUMES

Job Title	Resume Title	Page
Bank Collector	Focused	306
Bank Officer	Work History	308
Bookkeeper	Competency Cluster	314
Credit Manager	Work History	338
Financial Analyst	Work History	356
Investment Officer*	Focused	16
Securities Broker	Competancy Cluster	424

Note: Resumes marked * are found in Resume First Aid, Chapter 1.

HEALTH CARE RESUMES

Job Title	Resume Type	Page
Dental Assistant and Hygienist	Work History	344
Emergency Medical Technician	Work History	350
Hospital Administrator	Work History	366
Medical Records Technician	Focused	384
Nurse	Competency Cluster	392
Pharmacist	Focused	396
Physician Assistant	Work History	398
Veterinary Technician	Competency Cluster	442

INFORMATION TECHNOLOGY RESUMES

Job Title	Resume Type	Page
Computer Maintenance Specialist	Focused	326
Computer Operator	Focused	328
Computer Programmer	Work History	330
Computer Systems Analyst	Focused	334
Database Administrator	Focused	342
Internet Security Engineer	Focused	374
Network Administrator	Focused	388
Supervisory Systems Analyst	Focused	428
Web Developer	Focused	444
Word Processing Operator	Competency Cluster	446

LAW ENFORCEMENT AND SECURITY RESUMES

Job Title	Resume Type	Page
Corrections Officer	Work History	336
Private Investigator	Competency Cluster	400
Security Manager	Focused	426

MARKETING AND SALES RESUMES

Job Title	Resume Type	Page
Advertising Account Executive	Competency Cluster	298
Advertising Copy Writer	Focused	300
Advertising Sales Manager	Competency Cluster	302
Computer Sales Representative	Focused	332
Fund Raiser	Focused	360
Insurance Agent/Financial Planner	Work History	370
Manufacturers' Sales Representative	Competency Cluster	382
Product Manager	Work History	402
Real Estate Broker	Focused	408
Retail Buyer	Focused	412
Retail Salesperson	Competency Cluster	414
Travel Agent	Focused	440

SCIENTIFIC AND TECHNICAL RESUMES

Job Title	Resume Type	Page
Biological Technician	Competency Cluster	310
Biomedical Engineer	Focused	312
Business Machine Service Representative	Work History	316
Chemist	Competency Cluster	318
Civil Engineer	Work History	322
Electronic Engineer	Competency Cluster	348
Environmental Technician	Work History	354
Food Technologist	Focused	358
Heating, Air Conditioning, and Refrigeration Mechanic	Focused	364
Robotics Engineer	Work History	416
Technical Writer	Work History	432
Telecommunications Specialist	Competency Cluster	434

4 | ELECTRONIC RESUMES

Don't discard your conventional resume, but there is a new technique in the job search business: the electronic resume, an e-mail transmission of your resume that reaches the hiring official immediately and likely ends up in a database of applicants. Large companies commonly use automated applicant tracking systems. Service bureaus and Internet job sites use similar techniques to make your credentials available to a broad spectrum of potential employers.

A resume is still a resume, but there are special considerations to keep in mind if you want to benefit from the computer revolution. Successfully converting your credentials to a computer-friendly format gets you only so far. It won't compensate for your lacking the specific skills and experiences required for a position, but it may get you past the electronic gatekeeper and onto the to-be-considered-further list.

The electronic resume caters to the mass job market. If you have the wherewithal to present yourself directly to hiring officials who would welcome your credentials, you are a step ahead of Internet resume services and will find them to be unnecessary. On the other hand, if you need to cast your net broadly and see who expresses interest, post your credentials on an Internet resume service or e-mail text-formatted resumes to more than one company.

The upside to posting your resume electronically is broad exposure and the chance to be plucked from the database on the merits of your keywords. The downside is limiting your presentation to fit certain formatting conventions that are not terribly creative. There is also the remote possibility that the wrong people will access your resume. The chance of your job market initiative coming to the attention of your own company is reduced by procedures that allow you to authorize each release of your resume.

Computer-Friendly Resume Formatting

It used to be that human beings scanned resumes and sorted them according to their desirability. That is the way hiring still works much of the time, and it is where even electronic job searches end. The difference is in how the sorting is done. People screening resumes with their eyes have been replaced in the initial stages by computers doing the same thing electronically.

Whether you are asked to present your credentials in ASCII, .txt, or some other plain-text format, the goal is for it to be unembellished and, therefore, readable by any computer or software program. There are several approaches to preparing your resume or cover letter this way.

One easy approach is to use the Windows Notepad located under the Accessories option found under Programs on your PC (note: Mac users can accomplish the same thing using "Simple Text"). Notepad is a plain-text word processor that is free of most formatting. Either compose your document directly on Notepad or copy and paste it there from your regular word processing software. The result will be plain text that communicates universally well in e-mail.

Set the Word Wrap option, then mix small and capital letters, spacing your entries using the Enter key and space bar to achieve a straightforward, understandable version of your document. You can also use asterisks, dashes, and plus signs if they are helpful. Finally, copy and paste your document into an e-mail and send it to yourself to verify that the recipient sees what you intended. If your e-mail lacks a spell check, consider the added precaution of dropping your copy into a word processor to verify spelling.

Another way to the same goal is to work in your regular word processing program and save the document as a text file. Set your margins to 0 and 65 characters and work without formatting commands like columns, tabs, centering, or other special alignments, special characters, bold, italics, and so on. Use caps, asterisks, dashes, and plus signs, to the extent that they improve your presentation, and choose a common font like Courier. Do a spell check and read through once more before copying and pasting your document for a test e-mailing to yourself.

While most electronic resumes are deliberately solicited in plain text, you may occasionally be asked to include traditionally formatted word processor copy as an e-mail attachment. If you do, use a mainstream word processing program that should translate well if the recipient uses a different one. Unless it is solicited, don't count on e-mail attachments being opened and used. Many companies process only the e-mail, not its attachments. It takes time and companies know computer viruses enter their systems via attachments.

You run the risk of fonts and other formatting being corrupted when attachments are sent between different computers. Include a brief note in your e-mail offering to send a modified version if yours fails to open satisfactorily. Such problems are minimized by using universal fonts like Times Roman and Courier, and widely used software. If you know the recipient's computer configuration and software, save your document as a compatible file.

Keywords

Just as the human mind is impressed or not impressed by what it sees in a resume, so, too, is the computer that scans your credentials for specific content. Since even sophisticated computer applications lack the flexibility and judgment of a brain, narrow search criteria are used. That is why you must craft your resume to show the job search computer what it wants to see—keywords.

Every occupation has its own jargon, acronyms, and buzzwords. To make a list for your specialty, examine the Help Wanted listings in the employment publications in your field. Also read current professional publications to find the terminology that is being used to define and communicate what a successful practitioner does in your job. These keywords can be the belabored, lengthy terms of science and medicine or the crisp acronyms of computing, engineering, and government. It doesn't take a lot of imagination to find the keywords valued in your specialty—retailers might be looking for UPC scanner skills; a brokerage firm could be looking for an asset valuation analyst with NASDAQ experience. The terms and their variations are endless, so do your homework and define the keywords for the position you seek.

There are also general keywords that apply to such things as interpersonal skills. The computer may be programmed to find people who express a willingness to travel, are team players, delegate responsibility, possess organizational skills, speak in public, are innovative, are oriented toward customer service, or any of dozens, if not hundreds, of terms used to describe your work style.

If you are responding to a specific job announcement, analyze it for keywords. Next, design your resume to display the keywords the employer is looking for—within the limits of honesty and not pandering so blatantly to the advertisement that it becomes a turnoff.

Take care to get the acronyms right. The same advice applies to making your college and field of study recognizable. Job titles also need to contain terms that an automated sorting system will recognize and value: manager, trainee, supervisor, and the like. Computers recognize and analyze numbers well, and they are often programmed to do so. Make your year of college graduation a single date that can be read, not a range. A range is fine for job experience, which is expected to span a period of time and thus can yield meaningful results in the computer's evaluation of your work history.

If the concept of keywords is alien to you, help is readily available. One approach is to explore the Internet. You quickly learn the art of keyword searching—most search engines offer advice on how to conduct effective searches. But it isn't necessary to go online—any library with a computerized card catalog can provide you with worthwhile experience in keyword searching. Books, after all, have had indexes based on keywords for a long time—it is the same idea applied to computers and databases.

Electronic Resume Template

Bringing keywords clearly to the attention of the automated applicant evaluation system is a matter of formatting. The advice from those who run job database services is to have a plan or theme for your electronic resume. Rough out the essential content, and arrange it from top to bottom in categories and in order of importance. Within those categories, make your presentation concise and direct, respecting the need to communicate the keywords valued by employers.

On the following page is a recommended design for a successful electronic resume.

Sample Electronic Resumes

Full name
Street address
City, state, Zip Code
Telephone number (residence if you don't want to be called at work)
e-mail (personal is best since employers may access office accounts)

KEYWORD OVERVIEW

Begin with two or three sentences that say exactly who you are professionally and what you want for your next job. Include the keywords that make you recognizable to the electronic evaluator.

EXPERIENCE

Start with your current or last job and work back using this format:

Employer, Dates of employment

Title of position

Include several sentences that describe your job knowledge, skills, and experience followed by some accomplishments in a bulleted format. Include keywords.

Repeat the format for each significantly different position held with each employer. Limit the list to relevant experiences, but account for all periods of time. If you traveled for a year after college, explain briefly—postcollege travel abroad, dates.

EDUCATION

Name the degree and college, and state the year of graduation. Follow with other training valued in your industry—name the course of study, where it was taken, and the year. List professional licenses and certificates, including a license number that can be verified and the date awarded.

AFFILIATIONS AND ACCOMPLISHMENTS

List your professional memberships and dates joined. List significant awards and publications briefly—not everything you ever did or received. Use good judgment in separating entries of professional and personal value—omit the purely personal. Use keywords that denote leadership, such as *chairman*.

Don't waste space indicating that references are available upon request, that you are married, belong to certain nonprofessional organizations, have excellent health, are of a certain age, have a certain number of children, enjoy certain sports or activities, etc.—the computer doesn't care.

SALLY N. ANSON
8567 South Murray Lane
Columbia, SC 29208
803-222-9988 Office
803-333-9075 Residence
sanson@juno.com

OVERVIEW

Commercial lender with four years of successful experience in regional bank lending to middle market accounts as a credit analyst and corporate calling officer.

EXPERIENCE

Southland Banks   **Columbia, SC**
Assistant Loan Officer   6/2000–Present

Commercial loan officer with extensive business development responsibilities in the Carolinas, Georgia, and North Florida. Manage a $35 million portfolio, which includes $27 million outstanding and $8 million committed.

- Generated $11 million in new deposits and $19 million in new loans in 2.5 years.
- Number two performer on a staff of 12 regional lenders.
- Developed an on-line loan application on the bank's Web page that pre-qualifies candidates. Significantly reduced lending officer calls on unqualified prospects.

Coastal National Bank   **Sea Pines, GA**
Credit Analyst   6/1998–5/2000

Entry position upon college graduation. Credit review and analysis for middle market companies. Rapidly assumed full supporting activities for lenders prior to leaving to accept an officer position in the interest of professional growth.

Part-time college jobs   7/1994–5/1998
Various part-time positions while attending college, including seasonal retail sales, clerical positions, and summer employment as a bank teller.

EDUCATION

University of West Georgia   **State College, GA**
Bachelor of Business Administration,   6/1998
Banking and Finance

PROFESSIONAL AFFILIATIONS & TRAINING

- Professional Member, Robert Morris Associates, Secretary of Carolinas Chapter.
- Currently pursuing National Commercial Loan School, Norman, Oklahoma.

[Contrast this presentation with Sally N. Anson's conventional resume on page 309.]

Distribution Options

There are several options for making your electronic resume available. One is to send it directly to employers, with the caveat that unsolicited resumes are likely to receive little attention unless you are in a high-demand field. A broader approach is to submit your resume to professional associations and college placement offices that maintain electronic databases containing members' resumes. And executive recruiting firms often use electronic applicant tracking systems.

If you are looking for the latest in electronic resume distribution, go to the Internet. One place to start is your favorite search engine, using the keywords "resumes," "employment," "careers," or variations thereof. Find your way to the career section of something like www.yahoo.com and begin clicking topics that seem to meet your needs. On the Web, one thing invariably leads to another. Definitely check the Web page of major newspapers in your regions of interest; there you will find links to employment and careers that let you search for jobs, post your resume, and read career advice (e.g., for the Washington and Los Angeles markets: www.washingtonpost.com or www.myocjobfinder.com).

Internet Tip

The following links lead to some of the Web sites featuring electronic resume information and posting: www.eresumes.com, www.jobweb.com, www.10minuteresume.com, www.monster.com, www.ajb.dni.us, www.careerbuilder.com, www.nationjob.com, www.flipdog.com, and www.job.com. Similar sites can be found by entering "resume" in any search engine.

PART

II

JOB SEARCH COMMUNICATIONS

5 | A COORDINATED SERIES OF LETTERS

You have prepared a winning resume, and it is time to present it to those who might hire you. That calls for ongoing communications: "letters," printed and, perhaps, electronic; and conversations, in person and over the telephone. This chapter describes the cycles you are likely to experience and demonstrates the kinds of letters you might want to write. With the knowledge gained you will be better positioned to respond successfully at each step of the hiring process.

The letters you send with your resume are among the most important communications you have with a hiring official. They are tangible representations of you that are shared with others as candidates are discussed and sorted. These letters play a significant role in determining your fate throughout the hiring cycle.

People who screen resumes look for reasons to set them aside. Their challenge is to reduce a stack of hundreds to the dozen that will receive careful scrutiny. Among the first criteria used to judge your packet are letter content and presentation. At various levels of consciousness, reviewers consider these factors:

- Is the letter written on clean, neat paper of a conventional business size, weight, and color?

- Is the letter written on only one side of the page?

- Does the letter use a conventional business typeface or something too scriptlike and highly stylized for the purpose?

- Are the keyboarding, layout, and printing professional looking?

- Do the address and greeting match the letter's font and style or are they awkward insertions into a form letter?

- Are the spelling and grammar correct?

- Has the letter been proofread and corrected professionally—no misspellings, disconnects, obvious errors, or sloppy corrections?

- Is the letter phrased in a contemporary, unaffected style that sounds neither like a government regulation nor like a letter home from camp?

- Am I reading a letter custom-written for this position or is it bulk mail?

- Does the letter correctly address a specific person involved in the hiring?

- Does the letter make it easy to find what I want to know about the applicant?

- Does the letter signal familiarity with the employer's organization and mission?

- Is the letter personally signed?

Although an irresistibly attractive candidate might convey his or her credentials in a letter containing one or more of the problems mentioned above, don't count on being that person. In modern employee selection there are many applicants, and several of them usually are comparably attractive—so the quality of your correspondence matters.

Think of the entire stream of correspondence you will generate as you pursue leads, have interviews, field offers, and accept a position. Seat yourself on the final selection committee and picture the desirability of being represented by a matched set of coordinated, consistent correspondence. It speaks volumes about what can be expected as you complete work assignments on the job.

Put your resume and letters on the same kind of paper, use the same typeface, and remember that even your envelopes can find their way to the decision makers—avoid carelessly aligned labels and scribbled addresses that you assume won't be seen by anyone beyond the mailroom.

Although you may not use them all, here are a number of job search letters to consider. Each letter has a place in securing your next position and—nearly as important—preparing for hiring cycles to follow in the years ahead. Fully developed examples of the letters follow these descriptive sketches:

- **Response to a Classified Ad: Comparison Points Letter**—The response to an advertised position. In it you match what the employer asks for with your qualifications, point for point.

- **Response to a Specific Position Announcement: Conventional Letter**—Written in response to a position announcement.

- **Unsolicited Letter to an Executive Recruiter**—Announces your availability to an executive recruiter.

- **Availability Announcement Letter**—Makes your availability known broadly in your field.

- **Contact-Generating Letter**—Refreshes the memory of associates who are already in your network and asks them to suggest the names of others who might help.

- **Follow-up Letter**—Sent after a telephone or personal interview.

- **Bridge-Building Letter**—For leaving behind good feelings after a hiring cycle has not produced a job for you. The turndown might have come from you or the employer, but the objective is the same—leave everyone smiling and favorably disposed to hire you next time or, at least, to speak kindly of you.

- **Rejecting an Offer Letter**—Designed to say no to an offer but leave you in the employer's good graces.

- **Accepting an Offer Letter**—Used to say yes to an offer and reaffirm the conditions of employment.

- **Resignation Letter**—Gives notice to your present employer, offers your assistance during the transition, and lets you part friends.

- **Thanks for Helping Letter**—Closes the loop with everyone who helped you this time, to ensure they'll be there next time.

You will benefit from reviewing the summary points following all of the letters, whether or not you use the particular letter. The advice usually applies to many kinds of correspondence, and it is not necessarily repeated for each sample letter.

Examples of Letters

> # RESPONSE TO A CLASSIFIED AD:
> # COMPARISON POINTS LETTER

CAROL J. SEEKER
145 North Arlington Street, #903
Kingston, NY 12401
914-341-1001 Residence
cjs@juno.com

May 24, 2002

John H. Wilson
Collections Manager
c/o Human Resources, Attn: DF/CA
TEC State Bank
7100 Takoma Drive
Falls Church, VA 22044

Dear Mr. Wilson:

Please consider this letter and the accompanying resume to be my application for the Home Equity Collector position you advertised in the Sunday, May 26, 2002, edition of *The Washington Post.*

My resume provides more details, but here is a quick comparison of your needs and my preparation to meet them.

• YOUR REQUIREMENT: Independent, detail-oriented worker with excellent verbal and written communication skills in financial collections.

• MY PREPARATION: Prepared collection cases, crafted mail solicitations, and conducted follow-up calls for overdue credit card customers at the National Credit Union for the past three years.

• YOUR REQUIREMENT: MS Word experience.

• MY PREPARATION: Used MS Office applications, including MS Word, in case load management and direct mail solicitations.

• YOUR REQUIREMENT: Knowledge of bankruptcy, foreclosure, and collection laws and practices.

• MY PREPARATION: In addition to my bachelor's degree in marketing management, I have taken evening courses in real estate law and finance.

Thank you for your consideration, and I look forward to hearing from you. I would welcome the opportunity to provide additional information and to meet with you personally at your earliest convenience.

Sincerely,

Carol J. Seeker

attachment

Comments on Carol's Letter:

- This letter is written in response to a newspaper advertisement. It is easily modified to accommodate a different source announcing a different position.

- She correctly identified the position in her letter.

- She determined the name of the hiring official but respected the protocol of sending her letter in care of the human resources department cited in the ad. This is a judgment call; contact the manager directly if you have reason to believe your resume will not get past human resources. In this case, her qualifications are a good match to the position, and she should be considered. Another option is to send an information copy to the hiring official. Ideally, you want to avoid alienating human resources by going around them, but your objective is to have your application seen by the decision maker. If you can't determine internal company relationships, make follow-up calls to ensure your application made it beyond personnel.

- This letter abandons the popular practice of side-by-side columns in "your requirements/my qualifications"–style letters because electronic scanners digest single-column correspondence better than multiple columns.

- It is not necessary to give details such as college name since a resume accompanies the letter.

- If you prefer not to be contacted at work, add a sentence that says so and suggests the way to reach you.

- If you will be traveling, mention the dates and suggest a way to reach you.

RESPONSE TO A SPECIFIC POSITION ANNOUNCEMENT: CONVENTIONAL LETTER

CARL T. APPLICANT
145 South Response Street, #411
Kingston, NY 12401
914-341-1001
Cta411@aol.com

April 5, 2002

Kristina R. Bentrex
Project Manager (SYS/WF)
WinSystems Corporation
8931 Pinecrest Road
Atlanta, GA 30305

Dear Ms. Bentrex:

I am responding to your position announcement #2709-SYS/WF, dated April 4, 2002, for Systems Engineers. The opportunity was brought to my attention by Charles Planner, a project engineer at your firm. Mr. Planner and I collaborated on a contract at Research Signal several years ago.

As the accompanying resume details, I have the background you seek. In brief:

• I hold a bachelor's degree in electrical engineering from the University of Maryland.

• I have held a variety of positions in ISDN and Digital Signal Processing in worldwide telecommunications environments.

• My duties over the past ten years included project support, design analysis, specification identification, hardware and software allocation, and customized system design.

• I have performed these functions with a diverse product line that included both voice and data communications.

• My experience includes HOL, C, and Assembly (Intel 186/486) languages and a thorough familiarity with ISDN protocols.

I am familiar with your company's international reputation and market position since I have worked for your competitors in these markets. I genuinely respect and admire WinSystems Corporation, and I would welcome the opportunity to discuss the systems engineering position with you at your earliest convenience. In the interim, please feel free to discuss my background with Mr. Planner or anyone else in our industry.

Sincerely yours,

Carl T. Applicant

enclosure

Comments on Carl's Letter:

- He knows the name and title of the hiring official and communicates with her directly since he has inside information that this would be a welcome approach.

- He identifies by name and position a former colleague he knows would comment favorably about him if asked.

- He uses the language of the business to succinctly and authoritatively establish that he has the desired credentials.

- Going beyond the mention of an acquaintance in the company, he telegraphs that he knows the company culture and would function comfortably in it.

- He asks for the interview—like the salesperson who always asks for the sale.

UNSOLICITED LETTER TO AN EXECUTIVE RECRUITER

JOHN T. HARDER
145 South Response Street, #411
Kingston, NY 12401
914-341-1001 Office
914-341-2111 Residence
harderjt@erols.com

June 22, 2002

Robert G. Cumberland
Coldwell, Sampson and Associates
8931 Pinecrest Road, Suite 202
Lake Buena Vista, FL 32830

Dear Mr. Cumberland:

I am sending my resume with a request that you keep me in mind as you work with companies that may be looking for a business development manager in environmental services. My position for the past three years as director of sales for ABF Corporation prepares me well for a similar position in a larger organization.

The following things should interest a prospective employer:

· Successful penetration of new urban markets in the highly competitive mid-Atlantic Region—I have increased new client contracts by an average of 18 percent annually since joining the firm.

· Secured invitations to present marketing briefing on company services to growth sector companies—I am especially effective in reaching the institutional health care group, where contracts have grown by 15 percent during my tenure.

· Experienced in generating technical proposals and contracts, where my efforts have reduced closing expenses 8 percent by eliminating separate staffing.

· Particularly successful in telling the company's story in the public relations arena.

The resume that accompanies this letter spells out my precise work experience and educational preparation. My wife and I are particularly fond of the Southeast but would relocate anywhere except the New York metropolitan area for the right opportunity. I am currently earning $65,000 annually with benefits, and I expect approximately a 20 percent increase in salary and comparable benefits to justify a move, although I could be more flexible in a situation offering exceptional future growth potential.

Please call if you feel my credentials would be of interest to a client. You can reach me at home, or a discreet call to the office is fine. Please treat this contact confidentially and clear each release of my credentials with me. I look forward to hearing from you, and I will contact your office soon to determine the status of my inquiry.

Sincerely,

John T. Harder

attachment

Comments on John's Letter:

- A specific recruiter with an interest in his specialty was selected from a published guide or at the suggestion of someone in the industry.
- He immediately establishes that he is in the recruiter's area of interest, has been on the job a respectable period of years (he is not "job hopping"), and is a viable candidate seeking to make a logical progression in his field.
- He provides the recruiter with specific accomplishments that demonstrate his marketability.
- He identifies his salary and experience ranges, sets realistic growth expectations, and shows flexibility.
- He defines his geographic preferences and limitations and verifies that both he and his spouse are prepared to relocate. This is something a recruiter may be reluctant to ask but wants to know before expending effort that may come to nothing if the spouse vetoes the move.
- He okays telephone contact at the office, requests confidentiality, and asks that his resume not be broadcast without his permission.
- His personal e-mail address is used because of the privacy limitations of his company account.

AVAILABILITY ANNOUNCEMENT LETTER

W. EDITH DECKER, PH.D.
32 Lamp Post Lane
Towson, MD 21286
410-341-1001 Office
410-341-2111 Residence
doc-wed@aol.com

July 13, 2002

Connie H. Packard
Government Consultants, Inc.
86 Beltway Plaza, Suite 500
Arlington, VA 22202

Dear Ms. Packard:

I am writing to make you aware of my plans to pursue a professional growth opportunity in the coming months when my present project is completed. As a successful consultant supporting federal contractors fulfilling re-engineering, work group facilitation, and change management obligations, I knew our interests would be compatible.

As you can determine more precisely from the accompanying resume, I have:

• An earned doctorate in management from the University of Chicago

• Eight years of successful experience with three regional consulting firms specializing in short-duration service contracts with federal agencies having international operations

• A demonstrated willingness to work for extended periods of temporary duty overseas

• Performance assessment and technology standards experience

- CSI clearances

- Strong communication skills

My salary requirements are in the $70,000 range.

Hopefully these introductory comments will help you judge my potential, and I am confident that a meeting in which we can elaborate on these points would be beneficial. Thank you for your interest. I will call next week to see when we can get together.

Sincerely,

W. Edith Decker, Ph.D.

P.S. Please share my credentials with associates who might be interested.

attachment

Comments on Edith's Letter:

- The prominent display of an academic credential is not always desirable; in this case, however, it instantly satisfies a prominent criterion for the consulting position she seeks and is acceptable.
- She explains that this is a general notice of future availability and that she is presently employed in the kind of work she seeks.
- She presents the highlights of her credentials in a format easily digested and remembered by someone who will file her letter for future reference.
- She addresses potential reservations, such as willingness to travel.
- Valuable clearances are noted.
- She encourages future contact and takes the initiative in setting up an appointment.
- She asks that her availability be made known to others.
- She states her salary requirements to avoid unrealistic inquiries.

CONTACT-GENERATING LETTER

BLAKE K. NACKENOUR
5 Smith Street, #104
Prince Frederick, MD 20678
410-341-2111 Residence
bnac@ erols.com

July 15, 2002

Robert G. Sampson
Coldwell, Sampson and Associates
8931 Pinecrest Road, Suite 202
Lake Buena Vista, FL 32830

Dear Mr. Sampson:

I am writing to enlist your help in my job search. No, I am not asking you for a job, but I would appreciate it if you would review my resume, retain it for future reference, and share it with others who might be interested in someone with my background.

I was caught in the downsizing of XYZ Corporation's headquarters in nearby Baltimore, MD, last spring, about which you may be aware. Although I remain optimistic about the future, the job market for our career field is quite competitive at the present time. That is why I am taking the extraordinary step of contacting associates like you and requesting the same kind of assistance I would provide if our situations were reversed.

Although I have done my best to identify people who are influential in the business, your help in providing several more useful contacts would be most appreciated. I will call you in about a week to get their names and listen to any other advice you might like to offer.

In the briefest of summaries, here is what you will find explained more fully in the accompanying resume about my qualifications:

- Southeast Regional Field Training Manager, XYZ Corporation, 5 years
- Managed the growth and development of customer training
- Proven expertise in instruction and course design and development
- Highly proficient in the use of technologically advanced training media
- Innovative use of CBT, multimedia, self-paced, and online training tools

Thank you for your willingness to assist me in reentering the profession. I look forward to speaking with you next week. If you prefer to contact me sooner, you can reach me at the residence number listed above or through Smithson Outplacement Services, 410-444-0001, extension 307.

Sincerely yours,

Blake K. Nackenour

enclosure

Comments on Blake's Letter:

- Contact-generating, sometimes referred to as networking, letters often go to people you know well. Be as familiar and personal as the relationship allows, but when in doubt, keep the tone professional.

- A combination of candor about needing help and optimism about the future is an effective element in a contact-generating letter.

- He helps the other person experience the "there but for the grace of God go I" sentiment by drawing comparisons and mentioning his willingness to help if the tables were turned.

- He summarizes his qualifications.

- He asks for help like a salesperson asking for the sale. He promises follow-through and encourages the person to contact him.

FOLLOW-UP LETTER

WALDO J. STRIPE
145 Prospect Street
Waltham, MA 02154
781-341-1001 Office
781-341-2111 Residence
stripew@aol.com

September 29, 2002

Phyllis M. Xenia
Manager, Imaging Sciences Division
The Malcolm Deen Companies
8931 Dolphin Road, Suite 202
Coral Springs, FL 33065

Dear Ms. Xenia:

I am writing to thank you for the September 28th interview for the Image Scientist, Lead Engineer position at your Orlando plant. It was especially useful to meet you there and tour the new facilities. I was genuinely impressed with the color printer technology processes you have concentrated at this location.

As lead engineer on the focus team, I would look forward to the challenge of directing Deen's efforts in building optical measurement systems for image and color analysis. I came away from the visit and our stimulating conversations with ideas I look forward to sharing the next time we meet. Specifically, I would like to get your reaction to my thinking regarding the problems your staff discussed in the areas of vision systems hardware design and image processing software. I am confident you will find my comments useful in the crucial area of color reproduction evaluation methods.

You evaluate many people in the course of hiring, so let me recap my qualifications:

- MS in Engineering/Image Science
- Four years of imaging and color analysis experience with DEF

- Specializations in visual measurements and psychophysics
- Knowledge of home and business computers and printers
- High-level programming abilities
- Excellent management and communication skills

I was impressed with the facilities, the scientific and commercial challenges facing the lead engineer, and your vision for the position. If you end the search sharing my judgment that I am the person for the job, I am certain we can come to terms on a compensation package that would offer the growth I seek.

If I can further substantiate my ability to meet your needs at Orlando, please call me at home or work. My personal e-mail address is shown above, if that would be more convenient. Thanks again for your time. I look forward to hearing from you.

Sincerely yours,

Waldo J. Stripe

Comments on Waldo's Letter:

- Waldo was careful to get his interviewer's name and title correct, even if he had to call and verify them.
- He mentions specifics that demonstrate his grasp of her requirements.
- He specifically says how he relates to the challenges ahead and offers to share his insights at their next interview—as he increases its likelihood by suggesting what amounts to a free consultation on her problems.
- Waldo is realistic about not being the only candidate, and he restates his strengths.
- He explicitly welcomes the challenge and punctuates the thought by adding commercial sensitivity to the expected scientific one.
- He judges himself to be the person for the job but acknowledges that the choice is hers.
- He suggests that they can reach agreeable terms and invites further contact.
- He uses his personal, not office, e-mail since privacy on a company system cannot be ensured.

BRIDGE-BUILDING LETTER

GERALDINE P. HAYES
973 Stemm Creek Parkway
Palo Alto, CA 94304
650-341-2111 Residence
hayesg@ aol.com

January 22, 2002

Kirk B. Wonderly
Timberlane, Booth & Chairwood
9455-67 Manufacturers' Road NE
Fairfield, OH 45014

Dear Mr. Wonderly:

Although I was disappointed not to receive the merchandising management position for which I was considered, I want to thank you for the interview and wish you success with the person you hired. In today's fluid job market, we could well meet again, and I want you to keep me in mind the next time you or others you know in the industry are looking for management talent.

I value professional relationships developed in meetings like we had exploring this vacancy. I learned things from you, acquired respect for your way of doing business, and would welcome the opportunity to work with you in the future, possibly in another capacity. I hope that you feel the same and would be comfortable calling on me whenever such contact might be advantageous to either of us.

Thanks again for the courtesies extended during the selection process. I look forward to hearing from you in the future.

Sincerely,

Geraldine P. Hayes

Comments on Geraldine's Letter:

- Her personal e-mail address is provided because in today's business world that is an effective invitation to future contact—it is painless, avoids "telephone tag," is informal and confidential.

- For the cost of a stamp and the time to write a final letter, she provides a fileable reminder of herself and remains a player in the mind of someone with the power to hire.

- Her realistic observations about the job market and her place in it should register favorably with the recipient.

- The compliments are professional and not overdone, and everyone likes to hear them.

- She presumes a continuing professional relationship and invites future contact.

REJECTING AN OFFER LETTER

CLYDE I. PACKARD
145 South Response Street, #411
Kansas City, MO 64106
816-341-1001 Office
816-341-2111 Residence
cipack@erols.com

February 2, 2002

Samuel C. Rockbridge, Jr.
Vice President, Human Resources
Stovemaster Manufacturing Company
Jackson, MS 39201

Dear Mr. Rockbridge:

I spent last evening giving thorough consideration to your offer of a position as Safety Manager with Stovemaster Manufacturing. Although there are many attractive aspects to the opportunity, I came to the conclusion that it would not be the right move for me in my circumstances.

You may recall commenting Monday that one purpose of the interview process is to give both the candidate and the company the opportunity to make the right decision. I am grateful for that advice and for your candor in describing my prospects for growth in the position.

When I evaluated everything objectively, I concluded that I had not satisfied my own criteria for selecting my next position. You have an impressive organization, and if I were at an earlier stage of my professional growth I would relish a place on your team.

Thank you for the offer; but I must decline. All the best in your future endeavors. Please let me know if I can ever be of assistance to you or Stovemaster Manufacturing.

Sincerely,

Clyde I. Packard

Comments on Clyde's Letter:

- Although it may not matter in a rejection letter, note that his choice of a script typeface is unnecessarily difficult to read and potentially awkward for a computerized applicant tracking system—a standard business font is preferred.

- Clyde indicates that his decision was made after careful thought—he had been a serious candidate, not someone wasting the company's time.

- Insufficient prospect for growth is always an acceptable reason for saying no.

- Referring to the hiring official's comment that helped him reach the right decision makes the conclusion mutually acceptable.

- Saying he would have welcomed a place on the team at the right point in his career minimizes thoughts of broader negatives—the turndown was for specific and limited reasons.

ACCEPTING AN OFFER LETTER

HELEN B. JENSEN
Redoubt Street South, #881
Atlanta, GA 30346
404-341-1001 Office
404-341-2111 Residence
hbjenson@juno.com

March 2, 2002

Michael N. Arrowsmith
Senior Vice President, Marketing
The ABC Companies, Ltd.
Eden Prairie, MN 55334

Dear Mr. Arrowsmith:

I want to confirm our telephone conversation of yesterday afternoon in which you offered me the position of District Sales Manager with The ABC Companies, Ltd. The terms of employment described in the fax that followed are consistent with our negotiations, and I look forward to completing and returning the formal contract when I receive it in several days.

As was evident during the interviews, we share a mutual enthusiasm about the prospects of leading the company to new highs in sales and market penetration. I can't wait to begin.

Please extend my appreciation to your colleagues who informed me so thoroughly about the challenges and opportunities associated with the position. I look forward to confirming their confidence in me.

Let me know if there is anything I can do to get a head start or otherwise facilitate the transition.

Yours truly,

Helen B. Jensen

Comments on Helen's Letter:

- While being pleasant and properly enthusiastic about accepting the position, Helen confirms the conditions of employment and asks for the formal contract.

- She cites points of agreement and says she is ready to begin.

- Her letter extends kind words about others in the company on whom her success will depend.

- Concluding her acceptance with a commitment to start assuming responsibilities now makes her sound like a desirable employee.

RESIGNATION LETTER

NORWOOD D. BLACK
145 South Response Street, #993
Kingston, NY 12401
914-341-1001 Office
914-341-2111 Residence
norblk@att.net

February 7, 2002

Nadine V. Upland
Senior Scientist
Coldwell, Sampson and Associates
8931 Pinecrest Road, Suite 202
Kingston, NY 12401

Dear Ms. Upland:

Please accept this letter as my resignation from my position at Coldwell, Sampson and Associates. I begin new duties as senior scientist with the Benning Group in Green Spring, SC, on March 1, 2002. While some flexibility is possible, I intend to make February 22 my last day with the company unless a slightly different schedule is desirable from your perspective.

I'm sure you're aware of my favorable feelings about my Coldwell, Sampson experience. You and my other colleagues have been a pleasure to work with, both professionally and personally. The significant step forward that I am about to take is largely a result of my work here. I value your contributions to my development, and I will always be grateful.

If there is anything I can do, now or after I leave, to make things easier for my successor, just let me know. I look forward to our continued professional association in the years ahead, and I wish you and the Coldwell, Sampson family the best.

Yours truly,

Norwood D. Black

Comments on Norwood's Letter:

- Resignation letters generally follow a conversation in which the intention to resign is conveyed personally.

- He states for the record when he will leave, while extending whatever flexibility is possible.

- Two weeks is the minimum notice in most situations, but staying too long after announcing your departure is also unwise. The best advice is to leave promptly and offer to assist your successor or those who will assume your responsibilities.

- Resignation letters are for accentuating the positive, eliminating the negative. Few working relationships are perfect, but the focus should be on the future and a positive view of the past. Set the stage for future pleasantries as your professional paths cross.

THANKS FOR HELPING LETTER

FRANKLIN P. WARNER, JR.
45 South Depot Street, #11
Kingston, NY 12401
914-341-1201 Office
914-341-3111 Residence
fpwjr@ allnet.net

April 2, 2002

Roberta L. Calvert
Sampson and Associates
89 Crest Road, Suite 207
Amherst, NY 14228

Dear Ms. Calvert:

I wanted to let you know that I successfully concluded my job search and began my new position as an account executive with the Wilson Group last week. The job is just what I had been looking for, and it should provide the perfect outlet for the creative energies you so graciously recognized in me when we discussed my plans a few weeks ago.

The letters of recommendation you provided and telephone reference checks you accommodated were greatly appreciated. I have come to understand the value of professional friendships like yours and the important role they play in securing occupational advancement.

Thanks again for helping. If there is anything I can do for you in the future, please don't hesitate to ask.

Sincerely,

Franklin P. Warner, Jr.

Comments on Franklin's Letter:

- This is a letter to a reference. It could as easily have been written to anyone who assisted in the job search.

- Franklin personalized the note of thanks by relating a specific that the recipient would recall.

- He thanks the person for specific things he knows she did for him—letters and telephone calls.

- He offers to repay the favor.

Suggestions on Style: Things to Avoid

Although you might find the occasion to use nearly any style in your job search correspondence, the examples that follow are things you probably want to avoid.

1. Being presumptuous:

- Would you like to find the ideal person to fill your position? If you are, well here I am . . .

- It was clear to me that you were impressed by my . . .

- One of your clients needs me and . . .

- Eleven reasons to hire John Smith:

2. Passive voice:

- AWKWARD: Having spent many years . . .

  BETTER: I have spent many years . . .

- AWKWARD: Hoping to meet you personally when . . .

  BETTER: I hope to meet you when . . .

- AWKWARD: I was surprised to have been contacted by . . .

  BETTER: I was surprised when I was contacted by . . .

3. Making statements unnecessarily complicated:

- AWKWARD: With this letter and resume I would like to . . .

  BETTER: This letter and resume . . .

- AWKWARD: As you can see from the enclosed resume . . .

  BETTER: My resume shows . . .

- AWKWARD: Please feel free to share my credentials with any of your associates who you feel might be interested.

  BETTER: Please share my credentials with interested associates.

- AWKWARD: It is not that I would absolutely never . . .

  BETTER: I would not normally . . .

- AWKWARD: It is my sincere hope that this resume describes my qualifications for . . .

  BETTER: This resume describes my qualifications for . . .

- AWKWARD: I fervently wish I had the opportunity to express to you personally . . .

  BETTER: I wish I could tell you . . .

- AWKWARD: As per our conversation of . . .

  BETTER: When we spoke on . . .

- AWKWARD: I would like to take this opportunity to thank you so very much for . . .

  BETTER: Thank you for . . .

- AWKWARD: It was indeed my great pleasure to have joined you for . . .

  BETTER: I enjoyed joining you for . . .

- AWKWARD: As of this date it is my intention to . . .

  BETTER: Today I . . .

- AWKWARD: We in the software development community . . .

  BETTER: Software developers . . .

4. Clichés:

- I thrive on challenges, lead by my own example, am eternally optimistic, and will remain loyal to your organization through thick and thin.

- I represent the brightest and the best . . .

- I am a self-starter who . . .

- Gone but not forgotten, you surely recall speaking with me last month about . . .

5. Unprofessional:

- Let me be brief. I want a job with your company. Read my resume and call me! [This was the applicant's entire cover letter.]

- Hi John: Just thought I'd take a few minutes and . . .
- You are the best-looking woman I've ever had an interview with and . . .
- I'll give you a buzz next week regarding . . .

Strive for attention-getting introductory statements that are based on demonstrated familiarity with the job, company, current market conditions, a relevant bit of news, awareness of new technology, or the mention of someone whose familiarity with your work would be valued. For the balance of the letter, phrase your thoughts the way you would say the same things in polite, not overly formal or informal, conversation. The test: say it out loud, and if it doesn't sound like you speaking, simplify the sentence and be pleasantly direct.

6 PRESENTING YOUR CREDENTIALS

The way you learn about the availability of a position determines how you apply for it. While the list is not exhaustive, here are some of the possibilities and recommended ways to respond.

In each of these instances, you need a current resume that has been written in a style most appropriate to the situation. The other thing that is essential in almost every case is a cover letter that personalizes the resume and conveys information not included in it.

Source	Response
Newspaper advertisement.	Send a resume and cover letter, then follow their instructions—possibly completing their formal application or adhering to strict e–mail resume submission guidelines.
Internet Web page announcement.	Follow the instructions given, probably for submitting an electronic resume. Depending on how rigid the requirements (e.g., some literally want only an unembellished text-file resume), you might include an electronic cover letter as well. In less limited situations you could provide a formatted e-mail enclosure of your resume and cover letter.

Source	Response
Unsolicited inquiry.	Send your resume and a cover letter explaining your interest in the company.
A recruiter contacted you.	Send your resume through the recruiter who has already developed contacts within the company. The recruiter will interview you and provide additional information focused on the position.
Posted announcement.	Follow the instructions and include a resume and cover letter.

7 PREPARING RESUME COVER LETTERS

The cover letter has a mission as important as the resume itself—to get into the hands of the right person and to motivate that person to read it. Here are some points to consider as you prepare your cover letter.

Question	Answer
To whom should the cover letter be addressed?	The hiring official, if at all possible. There are times when you must respect the protocol of sending it through personnel, but the objective is to place it in the hands of the person to whom you would report if hired.
How do I know who that is?	Inquire. Don't call and say you are an applicant. Do your homework and find out enough about the organization to identify the right person. Call the department and ask one of your potential coworkers. While you are at it, get the full name, spelling, and title correct.
How do I get their attention?	Make a statement or two that indicates you know something about the company and the position. Say you were impressed by their Web page. Say how you learned about the vacancy.

Question	Answer
How do I learn how to get their attention?	Read newspapers, trade journals, business references in the library, call the public relations department of large firms for an annual report or recent news releases. Research the company on the Internet. Call the department and find a future peer willing to discuss the situation candidly. Call a competing firm and do the same.
What is your first priority for the cover letter?	To get your resume into the hands of the hiring official.
The next priority?	To get the hiring official's attention and impress him or her favorably enough to read your resume.
What would do that besides the company and position knowledge already mentioned?	Indicate how you can be of value to the company and the hiring official—how your skills and experience can solve a problem or contribute to company growth.
What is the ultimate objective of your cover letter?	To get an interview to state your case personally and have a chance at conveying the right chemistry, which only a personal interview can communicate.
What should the tone of the cover letter be?	Straightforward, positive, brief, in the language of the business in question—don't be overly obvious, but speak in terms meaningful to the hiring official.
How should the cover letter end?	Asking for an interview. Suggest a time when you will be in the area and offer to stop by, if convenient.
What other issues might be addressed in the cover letter?	Suggested times and places to reach you by telephone—whether or not a call to your office is okay. Whether or not your current employer is aware of your inquiry, or if confidentiality is required. Current compensation might be volunteered—but only if requested or if there is concern about the adequacy of pay for the new position.

Question	Answer
What about dropping names?	If there is a relevant common acquaintance who has agreed to be used as such a link, it can strengthen your letter. Be sure the reference is freely given and positive—enthusiastic is better.
Should I mention my reason for leaving?	It is not essential, but can clear the air on a point that is likely to require explanation eventually. Make it brief, general, and positive. If there is a serious problem that must be disclosed, do so as benignly as possible at this point and offer to elaborate at the interview.

8 UNDERSTANDING THE HIRING CYCLE

You need to understand the hiring cycle in order to participate in it most effectively—including your communications with the company. By knowing what to expect and having a realistic perspective, you will be spared some potential frustration and improve the odds of ending up with the position you want.

After your initial application, your resume and supporting materials are screened along with others and, if interest persists, you might be called for a telephone interview. If that goes well, a personal interview is arranged. Sometimes, the phone interview is omitted. Depending on the firm, you may speak initially with a human resources specialist (personnel officer) who will confirm that you meet the major job qualifications, appear genuinely interested in the position, and seem to have the standards of warmth, personality, and professional image that the company seeks.

A word about salary. The company will want to confirm that it can afford your services. This is an initial, general inquiry and not a negotiation of salary. Unless you are clearly out of range, the hiring process will go forward. Do your best to leave the salary question open until late in the game when the employer has developed a strong interest in you. An appropriate response early in the screening is that you are presently making $____ and that you would be expecting a reasonable incentive above that to justify the move. Leave it at that, if you can. A realistic expectation for a salary increase when changing jobs is the 10 to 15 percent range—sometimes 15 to 20 percent, rarely more. If that is inconsistent with what you feel you must have, you need to review the entire situation. While you might enjoy some unique status that commands more, serious differences in expectations should be resolved early.

Use your grapevine or, if necessary, directly determine early on that your goal is achievable. Unless realistic compromise is potentially possible, the prospects of your ultimately being hired become small.

The whole process may take a while. Timing between the cycles of the hiring process can vary widely and you must be prepared for some emotional ups and downs. Rarely is your application followed immediately by the employer's call, a personal interview, and an offer. It more often goes like this:

- You get reasonably enthusiastic about the prospect of something new and better. If you have been encouraged to apply, it is a compliment—your value in the marketplace is reaffirmed.

- A week or more goes by and no call—due to a number of good reasons that usually have nothing to do with how the employer feels about you. A key person got sick, had to take a trip, or had to deal with an unexpected development. Someone decided that they must all await the results of another ad. A decision was made to interview several local candidates first . . . and so on.

- Such delays can work on your morale and attitude. Initial enthusiasm can turn to posturing to avoid rejection—"I didn't really want it anyway . . . ."

- That kind of thinking is usually unfounded and unnecessary. Rarely is the delay anything more than a large organization trying to fit something that it doesn't do every day—hiring—into what it must do every day—deal with the business at hand and unexpected problems totally unrelated to your hiring.

- Be patient. Everything that was true on your most enthusiastic day probably still is. Well-founded personal and professional reasons attracted you to the position in the first place. Chances are they included a mix of opportunity, geography, and compensation. That is all still true and you have nothing to lose by seeing it through—possibly much to gain.

Your attitude means a lot. Whether you are competing for a CEO's position or something less, the company is trying to select the very best and will make the effort necessary to have an outstanding group from which to choose. You are well prepared or you would not have reached the point of serious consideration.

After the objective criteria have been satisfied, the selection process narrows to more subjective things. It is very important that you be yourself and do not attempt to play a role that you think will be popular. You have to come up with and maintain an honest, positive attitude that conveys something like this: "Yes, this sounds like an opportunity that could really be of interest to me—I want to learn more about it and help you understand just how I could become a very fine addition to your organization."

You might experience ups and downs in your enthusiasm for the position. Ask the necessary questions to resolve your concerns, but keep your positive interest apparent throughout. You are always in a position to say no to an offer. You are rarely able to revive interest once you have turned interviewers off with an attitude with which they are not prepared to deal. Keep it positive and keep their interest growing.

Final negotiations are best handled at the end when you are in the strongest position—they have selected you and made an offer. They want to see it work at that point and will be more apt to satisfy some concerns that you might have—assuming there are no big surprises that alter basic expectations that have been building from the beginning.

Impressions matter. When all is said and done and the final selection is made, you will have left impressions with a number of people. Good impressions can make you the winner in a group of relative equals. Consider how the following impressions can work for you:

- Quiet confidence and a good-natured interest in the company and future coworkers, consistently and naturally displayed with more than one person in a variety of settings.

- A general tone of openness and warmth. Say a genuine thank-you to the person who helped arrange your visit, send brief, positive letters of appreciation following interviews. Express your continuing interest. Employers want to feel comfortable with you and expect that their clients will feel the same.

- A display of poise and equanimity, not being overwhelmed by a single disappointment. Issues calmly resolved in a mutually satisfactory way.

- No up-front demands. Made sure that differences were potentially resolvable, but left their resolution for the proper point in the hiring process—at the offer stage.

- Had some things to offer for the good of the organization with an honest interest in accomplishing them.

- Positive attitude. Made no negative comments about past associations— even if warranted.

- Clean, crisp, well-groomed business image—traditional business wardrobe, obviously cleaned and pressed—the kind of person employers want representing their firm.

Employer fears. There is considerable risk, expense, and trauma for a hiring organization. It would like to avoid going through the same hiring demands again in the near future. You must be honest and genuine, but do not go in saying that you plan on leaving in two years. Before your interview, formulate a solid and positive career plan that shows your commitment to the organization will be long-term in nature—more than five years. Reality may dictate otherwise, but your incoming goal should be one with which the employer can be comfortable.

Finally, the counteroffer/buyback. The hiring cycle has been completed successfully, an offer has been made and accepted. Is it over? Maybe not. What remains is for you to tell your present employer. It is not uncommon for employers to make an unexpectedly good offer in order to retain you. Such counteroffers are usually for the purpose of buying them time to replace you. Why did it take your resignation to make you so valuable to the company? Were you only leaving because of a change in pay or some alteration of your duties? Or were there larger reasons? If so, it is doubtful that the counteroffer will change your mind about leaving. Think this all through and have your answer ready well before the emotional moment of actual resignation. Buybacks are seldom still in their jobs a year later. Decide whether or not you really want to move on. If the answer is yes and the opportunity presents itself, be prepared to follow through without anguishing over the final step.

PART III

INTERVIEWING SUCCESSFULLY

9

GETTING THE INTERVIEW

You have to make three things happen before an interview is possible:

1. find the job
2. apply for it
3. work your application to the top of the stack

To be really effective, you need to understand the dynamics of the preliminary selection process—the things that go on before the first candidate is selected for an interview. Elements of this were discussed in the previous chapter, "Understanding the Hiring Cycle." Knowing the process is necessary so you can judge when to make things happen, when to leave well enough alone, and precisely what to do when it is time to act. You must verify the true availability of the position and determine whether you stand a chance of being seriously considered—is it worth your time and effort? One way to get behind the scenes in a job search and generally improve your chances of turning an interview into a job is by networking to strengthen your candidacy. Finally, there are techniques that can improve your odds of getting that interview. This chapter addresses all of these tricks of the trade and more in these specific topics:

- finding the job
- preliminary selection process
- finding out if the job is really available
- sensing when to take the initiative

- networking your way to an interview
- improving your odds of getting an interview
- why your interview is important to the employer

Before you begin, look at the outline of the entire interview process in Figure 1 and orient yourself to what you are going to accomplish at the "Getting the Interview" stage. This is the stage where you find the job, determine how to apply for the job, and plan to make the most of the personal assets you will be presenting to your interviewer. At this point you lay the groundwork for everything that follows. What you learn becomes the basis for your personal preparations, getting ready to appear for the interview, what you do during the interview, the way you end your visit, appraising how you did, conducting your follow-up activities, and finally, negotiating the terms of accepting the position.

With that in mind, take a moment to review the stream of activity summarized in Figure 1 before going on to the particulars of "Getting the Interview."

Finding the Job

Unless you are in the unusual position of being actively courted by employers, you have to take personal initiatives to locate a job. Here are the options open to most people:

- reading newspapers and professional publications
- listening for word-of-mouth leads
- looking at bulletin boards
- distributing letters and resumes
- contacting executive recruiters to market you
- making cold calls
- self-advertising
- using an outplacement firm
- using an "expanded resume service"
- using the Internet

NEWSPAPERS AND PROFESSIONAL PUBLICATIONS

Go to the library and look through every current and recent publication that would logically advertise for people with your qualifications. Make notes on everything

GETTING THE INTERVIEW
- Finding a job
- Applying
- Networking
- Getting invited

You become aware of the vacant position, identify the person who makes the hiring decision, and determine the procedures of the application process. Next you prepare and submit the best possible combination of your cover letter, resume, and the application form. You network widely and determine whom you know who might tell you behind-the-scenes details about the job, company, and people involved—or put in a favorable word on your behalf. Finally, you make the right telephone calls, exert what influence you have, position yourself to be available, and generally do what you can to get invited for an interview.

PREPARING FOR THE INTERVIEW
- Researching the company
- Preparing personally
- Anticipating questions

APPEARING FOR THE INTERVIEW
- Reconnaissance
- Personal readiness
- Timing

DURING THE INTERVIEW
- Names and personalities
- Style and substance
- Satisfying agendas

LEAVING THE INTERVIEW
- Reading your audience
- Positive expectations
- Last impression

EVALUATING YOUR INTERVIEW
- Substantive match
- Personal chemistry
- Judging your chances

FOLLOWING UP AFTER YOUR INTERVIEW
- Thank-yous
- Additional information
- More networking

CONCLUDING THE INTERVIEW PROCESS
- The offer
- Negotiating
- Accepting

Figure 1. Getting the Interview.

that interests you or looks as though it might be close enough to get you noticed for something more appropriate. Note the names and addresses of points of contact—even if the job isn't what you are looking for at the moment. Set priorities and concentrate on current openings first. Get the big picture of which companies are hiring, and use that knowledge in your interview preparation. This kind of information helps you tap the "hidden" job market—positions that are not currently advertised but are ready to be filled. Executive recruiters rely heavily on such finds as they market promising candidates. Success often comes for them (and for you) when the right resume is presented at the right time—which is not necessarily limited to when everyone else is responding to an advertised vacancy.

BULLETIN BOARDS

Depending on your specialty, you can sometimes walk through buildings housing companies in your field and find jobs posted. Office buildings have lobby bulletin boards posted with index cards seeking everything from clerical help to managers—sometimes to fill short-term, grant-generated positions that can lead to a permanent job. You can also take advantage of in-house postings by having your friends look where they work. Government agencies and public employers have bulletin boards full of advertised positions—many require that you already be in the civil service system, but look and inquire. Doing so can generate other leads.

Don't overlook these obvious sources. Dress for business, have your briefcase full of resumes, and walk in if the posted vacancy lends itself to such an approach. If you don't see the bulletin board, ask where it is located. When you get to the receptionist, ask to see their job vacancy announcements. The worst case is that they have none. You should visit as many offices as possible, leave resumes, make contacts for the future, and have ad hoc interviews as they present themselves.

WORD OF MOUTH

Networking is one of your richest sources of current vacancy information. Talk to people who work where you would like to become employed. Let them know that you are interested in hearing about opportunities for which you might apply. Give them an informal sketch of your professional background if they are not already aware of it and ask them to serve as a listening post for you—give them a resume. As a rule, people are complimented and welcome the chance to help.

LETTERS AND RESUMES

Go to the library or the Internet and use business directories to research companies that might hire you. If you need help, examine the Directory of Directories or talk with the librarian about where to begin your search. On the Internet, use a good search engine and keywords relevant to your field. Mail the letter and resume on a speculative basis, noting your interest in the company. Show you know what the company does, and indicate how you could play a useful role in its operation. Be alert to company Web sites and opportunities to take advantage of its electronic employment gateways.

EXECUTIVE RECRUITERS

If you have a highly marketable skill, take advantage of an executive recruiter to comb the marketplace for you. The first test of a reputable recruiter is that you pay the recruiter nothing—the company that hires you pays the fee. You can bet that the recruiter will not waste valuable time on you unless there is a good chance of collecting that fee. A recruiter's interest is one of the most honest appraisals of your market value—assuming he or she isn't uninterested merely because you fall outside his or her narrow recruiting specialty. Should you encounter indifference, ask if it is because you are outside his or her field of interest, and seek a referral. Case History 1 (p. 106) illustrates the technique.

Don't confuse executive recruiters with placement firms that charge to find you a job—that is an entirely different business. Check the executive recruiter directories and contact a few of the firms that operate in your specialty. (See John's letter in Chapter 5 (p. 68)). Do not list yourself with every firm. Recruiters will inevitably bump into each other marketing you and could decide further effort on their part isn't worthwhile. First, pick one good recruiter, give him or her an exclusive for a reasonable period of time, and see what he or she can do. Ask whether you will be actively marketed or become part of a database for vacancies as they occur.

Case History 1—Situation

EXECUTIVE RECRUITER INTEREST TEST

Background

Nancy Johnston is in her third year as a systems analyst with a defense contractor. ❶ She is receptive to relocating nationally but reluctant to send her resume all over the industry without assurance of interest and confidentiality. She decides that if an executive recruiter will market her effectively, that is the best way to accomplish her move. However, she has heard recruiter promises before and wants to be sure she has a recruiter who will actively market her. ❷

Situation

❸ Nancy calls a recruiter who contacted her several times in the past seeking her advice on people who might be suitable candidates for positions he was filling. She knew that part of his strategy was to interest her in relocating, but ❹ she still feels comfortable with his way of doing business. ❺ He responds positively, and they talk that evening by telephone from her home so she can speak freely. That call is an exciting one, with the recruiter helping to target her interests and ❻ informing her about several opportunities he will explore right away. ❼ Within a few days, Nancy is having brief conferences with her recruiter every day or so—confirming something in her preparation that mattered to a particular employer, ❽ verifying the name of her supervisor so a prospective employer could make a professional inquiry, testing interest in certain kinds of jobs, and asking about the ❾ acceptability of relocating to a West Coast city within the month.

Conclusion

Nancy sees the activity of her recruiter grow from information-gathering to active presentation of her credentials in a few weeks' time. ❿ Her conversations turn to arranging telephone interviews, making appointments for face-to-face discussions with hiring officials in distant cities, and finally, negotiating an offer. She is not a passive file resume to her recruiter. This shows in specific activity and results.

Case History 1—Analysis

EXECUTIVE RECRUITER INTEREST TEST

General Strategy

Nancy knows the problem with sending her own resume and takes a more surgical approach to reaching prospective employers. She knows that a good recruiter could do the job, but needs evidence that the recruiter is convinced of her marketability. This evidence comes from a quick response to her statement of interest and almost immediate third-party interaction with employers showing actual interest from the field.

Specific Points

❶ Recruiters do what you cannot do for yourself—target your resume to the right people directly and discreetly.

❷ Your challenge is to find a recruiter who will do more than make you a routine "listing"—you want evidence that you will be actively marketed, or you might as well sign up with a national job bank.

❸ If you are in a high-demand field, you have already had contact with a recruiter or know of colleagues who have.

❹ Step one in deciding on a recruiter is finding comfort with his or her style.

❺ Agreeing on objectives and the realistic prospects for fulfilling them is essential to making progress together.

❻ Your first sign of valid recruiter interest is his or her questioning you about situations that he or she is actively working on. If you are really marketable, this conversation takes place up front.

❼ Your confirmation that real activity is taking place comes when you receive calls for more information and clarification from your recruiter.

❽ Actual contact arranged between principals means that you are being considered seriously as a result of the recruiter's efforts.

❾ Relocation inquiries come only from potential offers.

❿ Nancy's evidence of marketability and recruiter interest? Real activity.

If you find someone who will actively market you, you have arrived. When you are getting preferred treatment, there will be noticeable activity. You will get inquiries for more detailed information from the recruiter as he or she finds interest among the employers contacted. Telephone interviews will be scheduled. A good recruiter who is really interested in you will engage you in a very active process. Any status short of that with a recruiter is of limited value. The real action (and endorsement of your market value) is in being an actively marketed candidate.

COLD CALLS

If you are willing to take an active role on your own behalf, use the directories of your profession and call people who would have a potential interest in hiring you.

- Let them know that you are available.
- Tell them what your qualifications are.
- Ask if they have any vacancies.
- If they don't have any vacancies, ask who might need your services now.

In effect, you become your own executive recruiter. As you will learn, it isn't especially easy or fun—a lot of people say no. However, persistent cold calling to the right kind of people uncovers jobs you would never find in a passive, traditional job search. It puts you into an active mode that few of your job-hunting competitors will have the initiative to match—most people are uncomfortable at the very thought of this approach. If you can do it, you will greatly increase your chances of finding a good job. Here are some rules to keep in mind.

Rules for Being Your Own Executive Recruiter

- Know what you want to do and why you are hunting for a job. (Have a positive, professional, and career-oriented reason ready if asked.)
- Begin with a simple script that can guide you until it becomes automatic: "Good morning, Ms. Jones, my name is Penny Moss. I am a commercial loan officer with four years of experience successfully developing new business with mid-market companies. I'm looking for a professional growth opportunity, and I thought you'd be interested in talking with me." Then let the other person speak, but be ready to react and keep the conversation going as interest develops.

- Engage your contact's interest by a compliment about his or her company (if you have the basis for a valid one from your research) and a brief, convincing line or two about what you can do for the company.

- Respond to signs of interest: What's your major? Have you ever . . . ? How much are you making? (Stall this particular one by saying something like "I'm sure you could be competitive!," but recognize it as a "buy signal" and keep the conversation going.)

- Lock in the next step by setting up an interview, or at least another call. Never settle for "send me a resume" unless the request is linked to a more valid expression of interest, such as those just mentioned. Otherwise it's usually a brush-off and not worth your time and postage. Explain that you are only interested in current positions and are sensitive about circulating your resume without a specific job objective—then push for the particulars about what she or he has in mind. If nothing, forget it and make your next call.

- Gain "market knowledge"—find out what is going on in your industry, where the next opportunities are going to be in this contact's opinion.

- Identify another good lead somewhere else if she or he doesn't need you just now—don't be bashful about asking specific questions such as:

  ✓ Whom do you know who could use someone with my preparation?

  ✓ Who is expanding their operation and might be staffing?

  ✓ Is there someone elsewhere in your company who might have an interest in someone like me?

  ✓ May I say that you suggested I call?

SELF-ADVERTISING

The "Positions Wanted" columns of the classified sections are small because job seekers read these pages more than employers do. While some people may find work by advertising their own talents, a more active approach will get more leads in a shorter time.

OUTPLACEMENT FIRMS

Outplacement firms are a passive sort of executive recruitment organization at which you are assisted in identifying your potential and finding a place to use it. The firms are less worried about having a highly marketable candidate because they get paid for helping candidates, not placing them. A good outplacement organization has helpful knowledge of the job market and can assist, but it is not a service to purchase on your own. If your company provides it, use it and hope for the best; some are very good, others are little more than "feel good" oases for executives on the rebound.

"EXPANDED RESUME SERVICES"

Avoid this option, or approach it very cautiously. You have probably noticed the advertisements for companies that place "executives—$75,000 to $500,000" in the professional positions section of your Sunday paper. Some are legitimate services and can offer a helpful combination of career advice, resume preparation, and industry contacts, but you want to be keenly aware of what you are getting into. Find out exactly what the fees are and what they promise to do for you. Then go home and think about it before you sign the line for several thousand dollars' worth of fancy resume preparation and not much more than you can get from a good book or college placement office.

USING THE INTERNET

Online services are the electronic equivalent of traditional resume distribution and job posting. Free services are sponsored by specialized professional groups—inquire with organizations and publications that represent your field. Commercial services are also available where employers post jobs, individuals post resumes, and each can search databases containing the other. See Chapter 4, "Electronic Resumes," for additional information on using these services.

Companies, organizations, and government agencies routinely post available positions on their individual Web sites. When your research identifies a potential employer, find it on the Web and follow links to the "positions available" section. You may even have a slight advantage applying directly because the employer avoids liability for a headhunter or commercial Internet job posting service fee if you are hired.

While Internet job listings are heavily slanted toward high technology and other hard-to-fill job vacancies, much like executive recruiting, they are still a vast resource for shopping the job market that should not be overlooked. Check the advertised job posting sites, but don't ignore such less obvious possibilities as your college's placement service page.

| **Internet Tip** |
| To sample the job search possibilities on the Internet, try: http://www. job-hunt.org/ or enter the keywords "job listings" in your favorite search engine. |

The Preliminary Hiring Selection Process

Before the vacancy was ever announced, the people who will interview you for the position decided on how to fill it. They considered everything from eliminating the job and giving the responsibilities to other people, to hiring someone of twice your professional stature. They contemplated:

- what the ideal use of the new person would be
- what missing qualities should be brought in from the outside this time
- what kinds of flaws the last person had that should be avoided
- how filling this vacancy will affect the morale of the existing staff
- where the new person will fit into the organization

In-house considerations set the stage for the attitudes you encounter at the interview.

KNOWING THE HIRING SITUATION

The more you know about the background of the hiring, the better able you are to appreciate it and respond appropriately at the interview. For example, you would know why it's important to be sensitive to a division head who fought to eliminate the position, or a manager who wanted a person with more experience than you have for the job.

Learning such things from research and networking will help you to have a successful interview. This is not information you find printed in position announcements—you can only get it via personal contacts on the inside.

While many hirings are still spontaneous, more companies are going to great lengths to define employee qualifications and determine if you possess them during your interview. If you expect that and prepare for it, you will have a leg up on your competition. You will improve your chances of remaining a contender after equally qualified but poorly prepared candidates slip to the background during the important preliminary selection process. Here is a step-by-step look at how a typical hiring develops.

THE POSITION IS ANNOUNCED

You find that most jobs are posted internally for the benefit of present employees. This is a way for a company to make growth opportunities available to its own people. It is also done to encourage employees to refer qualified acquaintances—a way to find you without paying a recruiting or placement fee. You sometimes earn your friend a finder's fee if you prove to be the successful candidate—this is a popular in-house practice that generally costs much less than paying an employment agency. A recruiter is engaged only if the position calls for skills that are not easily found by referral or routine advertising. The recruiter might come from the company's own human resources department or a consulting firm that specializes in the kind of person being sought.

Newspaper and professional publication advertising is used to reach a broad cross section of candidates—often to satisfy equal opportunity hiring requirements. Listings with public employment agencies and college placement offices are also popular approaches for certain levels of hiring and in addition help to substantiate a firm's efforts to hire from a broad pool of applicants. The Internet is also used to post job vacancies to an international audience of millions of potential candidates.

RESUMES, LETTERS, AND APPLICATIONS

How you learned about the vacancy determines what steps you take in applying for it. When a position is announced or advertised by a large organization, you can usually expect to make formal application through the personnel office. The manager you will be working for becomes involved in the process only later. The human resources department screens applicants, sees to it that the company's hiring procedures are followed, and then presents the line manager with a group of "prequalified" candidates from which to choose. Your first point of contact in the interview process is probably going to be a human resources person and not someone from the department where you will be working—that comes after you survive the first cut of the selection process.

RESUME AND COVER LETTER

You need a professional-looking resume that puts you in the most favorable light for the job. Part I, Preparing a Winning Resume, should be your detailed guide to preparing the right resume, and Part II, Job Search Communications, explains the intricacies of job search letters

THE COMPANY APPLICATION FORM

You are expected to complete a company application form so there is a formally signed record of how you represented yourself to the company—your academic background, experience, and answers regarding criminal convictions and substance abuse. Sometimes the application is just a formality that comes late in the hiring process—but that privilege is increasingly limited to higher-level positions or when you have a well-established professional reputation.

When the application comes early in the employment cycle, complete it neatly and thoroughly, and top it off with a personalized cover letter and resume. Address the package to someone specific, and refer to the job for which you are applying.

One question on the company application form deserves special attention: salary. If you are asked to enter each job in your work history and the associated salary, give a range (e.g., mid-$40s to upper $50s; or, began lower $30s, left earning in the mid-$40s). When completing the information for your present position, put the beginning salary followed by a dash indicating clearly that the upper limit has not been shown. Another option is to note that present salary will be disclosed at the time of an offer. If asked what your salary requirements are, respond "open" or "negotiable." These salary questions can only hurt you and help the company in salary negotiations when an offer is made. Give them a range so they know they can afford to consider you—that is all they really need to know during the screening phase.

HUMAN RESOURCES, PERSONNEL, AND THE LINE MANAGER

You need to cater to each of the people you will be dealing with. Don't expect the human resources person to know detailed buzzwords of a specialized job. He or she will have the big picture, know the general requirements, be oriented toward some firm criteria that have to be met (and a few turnoffs that mean certain rejection), but the nitty-gritty professional discussions come when you meet your working colleagues.

The terms "human resources" and "personnel" are used interchangeably, although human resources is the more contemporary one. In either case, it refers to people, usually in large companies, whose full-time job is to hire, train, and administer benefits to the employees. They work cooperatively with the line managers who actually supervise employees. Personnel is a support function; keep that fact in perspective as you go through the job interview process. Don't lose sight of the fact that it is the line manager who makes the hiring decision and for whom you will ultimately be working.

The relationship between human resources and line managers varies by the company's size and the way it operates. In some firms, managers do their own hiring, and personnel handles the paperwork. In others, human resources has a mandate from top management to keep line managers honest when it comes to everything from equal opportunity compliance and salary guidelines to rigorous screening, interviewing, and background checking.

Your best strategy is to work through personnel, respecting its role, but also try discreetly to establish contact with the person who will eventually hire you. If you are rebuffed and told you have to deal only with human resources, don't press the issue. Wait for the hiring to rise to the working manager's level. On the other hand, if you find the line supervisor receptive to your inquiry, cultivate the link and find out as much about the actual requirements as you can. Respect the fact that you don't need any enemies in the hiring chain, and never blatantly bypass anyone. With a little discretion you can keep them all happy and supporting your application.

THE SCREENING PROCESS

THE FIRST SORT

After the deadline for accepting applications has passed, you and the other candidates are sorted into stacks that reflect how well you satisfy the objective requirements. Those who don't have the necessary education and experience are set aside and thanked for their interest. Applicants with too much or the wrong kind of preparation meet a similar fate. Ineptly presented candidates who lack extraordinary talent are bypassed. And those doing the selection eventually settle on a group of applicants who best satisfy the needs of the company on paper. These are ranked, and a small group is selected for further scrutiny—the interviews begin.

TELEPHONE INTERVIEWS

Chances are good that the first round of personal contact will come by telephone. A human resources person will call you and begin the subjective process of determining whether you seem to "fit." There are plenty of objective questions asked, and they certainly matter, but for the first time the hiring process also contains a personal element that can help or hurt your chances of getting the job. This is where your intangible qualities begin to impress those examining you for hiring—warmth, confidence, articulate speech, believable enthusiasm, knowing the language of the business, and the good judgment to say the "right" things.

Saying the Right Things in Your Telephone Interview

- Sound composed and in control even if the call was not expected—sometimes they are prearranged, at other times they come out of the blue from a resume you had sent and forgotten about.

- Have your supporting job search and note-taking materials readily available at the telephone so you can retrieve company information, respond to questions about your resume or application, and take notes during the call.

- Be businesslike but pleasant. Your goal is to command respect and be likable: no first names unless invited, no nervous chewing-gum popping, cigarette lighting, or throat clearing.

- Use the interviewer's questions as opportunities to present your strengths and not just respond to what they ask, but keep it brief.

- Try to learn what they want—the problem to be solved, the job to be done, the personal and professional qualities being sought. Then build your case in response to the needs expressed.

- Avoid the temptation to ask about salary and benefits. Unless you are forced to answer, tap dance if you are asked what your requirements are ("I'm sure XYZ Corporation pays competitive salaries, and we'll have no trouble in that area"). If forced, answer: "My present salary is in the midthirties [or whatever], and I would, of course, expect a reasonable incentive above that."

- Get the interviewer's name and title correct, verify the spelling, make notes on everything significant so you can follow up and be well prepared for the face-to-face interview that should follow. Identify other principals, too, if you can do so gracefully (e.g., if talking to the personnel official, get the name of the line manager who will interview and hire you).

- Be ready with a few intelligent questions of your own when the interviewer finishes:

  ✓ What projects and challenges could you expect to face when you begin?

  ✓ What qualities does he or she see as crucial to meeting them successfully?

  ✓ Could we set an appointment for the interview now?

  ✓ What is the status of the XYZ initiative you read about in the *ABC Journal*? It sounds like a fascinating project! (Use only if your research has provided you with solid information for such questions.)

  ✓ Where do we go from here? (Push for scheduled, continuing contact—an interview, an invitation to check back in a week or so, at the very least.)

  ✓ Would you mind clarifying something I saw on your Web page? (Be careful not to make this appear contrived; use only if you find something you genuinely would like to know.)

- Say thanks!

- Accept the interview if offered, even if you are less than ecstatic about what you heard—it could be better than you think, it could lead to something else, you can always use the practice and end up saying no.

These are the preliminary rounds of getting the actual face-to-face interview. As you will soon see, there are ways to ease your passage to that point. You can learn things during the preliminaries that will influence your success at the advanced stages of the job interview process.

Finding Out If the Job Is Really Available

The founding editor of a successful national professional newspaper once told me that the financial turning point for his publication was implementation of the Equal Employment Opportunity Act of 1964. Overnight his classified advertising section became the gold mine it remains today. Every employer in the country was placing ads for positions to satisfy affirmative action reporting requirements. A lot of good people were undoubtedly hired as a result, but to no one's surprise, many of the jobs were (and are) advertised when the position had already been filled.

The truth is that many advertised positions are anything but available, and it is naïve to spend your valuable job-hunting energy on someone's compliance drill. One of the first things you need to determine in your job search is whether your interest in the position would be welcomed or merely tolerated. Whether it happens in-house or as the result of a national solicitation, do not let yourself become a "can't win" candidate. Here are a few ways you can sort out the legitimate opportunities.

THE "NO VACANCY" VACANCY

Ask some early questions. There is nothing wrong with inquiring, "Are there any in-house candidates for the position?" And, although you almost certainly won't be told outright that someone has the job wrapped up, the tone of your discussion may give you insight into how serious the company is about bringing someone in from the outside. Use your network to find out whether the hiring committee is just "kicking tires" to see if there might be someone out there more desirable than their candidate, fleshing out the "we advertised the position" file for a prearranged hire, or whether you would be an honest contender for the job. If you end up with serious doubt about the legitimacy of the opportunity, don't waste your time unless you want interview practice.

CAN YOU HIRE ME IF YOU SELECT ME?

Another question to ask is, "Has this position been funded?" Without the right answer, you could find yourself applying for a job and going through the full screening process only to find that there is no money available to hire you. Find out at the beginning if you are part of some department head's gamble to add a position by the time he or she has advertised and interviewed a batch of candidates.

Just as all advertised positions are not available to everyone who might apply, so every candidate doesn't see his successful job interview turn into employment. Be skeptical enough to determine whether you are competing for a fully funded position before you commit to the application process. Being the darling of the job interview will not count for much if the departmental budget fails to include a line for your salary and benefits.

HOW WILL YOUR INSIDER APPLICATION BE RECEIVED?

"Genuineness of opportunity" questions are there for you as an in-house candidate, too. Sometimes it is even more difficult to ferret out the monkey drill when you are to be the stalking horse in an internal hiring.

To avoid the problem, you must begin with a candid self-appraisal of your qualifications—especially your status in the political structure that controls the hiring. If the only person openly encouraging your application is the person who is leaving and you know they're glad to see him or her go, that speaks volumes about your chances of success. Sterile, objective responses to your inquiries by those in the hiring chain are another sign that your pursuit of the position is doomed. Most successful inside hires are warmly encouraged, and there are plenty of winks and nods to reinforce faith in your ultimate triumph.

Still, judgment is necessary in deciding what you should do, even when it appears that you are not the chosen one. Often a gracious run for the roses and magnanimous acceptance of defeat leave you nicely positioned for the next time or simply enhance your present desirable status. Not to compete may have branded you as lazy and complacent and put your present status at risk. There is also the possibility that the chosen candidate will not accept and you turn out to be the best bet after all. If promotion is critical to your career or ego, plan to move on instead of up in any organization that fails to recognize your potential quickly. If not, go with the flow and enjoy your work while relegating the politics to its rightfully limited place.

Your course of action depends entirely on your objectives, but a little reconnaissance before throwing your hat into your own company's ring can eliminate unpleasant surprises and position you well to deal with realities. One sure career wrecker is to be a poor loser. Appraise your situation realistically, play the role you are given in the circumstances, then prepare to be a magnanimous supporter of the chosen one—or quietly, systematically find a new job.

When to Take the Initiative

There is a fine line between being interested and being a nuisance as the hiring unfolds. You need sensitivity to tell the difference and bring yourself to the attention of the people sorting the candidates at only the right times—and in the right ways. The proper call at the correct time can keep your resume in play just when it was about to head for the circular file. On the other hand, if you overdo it you also risk giving yourself an unwanted nudge toward rejection.

Your initiatives can be classified in two ways:

1. *Reconnaissance*. This is when you call to get general information that could apply to any candidate (e.g., What is the deadline for applications? Is there an in-house candidate? Whom would I report to? What is the spelling of the hiring official's full name? Her (or his) title? Where can I request a copy of your annual report?).

2. *Status checking*. This is when you ask where you personally stand at a particular point in the hiring cycle (e.g., Is my application still under active consideration? Will I be asked to appear for an interview? When will you be making me an offer?).

Reconnaissance questions are generally better tolerated than status checking ones. There is a distinction made between the conscientious candidate trying to learn all he or she can about the opportunity and the overly anxious applicant constantly trying to determine where he or she stands. Most employers are prepared to deal with you a reasonable number of times when your questions relate to knowing more about the position. Few companies are willing to tell you where you rank in the pack of interested applicants. Reconnaissance questions can usually be asked of third parties who may know names, positions, and information about the company and the job but who have little involvement in the hiring decision. As you will learn later in this section, these are the people to cultivate when preparing for your interview.

The opportunities for you to express personal interest during the preliminary stages are limited. If you know the people doing the hiring, by all means follow up your application package with a friendly but businesslike call expressing your sincere interest in the position. Offer to make yourself available for questions and to provide additional information if it might be helpful. Once you have done that, excessive communication will detract from your appeal. An exception might be if someone on the inside indicates that the job emphasis has changed or that some aspect of your qualifications is not clearly understood. In such instances a brief follow-up letter to clarify the matter could be both helpful and appropriate.

Networking Your Way to an Interview

Your ability to influence the hiring decision isn't limited to what you can do personally; third parties can also help. A friend employed by the company can put in a good word for you or introduce you to someone involved in the hiring. An influential reference can take an initiative on your behalf instead of your waiting to be called by the employer. Using the knowledge and influence of friends and friends of friends is called "networking," and it can help you get the interview.

Another side of networking involves your laying the groundwork for solid reference checks and inquiries. Employers know that your resume is a personal sales document and that your references are almost certainly going to be favorable ones. They also know that in our litigious society they aren't going to be getting very candid opinions unless they actively seek them. For all of these reasons, expect employers to network to find out about you.

You should initiate your own contacts within the same group of people and prepare them to respond favorably. Let your former supervisors and colleagues know that they might be contacted, whether or not they have been listed as formal references. Tell them why you feel qualified for and enthusiastic about the position so they can feel motivated to help and mirror your interest. Some interviewers now make it a practice to ask for "negative references"—people you had problems with in an earlier job. Networking can prepare such unlikely "references" for an unexpected call. Whether such an encounter ends up amounting to damage control or actually putting a positive spin on what used to be a strained relationship depends largely on your diplomatic skills before the reference check occurs.

You will learn more about networking in Chapter 10 as you go beyond the preliminary task of getting the interview. For now you must recognize the potential for networking your way to the interview, systematically working the crowd, and seeing that your application is evaluated personally by the people who count. A word to the line manager from a respected colleague can trigger a call to human resources suggesting that you be interviewed. Without that little bit of outside help you might have been relegated to the second round of interviews that often never take place.

Your network humanizes the hiring process before you are able to do so yourself. The network call is from someone with a face and a name, a personality and a reputation, a known quantity who ranks above the faceless resumes being sorted down to a reasonable number for interviewing.

Improving Your Odds of Getting an Interview

Remember that your main objective during the preliminary stages of the hiring process is to get the interview. Following are suggested actions to improve your chances of being interviewed. Keep in mind that only you can determine which ones are appropriate to your particular hiring situation. Implemented sensitively and with skill, they can help you get through the door, to where your talents can finally be showcased. Used as obvious gimmicks, they can actually work against you. So before you begin, plan your activities and consider the impact they might have.

BE IN TOWN ON BUSINESS

Interviewing candidates from out of town is costly for companies. One sure way to increase your chances of being on the interview list is to make yourself available at no cost to them. When you learn that interviews are scheduled for a certain time period and you haven't been invited, a call to the hiring official announcing your availability can sometimes do the trick. Just tell the official you will be in town on business on the same date and have time to schedule an interview. You may have been a second- or third-round interview, but by making it easy for the company to have a look at you along with (or even before) the first-round candidates, you rank yourself a cut or two higher in the selection process and increase your chances of being hired. Case History 2 illustrates this technique.

FAX OR E-MAIL A REVISED RESUME

If you omitted something like a significant course, workshop, or completed degree, or have learned something about the company or the position that lets you recast your qualifications in a more favorable light, take the occasion to send a revised resume. Fax and e-mail add urgency and grab immediate attention. Follow up with a printed copy by mail, but get yourself noticed by sending a time-sensitive update while the selection process is going on. You increase your odds of interviewing because of improved credentials, initiative, and a demonstrated awareness of the impact of current business technology. Take the trouble to make the revision objectively better—not just a ruse to get attention. The fax machine is not always the most private way to communicate, since one often serves the entire office. But with that in mind, use it to get attention and keep your application package up to the minute. E-mail, on the other hand, can be precisely targeted. Make the most of e-mail carbon copies and blind carbon copies to cultivate your network.

HAVE A REFERENCE CALL OR E-MAIL THE INTERVIEWER

You might have a reference listed on your application who is sincerely interested in helping you. Rather than passively wait for a reference check—which often doesn't take place until after you've interviewed and are on the verge of being offered the position—ask your reference to call or e-mail the interviewer to verify if the letter of reference has been received. This can accomplish several things:

- It shows that your reference holds you in high enough regard to go the extra distance for you. But more important,
- It sets up an informal reference check before the selections for interviewing have even been made.

Your mentor can take the occasion to speak highly of you and your appropriateness for the position. He or she can also respond to any questions the interviewer has about your qualifications. That little bit of added endorsement might keep you in the "must interview" stack. You can really gain points if the reference has status in your field and is either acquainted with or admired by the hiring official. Your status rises instantly by association. This technique is illustrated in Case History 3.

DO BUSINESS WITH YOUR INTERVIEWER

If you can take an initiative that would put you in legitimate business contact with the person considering your application, do it. There is no better showcase for your talents than doing what you do in real life before the person interested in hiring you. Whether it is a sales call or a professional presentation, nothing surpasses the impact of a de facto "interview" that consists of you and the prospective supervisor actually doing business together. You can't let it look contrived, but you can alter the timing of appointments or trade assignments with a colleague if the result is an opportunity to appear before the hiring official. While you are there, the person should make the connection between the coincidence of your presence and your pending application; if not, find a discreet way to raise the issue and express interest. As in earlier interview-enhancing techniques, you have to use good judgment and walk the fine line between being offensively brazen and being attractively filled with initiative. The technique is illustrated in Case History 4.

Your Interview's Importance to the Employer

The hiring ritual is as full of risk and expense for your employer-to-be as it is for you—sometimes more. At Apple Computer the typical executive hire goes through at least a dozen, and as many as fifteen interviews. According to *Industry Week*, a New Jersey consulting company reported that "every 100 resumes produce three telephone interviews, or 'screens,' every three screens produce one initial in-person interview, and every six or seven first in-person interviews produce one hire . . . . Each person hired costs an estimated $20,000 in transportation and interviewing expenses." That figure goes higher if the employment contract guarantees six months' salary for a new hire who doesn't work out, or if you count the "opportunity costs" of not having the right person in the job for a period of time. Still more costs occur if in-house morale and effectiveness suffer when an outside choice is made and staff candidates move on because they did not move up. Harry Bacas reported in *Nation's Business* that "half of all new hires stay with a company no more than six months, and each mis-hire can cost 30 to 50 percent above annual salary in lost productivity and the expense of replacement." Finally, a more broadly focused *Fortune* article by Brian Dumaine quotes authorities who place the cost of an unsuccessful hiring at between $5,000 for an hourly worker and $75,000 for a manager.

These numbers explain why you are not the only person experiencing anxiety at your job interview. The company and those responsible for your selection have a major stake in things working out right. In getting ready for your interview you can increase your attractiveness by making that job easier for the person facing you across the hiring desk. Do it by presenting him or her with a purposeful, well-informed, "self-qualified" candidate. Demonstrate from your first expression of interest to your final response to their questions that you know what they need and are in a position to prove that you can deliver it. Show them a winner they don't have to struggle to understand. Give them reason to believe it's going to be a long time before they have to go through this particular staffing hassle again.

Case History 2—Situation

IN TOWN ON BUSINESS

Background

Sam Wilson works for a small investment firm in South Carolina as a financial analyst. His job search for a career growth opportunity is at a standstill. ❶ Travel funds are tight, and the money center banks interested in his talents are reluctant to fly him in for an interview, concentrating on local applicants instead. ❷ He decides that the next favorable telephone interview that doesn't result in an invitation for a personal visit will be treated differently—even if it costs him money.

Situation

Sam finishes an exciting forty-five-minute telephone interview conversation with Tom Holder, the chief trust investment officer at National Bank in Baltimore. ❸ He wants an equities manager with just the kind of track record Sam is offering. ❹ As they conclude, Mr. Holder says he'll get back to Sam in a week, after he talks with two local candidates he has to interview first. ❺ A few days pass and Tom decides to take the initiative. He calls the man he knows is very interested in him and makes his job easier. ❻ "Mr. Holder, this is Sam Wilson in Charleston—we spoke last week regarding the investment position in your department," Sam begins. "I'm going to be in Baltimore next week on some other business and I wondered if we might be able to get together." ❼ "Yes, I'd like to meet you, Sam. What day are you available?" Holder replies. ❽ "Actually, I have some flexibility, since I'm still making the arrangements for the trip. What would be best for you?" Sam asks. "As I mentioned in our earlier conversation, I'm interviewing two local people at the beginning of the week. If you could be here Wednesday afternoon, ❾ we could consider it an interview. I'll be able to involve some of my people then," Holder says.

Conclusion

Sam makes the trip to Baltimore at his own expense and has a very sucessful interview. The chemistry is right, and he goes home confident of getting the offer. ❿ He learns later that he nosed out one of the local guys who would have almost certainly been hired before National Bank spent the money to see him in person.

Case History 2—Analysis

IN TOWN ON BUSINESS

General Strategy

Sam can see that he is being placed in the second tier of interviews not by a weak resume or poor performance during the telephone screening, but because it costs the employer money to bring him to his or her city. He decides to make himself available without cost, but doesn't want to come right out and volunteer to pay his own way, afraid he'll appear overly anxious. So he arranges to be in town on other business.

Specific Points

❶ When your interview is in another city, don't be surprised to find the employer reluctant to invite you if he or she has qualified local candidates.

❷ You might have to spend some money on your own travel if you can't honestly arrange a related business trip at a convenient time.

❸ Your qualifications have to be right, but other factors can still keep you from getting the job.

❹ Sam learned what was apt to happen when he was told that local candidates would be interviewed first. If one of them was qualified, Sam would never see an interview.

❺ After giving the employer a chance to call him, Sam took the initiative.

❻ A quick reminder about their favorable telephone interview was followed by the real test of where he stood—making himself available at no cost.

❼ Favorable interviewer response, but with the possibility that the time would not work out.

❽ Put the employer first when possible—his or her choice of day and time.

❾ Confirmation that it's to be more than a courtesy call—Sam has an interview.

❿ He got the job thanks to the fine qualifications he started out with and the quality that only the personal interview his initiative prompted could convey: he had the right chemistry.

Case History 3—Situation

A REFERENCE CALLS THE INTERVIEWER

Background

Ed Masden is a credit manager in the wholesale restaurant supply business with an application pending at one of the fastest-growing companies in the state. He looks good on paper ❶ but doesn't have name recognition in hiring circles. When he sees no interview developing, Ed decides to ask a friend who was already serving as a reference to ❷ intervene discreetly by initiating an unsolicited call on his behalf.

Situation

Ed calls Tim Howe, a longtime ❸ friend and one of the leading credit managers in the state. He ❹ recounts how his application is dead in the water in spite of his fine qualifications and asks for suggestions on how it might be revived to win him the opportunity to impress the company in person. ❺ Tim mentions that he has worked on a number of professional association projects with the person doing the hiring and that he will give her a call. "Cindy! This is Tim Howe calling. Listen, I know you are hiring a senior credit manager, and ❻ I want to give my active endorsement to someone." ❼ "Tim, I must have a hundred applications for that job, and most of them are good people . . ." she begins to explain. "I can appreciate that," he continues, "but I'm sure you want to end up with the best person, and I honestly feel strongly about this guy. ❽ Let me tell you a little bit about him." The conversation goes on, and while she recognizes that influence is being brokered, she respects Tim's opinion and, with promises of nothing more, ❾ adds Ed to her list of people who will be interviewed.

Conclusion

Ed achieves his objective. By having a respected member of his profession take an active role, he gets the interview that leads to a rewarding new job. ❿ Without doing something special to relate his excellent professional and personal qualifications, Ed might never have risen from the stack of applicants.

Case History 3—Analysis

A REFERENCE CALLS THE INTERVIEWER

General Strategy

Ed Masden senses correctly that his application is not moving any closer to an interview appointment on the merits alone. He has a reference with the clout and political skills needed to intervene effectively, so he sets the process in motion. All he asks is the chance to be interviewed; no special favors beyond that are requested.

Specific Points

❶ When you know that your qualifications alone are not going to move you to the interview stage in a crowded field of candidates, you need to act.

❷ If you can move the influence of a powerful reference to the front instead of the end of the hiring process, do it.

❸ A friend with professional stature committed to backing your candidacy is an ideal prospect to take an initiative on your behalf.

❹ Make your case for being well qualified and ask nothing more than a chance to be considered seriously for the interview.

❺ Your ideal mentor already knows the hiring official and can trade on an existing relationship instead of reputation alone.

❻ Your advocate should be strong enough to make a straightforward approach to pushing your candidacy.

❼ It doesn't matter that the field is packed; you are well qualified, and all you ask is to be heard in person.

❽ You benefit by having your sterling qualities actively personalized by a respected third party.

❾ Your friend is asking only for a professional courtesy that can be painlessly granted—an interview, not a job.

❿ By getting the interview, you can get the job. Special effort to get that far is worthwhile.

Case History 4—Situation

DOING BUSINESS WITH YOUR INTERVIEWER

Background

Dorothy Ward is an emergency medical technician who wants to teach in her specialty at a local college. ❶ Her efforts to apply have not met with success for several years. ❷ She learns that the present instructor will be leaving at the end of the year and decides to personalize her application by demonstrating her professional talents at the college.

Situation

Dorothy had responded to emergencies at the college on a number of occasions and knows some of the staff. ❸ When she hears that they are planning a career night, she volunteers to represent her profession. Among the preliminaries is a requirement that each participant come for an interview with the dean. ❹ It is an opportunity to screen the participants for desirability and say thanks for helping on a community service basis. Dorothy has her appointment with Dean Grundy and impresses him with her professionalism.

❺ The career night passes successfully, and he contacts her to teach an evening class. ❻ The class showcases her abilities to teach, order materials, add overload students, and process final grades. ❼, ❽ When the full-time position is advertised the next spring, she is an applicant with an already established reputation for competence, initiative, and a strong motivation to serve the students. ❾ While the usual competitive hiring cycle has to be completed, only an extraordinary turn of events will deny Dorothy the position this time—and there is none.

Conclusion

Dorothy takes the trouble to demonstrate her competency to the person she wants to hire her. In this instance there is time to do it over a period of months. ❿ The same effect can be achieved by making an immediate sales call or scheduling a technical consultation in other fields. The objective is to showcase your talents in the setting where they will be used.

Case History 4—Analysis

DOING BUSINESS WITH
YOUR INTERVIEWER

General Strategy

Dorothy needs an inside track to get the teaching position she wants. The most effective way to do that is to show the person doing the hiring that she can do the job. She decides to put her professional talents to work at the college without pay. She parlays that into a part-time position, and finally becomes a "known quantity" candidate for the full-time job she really wants.

Specific Points

❶ You need the required talents, but some situations require special strategies.

❷ If you see a vacancy developing, position yourself to be an obvious candidate.

❸ You need an occasion to present yourself, which doesn't have to be a formal working situation.

❹ The right volunteer setting or business call can provide you with a de facto job interview—or at least a foot in the door.

❺ After your initial working contact, try to sustain the relationship if possible.

❻ The impact is particularly strong when you can repeat the work exposure in different settings.

❼ The ideal outcome is to establish a real-world professional bond.

❽ Your efforts pay off when the informal exposure connects with an actual hiring situation for which you are already a known quantity.

❾ You still have to complete a regular competitive hiring, but are positioned as the candidate with the built-in advantage of having been observed and appreciated on a professional level.

❿ If time is short, the same technique works while you are actively under consideration. Arrange to make a business call while your application is pending, and turn the occasion into an invitation for a formal interview.

SUMMARY CHECKLIST: GETTING THE INTERVIEW

- Learn everything you can about the hiring situation: Who is involved and what are their biases?

- Verify that the position is realistically available to you. Or is it already a "done deal" on which you would be wasting your time?

- Find out if the position is fully funded and whether you could begin working right away if selected.

- "Self-qualify" with an honest match of your qualifications to the employer's needs, and increase your odds of interviewing successfully by pursuing only realistic situations.

- Determine the role of human resources and line manager, and craft your application package and personal initiatives to respect all the players while keeping the emphasis on the ultimate decision maker.

- Focus your application on the specific needs of the position for which you are applying. Personal computers make it easy to personalize your resume and letter of application.

- Be prepared for a telephone interview—scheduled or otherwise.

- Be sensitive to the differences between "reconnaissance" and "status checking" initiatives, and use both to your greatest advantage without wearing out your welcome.

- Discreetly use your networking capabilities to learn what is going on in the mind of the hiring official, and make him or her aware of your interest through third parties, if that can be done effectively.

- Use networking to prepare your references (even a few "negative" ones) for a possible call from the employer.

- Implement your own strategies for increasing your odds of getting the interview if you are not scheduled for one early in the hiring cycle.

- Appreciate the importance of the interview to the employer, and do your part to make it worthwhile for both parties.

10 PREPARING FOR THE INTERVIEW

Whether you already have an interview scheduled or are still trying to arrange one, you have some preparing to do. The knowledge you gain in the process helps you in either situation—(1) by being impressive enough during the preliminary selection process to get the interview or (2) by doing well enough when you face your interviewer to get the job. You make your preparations with a four-part approach that involves learning about:

- sources of information
- the company and its people
- what you want and what you have to offer
- the interview process and how you can influence it

The four approaches blend and overlap, but the knowledge that you gain in each strengthens your overall preparation for the job interview. Your objective is to learn as much as you can about the information sources for the position you are pursuing, the company and the people working for it, your own talents and what you expect from your career, and what you are apt to encounter as you move through the job interview process.

You are going to use information that is all around you but may not have mattered to you until now. Everyday sources, none of them created with your particular job search in mind, become useful and make you a more successful candidate once you become aware of their potential. Some of your sources are passive—books on the shelves of libraries. Others are active—people you'll contact, places you'll go,

GETTING THE INTERVIEW
- Finding a job
- Applying
- Networking
- Getting invited

PREPARING FOR THE INTERVIEW
- Researching the company
- Preparing personally
- Anticipating questions

You get ready for your interview by becoming informed about the company in order to be a knowledgeable candidate and to evaluate the desirability of working for it. You must first convince yourself that you are the best person for the job in order to convince others with your confidence, knowledge, and motivation. Next you prepare yourself for the interview process by knowing questions you are likely to encounter. Finally, you get ready to ask some questions yourself. Impress the interviewers with your informed interest and also learn about the promise and problems of the working situation.

APPEARING FOR THE INTERVIEW
- Reconnaissance
- Personal readiness
- Timing

DURING THE INTERVIEW
- Names and personalities
- Style and substance
- Satisfying agendas

LEAVING THE INTERVIEW
- Reading your audience
- Positive expectations
- Last impression

EVALUATING YOUR INTERVIEW
- Substantive match
- Personal chemistry
- Judging your chances

FOLLOWING UP AFTER YOUR INTERVIEW
- Thank-yous
- Additional information
- More networking

CONCLUDING THE INTERVIEW PROCESS
- The offer
- Negotiating
- Accepting

Figure 2. Preparing for the Interview.

and information you'll come across while aggressively researching a company on the Internet.

Before getting into the specifics of preparing for your interview, look at the whole process and see where it is leading you. Understand that what you are about to do in "Preparing for the Interview" continues steps that you began in Chapter 9, "Getting the Interview." Look ahead on the job interview continuum and see how valuable your preparation is going to be as you move through the job interview cycle.

Sources of Information

The information you need comes from many sources, including community organizations; regional and national publications; the Internet; and, among the most valuable, your network of friends and professional acquaintances. The following selective list is an overview of the kinds of resources that can make you a better-informed job candidate. Use this as a starting point for your own imaginative search for print and electronic publications and people who can tell you what you need to know about your job opportunity.

Internet Tip

Many information sources have their own Web pages. For example: http://www.bbb.org will link you to individual Better Business Bureaus, and at http://www.chamber-of-commerce.com you can find Chambers of Commerce all over the world. Enter a business reference, company or newspaper name, or other keywords that interest you into a search engine for results that may be of particular value to you.

BETTER BUSINESS BUREAU

The Better Business Bureau (BBB) is listed in your telephone book or you can access it directly at the BBB Web site. If you are investigating a company in another part of the country, the Internet is the easiest approach; you could also check the library for that city's telephone directory, call long distance directory assistance, or ask your local BBB for a referral. Don't expect an elaborate report, but what you get will be useful. The Web query or spokesperson checks to see if the company you ask about has been the subject of complaints from customers and clients, and she or he will discuss the general nature of any problems with you. The BBB will not recommend whether you should work for the firm, of course. Finding a company with a derogative file should be a red flag to you. Dig deeper to find out whether this is the kind of organization you want to be affiliated with, depend on for a living, or add to your resume.

CHAMBERS OF COMMERCE

Most cities have a Chamber of Commerce office, and there is a national Web site with links to local chambers. It is an advocate for the local business community and an excellent source of basic information on the company you are investigating. The Chamber of Commerce is listed in the telephone book and is usually located in a community's business district. You can purchase an inexpensive directory of members that includes almost every enterprise in the area, public and private. Each company pays dues to belong, and the directory tells you how many employees it has, what it does, how long it has been in business, and whom to contact for more information. Regional directory companies publish a more extensive guide, and you can examine a copy at the chamber office or library. In addition to information on your prospective employer, the Chamber of Commerce can also help you evaluate the community as a place to live and work.

The chamber staff is usually well informed on regional trends and personalities. Start a discussion about the company that interests you and see what they have to say. You might learn of plans to expand or close the plant, for example. Think about what you would like to know, and ask. Interesting tidbits about company executive officers can often be picked up from people who meet them socially. Ask what kind of reputation your prospective employer has as a place to work—you usually get an honest opinion if you ask in the course of a casual conversation. A written inquiry will probably get you a list of members, a local map, and maybe a community brochure for your trouble. But you have to dig for what you really want to know. Visit the office personally or, at a minimum, telephone and put the force of your personal interest behind your inquiry.

CREDIT CHECK

If you are looking for information on an established, mid-size business, you can see how the company rates in Dun & Bradstreet or Moody's by checking the reference section of your library. Both references tell you whether the company is considered to be a good credit risk, and that, of course, indicates something of its overall strength and character. If you are considering a position with a small organization or an individually owned firm, the same kind of credit bureau that rates your personal credit rates theirs. You may need a business or legal connection to get a report, but if you are concerned about the firm's financial stability, pursue the matter with your attorney, who can either get the information or advise you on how to do it ethically. Credit bureau reports are not routinely available to individuals, but there are ways to get the information if you have a legitimate need to know.

You can also ask your prospective employer for banking and accounting references to verify the condition of the company. While these are usually perfunctory contacts that tell you little more than that the firm is a client, it can uncover a "worst case" scenario if the organization is on the verge of disaster. For example, you can ask if the company appears to be sound financially. A hedged answer is an invitation to look more closely. Standard business references list the professional and financial affiliations of major companies; you have to ask smaller companies for the names of their accounting and law firms and their banks. If they refuse, consider it to be a red flag, and investigate further before you make a career commitment.

Credit checks are not needed in many job searches, but they are a reasonable precaution if you sense there might be problems. You don't want to end up like a major hotel chain executive who recently accepted a high-level position, relocated his family, purchased a new home, and was soon informed that his position had been eliminated to meet financial exigencies. You can spare yourself the career disruption by checking the financial health of your employer-to-be ahead of time. Many inquiries can be accomplished on the Internet using commonsense keyword searches (e.g., the names of standard business and credit reference firms, business intelligence and information services, etc.).

STANDARD BUSINESS REFERENCES

Thomas' Register of American Manufacturers, Standard & Poor's Register of Corporations, Directors and Executives, MacRae's Bluebook, and other references geared to specific industries or regions of the country can help you determine what a company does, the scope of its operations, its business affiliations, the names of officers heading its major divisions, and much more. For other sources, ask your librarian or call a local college professor teaching in your field—he or she will usually point you in the right direction and be complimented that you asked. Here is a sampling of what can be found in *Standard & Poor's Register* (adapted from "User's Companion to *Poor's Register*"):

- ✓ accounting firm
- ✓ address
- ✓ affiliates
- ✓ bank (primary)
- ✓ directors (including personal information)
- ✓ divisions
- ✓ employees (number of)
- ✓ executives (including personal information)
- ✓ law firms
- ✓ officers (including personal information)
- ✓ personnel (key)

- ✓ products
- ✓ sales (annual)
- ✓ services
- ✓ Standard Industrial Classification (SIC) codes

- ✓ stock exchanges (where traded)
- ✓ subsidiaries
- ✓ telephone number

PUBLISHED INDEXES AND COMPUTER DATABASES

Magazine, newspaper, and professional journal indexes give you leads to articles about companies and the people who run them. Libraries have computer terminals for accessing databases. Use them to find information on the company, its products, people, and competitors—the industry itself. Try entering the name of your interviewer or industry personalities—one of them may have just published an article or given a speech that made the trade news. Maybe your human resources contact wrote something for a personnel journal. Reading it could give you insight into how he or she will deal with you—and present you with an opportunity both to compliment him or her and demonstrate your awareness of the industry. Some computer indexes catalog the speeches of leading business personalities. Locate a few that apply to your specialty and you have the makings of informed, businesslike conversation during your interviews. This kind of "knowledge initiative" impresses employers in an era when finding and using information is increasingly important. The Internet also contains useful current and recent past information, but don't expect to find many free library-grade archives there.

Internet Tip

To examine a fee-based research service try http://ask.elibrary.com for Electric Library; for an investor-oriented site try http://www.corporateinformation.com/; or enter the keywords "company information" in your favorite search engine to locate other choices.

COMPANY INFORMATION

Public relations departments will answer your questions and mail you information such as annual reports. You may actually be expected to familiarize yourself with such publications before your interview. Annual reports are also often available in the business section of the library, at your placement office, or on the company's Web site.

You read them to learn what companies do, what they take pride in doing especially well, what they plan for the future—and to get a flavor for their corporate culture. Pride in a child care program for a company's employees might be noted, for example. The company's attitude toward the environment will often be stated. Where the firm sees itself in ten years is a regular feature of such publications.

Annual reports are free public information that tell you a lot about where the company stands, where it hopes to go, and how you might make a contribution. You can also get financial and compliance reports from regulatory agencies.

Candidates entering interviews today must be thoroughly familiar with the company's Web page. Information of every description is found there: mission statements and objectives; news, leadership, and personalities; investor information and financials; organization charts and annual reports; planned initiatives, and much more. Little things like recognizing key people from their photographs on the company Web page can subtly change an interview for the better.

NETWORKING

After you have exhausted your formal sources and know where to begin, get more personal. Talk with people. Finding them is the function of your network. When you network correctly, one contact leads to another until you learn what you need to know. You will see examples of networking used in specific situations throughout this book.

THE COMPANY AND ITS PEOPLE

The information you need to know depends on the position you are pursuing. If you are going into general management, your interests are wide-ranging and you want the big picture. You need to know about the different operating divisions of the company, but not in-depth. On the other hand, if you are going to work in a specialized part of a firm, your interests will be focused, and you need just enough overall company knowledge to be informed about and appreciate the role your division plays.

Regardless of whether your needs are for broad or focused information, the accompanying chart will start you thinking of the kinds of questions you want to pursue, why they are important to you, and where you can find the answers. Researching them helps you decide whether the opportunity is worthwhile and, if it is, understand both what your interviewers' questions mean and how to respond.

THINGS YOU WANT TO KNOW ABOUT THE COMPANY

What You Want to Know	Why You Want to Know It	How You Can Find Out
What does the company do?	• To be a knowledgeable candidate • To decide whether you want to be a part of such an enterprise • To judge future opportunities	• Annual reports • Chambers of Commerce • Library business references • Internet • Network contacts
Who owns the company and what other companies does it own?	• To be a knowledgeable candidate • To avoid overlapping applications and references • To judge its strength and character • To judge future opportunities	• Annual reports • Library business references • Internet • Network contacts
How big is the company?	• To be a knowledgeable candidate • To judge the strength of the company • To judge future opportunities	• Annual reports • Chambers of Commerce • Library business references • Internet
What kind of image does the company have?	• To be a knowledgeable candidate • To decide whether you want to be a part of such an enterprise • To judge its strength and character	• Journals, periodicals, and newspapers • Better Business Bureau • Chambers of Commerce • Credit checks • Internet • Network contacts
Who runs the company?	• To be an informed candidate	• Annual reports

(cont'd)

What You Want to Know	Why You Want to Know It	How You Can Find Out
Who runs the company? *cont'd*	• To judge its strength and character	• Chambers of Commerce • Library business references • Journals, periodicals, and newspapers • Internet • Network contacts
Is the company in trouble?	• To be a knowledgeable candidate • To judge the strength of the company • To judge future opportunities	• Chambers of Commerce • Library business references • Credit checks • Internet • Journals, periodicals, and newspapers • Network contacts
How does the company's future look?	• To be a knowledgeable candidate • To judge the strength of the company • To judge future opportunities	• Annual reports • Chambers of Commerce • Credit checks • Library business references • Journals, periodicals, and newspapers • Internet • Network contacts
Has the company been in the news recently?	• To be a knowledgeable candidate	• Chambers of Commerce

(cont'd)

What You Want to Know	Why You Want to Know It	How You Can Find Out
Has the company been in the news recently? *cont'd*	• To decide whether you want to be a part of such an enterprise • To judge future opportunities	• Journals, periodicals, and newspapers • Internet • Network contacts
What are the company's products or services?	• To be a knowledgeable candidate • To decide whether you want to be a part of such an enterprise • To judge future opportunities	• Annual reports • Chambers of Commerce • Library business references • Journals, periodicals, and newspapers • Internet • Network contacts
Should I be aware of the reputation and accomplishments of anyone working for the company?	• To be a knowledgeable candidate • To decide whether you want to be a part of such an enterprise • To judge future opportunities	• Annual reports • Chambers of Commerce • Library business references • Journals, periodicals, and newspapers • Internet • Network contacts
What is my interviewer's name, title, and place in the company's organization?	• To be a knowledgeable candidate	• Formal company contacts • Internet • Network contacts
What is my interviewer's background?	• To be a knowledgeable candidate	• Library business references

(cont'd)

What You Want to Know	Why You Want to Know It	How You Can Find Out
What is my interviewer's background? *cont'd*		• Chambers of Commerce • Internet • Network contacts
Is it a smoking or non-smoking organization?	• To determine whether you fit this aspect of the corporate culture	• Formal company contacts • Network contacts
What are the social expectations for my position?	• To determine whether you fit this aspect of the corporate culture	• Formal company contacts • Network contacts
How much business travel is involved?	• To determine whether you fit this aspect of the corporate culture	• Formal company contacts • Network contacts

APPLYING THE NETWORKING TECHNIQUE

Some of the most useful information comes through networking. Much of it happens while you are comfortably interacting with your colleagues in routine business and social settings. That's the easy part. But to push beyond that and open up new sources, you have to do what is referred to in sales as "cold calling":

- Your network acquaintances mention others who probably know what you need to find out.
- They suggest that the person would be willing to talk with you.
- Some introduce you to the source or tell you to mention their names to break the ice.

Asking for something from someone you don't know—cold calling—can be unnatural and stressful. Still, it's worth the discomfort because it opens up opportunities not available to your competitors who never network beyond their own comfortable circle of friends and acquaintances. Extend yourself, and your broadened base of contacts will improve your odds of having a successful interview. In the process you open up the possibility of finding opportunities that you might not have even been aware of otherwise. The technique is illustrated in Case History 5.

Case History 5—Situation

COLD CALLING WITH LEADS AND INTRODUCTIONS

Background

Pat Lyle is a graphics artist who has developed new abilities in the computer graphics side of her profession. ❶ Most of her contacts, however, are in the traditional pen-and-ink firms. She needs to find a place for her newly developed and highly marketable skills and network a new group of people. ❷ Her few acquaintances in the specialty authorize her to use their names freely but are too busy to help actively. She needs to take the initiative personally.

Situation

Pat gets the ❸ directory issue of her professional journal and identifies people positioned to help her in the kinds of firms she seeks to join. She compares the names to those provided by her friends who agree to vouch for her. ❹ With her list of prospects, she makes calls to people she doesn't know but whose help she needs. ❺ "Good morning, Mr. Wilson, this is Pat Lyle. I'm a graphics artist with eight years of experience with Sun Graphics. I've been taking courses in computer graphics, and I'm looking for a position that can use my skills. ❻ Mike Barrett said to mention his name and ask if you might help steer me in the right direction. He says you have a strong computer graphics operation and would know about opportunities if anyone would." Wilson responds that he doesn't anticipate any openings, ❼ but suggests that she call Mary Chun at Island Graphics—❽ and say that he suggested calling. Pat places the call and finds that Mary is indeed interested in talking with her. She is thinking of advertising a position in a few months and welcomes a viable candidate. ❾ They have an informal interview, Mary suggests a few other possibilities, but Pat accepts a position with her a few months later.

Conclusion

Pat takes the trouble to meet people at the working level in her new field before their needs are advertised. A colleague's reputation helps break the ice and position her to ❿ get a job for which she would have been just another routine candidate had she not taken the initiative.

Case History 5—Analysis

COLD CALLING WITH LEADS AND INTRODUCTIONS

General Strategy

Pat knows that she lacks the contacts to break into the computer graphics side of the business. Her few friends in a position to help are too busy to take an initiative for her, but are willing to have their names used. She uses that little bit of assistance and parlays it into a job by getting on the telephone and finding out where the vacancies are developing.

Specific Points

❶ When you have talent but lack the personal contacts to make them work in a new setting, you need to identify people at the working level who might appreciate what you have to offer.

❷ Mutual professional acquaintances can make cold calling easier.

❸ Your industry almost certainly has a professional directory that identifies people to call in your specialty. If not, call the company and ask who does your kind of work there.

❹ Coordinate your lists and start calling the people who are most apt to be responsive because of an even remotely shared acquaintance.

❺ You need a short script that will pitch your strengths in a brief introduction.

❻ Take advantage of name-dropping and increase your chances of getting helped by someone who might say no to you, but not you and a friend.

❼ Cold calls that generate leads are the next best thing to job offers.

❽ Always try to keep the linkage of third-party referrals going—ask to use his or her name when you call the person he or she suggested.

❾ You have succeeded in finding someone who needs you.

❿ Your cold-calling initiative got you the interview and a favorable predisposition to hire before the vacancy was even advertised. The same technique works when trying to find inside information about a job for which you have already made an application—instead of an opening, ask for information.

APPLYING THE "CONSULTANT" TECHNIQUE

When you don't have leads and introductions, you can always call in the capacity of a "consultant." This is a telephone technique for uncovering useful information. While you should never use the technique unethically (blatantly misrepresenting yourself, for example), don't be afraid to talk with people inside the company you want to join. If you don't have an individual's name, just ask to speak with someone who is knowledgeable about your specialty. Such conversations can lead to everything from vacancies that have yet to be announced to an insider's perspective on a position for which you've already applied.

Avoid using your name, since that might prejudice a future interview. If asked, just respond that you are an independent consultant with an interest in conducting your inquiry confidentially. That will satisfy most people. In fact, few ever ask. If you approach them correctly, people will gladly share information. Be businesslike—have your objectives in mind, pursue them professionally, and respect your source's time. You can conduct yourself in such a way as to probe and find out what you need to know without ever being dishonest or saying anything you wouldn't have said in person. Remember that many businesses routinely use "caller ID" and note the telephone number of the calling party. Never rely on your call being an anonymous one, but unless you anger someone, a brief call made in confidence remains simply that. Case History 6 illustrates the technique.

Evaluating What You Have to Offer

When the time comes for your interview, you want to focus attention on your strengths. You do that by building your knowledge about the company's needs and your qualifications into a solid case for why the hiring will be good for the company and you. Spontaneous responses alone might not accomplish that goal during your interview. You need to think through the possibilities and make decisions ahead of time. Here are some questions that will help you do that. You should expand the list to cover other topics that define a mutually beneficial relationship between you and your prospective employer.

EVALUATING YOUR POTENTIAL RELATIONSHIP WITH THE COMPANY	
The Company	**And You**
What does the company need?	Do you offer those skills, and are you interested in applying them in this kind of situation?
Will you be in the mainstream or in a support function?	Does it matter to you and your future that you have the potential to reach the top, or is a solid supporting position satisfactory?
What does this company do?	Do you feel good about it, and can you get enthusiastic about being part of the effort? Would you be proud of your work, feel good about telling others what you do and comfortable having it on your resume in the future?
What kind of people succeed in this company?	Do you see yourself as "that kind of person"? Can you identify with the values and behavior of the people who are the visible winners?
Where are the growth opportunities in this company?	Do your skills and personality fit, and is the division to which you are applying an integral part of the company's future growth?
What kind of training or staff development program does the company have?	Will you be helped or hindered as you pursue further education and professional growth? Will you be viewed as doing the right thing, or diluting your efforts for the company? Do you care?
Who will the company be competing with in the course of your time with them?	Are you picking a winner, or are you joining a company that will be bowing to the competition?
What are the growth and profitability histories for the company? What are the projections?	Are you joining a company with solid financial prospects?

Case History 6—Situation

COLD CALLING WITHOUT LEADS AND INTRODUCTIONS

Background

Marla Oakton is an account executive with a mid-size brokerage firm and is applying for a position with a large one. ❶ She knows the job description and projected earnings, but before deciding wants to confirm things about the corporate culture—especially the attitude toward women. This kind of information isn't put in writing or honestly discussed at formal interviews.

Situation

❷ Marla knows she needs to talk to her counterparts in a candid and nonthreatening way. Testing company practices that relate to sensitive issues calls for informal, confidential conversations. ❸ She uses her industry directory to identify men and women, account executives and managers, to call. ❹ It won't work to say "Hi, my name is Marla Oakton, a candidate for a position in your company, and I want to know if women are treated professionally and have a fair shot at senior management positions." She knows that a more subtle approach will serve her purposes better. ❺ She starts calling in the capacity of a consultant doing a survey of the industry. ❻ She promises anonymity and asks for it in return; to her surprise, her terms are almost universally accepted.

❼ Callers give their candid impressions on the questions that are of interest to her. ❽ When she finishes, Marla has a broad, candid survey of attitudes on a sensitive subject ❾ that matters greatly in her career decision. She approaches the subject as directly as the realities of current social conditions in the workplace permit—and does nothing dishonest.

Conclusion

Without direct referrals, Marla is able to get inside her future workplace and determine whether prevailing attitudes will suit her needs. ❿ She acts ethically by doing nothing more than creating the circumstances of confidential inquiry needed to gain essential career information for her private use.

Case History 6—Analysis

COLD CALLING WITHOUT LEADS AND INTRODUCTIONS

General Strategy

Marla decides not to risk a career move to an organization that holds traditional attitudes toward the advancement of women. She wants to have honest conversations up front before making a final decision. So she identifies future colleagues and telephones them to survey their attitudes on things that matter to her professionally.

Specific Points

❶ There are issues that cannot be judged accurately by such traditional sources as job descriptions and structured, official conversations.

❷ You sometimes need to talk candidly about private things before deciding to pursue employment in a particular organization.

❸ Most professions have directories that let you identify the people you should be talking with for certain kinds of information.

❹ Ideally, you can raise any issue in an open conversation. Practically, you cannot. This hypothetical lead-in demonstrates how naive it might be.

❺ Anyone can rationalize being a consultant—even working for oneself.

❻ Confidentiality is standard operating practice in business conversations and is easily invoked for your own purposes.

❼ People will generally try to help you; try asking sincere, reasonable questions and see for yourself.

❽ Nothing compares with direct, confidential calling for finding out what you need to know.

❾ Callers sense a valid inquiry; this one had conspicuous relevancy for the caller, and that eased her way in getting useful responses.

❿ Ethical approaches to sensitive issues are very important. In this case nothing was misrepresented, and only the caller used the information.

The Interview Process and Your Influence on It

You might find yourself in one or more of several job interview environments. By knowing what to expect, you can avoid being surprised or intimidated. You are dealing more with variations in technique than in substance in different interview formats, and if you are well prepared, are a good fit for the position, and know what is coming, you will be able to impress interviewers regardless of their approach.

You need to recognize the interviewer's technique and how it applies to you. An aggressive natural leader and a good team player may show very different traits and each still walk away with a successful interview—depending on what the interviewer wants. To make your strongest case, you need to know what is expected, decide whether you can honestly provide it, then deliver it effectively, using your knowledge of the company and what the interviewer is trying to accomplish.

The accompanying table lists different types of interviews. Most interviews are a combination of the following techniques:

- A telephone interview might be either structured or informal—or a hybrid mix of the two.

- A face-to-face interview might be with an individual or a group.

- The interview may require a meeting with a formal panel, and it may or may not incorporate stress to reveal your character.

- The same is true of the interview's purpose—whether screening, selection, or hiring, it could be

  ✓ informal or structured;

  ✓ in person or by telephone (or satellite or computer, for that matter); and

  ✓ individual or group.

Your best strategy is to be aware of the possibilities and then play your role as comfortably as you can. While you should never smile smugly and indicate that you know exactly what is going on, you can put aside the stress that being surprised might have brought on and concentrate on being a poised, well-informed candidate.

TYPES OF INTERVIEWS

Interview Type	Description/Purpose
Face-to-face	Interviewer and candidate physically present at the same site for personal interaction.
Group	Candidates are put into a group situation to see how they react in a common task. Leaders and team players emerge.
Hiring	Purpose is to make the offer and negotiate terms of employment.
Informal	Nondirective; interviewer serves more as a moderator; purpose is to bring out the interviewee's personality.
Panel	Also called a "board" interview. A number of interviewers evaluate a single candidate. Example: a college president being selected by a panel consisting of faculty, administrators, and the governing board.
Remote	Telephone, satellite, videotape, computer—an interview where the interviewer and candidate do not encounter each other personally.
Screening	Purpose is to narrow the choices. Weed out anyone with less than complete qualifications or a flaw—look for a reason to reject candidates. Impersonal, fact-oriented, to assess qualifications. Conducted by a human resources specialist using formal interviewing techniques and strategies. Candidate initiative not a good idea—respond to what you are asked, and don't provide a reason to be judged unlikable or inappropriate. Not a time to introduce controversy.
Selection	Purpose is to pick the person to hire—look for a reason to accept the candidate. Intuitive, personal, professional task-oriented. Conducted by a line manager or supervisor often not paying much attention to interview techniques. Candidate should use interview preparation to good advantage. Impress interviewer with job knowledge, personality, skills needed for the actual job.

(cont'd)

Interview Type	Description/Purpose
Situational	Individual is put in a hypothetical situation and asked to re-solve it. A one-person variation of the group interview.
Stress	Purpose is to challenge the candidate's opinions and qualifi-cations; use silence to make her or him uncomfortable; curt responses; staring for effect. Onset and end of stress segment are usually apparent—change of interviewer's character and approach.
Structured	Checklist interview where the routine is set and you respond to preconceived questions—no room for spontaneity by in-terviewer or candidate.

Next in your preparation comes an awareness of what you can expect from your interviewer if he or she follows the traditional rules provided below. The interviewer can be expected to have these ground rules in mind when trying to get to know you. Remember the rules as you prepare for your interview. They tell you where your interviewer is coming from and what he or she is trying to do at various stages of your interview.

Rules the Interviewer Follows

- **Works from a job description**—expect your interviewer to have a list of the job duties, qualifications, and work experience needed.

- **Relaxes the candidate**—your interviewer will make some small talk and ask something about your personal interests to make you feel comfortable.

- **Has an interview schedule**—your interviewer can be expected to move through phases that go from telling you about the position, to examining your background and motivations, to ending with asking for your questions about the position.

- **Listens more than talks**—your interviewer will stress getting you to express yourself and provide information, trying to avoid filling the time with his or her own comments.

- **Conducts a truthful and legal interview**—your interviewer will try to keep his or her comments about the company honest and avoid asking you questions prohibited by equal opportunity regulations.

- **Inquires about salary**—your interviewer may inquire about your salary history but will probably avoid any definitive discussion of anything but the salary range until the time of an offer.

- **Gives the next step**—your interviewer should conclude the interview by making you aware of what comes next in the hiring cycle.

According to an expert quoted in Harry Bacas's *Nation's Business* article on hiring, you can expect the interviewer to "find out whether [you] can do the job; whether [you] will do the job the way [the company] wants it done; and whether [you] fit into [their] organization."

The interviewer comes to the interview with a plan. Some are very thoroughly prepared; others are less formal and give the appearance of just wanting to get to know you. Nearly all of them have some standard questions that you should anticipate. You don't want to be armed with tape-recorderlike responses, but you should be ready with a well-reasoned, natural answer to the questions that follow.

QUESTIONS YOUR INTERVIEWER MIGHT ASK	
Question	**Suggested Response**
Can you answer this question the way you think your references will answer it?	An implied notice that your response will be verified. Welcome the challenge and suggest asking a certain person to corroborate.
Aren't you overqualified?	You won't waste time training me. Use company knowledge to show you know where you'd fit in if hired. Imply that rapid growth will take care of any problem with overqualification.
Could you give me some references that you didn't get along with?	Be ready. Have a few people in mind who differed with you but with whom you learned to share a mutual respect. Prepare these references for possible contact.
Have you ever had more to do than you could accomplish? How did you handle it?	Yes, you have, and you solved the problem by setting priorities and negotiating new terms when you had to.

(cont'd)

Question	Suggested Response
How did you accomplish that (some specific thing you claim to have done)?	Be ready to back your claim with demonstrable proof that you did it; be able to talk in specific, operational terms.
How long would it take you to make a contribution here?	Be realistic, but offer an attractive hypothetical accomplishment based on your research, if the situation lends itself.
How much did you save the company when you implemented your new procedure?	Do your homework—have the figures and suggest that they can be verified by checking with a reference.
How much money do you need?	Try to turn the tables; ask what they pay for similar positions. Or you'd like as much as your experience would qualify you for—confident that they'll be fair.
In what area have you shown your greatest improvement in the past two years?	This question is designed to get you to admit a shortcoming and, hopefully, show growth in overcoming it. Try to have a favorable example in mind.
Is there something in your past that you feel less than proud of that you'd rather discuss now than have us discover later?	Don't do your best to come up with something bad to satisfy the question, but if there was an incident that is apt to come to light, say so. Give it as brief and positive a mention as you can.
Name three accomplishments that you are most proud of.	Be ready with some good examples, including how your accomplishments helped others, including your last employer.

(cont'd)

Question	Suggested Response
Name three things you like about your job and three things you don't like about it.	Accentuate the positive, minimize the negative. Acceptable negatives include limited opportunity for growth, desire to take on a new challenge, maturing priorities that called for a change professionally.
Tell me about your faults.	Don't overdo the honesty here—something like "I work too hard . . ." is fine if you elaborate a little and make it more than a glib response. Don't feel obligated to give them reasons to eliminate you.
Tell me about your professional experience.	Keep it brief and don't make yourself appear too narrow and specialized. Let the interviewer ask for more detail.
Tell me about (open-ended question) . . .	These questions are to keep you from responding yes or no. Be prepared to explain something briefly.
That sounds great! Were there any negatives?	Sure there were, and mention some minor things, but stress that they were outweighed by the positives.
What are you looking for in this position?	Stay general enough to fit what the company may need. Don't make it more than they can deliver.
What do you and your current supervisor fight about?	"We don't fight—we discuss our differences, I make my views known, and he or she has the ultimate authority—which I respect."
What do you know about our company?	A brief, positive response based on your research that shows you know what they do and their position in the industry. Be ready to go into more detail if asked.

(cont'd)

Question	Suggested Response
What do you think you could contribute to our firm?	Match your skills to the company's needs.
What is the name of the person you reported to in that particular situation?	Have your references ready. A typed list in your briefcase is a good idea. You can produce it when asked.
Why do you switch jobs so often?	Minimize the changes by citing broad experience gained, purposeful progression, and a desire to reach a point quickly where you can stabilize your career—now, with this company.
Why do you want to be part of this organization?	A response that shows realistic ambition and identification with what the company does.
You brought the production figures up to record levels in six months?	This is the "echo question" used by the interviewer to seek more detail. Pick up on the question and establish how you did it.

Have your own agenda when you enter the interview. Granted, the interviewer is in charge, but you have a lot of influence over what the substance of the interview ends up being. You do that to a degree by answering questions, but you really accomplish it with the questions you ask.

QUESTIONS YOU MIGHT ASK YOUR INTERVIEWER	
Questions to Ask	**Why You Want to Know**
Well, where do we go from here? Whom will I be seeing next?	These questions will give you some indication whether you are finished or will be moving on up the interview chain; look for body language, enthusiasm, discomfort.
How many people work in this department?	To determine its importance in the overall organization and your relative status in the company.
Exactly where do I fit into the organization?	To learn the role you will play relative to others and to attach real meaning to your job title and description.
To whom do I report, and what are the overall reporting relationships within the department?	This is another way to determine your true status.
Who reports to me, and what does that mean in terms of authority?	This defines your status and power relative to others in the organization.
How important is this division to senior management?	To judge whether you can get noticed there by higher-ups.
How do you see this company developing over the next few years?	To judge your opportunities for growth.
What are your plans for expansion that would affect my future?	To judge your opportunities for growth.

(cont'd)

Questions to Ask	Why You Want to Know
How would you describe the working relationship between this division and senior management?	To establish whether you will be interacting with the leaders directly or screened by others.
How would you describe the management style here?	To see if you fit.
Why did my predecessor leave?	To see if there was a problem that you might have as well—maybe a pattern of people not being able to succeed in the position.
How long has this position been open?	To determine whether others are finding good cause to reject the opportunity; if they're having trouble filling it, find out why.
How many people have held this job in the past five years?	To see if the position is a difficult one to succeed in.
How many people have been promoted from this position in the past five years?	To determine whether the job is a springboard to bigger and better things.
What would be your highest priority for me to accomplish if you hired me?	To get an idea about what your real priorities will be.
How independent is this department? Do global responsibilities translate into substantive tasks or something less?	To judge whether you will be able to get things done.
Why did you join the company? How long have you been here? Why do you stay?	To test your interviewer's enthusiasm for the company or reservations about it.

(cont'd)

Questions to Ask	Why You Want to Know
What kind of travel is associated with the job? Where would I be working most of the time? Tell me about the company's travel policies.	To avoid surprises about working conditions you might not be aware of unless you ask.
Will I be attending a training program? Where and for how long?	To find out both the opportunities and limitations in the staff training area.
Is there a formal job description? Can I see it?	To determine if what you are hearing matches what is on paper.
Tell me about the evaluation process at this company. When will my first review come, and how important is it?	To find out how the reward and advancement structure link to performance.

Don't ask things that you could have looked up in the annual report or a standard business reference. Don't put your interviewer on the spot. Orient your questions toward things that you need to know to make an intelligent career decision. Leave salary and benefits questions for the negotiating stage. Keep your questions, attitude, and expectations positive. Don't ask how you did in the interview!

DEALING WITH INTERVIEWERS

You don't want to make your preparation too obvious. There is something disconcerting about the overprepared candidate, so avoid giving that impression. Make sure your interviewer walks away with the feeling that he or she has communicated with the person you will be day to day on the job, not an actor who learned his or her lines. Let your knowledge of the company show as the interview unfolds—not all at once.

The same is true of asking your own questions. Wait until they fit. Don't fall into the coached-candidate trap of dropping an obviously planted question and awkwardly trying to make it mean something when it doesn't. You will have your chance to ask real questions in the course of your interview and at its conclusion.

TYPES OF INTERVIEWERS

You can expect to encounter two basic types of interviewers:

1. the personnel or human resources professional
2. the line manager, supervisor, or senior executive

This division separates the people who do the work of the company: the managers, supervisors, and executives; and the personnel or human resources people who support them.

The personnel staff is most heavily involved in the screening stage of hiring. Their job is to select a basically qualified group of candidates from which the decision makers can hire. The line manager is the person you end up working for after the hiring is over. Personnel's continuing role includes employee benefits administration and maybe some training. Each of the two types of interviewers has an orientation you should be aware of.

When it comes to interviewing, expect managers as a group to be commonsense generalists—they will use fewer interviewing techniques, such as deliberately adding stress. Managers are more interested in getting to know you and determining whether you know your stuff, want to do the work required, and would be nice to work with.

Human resources people are more apt to use interviewing technique tricks. They read the journals, think more like psychologists, and, as a group, are more interested in sorting applicants in seemingly objective ways. They want to get the verifiable facts about you. Personnel interviewers apply the objective hiring criteria given to them by management and weed you out if you give them an obvious reason to. They also give you basic information about the company—everything from the corporate culture to employee benefits. In short, they save the line manager the time and trouble of doing the preliminaries. In smaller organizations the manager often performs some of the roles left to personnel in larger corporations.

With the distinction between the two kinds of interviewers in mind, you can see how their approaches will differ. Expect personnel to test your fit against formal job criteria. Expect managers to have a more hands-on approach to evaluating your suitability. Increasingly, personnel interviewers are trained to get beyond the defenses of the prepared candidate. In many companies, the interviewing skills of human resources professionals are taught to managers and supervisors as well.

INTERVIEWERS' TECHNIQUES

No sooner does the candidate learn the tricks of the interviewer than the interviewer develops new ones. Articles in personnel journals and business magazines are now busy telling human resources managers how to train interviewers to get beyond the hype of the well-prepped candidate. Dan Moreau, in *Changing Times*, writes:

> Oh, for the good old days, when job interviews were job interviews, and you could whiz through one by volleying the stock questions with your glib, prepackaged answers. Today it's not so easy. Job interviewers have wised up. Now they're more apt to press a point—to take a line from your resume, for example, and ask you in depth about it. Why did you choose that college? What projects did you complete there that would make you a better candidate for the job we have?
>
> Looking good in your job interview today means preparing for the unexpected.

A number of managers are being prepared to take more than an impromptu approach to their role as interviewers. In an *Industry Week* article on hiring, James Braham quoted a TRW, Inc., director of management development who said, "we're trying to make sure that our managers know how to ask some follow-up questions, probe deeper into the subject area, and get away from that practiced answer—really get to know the candidate better. You look for how he deals with others, what are his communication skills, his motivation? Does he set goals? Have high energy? How does he solve problems?" Here are some techniques currently being used to get beyond your preparation for the standard interview questions and find out what you are really like.

NEGATIVE REFERENCE CHECK

Routine references and letters of recommendation are notoriously positive—otherwise you wouldn't provide them. At the most, they may damn with faint praise, and they rarely describe a truly negative incident or characteristic. To get around that, employers will sometimes ask, during the interview, for the names of several people whom you did not get along with very well. The practice was described in Bruce Posner's *INC.* magazine article by consultant Phil Thomas:

> While most job applicants will say initially they can't think of anyone who didn't like them, persistence will almost always result in some names—names that the surprised applicant probably hasn't had time to screen mentally. Those negative references and the potential hire's explanations of the problems invariably give . . . a more balanced picture of the person's strengths and weaknesses.

Your best tactic as an applicant going into such a situation is to have several people in mind who were not your soul mates in previous work settings but whose respect you ended up commanding. Think of people with whom you had honest differences, never really won over, but who would respond when asked that you were a bright, fair-minded person who just happened to see things differently from the way they did.

NETWORK REFERENCE CHECK

Networking is a two-way street in hiring. While you can enhance your knowledge of the company and the interviewing process, so, too, can the company investigate you and verify your claims. Consultants interviewed in Braham's *Industry Week* article expressed the belief that people applying for professional positions have reputations within their industry. Personnel staff, managers, and executives can check you out on a quiet, personal level by contacting professional acquaintances and seeking candid opinions about you and your work. Consider the connections that might logically exist between your professional associates in your present and past positions and those who will want to know more about you at the new firm. Anticipate calls that might take place, and consider preparing people who are not among your formal references for the possibility of being contacted about your application for the new position. The less people are surprised, the better are your chances of getting favorable reviews on impromptu reference checks.

TWO-SIDED COIN QUESTIONS

A smooth reference checker will put the person being queried at ease by asking mostly positive questions about you. Of course, even positive questions can probe things that are not apparent in the sometimes complimentary but revealing responses they bring out. An example might be, "Tell me the area in which Jill showed her greatest growth during the period she worked with you." In answering, the reference often doesn't think about the mirror side of that question, which is that he or she is also revealing your area of greatest weakness—the thing you had to work on. This is not bad—you overcame the problem—but it illustrates how a seemingly harmless question can have a hidden agenda.

BEHAVIORAL INTERVIEWING

Jim Kennedy, a San Francisco consultant quoted by James Braham in *Industry Week*, thinks that the hiring advantage has swung from the employer to the candidate. The reason is the current emphasis on preparing candidates to ace the standard interview. College placement officers, outplacement companies, executive recruitment firms, and self-help books have made a concerted effort to train candidates for their interviews. Companies have reacted by turning to interviewing techniques designed to do more than just hear what the candidate says about his or her job performance and training. Now they expect candidates to reveal how and what they did in concrete terms—less fluff, more verifiable substance. What you did and how you did it are what your interviewer wants to know to visualize your behavior on the job.

CONTINUUM QUESTIONS

One way interviewers draw you out is to give you a question that has no right or wrong answer—no boundaries—and see what you do with it. It is merely designed to "work you" and let the interviewer judge how well you do everything from "handling yourself" to fitting in with the company. You are also given the rope with which to hang yourself, if you are so inclined. The question might involve asking you what kind of relationship you prefer with your boss—highly structured or unstructured, for example. Either approach to answering it could be productive and "correct." What the interviewer wants to explore is your values, work ethic, and style—as well as your ability to deal with an ambiguous question.

A TO Z QUESTIONS

Consultant Kurt Einstein's A to Z method is described in Bruce Posner's *INC.* article. It recommends getting you to open up by describing your three most sterling accomplishments in as much detail as possible. "What are the three professional highlights of your career so far? Tell me all about each one of them. What did you do? How did you do it? Why is it so important to you?" The approach puts the focus on you, the candidate, what you personally did and how you did it, instead of the accomplishments of your department, boss, or other third parties. It is a combination open-ended and follow-up question that is supposed to get you away from scripted responses and provide more in-depth information about yourself. The A to Z question is open enough to give you a chance to demonstrate what is important to you, what you can get enthusiastic about, and so on.

TARGETED SELECTION QUESTIONS

Kirsten Schabacker, writing in *Working Woman*, mentioned a Pittsburgh consulting firm that uses an interviewing technique called *targeted selection*, designed to reveal how a candidate thinks and acts. Some questions illustrating the technique included

- "Tell me about a particularly successful presentation you made in your last job and why it was such a success. What about a not-so-successful one? What went wrong?"

- "Tell me about a project you worked on in which one of the team members was not really pulling his or her weight."

This technique is designed to put you on the spot for a specific issue and force a revealing response. It puts you into a situation of having to acknowledge that everything isn't perfect in your work experience and makes you tell how you handled the problems and were affected by them.

Handling Inappropriate Questions

There are some things you are protected from answering, and most interviewers are aware of that. Your religion; political beliefs; ancestry; national origin; birthplace and naturalization status of your parents, spouse, or children; native language or language spoken at home; age (except to say that you are over eighteen); ages of your children; marital status; maiden name; spouse's occupation; and number of dependents—these are among a long list of questions you should never be expected to answer. If an interviewer stumbles across one of them, you have several choices:

- Politely ask its relevancy for the position in question.

- Refuse to answer, and cite your rights protected by the Equal Employment Opportunity Commission.

- Volunteer the information if you think it might be helpful and the interviewer seems to want to know.

It is a judgment call on your part. The whole issue of equal opportunity is discussed more fully in Chapter 16, "Working and the Law." The area of sexual attraction can also bring about inappropriate lines of questioning, comments, and innuendos; Chapter 16 also advises you on how to deal with that problem if it arises.

SUMMARY CHECKLIST: PREPARING FOR THE INTERVIEW

- Your preparations begin with an examination of the standard business references and proceed to sources unique to your region and industry.

- Your objectives in preparing for your interview are to secure the interview and do well during it.

- Your focus in preparing for your interview should include sources of information, the company and its people, what you want and have to offer, and the interview process and how you can influence it.

- Your sources of information include library and other business references, community organizations, regional and national publications, the Internet, and your network of friends and professional acquaintances.

- Sort out what you need to know about the company, why you want to know it, and where you can find the answers.

- Your interview can assume a variety of formats, and familiarity with each of them helps you prepare for and avoid surprises.

- Interviewers follow expected procedures, and knowing them can make you a more effective candidate.

- Interviewers ask certain kinds of questions, and anticipating them can help you answer effectively.

- You are expected to ask some questions of your own, and there are certain ones that both impress interviewers and help you understand the job.

- You can cause problems for yourself by appearing to be overly prepared.

- Interviewers are either personnel/human resources types or managers, and they have different approaches to interviewing.

- Interviewers have developed techniques designed to get beyond your prepared answers; you should know what they are and how to handle them.

11 APPEARING FOR THE INTERVIEW

Much of the impression you leave with your interviewer is subjective—it is the gut feeling he or she gets when you walk in the door. You can improve that impression by being at ease and free of distractions when you become the focus of attention. Some things that can help you do that include:

- dressing properly
- being comfortable with your appearance
- knowing exactly where you are going
- knowing the procedures
- being aware of whom to expect
- being aware of what to expect

In this chapter you review the accepted way of doing everything from shaking hands to saying hello and good-bye. You learn the procedures for dealing with interviewers' names, judging the right time to arrive, sensing when to leave, and everything else that makes your entrance, presence, and exit smoothly executed events. When you do all of these things well, it leaves the focus on you and your positive attributes instead of on memorably awkward moments that could have been avoided.

Before you go on to the detailed suggestions about showing up for your appointment, review Figure 3 below and put what you are about to learn into context.

165

GETTING THE INTERVIEW
- Finding a job
- Applying
- Networking
- Getting invited

PREPARING FOR THE INTERVIEW
- Researching the company
- Preparing personally
- Anticipating questions

APPEARING FOR THE INTERVIEW
- Reconnaissance
- Personal readiness
- Timing

You have done your research, have prepared yourself as best you could, and now it's time to meet the interviewer. You are confident about your company knowledge and your own qualifications, and don't want an awkward arrival to detract from your positive image. You discreetly check out the interview site so there's no chance of getting lost or being late. You know what the appropriate interview dress is and wear it. Good grooming, manners, and knowledge of what to say and do complete your preparations for a relaxed, on-time arrival.

DURING THE INTERVIEW
- Names and personalities
- Style and substance
- Satisfying agendas

LEAVING THE INTERVIEW
- Reading your audience
- Positive expectations
- Last impression

EVALUATING YOUR INTERVIEW
- Substantive match
- Personal chemistry
- Judging your chances

FOLLOWING UP AFTER YOUR INTERVIEW
- Thank-yous
- Additional information
- More networking

CONCLUDING THE INTERVIEW PROCESS
- The offer
- Negotiating
- Accepting

Figure 3. Appearing for the Interview.

Understand how your efforts to apply for the job, secure the interview, and research and otherwise prepare for it have advanced you to the point of appearing for the culmination of all that effort—the face-to-face job interview.

"Appearing for the Interview" covers the practical matters of getting to your interview session looking good, feeling good, and being situated to do your best. It is the chance to make your pitch for a job you really want. You have enough on your mind without worrying about how to find the building, what the parking arrangements are like, and the location of the last unlocked rest room before you become identified as "the candidate." You don't want to be lost, late, inappropriately attired, or have your first words be "May I have the key to your rest room?"

This chapter is filled with practical, commonsense suggestions. Many of them are precautions you might have taken anyway. Others are things you may never have thought about. But before you decide that it sounds all too obvious, look at some true stories of what takes place at job interviews.

As the titles imply, the authors of these two articles were looking for the extreme cases and found them, but in doing so they make the point that there are codes of behavior for job interviews that you want to be sensitive to. After you see how far some people go in the wrong direction, learn this chapter's down-to-earth lessons about how you should behave.

According to an article called "Foolish Interviews" in *USAir Magazine*, Accountemps surveyed two hundred executives, asking them to cite the most unusual things they ever saw or heard of happening during job interviews. Here are some highlights:

- She returned that afternoon asking if we could redo the entire interview.

- He said if I hired him, I'd soon learn to regret it.

- She wanted to borrow the fax to send out some personal letters.

- He brought in a mini tape recorder and said he always taped his job interviews.

- She took three cellular phone calls. Said she had a similar business on the side.

- He left his dry-cleaner tag on his jacket and said he wanted to show he was a clean individual.

- When asked about loyalty, he showed a tattoo of his girlfriend's name.

- The candidate was told to take his time answering, so he began writing down each of his answers before speaking.

In a similar article in *Harper's*, "Unemployment Strategies," are excerpts from a survey sponsored by Robert Haft International, a major recruiting firm. Vice presidents and personnel directors of a hundred large corporations were asked to describe their most unusual interviewing experiences. Here are several techniques you might want to reconsider if you planned to include them in your job interview:

- Applicant challenged the interviewer to an arm wrestle.
- Interviewee wore a Walkman, explaining that she could listen to the interviewer and the music at the same time.
- Candidate fell and broke a bone during the interview.
- Candidate announced she hadn't had lunch and proceeded to eat a hamburger and French fries in the interviewer's office.
- Applicant explained that her long-term career goal was to replace the interviewer.
- Candidate said he never finished high school but was kidnapped and kept in a closet in Mexico.
- Balding candidate excused himself and returned to the office a few minutes later wearing a hairpiece.
- Applicant said if he were hired, he would demonstrate his loyalty by having the corporate logo tattooed on his forearm.
- Applicant interrupted interview to phone his therapist for advice on how to answer specific interview questions.
- Candidate brought large dog to the interview.
- Applicant refused to sit down and insisted on being interviewed standing up.
- Candidate dozed off and started snoring during interview.

Amusing? Yes. All that unusual? Not really. I remember a colleague coming to lunch one day following a busy morning of interviewing candidates. He told of his surprise—and only later, amusement—when a candidate entered his office and sat down in the interviewer's chair! He conducted the interview from the candidate's chair, and none of us ever forgot the incident. The prospect was not hired, and all that any of us recall is the chair incident—it obliterated any other impact that candidate might have made on us. The message to you is that it is worth being aware of and respecting the seemingly obvious protocols as you appear for your job interview. You have a role to play, and if you get too far out of character, you lose.

Clothing and Grooming

It is only common sense to come to your interview well groomed and properly dressed. But that takes judgment and sometimes presumes knowledge that you might not have. While the general rules are known to most candidates, a surprising number of us miss a link or two in the chain of perfect social graces as we make our way to becoming reasonably sophisticated adults. It is worth reviewing the suggestions that follow and doing a bit of research on what is expected where you plan to interview.

Internet Tip

Illustrations of currently fashionable professional wear can be found on the Internet at catalog sites like http://www.landsend.com and retailers like http://www.menswearhouse.com (the "Guy'dLines" section is excellent). Women may find http://womencentral.msn.com/ and http://www.style.com/ useful. Check your favorites using brand names or keywords like "fashion advice" and a search engine.

PROPER DRESS

If you are a military officer interviewing for a command position, there is no doubt about what you will wear. There is a correct uniform designated for the season and the occasion. All you need to worry about is having it fit well and be clean, pressed, and complete with the proper embellishments. In many instances it is actually designated the "uniform of the day"—you can't go wrong.

The same is nearly true in most businesses. Each situation has its "uniform," and with some effort you can determine what it is and comply. In the jargon of college town clothiers, what you are trying to describe is an "interview suit." Graduating seniors, certainly from business and law schools, invest in one. It is a tradition, a necessity, and an expectation of the recruiters who will interview them.

In selecting your interview suit, find safety in the norm. Your job interview is no time to stand out in either direction. Good-quality business clothing, clean and well fitted, is your goal. Respect the seasonal nature of certain items by avoiding inappropriately light-colored garments except in summer—and then only if they are accepted in the group in which you will be interviewing. A perfectly proper summer tan business suit might be totally out of place in certain corporate or government offices even on a humid, ninety-eight-degree Washington, DC, day. The same goes for short-sleeve shirts, as illogical as that may sound.

If you can't find out by observation what your interviewer and his or her colleagues will likely be wearing, call and ask the secretary what the usual business dress is for the office. There is no need to identify yourself. Just say you are coming to town on a future business trip and wanted to inquire. You can't go wrong with a moderately conservative dark suit (dark blue or gray is better than brown) that meets the current lapel width and fabric standards (natural or a blend), solid white or light blue shirt (cotton or a blend, never polyester, never a dark color), and a businesslike tie of current vintage, color, and width. A suit is preferred to a sport coat or blazer.

For men, dark dress shoes would usually be better than loafers, although dress slip-ons giving the appearance of wingtips or other business standards would be fine in most settings. Dark socks are essential—preferably the same color or a darker shade than the pants. Never, ever white! Over the calf is the preferred length. A dark belt of reasonable width for the suit and color match for the shoes is good—no casual belts with dress suits, please, and no dominant, attention-getting buckles.

Leave your gold chains and turquoise ring or watchband at home—avoid any jewelry that would be distracting. Men's earrings are increasingly common, but not recommended; even the unadorned pierced male ear can raise eyebrows.

Women have much the same situation as men, except it isn't as easy to select a "standard" business uniform. This is truer today than it was a few years ago, when women were into the male business look. You want to appear as an attractively attired woman avoiding the extremes of fashion. It is perfectly acceptable that you look pretty and feminine. It might not be wise to emphasize sex appeal, although that is a matter of personal judgment and varies by situation. (Chapter 16, "Working and the Law," discusses this more fully.) For most women, a modest, well-fitting dress or suit would probably be fine. Slacks are not a good idea. Tasteful, interesting jewelry is fine, but choose things that will not be a distraction for your interviewer.

GOOD GROOMING

The starting point is cleanliness. Above all else, be freshly bathed and have your hair recently cut, shampooed, and styled in some acceptable business fashion. Avoid the extremes, whether you are a man or a woman. If your hair is colored, have it done by a professional. On the job you will be representing the company to its clients, and you will be silently judged during the interview on the image you project. Do-it-yourself hair coloring, extreme haircuts, and overdone makeup all contribute to a silent selection-out process that can destroy what is otherwise a substantively good interview.

Use deodorant—unscented is fine, even preferred. Don't use heavy perfume, cologne, or aftershave. A touch of something is fine, especially on women. Men:

when in doubt, opt for the clean, unscented image that doesn't raise the question of whether your interviewer likes what you are wearing—or, for that matter, whether she or he thinks you should be wearing it. If you insist on splashing on the after-shave at the last opportunity (and I recommend against it), wash your hands! The last thing you need is for the interviewer with whom you have just shaken hands to sit there smelling your overpowering scent on his or her own hand throughout the interview.

Facial hair for men is usually a negative. If you are coming for an interview in the traditional business world, leave the full-face beard behind. A reasonable-size and well-kept mustache may be acceptable. When in doubt, come clean-shaven for a serious job interview. If it is important to you, check the situation out beforehand by asking someone not in your interviewing chain if beards are not unusual in the organization.

Visible body hair on women can be distracting in our culture. Without arguing the merits, I recommend adhering to the usual expectations: shaved underarms, legs, and appropriately removed noticeable facial hair.

DO'S AND DON'TS OF CLOTHING AND GROOMING	
Do	**Don't**
Select moderately conservative business wear for your interview—wear the "uniform."	Try to make a fashion statement or express your individualism.
Choose blue, charcoal, gray, or possibly black, solid or modest pinstripe (women have more flexibility, but these are always correct).	Choose brown, or another color.
Wear a long-sleeve solid (or very muted pinstripe) white or light blue shirt (women have more flexibility but can't go wrong with these).	Wear dark shirts, bold colors or patterns, or short sleeves.
Dress with the season and situation in mind. Wear a dark business dress in the summer if that is the accepted style.	Wear summer colors in other seasons.

(cont'd)

Do	Don't
Wear dress shoes—tie or slip-on (men).	Wear "comfort sole" dress shoes.
Coordinate shoes and belts—both should be leather, a deep brown or black (women are safe adding navy, burgundy, or even red). For women, choose moderate heels or flats.	Wear casual accessories with dress clothes or showy belt buckles.
Men: wear over-the-calf socks as dark or darker than your suit. Women: wear conservative skin-tone hosiery.	Men: wear white socks or inappropriate lengths (crew or midcalf) or colors (especially light ones). Women: wear highly styled, patterned, black, white, or colored hosiery.
Wear natural or blended fabrics—modern wools are best.	Wear polyester fabrics.
Wear a suit or business dress.	Wear a sport coat or pantsuit.
Men: wear a reasonably conservative, good-quality, contemporary-style tie. Women: optional with some business fashions—same standard if a scarf is selected.	Wear a bow or a too wide/narrow light or patterned tie or scarf.
Wear modest jewelry and accessories—analog watch and leather band.	Wear garish, dominant, or ostentatious jewelry and accessories—skin diver watches or fraternal/political pins.
Let your natural attractiveness show modestly.	Make your physical attractiveness a feature of your presentation.
Dress for the position you want.	Dress for the position you have.

(cont'd)

Do	Don't
Dress to the accepted standard of your industry—conservative business dress is right for most but not all situations. Inquire if in doubt.	Show your individuality by expressing a personal standard at interview time. Wear regional fashions such as western wear—even of the finest quality—unless you are where it will be unquestionably accepted.
Carry a plain brown or burgundy leather briefcase (blue or black may also be okay for women with the right outfit).	Carry a "stand-out" briefcase full of embellishments or a soft-sided fabric model with your initials monogrammed on it. Juggle both purse and briefcase (use a small clutch in the briefcase instead).
Carry only what you need.	Carry an overcoat, a newspaper, book, or other accessories that are not essential. Stuff your pockets with bulging, inessential things.
Choose a light scent or unscented grooming and beauty products for your interview.	Wear something that is bound to get attention—it might be the thing that is most memorable about you.
Emphasize cleanliness in preparing yourself for the interview—body, hair, and clothes.	Present an unkempt appearance or show any signs of poor hygiene.
Brush your teeth. Visit your dentist for a professional cleaning if it has been a while.	Eat offending foods before the interview.
Men: appear clean-shaven—although a well-kept mustache will usually be okay.	Appear with a beard unless you have prior knowledge that it will be well received.
Present the appearance of a non-smoker.	Show the telltale signs of being a smoker—stained fingers and teeth, the smell of stale smoke on your clothes and papers, smoking materials in your briefcase or pockets.

Familiarizing Yourself with the Interview Site

For a comfortable arrival, know where you are going and what conditions to expect when you get there. You can remove this form of anxiety by checking out the site ahead of time. Locally you do that by deliberately going across town for a dry run one afternoon. If you are traveling to a distant city, you might find it necessary to arrive the evening before. This is not always necessary if you know the setting from previous business trips. You may also have a totally straightforward situation that leaves no room for doubt. However, you will arrive more relaxed if you inquire about the exact location, parking arrangements, and special considerations of which you should be aware—such as highway construction that may make you late, for example.

RECONNAISSANCE

If you live in the interview city or can arrive at an out-of-town site early, go to the building where your interview will be held and satisfy yourself on these matters:

- Is the office easy to locate, or will special instructions be necessary?
- If you're driving, is parking available, or is it available only to people working in the building? If so, ask your interviewer to arrange with the garage to expect you or to suggest an alternative.
- Is the traffic pattern at the time you will arrive the same as when you checked the site? Are some streets one-way during rush hour? etc.
- Is public transportation available if you don't plan to drive?
- Are there any special building security arrangements? Have you been listed as an expected guest for the day of your interview?
- What time do the facilities you plan to use open and close if you will arrive early and/or stay late?

These matters are not always taken care of by your host. If the information isn't volunteered by the time your interview draws near, find out for yourself and ask for assistance.

Internet Tip

Internet map sites will help you find your way to an interview. Enter the employer's address and get back a detailed map and driving instructions—but remember to check it for real-world accuracy. Suggested sites include mapquest.com or the map feature on yahoo.com. You can also enter the keyword "maps" and locate others.

In addition to putting your mind at ease about these matters, your comfortable arrival gives you time to learn more about the job and the company. A chat with the doorman could reveal that the company will be in its new suburban headquarters this time next year. Or small talk with the parking lot attendant tells you about a commuter bus that leaves the shopping center near your apartment to that suburban complex every weekday morning.

If your plans include an overnight stay before your interview, ask if your hotel room is quiet. I once arrived for a critical business meeting in Cleveland and retired for the evening early in a nice hotel room only to be awakened at midnight by workmen using jackhammers to tear down a massive parking garage across the street. This is not the sort of thing reservations clerks volunteer, but they will usually admit it if you ask. Don't go into your interview tired and aggravated when problems like these can be avoided.

PIT STOPS AND PRIMPING

You can't expect to arrive for the interview and discreetly duck into the rest room. It is increasingly common to find them locked. The answer, short of beginning your visit with an awkward request for the bathroom key, is for you to learn ahead of time where a public rest room is available. That kind of information can be picked up during your preliminary walk-through.

You should not overlook the practical side of interviewing—rest rooms and otherwise. Your best-laid plans for what to say and how to say it in the interview session can be rendered less effective by being personally uncomfortable. Foresight can eliminate the problem entirely, leaving the interview itself as the focus of your valuable energies and attention.

Interviewing Procedures

There are things that you just need to do "right" when it comes to interviewing. They are not written in stone and there are exceptions, but you should have a sense of what will be well received and what will be offensive. You don't want to detract from your otherwise favorable impression at the interview by doing the little things wrong. Here are some examples.

TIMING YOUR ARRIVAL

You don't want to be late for your interview, but neither do you want to be uncomfortably early—for you or your host. If you arrive more than ten minutes ahead of schedule, plan to kill time inconspicuously somewhere besides the reception area of your interviewer. The ideal situation is to walk in about five minutes early. You run the risk of awkwardly encountering the person interviewing before you if you are too far ahead of schedule. That could prove embarrassing for everyone concerned in certain situations. Avoid the problem by being only slightly early.

WHAT TO BRING AND WHAT TO LEAVE AT HOME

In the interview "bloopers" that introduced this section, you learned not to bring your lunch, a Walkman, or a large dog. It is almost as bad to come with your spouse and children or anyone else whose presence is a distraction. If your interview is extended or you are taken to lunch, you then have an added problem.

On the practical side, bring a briefcase or folio with you with a copy of your resume, a completed application if you have one, a list of your references (possibly several letters of reference), and a few samples of your work if you need to exhibit it. It is a good idea to have a small pad on which to take notes if that becomes appropriate during your interview. You should also have the telephone numbers of your contacts in case you are unexpectedly delayed. A list of questions you would like to have answered is also an appropriate thing to have readily available. Don't forget your directions for finding the interview site, and a map if you need one.

HANDSHAKES AND GREETINGS

You wouldn't think that saying hello or shaking hands would present a problem, and usually they don't. However, done memorably wrong, they can mark you as an inept candidate and detract from an otherwise good impression.

Your handshake should be extended only in response to one offered by your interviewer. Never initiate it. Make your grip pleasantly firm—neither crushing nor limp. If you in fact have "sweaty palms," inconspicuously dry them before coming into the greeting situation—fold your handkerchief and replace it in your pocket, for example, and discreetly dry your handshaking palm in the process. Reach inside your briefcase and find a freshly folded cloth handkerchief there that will accomplish the same thing. It would be an unusual business interview that began with a "high-five," so resist the urge to greet even a long-lost friend with other than the traditional handshake until the two of you are in a less formal situation.

When greetings are made, your host or hostess should be allowed to take the initiative. If you are sure you know names, use them. When in doubt, pause until everyone's identity is made known. The use of first names is inappropriate unless you are invited to do so by the interviewer; even then, switch back to more formal address if someone else joins the interview. If you are in a panel interview and know only some of the people well, use formal address for everyone until a more relaxed atmosphere has been introduced. While you will almost certainly be met and escorted during the course of your interviews, if you find yourself directed to a series of offices, rely on the secretary at each location to introduce you. If you end up truly on your own, just do the natural, polite thing and say: "Ms. Jones? My name is John Wilson, and I was asked to talk with you about the accounting vacancy. I am a candidate for the position." She should take it from there; follow her lead.

You need to handle the question of personal titles carefully. Mr. and Ms. are the safest these days—Mrs. is fine if you are certain of its correctness. If a genderless functional title makes for a comfortable greeting—such as the dean of a college—use it: "Good morning, Dean Roberts, it is a pleasure to meet you." "Dr." is fine if you are sure that the title is correct, but don't put a person into the awkward position of having to explain that he doesn't have a doctorate. In terms of your own title, modesty is best. "Good afternoon, I'm Don Jackson" is usually better than "Good afternoon, I'm Dr. Jackson," unless you are a medical doctor. Academic doctoral degrees are often best understated. Outside the military, that rule is doubly true for rank—you should be "Colonel" Smith to your military associates only, not to your civilian colleagues, unless it is a situation that clearly warrants using the title.

The best use of titles—academic, military, and otherwise—is to have other people "discover" you have them; never announce them yourself. In job interviews this can have practical implications for you. For example, your interviewer may be a very accomplished person with no formal titles. While she or he would not likely say so, chances are it would be appreciated if you don't emphasize them either. The fact that you have them speaks for itself via your credentials; soft-pedal the issue in person and you will appear the more gracious for doing so.

SEATING

The natural and correct approach is to let your interviewer show you where to sit. The same is true of timing your seating—follow the lead of your interviewer, who will indicate that you should be seated. If none of this materializes, just wait the interviewer out and take the most obviously correct chair after she or he has been seated. When someone else enters the room, stand and be prepared to shift chairs to accommodate the individual if he or she stays.

PHYSICAL CONDITION

You relate better to your interviewer if you feel and look well. One of the most telling things about first impressions is the image of your overall condition that you telegraph by your appearance. Not just the suit and haircut, but also the clarity of your eyes, the erectness of your posture, the spring in your step, your engaging smile. Taken together, things like these tell the interviewers important things. Here are a few tips on how you can make that subjective impression a positive one.

- *Rest.* You want to look rested. It shows when you are worn out. Obvious fatigue can be taken as a sign of a lifestyle and personal habits that might detract from your ability to work effectively. Get a good night's sleep each night for a week before interviewing. Avoid emotional aggravation—the week of the interview is not a good time to leave your spouse or bring on other weighty problems. Such things show on your face. You want to present your interviewer with the peaceful, rested look of someone whose life is in good order.

- *Exercise.* A tiring workout just before the interview is a bad idea. An ongoing exercise program that gets you in shape by the time of the interview is a good one. If your career move lends itself to long-range planning and exercise is not yet part of your routine, add it to your lifestyle six months before you get serious about the job search. You will look better, feel better about yourself, and have something in common with your interviewer, who might well be doing the same thing these days. In a dynamic office of the 21st century you are probably the exception if you are not into some kind of fitness routine. The topic may very well come up in the course of your interview, and you will fit the office culture more comfortably if you have the established habit. Today, showing a personal concern for one's own health and fitness is the norm. You can do that with an individual training program that requires no particular athletic orientation, personal expense, or sacrifice of time; extended lunch hours often accommodate the office exerciser. Company benefits and even compensation packages are increasingly geared to your willingness to stay fit. It can have a favorable impact at interview time as well.

- *Relaxation.* You want to strike a businesslike balance between being hyperkinetic and too laid back. The two preceding topics, on rest and exercise, are an integral part of relaxation. The third component is a personal attitude toward your life and work. What you want to convey at your interview—not with expository statements in most cases, but by example—is that you are a high-energy performer who knows how to relax. The workaholic image is passé—you are still expected to go the extra mile, but with a degree of grace that leaves you looking and feeling good. Appearing appropriately relaxed at your interview is your best way to encourage this favorable impression. You do it by pulling together all the suggestions that have been made so far—be prepared for the interview, dress right, know where you are to be and arrive on time, be rested and fit. With those things done, the image you want to convey will come through naturally, and you will be ahead of the game because your competition can't fake it or put it together on short notice.

THINGS TO AVOID

Don't smoke, chew gum, make nervous gestures, or fail to respect people's personal space (getting too close when you speak, etc.). Articles and books can advise you about the power of body language and eye contact, but it all boils down to your exhibiting reasonable, normal behavior. While a more detailed discussion of body language follows under "Interview Psychology" in Chapter 12, here are some things to keep in mind:

Most interviewers will be uncomfortable with you if you don't look them in the eye. They will probably be just as uncomfortable if all you do is look them in the eye! Relax and interact as comfortably and naturally as you can, looking at the interviewer most of the time but casting your gaze elsewhere at intervals. Do not lean awkwardly forward for the whole interview. Again, relax, and sit as you would normally in a business conversation. Grow animated when the situation calls for it; sit back and be pensive when that is appropriate. Come across as a normal human being and not an actor at an audition.

You should be evaluating those who interview you on these same criteria. If an interviewer's desk has an ashtray overflowing with cigarette butts, you are in the wrong place if you are a nonsmoker. An interviewer whose gaze never leaves you could be an awkward supervisor in the workaday world. With the rare exception of "stress" interviews that should end with a return to normal interviewer behavior after you've been "tested," interviews should be an accurate window on the work environment. If anything, people are on better behavior during interviews, so take that into account in your follow-up evaluation of the session.

Whom and What to Expect

Internet Tip

Find the company's Web page by entering its name in a search engine or by using a site especially designed to locate company Web pages like http://www.switchboard.com/.

If you have not been given a list of people you can expect to see in the course of your interview, make your own list. This can reduce your anxiety level. Everything you can put in the "expected to happen" column takes something off the list of possible surprises—and it really doesn't matter if they actually occur or not. For example, if the chairman of the board stops by for an urgent word with your interviewer and you had considered the possibility of meeting him, you take it comfortably in stride when he gives you a polite handshake. Had you not even considered the possibility, your response might have been more awkward.

Some people benefit from laying out their whole interview day complete with a cast of characters that includes everyone from the parking lot attendant to the boss's boss. You can plan to remember the receptionist's name—and do it because it is a deliberate, planned event. Remember that the receptionist, while not one of your raters, can be a positive influence with those who are. Also, how you treat support staff can influence your hiring. Your behavior toward other people may be scrutinized by your interviewer. Don't even slight the parking garage attendant—he or she just may have an informal vote before the day ends, when your interviewer heads off into the evening rush hour.

SUMMARY CHECKLIST: APPEARING FOR THE INTERVIEW

- To make your interview appearance effective, dress properly, be well groomed, know where you are going, handle the social protocols graciously, and be aware of whom and what to expect.

- Be aware of legendary job candidate "bloopers," avoid them yourself, and steer clear of less obvious but potentially disastrous missteps of your own.

- You should plan to dress in normal business attire; when in doubt, wear your "interview suit."

- Your grooming should emphasize cleanliness, a lack of extremes in scents and accessories, and modest good taste.

- You should make a familiarization visit to your interview site if practical and you haven't been there before.

- You should attend to your personal comfort and primping before arriving at the interviewer's office.

- You should arrive a few minutes ahead of time, never late or more than ten minutes early.

- Bring something on which to take notes, a copy of your resume, application, and references—and little else (no companions).

- Follow your interviewer's lead on handshakes and greetings, never initiating them yourself.

- Use your personal titles modestly and other people's professional titles correctly—avoiding first names unless their use is clearly indicated by your interviewer.

- Follow your interviewer's lead and gestures in seating.

- Appear for your interview rested, relaxed, and physically fit—qualities that speak volumes for your character and potential.

- Make a list of probable characters for your interview day and treat them all with interest and respect—not just your interviewer and his or her superiors.

- Use your interview to evaluate the corporate culture and decide whether you want to be part of it—smoking or nonsmoking, relaxed or formal, philosophically compatible with your values, etc.

12 DURING THE INTERVIEW

You now know about the preliminaries. You have located the job, successfully applied for it, researched the situation thoroughly, secured an interview appointment, and even studied the art of making an effective appearance. It is time to learn how to conduct yourself during the interview.

Your role at this point is to command the respect of the interviewer with your qualifications, honesty, motivation, and knowledge of the working situation. Your interviewer subtly tests each of these factors and at least informally evaluates your personality. And since an interview is only partly objective, you want:

- to be interesting and likable—an employer rarely hires anyone she or he doesn't first "like"

- to be your own strongest advocate, in a tactful and courteous way

- to control a large part of the interview by injecting your own points as you answer the interviewer's questions and ask some of your own

- to use your voice and personal style to impress the interviewer in ways that were not possible on paper

- to avoid leaving intangible negative impressions

These are subjective aspects of the interview—things that don't necessarily fit on checklists but that have a way of registering with the interviewer and influencing his or her final judgment.

GETTING THE INTERVIEW
- Finding a job
  - Applying
  - Networking
  - Getting invited

PREPARING FOR THE INTERVIEW
- Researching the company
  - Preparing personally
  - Anticipating questions

APPEARING FOR THE INTERVIEW
- Reconnaissance
- Personal readiness
  - Timing

DURING THE INTERVIEW
- Names and personalities
  - Style and substance
  - Satisfying agendas

You are facing the interviewer and are engaged in an exchange that will leave a personal impression of your qualifications and desirability for the job. It is the interviewer's task to verify your credentials and clarify points—with an interest in both the substance and style of your responses. This is where you show knowledge, display judgment, assert values, demonstrate restraint, and exude charm. You and the interviewer estimate how well you might fit into the organization as well as how you'd actually perform the tasks involved. Information on paper and voices on telephones become real people interacting and subtly judging capability, likability, and promise.

LEAVING THE INTERVIEW
- Reading your audience
  - Positive expectations
  - Last impression

EVALUATING YOUR INTERVIEW
- Substantive match
- Personal chemistry
- Judging your chances

FOLLOWING UP AFTER YOUR INTERVIEW
- Thank-yous
- Additional information
- More networking

CONCLUDING THE INTERVIEW PROCESS
- The offer
- Negotiating
- Accepting

Figure 4. During the Interview.

You are ready to use the information found during your research on the company, the position, and the people interviewing you. You already know about the different kinds of interviews that you might encounter, the questions you can expect to be asked, and the answers you might give from reading about them in Chapter 10. Now you are going to concentrate on dealing with the person asking them—the practical, applied psychology of the interviewer interacting with you, the job candidate. Specifically, you will see how to:

- project your personal qualities during the interview
- understand the reasons for background checks
- use your research from the preparations stage
- deal with the interviewer's questions
- understand basic job interview psychology
- communicate technological awareness

Figure 4 shows where these steps fit into the total job-hunting and interview cycle. Examine it before you go, then learn how you can perform at your best during the interview.

Projecting Personal Qualities

It is time for you to come off the resume sheet and become flesh and blood. You are about to get your chance to fill in the blanks that remain for the people who already like what they see on paper but need confirmation. They want to be assured that you are someone with whom they would like to share their working hours. You have to satisfy their concerns in the total communication experience that is the face-to-face job interview.

BACKGROUND CHECKS

You succeed in a job interview by establishing your credibility. It is one of the first things you do, and it becomes the baseline from which all of your other claims are judged. Much of the interviewer's assessment of your honesty is a gut feeling, but the measures are becoming increasingly objective. You can expect to encounter varying degrees of "resume analysis." A conscientious interviewer will look for and then probe any inconsistencies in your resume and personal comments.

As you learned in resume writing, you have to account for all time periods. Your dates of schooling and employment should connect logically, or you need to explain the lapses. Breaks in employment can be as innocent as student travel before beginning a career or as serious as a prison term. You have to assume that your job application will be formally investigated. No one is exempt. In December 2001, George O'Leary was appointed the football coach at Notre Dame, the biggest job in the college game. But he had to resign immediately once the university found that parts of his resume didn't check out.

In the 1980s, resume checking became a growth industry. In the new century online services like VeriRes, Inc. (http://www.verires.com), provide a wide range of verification services for nominal fees. For $15 the employer can verify your date of birth and do a national search for aliases and other Social Security numbers you may have used. A criminal records check costs from $25 to $79. Dates of employment, position, duties, pay, reason for separation, and rehire status go for $10. Ten dollars will also verify your dates of college attendance, course of study, and type of degree earned. Credit reports, bankruptcies, liens, judgments, marriage and divorce records, professional license, business affiliation, criminal records, and more are also available, often on a same-day basis. So don't assume only high-security employers like the CIA will check you out. Represent yourself honestly.

One reason for this growth is the liability employers can incur if you misrepresent yourself before they hire you, and you do something wrong after they hire you. Avis Rent A Car was sued for not checking the jail record of an employee who committed a crime while working for the company. Here is what one large background checking firm listed as the most common lies by job applicants. In checking 100 resumes for a high-tech manufacturer, they found the following discrepancies:

- Wrong dates of employment—41
- Wrong dates of study—26
- Wrong size of previous salary—13
- Nonexistent employer—11
- Wrong grade point average—7

According to *INC.* magazine, there's a 30 percent chance that a resume will be wrong and a 3 percent chance that an applicant will fail to disclose a criminal record. The best way for companies to prevent such misrepresentations is to ask the right questions in writing and have you sign the application—with notification that it will be verified. When that is done, says Barry Bergman, president of the security firm interviewed by *INC.*, it "makes it less likely that a degree in political science will become an engineering degree, or that three months at a previous job will become three years."

Margaret Mannix, writing in *U.S. News & World Report*, said that a 1991 study by Northwestern University found that 46 percent of the 320 companies surveyed don't request a transcript when hiring a new college graduate, 56 percent don't check faculty references, 37 percent never speak with personal references, 21 percent fail to verify the degree, and 18 percent don't check past employment. Looking at the other side of those statistics, it is apparent that you still stand an excellent chance of being found out if you are dishonest. There is a lot of checking going on, and you should come to your interview comfortable that your resume and comments will stand the test of verification if it comes.

The way you phrase your responses can affect the way an interviewer judges your honesty. According to Brian Dumaine, writing in *Fortune*, employers are weary of sweeping statements such as "I was in charge of" or "I created"—these are often signs that the candidate is exaggerating. You should approach your interview with an unembellished, positive, objective version of what you have done and what you expect to be able to do for the employer. With every claim made you should be ready to offer a reference or data that will vouch for your veracity. There is no way for you to anticipate what the interviewer already knows about you; it is not worth stretching the truth and risking failure on the grounds of dishonesty or exaggeration. None of which is to say that you should accentuate the negative or turn your interview into a confessional; act in your own best interests, but do it honestly.

MAKING YOUR POINTS

Make the interview a platform for presenting your own case for being hired. While the interview takes place at the invitation of the hiring company whose employee is conducting the session, you are still half the show, and communication is a two-way street. You certainly shouldn't appear arrogant, but you should show confidence. You have two direct ways to communicate at the interview:

1. *Answering questions*—lets you modify the interviewer's approach and enables you to stress your own agenda. Anyone who has ever watched a politician respond to an interviewer's questions knows that the answers don't have to be limited to the questions. While you should not make exaggerated use of the technique, there is room for you to maneuver. Rehearse your answers if some of the easy-to-anticipate questions come your way. Case History 7 illustrates this technique.

Case History 7—Situation

CONTROLLING THE INTERVIEW WITH YOUR ANSWERS

Background

Nick Clayton is a publicist at a large trade press who is seeking the director of publicity position with a small, independent book publisher. ❶ He knows that his interviewer will probably inquire why he wants to step off the career ladder at a major organization to join a small one. He plans to use every occasion he can during the interview to communicate his intention to make a purposeful lateral move. ❷ One way to do that is by expanding his answers to promote his own agenda—establishing that he has a sound rationale for making the move.

Situation

❸ Nick takes his place in the interviewer's office, exchanges pleasantries, and begins to deal with questions. "Tell me what kind of clients you've been handling at Hilton Press," the interviewer asks. He responds, "I've been arranging promotional tours for nonfiction authors for the past three years. ❹ As I understand it, about 85 percent of your production is nonfiction. ❺ I'd love to take a highly personalized package to the media contacts I've had to work with all this time on a mass-production basis—what a difference it would make!"

❻ "Where have you established contacts, Nick?" the interviewer asks. ❼ "Most of the major market talk-radio producers are professional acquaintances, and the top half-dozen or so national TV talk shows. ❽ I think they'd really light up if they had a look at your stuff—even the backlist titles are refreshingly different," he answers. "So you think you'll still be listened to when you're representing us?" the interviewer inquires. ❾ "You bet I do! What I can do for you is get my foot into doors I've already entered. Once inside, I will have the chance to do what I've always wanted to do—promote some things I feel strongly about and not just the next project on my calendar!"

Conclusion

So in the routine discourse of his interview, Nick explains again and again his heartfelt ❿ answer to the hiring firm's biggest question, "Why does this guy want to work for us?"

Case History 7—Analysis

CONTROLLING THE INTERVIEW WITH YOUR ANSWERS

General Strategy

Nick has the challenge of explaining why he wants to make a lateral move from a fast-track career in a large organization to a small one. He has already said he wants to; he is now going to demonstrate it by weaving the rationale into a number of his interview responses. That will show the interviewer that Nick knows what he is doing.

Specific Points

1 You often sense issues that call for elaboration.

2 You have the floor when answering questions and, with some good judgment, can stretch most answers to address your own agenda.

3 Let your interviewer set the pace of the interview, but be ready to interject your points in addition to what is specifically asked.

4 After answering the question, Nick established linkage between his past and the organization's present missions.

5 In the same conversation he made clear his view of how his work would be more rewarding in the new situation.

6 The interviewer asks another limited, direct question.

7 Nick proceeds to answer the direct question objectively.

8 Without yielding the initiative to the interviewer, Nick proceeds to explain why his past experience and new setting will make for a profitable marriage.

9 Reading the "buy signal" indicating that the interviewer is hearing his message, Nick comes right out with his prime motivation for the change from big to small company roles.

10 Let your answers address what you understand to be the real concerns, not just the formally worded questions. Do it by expanding your answers.

Case History 8—Situation

CONTROLLING THE INTERVIEW WITH YOUR QUESTIONS

Background

Rene Fitzgerald is an operating room nurse who has not been working for several years and is ❶ interested in returning part time. She once suffered from "burnout" and wants to be certain that the working environment at the hospital suits her ❷ lifestyle, which now calls for a high degree of independence and an ability to leave the job at the hospital door.

Situation

Rene's talents are very much in demand, so she has the luxury of shopping for the right situation. ❸ A nurse placement agency arranges an appointment for her with the director of nursing at Fern Memorial Hospital. She is given an opportunity to ❹ introduce herself and say why she is interested in working as an operating room nurse at Fern. While she takes the occasion ❺ to voice her concern with limiting stress, it is the ❻ questions she asks later that clearly indicate her agenda. The director ends the session with the customary "Thank you for answering my questions. ❼ Now are there any that I might answer for you?" Rene has ❽ laid the groundwork, so it is not a surprise when she asks: ❾ "Do you consistently have enough staff to let me work three days a week, not making me feel guilty when I say no to additional hours? What happens if I want to accompany my husband on a business trip and I give you several weeks' notice that I'll need a replacement on a certain day? Do you have operating room nurses who have worked part time and stayed in that capacity for a number of years? Could you suggest a few I might talk with about working conditions? I have to limit the intensity of my involvement. Talk with my references and verify what I can do for you, and why I have to do it this way."

Conclusion

Rene has special needs of her own. She communicates them with questions whose relevance was made clear earlier in the interview. ❿ In doing so she steers clear of mismatched expectations and gets the type of working situation she can sustain successfully.

Case History 8—Analysis

CONTROLLING THE INTERVIEW WITH YOUR QUESTIONS

General Strategy

Rene is in a position to be frank but does not want to be offensive or appear to be indifferent to the needs of her potential employer. She is using her interview as an occasion not only to respond to the employer's questions but also to ask important ones of her own. She does this with sensitivity by putting her questions into the context of her special needs and providing references to substantiate her unique circumstances.

Specific Points

❶ When you are in a high-demand field, you stand a better chance of customizing your working situation.

❷ You have reasons to limit your professional activity and need to say so.

❸ Your agency prescreens the situation and establishes the fact that the employer has an interest in talking with you even with limitations.

❹ When interviews begin with a personal introduction, this can be an opportunity to begin sketching the parameters of your special needs.

❺ In this instance, mentions the need for limiting stress in her work.

❻ You get the opportunity to go beyond generalities by asking well-thought-out questions that address your specific needs.

❼ While you can ask periodic questions during the interview, generally your opportunity comes by invitation at the end.

❽ It helps to have set the tone, especially if your questions are limiting.

❾ Then, in a series of targeted questions, you explore your concerns with the interviewer.

❿ The objective of asking questions is to get a realistic job picture.

2. *Asking questions*—presents you with an opportunity to focus the interview in your favor. By asking the right questions you can do more than gather information; you can also make your own case and create "readiness" in your interviewer's mind for accepting your point of view. Your well-chosen questions can set the mood or shift the emphasis of the interview. You should anticipate this and have several questions prepared. Case History 8 illustrates this technique.

MAINTAINING A POSITIVE ATTITUDE

Bring enthusiasm and energy to your interview. Don't dread the occasion and come across as though you would rather be anywhere else. That is exactly how some candidates hurt their prospects.

Enthusiasm is something you can generate and control. It is a matter of personal attitude. You are the one who sends the internal messages that make you feel a certain way—"self-talk" is a term sometimes used to describe the process of initiating your own moods and feelings. No one is proposing that you adopt an unrealistic long-range view of your life; if you have problems, get to work on solving them. But for something as limited in time as a job interview, which is rich in potential for helping you solve other problems, it is worth talking yourself into an enthusiastic position instead of accepting the negative one. You can stop the internal process that repeats the negative message and dampens your enthusiasm. Replace it with a positive one that will sustain you through the interview. You will be amazed at the difference in how you feel, act, and appear to other people.

There is nothing mysterious about the power of a positive attitude. Interviewers are attracted to positive candidates who radiate that they look forward to the challenge of the new job and are sure they can make a contribution. Along with a capable employee, they are looking for a fresh attitude that will contribute to the overall mood of the company—a "can do" attitude that might be infectious. In addition to your fine qualifications, that is what they want to see in you, and you can deliver it if you try.

TRANSFERRING YOUR ENTHUSIASM

Your enthusiasm can transfer to the interviewer as well. It is a quality you can bring with you to an interview that might otherwise have remained uninspired. It is your own very personal touch—the way you introduce a favorable measure of yourself that no one else can duplicate. You personalize your interview and become memorable in a way that no competing candidate can exactly match. You become unique in the interviewer's eyes, and that can be quite valuable at selection time, when the choice comes down to one among many who are technically qualified.

SELLING YOURSELF AS LIKABLE

Put yourself in the interviewer's position. You are both there for a business purpose, but any meeting of two people is also a social transaction. Literally everyone wants to be liked, including your interviewer. The easier you make it for her or him to feel liked, the more highly she or he will regard you as a candidate. You never escape the stratification of the interview where you each have separate roles, but neither do you get away from the human interaction that weighs so heavily in the final subjective act of one person selecting or rejecting another one.

Like all techniques in interviewing, you can get into trouble by awkwardly applying the likability approach. Don't try to make the interviewer your buddy. Actress Julia Roberts is quoted in *Playboy* magazine as saying that one of the best pieces of advice she received from her brother, actor Eric Roberts, was: "You have to remember that this is show business, not show friendship." Keep the businesslike air and the appropriate professional distance. But with those boundaries in place, let the likability factor come into play between the two of you. If the situation lends itself, find a common interest and share a properly limited appreciation of it. Look for the things about which you can honestly share some enthusiasm.

Attitude is very important. If you expect to like someone, you probably will. Go into your interview expecting to find a person there ready to interview you who has your best interests in mind—someone you can have good feelings about and with whom you will relate easily.

CONVEYING PERSONAL STYLE

Common courtesy is expected; it is something that can win you points with the interviewer and support staff. Say some genuine thank-yous for the nice things that everyone along the way has done for you. Be tactful and self-effacing when it comes to potentially embarrassing statements or incidents. Take them in stride, and seize the opportunity to give your hosts a comfortable way out if they have caused an awkward moment. Your courtesy stands an excellent chance of being both appreciated and remembered—it is the kind of quality they would appreciate seeing in a colleague. Look for opportunities to demonstrate what you are like during the interview.

ADAPTING TO YOUR INTERVIEWER

Part of making your interview a success is your ability to complement the style and energy level of your interviewer. Pace yourself to the interviewer—if he or she is laid back and casual, be ready to accommodate that style with more informal responses than you might normally give. However, avoid the trap of joining the informal interviewer in a personal style that is so relaxed as to make you appear indifferent or disrespectful. What is normal behavior for the interviewer may not be suitable for you. Look for straightforward invitations to informality before fully joining in.

DRINKING AND SMOKING

If you have a meal with your interviewer, be cautious about too much relaxed familiarity. Order something simple that you can easily eat while carrying on a business conversation. You can decline the second drink or skip alcohol entirely. It is no longer awkward to decline a cocktail; most people are now perfectly comfortable ordering a nonalcoholic drink. While this is an opportunity to establish that you drink socially (if indeed you do), you do not have to provide excuses for not drinking.

However, for recovering alcoholics, this can create a problem. It is one of those things that requires judgment on your part. If substance abuse is bound to come up in a background or reference check, or if the application required you to acknowledge the problem, take the initiative and explain that you have solved it. If your drinking was a very private thing that is not apt to be passed along by others, you may want to let the matter pass unless you are asked.

Smoking can pose an interesting challenge for a candidate. In what is increasingly a nonsmokers' world, it can be an emotional issue for you or the interviewer. If the interviewer is a smoker, she or he will probably have the discipline not to do so with you—even at lunch. If the interviewer asks whether you mind if she or he has a cigarette, you have to make a judgment call. The best response may be to say that you are not a smoker, but have no objection to the interviewer's smoking. Be sensitive, make your point that smoking is not your thing—but don't get on your soapbox. If you are the smoker, definitely forget it unless your interviewer is a smoker, too, and you can both light up without offending others. While many people wouldn't say so openly, they would not hire a smoker if it could be avoided. If you are working on breaking the habit, say so. If you expect to smoke only on your breaks outside the office, say so. If smoking is of emotional importance to you, you may have a problem in many contemporary offices.

ACCEPTING DIFFERENT PERSONALITIES

Be ready to accept a contrasting personality when you meet your interviewer. It isn't necessary that you be of the same ilk to get along well together. Tolerance should be your byword as you interview with a company. Expect to meet different kinds of people, and make up your mind ahead of time that you are going to accept those differences.

SENIORS INTERVIEWED BY JUNIORS

Age or experience differences shouldn't separate you from your interviewer. While there are many potentially awkward combinations, let's assume that you are a senior person interviewing with a relatively junior human resources officer. It may be necessary for you to set the mood by being relaxed and pleasantly respectful of your interviewer's position. Keep the interview an objective business affair with a natural extension of the kinds of friendly interaction you would have with a similarly experienced person anywhere else in life. Be nice. Take care of business. Avoid resenting the gap in age and experience, and make your interview a positive experience for both of you—instead of an unspoken contest over who should be interviewing whom based on the merits.

SEXUAL CHEMISTRY

Another area of human interaction that is no stranger to the employment interview is sexual chemistry—pleasant and unpleasant. Chapter 16 deals with the topic more thoroughly, but you should not be surprised if it happens. There are gracious and effective ways to keep it from becoming a problem, except in the most extreme cases.

Using Your Research

You made an effort to research the company, the position, and the people you might meet or discuss at your interview. Now is the time to use your research. The trick to doing so effectively is letting it enter into the dialogue naturally. It has to flow and complement points that would normally be made anyway. The exception is when you have an opportunity to ask a question that can use new information as its basis. That is an acceptable way of opening new lines of inquiry and ideal for exhibiting your knowledge of the company.

SHOWING INTEREST IN THE COMPANY

Your starting point for showing interest in the company and the job is in demonstrating a clear understanding of what it does—and what you expect to contribute. This is a two-sided proposition. You want to be cautious about your interests appearing to be too narrow. Use the following general guidelines. Dispense your company knowledge incrementally. Take your time and let the interviewer set the stage for how specific you can safely become.

As the situation is drawn more clearly by the interviewer, use your answers—and questions—to show your company knowledge, working your assets into a plausible model for satisfying the company's needs.

GUIDELINES FOR SHOWING COMPANY KNOWLEDGE

- Mention specific instances where the company has been successful—or unsuccessful—and how your skills and sensitivities could have contributed to or changed the outcome.

- If you know the key personalities of the organization, associate yourself with the winners, distance yourself from the losers—all in the course of the interview and in such a way as to come across as a candid observer rather than an all-knowing critic.

- Have alternative solutions for each problem—make these positive, and position the company as the beneficiary, with you profiting only as a member of the team.

- Respectfully subordinate yourself to the organization, and don't come across as a one-person act with an answer for everything.

- Pose as an aware observer with some tentative theories about how things work at the company, but with humility and respect for the knowledge of the insiders.

- Appear interested, aware, and anxious to test your preliminary solutions with people in a position to give you the feedback needed to make them realistic.

LEARNING ABOUT THE JOB

Use your knowledge of the company and its people to find out exactly what the employer wants to accomplish by filling this position. If your network and research have given you incomplete or conflicting readings about this, now is the time for clarification. Do it early in the interview, because you run the risk of exhibiting faulty knowledge. Also, the earlier in the interview you do it, the better positioned you are to use the remaining time to make your case for why you are the person to hire.

IDENTIFY THE DECISION MAKER

You want to identify the decision maker as soon as possible. Your ability to sort differing opinions of the job and the priorities surrounding it can be crucial to your hiring. It is not uncommon for the boss to expose you to others on staff who obviously have differing approaches to the problem. When it comes time to interview with the boss, you can expect to be asked your own opinion as to the most productive solution. Choosing his or her direction, or making a sensitive case for not doing so, is important. By questioning others in the interview chain before reaching the decision maker, you can have the information you need to react intelligently. Keep in mind that the right answer doesn't always agree with what you know to be the favorite solution. If in your interview with the boss you have made sense out of differing staff opinions, you have gained more than you would have with an obedient answer. Be willing to take a well-reasoned risk in situations that let you demonstrate your ability to distill information into an original solution. The technique is illustrated in Case History 9.

SALARY QUESTIONS COME LATER

Save the salary questions for later. It is the one thing about the job you don't want to pursue at this stage. Again, you face the problem of casting yourself too narrowly. If you place an emphasis on salary early in the selection process, you make it a premature priority for both sides in the hiring. Case History 10 shows you how to handle the situation.

SHOWING INTEREST IN YOUR INTERVIEWER

In addition to approaching your interviewer as a potential friend instead of as an adversary, this is the time to apply any knowledge you've gained that might strengthen your relationship. If your research revealed an article he or she wrote, mention having read it. If she or he has things in his or her office that betray a common interest—for example, aviation—share the interest honestly. Don't overdo it, but use the occasion to express respect for the avocation. Use knowledge of your interviewer to personalize the relationship early. It will give you a better platform for selling yourself as the right person to hire. You create an expectation of good things to come, and that can be helpful. Case History 11 shows you how.

Dealing with Questions

Your greatest influence on the interview's outcome is in how you deal with the questions you are asked. What you say is important, but so is how you say it—demonstrating your poise and ability to think under stress is as much a part of the process as the objective questions and answers. Here are some guidelines that you should be familiar with and use to your advantage:

Case History 9—Situation

SOLVING A PROBLEM AT
YOUR INTERVIEW

Background

Bob McClay is a successful group sales specialist with a major national insurance company. ❶ He is tired of frequent travel and is seeking a partnership interest in a hometown agency where he and his bride plan to relocate and raise a family. His background is impressive, but he is going to have to ❷ make a special impression to jump from sales representative to partner.

Situation

Bob enters his interview with the senior partner of Edgewright Agency as he finishes ❸ a day of informal interviews with several key people. As he takes his seat and they make the transition from small talk to substantive issues, his prospective boss and partner asks, "Well, Bob, if you're going to own a hunk of this business, ❹ you're going to have to deal with its problems. You've been around for a few hours now. Which one do you suggest tackling first?" ❺ While he is a little surprised by the question, Bob ❻ recalls a few things that seemed to have the staff perplexed. ❼ One of them was the onslaught of out-of-the-region telephone solicitations to certain segments of their traditional client base. He decides to place ❽ sales and service above operational matters and makes this his problem to solve. "Mr. Edgewright, your folks are having a problem bucking the telemarketers from Pennsylvania. Just getting defensive about it isn't going to make things better—and that's the main response I was hearing today. ❾ I have an idea about local telemarketing that I'd like to develop for you." And Bob goes on to introduce the local agency to a kind of marketing that suits its situation very well but was not something the agency had thought of trying. His experience with the technique on the national level makes him the perfect person to lead in that new direction.

Conclusion

Bob ❿ enters the interview an outside observer and leaves it on the verge of becoming an inside problem solver. An opportunity is presented that vaults him beyond his resume and puts his abilities to work in a way that matters to the bottom line. He can do more than close sales; he is also partnership material.

Case History 9—Analysis

SOLVING A PROBLEM AT YOUR INTERVIEW

General Strategy

Bob comes into the interview with a sixth sense that says, "I've got to become a player here right away if I am to become a partner. Otherwise I'm going to be what I've already been—a salesman." He looks for his opening and finds it when the senior partner asks his opinion on something he can make a contribution to directly.

Specific Points

❶ Lifestyle changes can alter your career path—a job interview is often one of the first places that you realize how significant the change will be.

❷ When you are attempting to make a significant impact on top management, it helps to be in a position to "fix something"—be ready to solve a problem.

❸ Your interview day often begins with the "lesser lights" and ends with the boss. Appreciate the difference in how you should perform in each setting.

❹ Expect a blockbuster. He or she assumes you've already covered the routine things with others.

❺ When you aspire to a role that is different from that of the regular employees, expect questions that reflect values different from those they reflected.

❻ Be a keen observer and listener in the preliminary interviews in order to be prepared to make a contribution if the opportunity presents itself.

❼ Pick a problem that seems to lack an in-house solution.

❽ Given a choice, go for the bottom-line issues, not the organizational or philosophical ones.

❾ Present your tentative solution and make it clear that you don't presume to solve it on the spot—entice the boss to hear the rest of your story as a partner.

❿ The task is to change your image from that of an outside observer into a problem solver intimately involved in structuring a real solution.

Basic Rules for Handling Questions

- Learn as much about the job as possible so you can answer questions in the proper context and steer the interview toward your strengths.

- Pay attention to the interviewer, and be ready to react to her or his interests, rather than concentrating on a rigid agenda of your own.

- Expect more than one-word answers and stock interviewer questions—be prepared for questions that require you to be more expansive.

- Be ready to appraise your own job performance, give reasons for your opinions, and tell how you accomplished specific things.

- Understand the reason for open-ended questions and other techniques used to prolong your responses in hopes of gaining more depth; use them to amplify your strengths and promote your own agenda.

- Be an attentive listener; it will give you a chance to read the situation and adjust your strategy to the dynamics of the interview, not just react.

- Use hypothetical questions about how you would solve problems as opportunities to project your strengths and show awareness of the company's needs, how it operates, and how you can make a contribution.

- Be ready for surprise questions like, "We all have things we'd rather not have known about us. What is there in your background that you'd rather tell us about now than have discovered later?" (See Chapter 10 on how to respond.)

If you know these rules, you are better prepared than the average candidate. They put you in the enviable position of having been "taught the test." You are freed from the anxiety of wondering what is happening during your interview. You can face the interviewer's questions calmly and frame the kinds of responses that leave a favorable impression—both in style and in substance. As important, perhaps, you can avoid the traps that have been laid out for you. With your thorough knowledge of questioning procedures, you can sidestep the awkward moments and focus the interviewer's attention on what you have to offer.

BEHAVIORAL INTERVIEWING

Business Week's John Byrne has reported that "behavioral interviewing" is the in thing for human resources experts and personnel consultants from coast to coast who stress finding out what a person is going to do on the job, not just verifying that he or she has the credentials to do it. The article quoted Jim Kennedy of San Francisco's Management Team Consultants, who says you can expect four categories of questioning in a behavioral interview:

- **Problem question**. "Give me an example of a problem in which you and your manager disagreed over how to accomplish a goal."

- **Continuum question**. "Do your talents lean more toward strategy or tactics, being creative or analytical?"

- **Comparison question**. "How would you compare, say, the marketing of consumer goods versus financial services?"

- **Future question**. "A year from now, what might your boss say during a performance review about your work for the company?"

Each of these questions is designed to draw you out and make you demonstrate your ability to deal with problems, show your strengths and weaknesses, and help interviewers judge whether you have the skills and personal characteristics that will make you a successful transfer into their organization. Review them and practice changing the wording and settings to suit your own professional situation. Rehearse the kinds of answers you might give, and be ready to respond with ease if you are faced with this new interviewing technique.

ADJUSTING TO THE INTERVIEWER'S REACTION

As your interview progresses, it is up to you to appraise the impact your answers are having and calibrate your responses accordingly. You can compare this to an artillery battery firing early rounds and having a spotter near the target call back instructions for improving accuracy. In the interview, you have to be your own spotter and look for clues for adjusting the interview in the face, words, and body language of your interviewer.

You have several choices on how to make your adjustments. If the response is positive, continue in the same vein. If the interviewer is getting bored and appears just to be going through the motions, you have nothing to lose by livening up the interview with a more controversial answer. Judgment is needed not to go from bad to worse, but the right move can save you. If you can break the monotony in some positive way, you are ahead of the game.

Case History 10—Situation

DELAYING THE SALARY QUESTION

Background

Wanda McFee is a landscape architect ❶ making the transition from working in the public sector on a scaled government salary to a position with a commercial developer. Part of her motivation is financial, and ❷ she wants to establish her value objectively and not on the basis of what she currently earns.

Situation

Wanda is going for an interview with the head of exterior design for a leading developer of commercial properties in a major city. ❸ She is well qualified for the position advertised and even has experience with government projects of a similar magnitude. As her interview progresses, ❹ she is asked the salary question early on. "Ms. McFee, ❺ we like the qualifications you're bringing to the position. What do you think it would take to retain you?" the interviewer asks. ❻ "Thank you for recognizing my potential, Mr. Smith, and I'm sure XYZ Development has a salary in mind that would be more than competitive for the work to be done." ❼ Other questions of a general nature follow; then the interviewer returns to salary: "What are you currently earning as a GS-12 with the Park Service?" he asks. ❽ "Well, GS-12s are paid in a range from $22,000 to $38,000, and I've been in the system for quite a few years." More general questions; then: "Frankly, Miss McKee, I need to establish whether we can afford you. Can you tell me your financial expectations?" he asks. "I don't have a dollar figure per se, but it would help me to know what XYZ normally expects to pay a person with the responsibilities we've discussed this afternoon. ❾ What do you plan to offer someone in my situation?" she responds. "We have a range that runs from the mid-$30s to upper $40s, depending on the circumstances," he answers. "I see no reason why we can't reach a suitable figure when an offer is made," she says as the topic changes.

Conclusion

Wanda wants to avoid having the developer add 15 percent to her government salary and bring her in at a low salary. ❿ She dances around the increasingly direct questions until he is satisfied that, short of insisting, he is going to get nothing but agreement that they are within each other's range.

Case History 10—Analysis

DELAYING THE SALARY QUESTION

General Strategy

Wanda needs to walk the narrow line between being obstinate and acting in her own best interests. She does that by turning the interviewer's questions into generalized responses, loosely defined ranges, and questions of her own.

Specific Points

❶ Your salary expectations can differ when changing categories of employer.

❷ In such a situation you want to avoid having your future salary determined solely by your past salary in a lower-paying industry.

❸ Your best strategy for a fair salary adjustment is to focus on your qualifications, not past salary, so prepare to put emphasis on the potential employer's compensation standard, not on your old salary.

❹ An early attempt to get you to name a salary figure should not be unexpected, but a definitive response is unnecessary.

❺ This is a "buy signal"—the interviewer wants to hire you. It is your license to dance a little on the salary question.

❻ Begin with appreciation and end by stating your expectation that they will treat the salary question fairly.

❼ It is common practice for the interviewer to back off on the salary question and then revisit it a few minutes later.

❽ Don't try to make a secret out of public information, but you can avoid telling precisely where you stand and probably get away with it.

❾ If you have the opportunity, shift the question back to the interviewer—chances are you will end up stating overlapping scales and leave the figure for later negotiations, as it should be.

❿ While a totally insistent inquiry should get an honest answer, most salary questions early in the interview can satisfactorily end with a defined range.

Case History 11—Situation

SHOWING INTEREST IN YOUR INTERVIEWER

Background

Barry Warren is a library technician looking for his ❶ first permanent position after working as a student assistant during four years of undergraduate study. He has his basic credentials and clearly relevant student work experience, but what will ❷ make the difference in a competitive interviewing situation against similar candidates is finding a basis for standing out positively in the mind of his interviewer.

Situation

Barry appears for his interview with a little bit of ❸ apprehension about the person scheduled to conduct it. He will be interviewed by the woman who used to supervise him as a student intern at the college library. Even though this is quite a different setting, a large municipal library, he ❹ remembers her as a distant person he never felt he knew. "Good morning, Mr. Warren," she begins. "I see we have something in common." ❺ Assuming she was referring to the college library, he answers, "Yes, we spent some hours together in the professional reference division at State College." "That's true enough, ❻ but I was thinking more along the lines of gemstones—I see you're wearing sapphire cuff links and a class ring. The stone must mean something to you!" she concludes. Caught off guard, he forgets about libraries entirely for a moment and ❼ enters into a lively discussion of gem- and birthstones. She points out a mounted set of specimens she has treasured since her college days, and they enjoy a few moments of ❽ talk that only gem collectors could possibly appreciate. It sets the stage for what is ❾ otherwise a routine interview. But it establishes that his experience, training, and aspirations suit the position well.

Conclusion

Barry is fortunate enough to stumble on a common interest with his interviewer that serves as an ice breaker and basis for identifying with each other. ❿ Without it he and the otherwise dissimilar interviewer might have failed to connect in any meaningful way, and the job might have gone to someone else.

Case History 11—Analysis

SHOWING INTEREST IN YOUR INTERVIEWER

General Strategy

Barry realizes that his credentials for the job are adequate but not outstanding. He hopes to find some spark of common interest with his interviewer so he will stand out from other candidates. While he knows of no such link, when it is presented he seizes on the opportunity and shares her appreciation of a hobby.

Specific Points

1 First positions in particular are helped by common interests between interviewer and applicant because there is no great base of professional experience to share.

2 You are looking for some comfortable way to stand out in a field of similar candidates, any of whom could do the job.

3 Apprehension is normal in interviews, and you need to acknowledge it but be ready for positive developments.

4 Try to remove past impressions when you interview with a previous acquaintance. Be ready to see something new in the interviewer.

5 It would not have been Barry's place to shift to a nonprofessional topic even if he had noticed the collection of gemstones.

6 But when the interviewer gives an entrée, you are free to join the off-the-topic discussion and promote the mutual interest.

7 Since the opening was provided, it is perfectly appropriate to follow the line of discussion at the interviewer's invitation.

8 Shared language or specialized vocabulary is one of the quickest ways to establish commonality between yourself and an interviewer.

9 An interview that had little promise beyond ordinary fact verification has taken on shades that will make Barry memorable at decision time.

10 Unless revealed by your research, interests are usually spontaneous, and you just have to be ready to develop them as they appear.

LISTENING, UNDERSTANDING, AND CLARIFYING

You need to settle down and listen to what is going on around you during your interview. If you are too rehearsed, nervous, or insensitive to the signals being sent, you might miss important cues from your interviewer. Often the interviewer will signal the kind of response that is wanted—all you have to do is be alert enough to receive the message. If you find yourself receiving mixed or unclear signals, or just don't understand the question, ask for clarification. If you need time to compose your thoughts, ask the interviewer to clarify his or her question.

TAKING TIME TO THINK

You don't have to give an instant response. It is expected that you might need to pause for a moment to think about what is being asked. You can actually create a negative impression by immediately shooting back an answer every time, suggesting that you are so heavily rehearsed as to leave no room for an original thought, or that you don't think the question is worthy of serious thought. In either case you stand a chance of impressing your interviewer negatively. Even if you are ready with an immediate comeback, show respect for the question, give it a pensive moment, then answer. The interviewer wants to think that she or he has caused you to think and has elicited the best you have to give, not an immediate reaction. Judgment is always necessary, and you have to vary your pattern to keep things interesting.

DELIBERATELY DIFFICULT QUESTIONS

Some interviewers deliberately put you on the spot with questions like:

- "We all have things we'd rather not have known about us. What is there in your background that you'd rather tell us about now than have it discovered later?"
- "Tell me what kinds of things you and your last boss used to fight about."
- "What do you consider to be your greatest weakness professionally?"

Be ready for the surprise question. (See Chapter 10 for further advice.) It doesn't always come, but when it does, your best weapon against it is sidestepping the expected shock; don't fall into the trap of an embarrassed confession that is neither necessary nor expected. Be composed, think for a moment, and respond in some inoffensively circumspect way that deals with the question safely and demonstrates your ability to cope with surprise. Case History 12 illustrates how to deal with difficult questions.

STANDING YOUR GROUND

It isn't necessary for you to be a doormat during your interview. If the interviewer is aggressive in his or her questioning, field the questions as objectively and unemotionally as you can. If something is offensive or wrong, defend your position as graciously as you can, then ask what the question is intended to reveal. Is there some suspected problem that you might better discuss more directly? Express your willingness—your preference—to do so in a forthright manner instead of risking misunderstandings by innuendo. Don't go looking for a fight, but if the interview is clearly in jeopardy, you have little to lose by challenging the line of questioning and then offering your full cooperation if there is a problem that needs to be addressed. Case History 13 shows you how this can be done.

MOTIVES FOR QUESTIONS

Your reaction to a question often depends on why you think it is being asked. A seemingly hostile question can be taken in stride if you understand the interviewer's motivation. Put yourself in the interviewer's position and imagine why she or he might take a certain tack in the questioning. Usually you will be able to see the reason and lend your cooperation without emotion or offense. Sometimes the interviewer will actually end a line of required difficult questions with the disclaimer "You know those are things we have to ask." Generally speaking, you are better advised to tolerate the questioning and realize that it is just part of the process of testing you for the position. Assume the question is relevant to the job and do your best to answer unless the question is clearly improper or damaging.

AVOIDING NEGATIVE COMMENTS ABOUT OTHERS

The fastest way to turn a former nemesis into an object of sympathy is to malign the person, making him or her the reason for your failure in a former position. Be objective and positive about the people with whom you have shared your career. It goes without saying that you've had your differences with people. Your interview for a new position is no time to stress this. If there was ever a time to look for the silver lining, be charitable, magnanimous, and forgiving of human frailties, this is it.

Future employers want to hire team players. People who can get along with others are in demand; those who can't, aren't. You should emphasize two characteristics for the new employer:

- your ability to learn from your mistakes
- your ability to put unpleasant things behind you

Case History 12—Situation

DEALING WITH DIFFICULT QUESTIONS

Background

Susan O'Hare is a pharmacist who is looking for a position with a supermarket chain after being fired from her last position ❶ after only a few months on the job. She is well qualified and has an excellent record as a retail pharmacist prior to ❷ the unfortunate incident that ended her last employment. Difficult questions are expected as she interviews for a position she hopes will put the whole thing behind her.

Situation

Susan enters the office confidently and takes her place across the desk from the woman who will question her. She makes easy conversation as the interview begins in earnest. Everything is relaxed until she is asked the question ❸ she was beginning to think would never come. "You were let go from your last position, Ms. O'Hare. ❹ Tell me about it," her interviewer inquires. "I was fired after a personal misunderstanding with the manager of the store where I worked," she explains, ❺ hoping it will end there. "What kind of 'personal misunderstanding' would be serious enough to cost you your job?" the interviewer asks, pressing the point. ❻ "I was being sexually harassed," she replies without elaborating. "And you got fired?" the interviewer asks, implying that it should have been the other way around. ❼ "I couldn't prove it—it was his word against mine. When I became an embarrassment, he made my working situation difficult and terminated me without cause as my probation period was about to end," she explains. ❽ The incident was one that didn't lend itself to a fully objective resolution, so Susan only reluctantly elaborated when asked specific questions about it and ❾ turned the conversation toward the contributions she hoped to make to this organization if given the opportunity.

Conclusion

Susan is in the difficult position of not wanting to dwell on a negative incident or speak ill of a past employer. But ❿ she has to explain something that mars her record and damages her employability. The best approach is to tell the truth and show her intention to put the problem behind her.

Case History 12—Analysis

DEALING WITH DIFFICULT QUESTIONS

General Strategy

Susan knows that her last period of employment is too brief to be explained in any positive way. She decides to let the interviewer ask for an explanation and to provide the details in as limited and unemotional terms as she can. Her plan is to confront the incident directly without more elaboration than necessary. She will honestly tell her side of the story and place the focus on the future, not the past.

Specific Points

❶ Brief tenure in a position can be expected to bring on tough questions if there is no accompanying explanation.

❷ Incidents such as unsubstantiated sexual harassment are difficult to express routinely in a resume or cover letter, so they are left for the interview.

❸ Interviewers often hold back the hard questions to see if they are made unnecessary by other developments in the course of the interview.

❹ This is the kind of open-ended question that puts you in a position to give the incident the tone you feel it deserves.

❺ It is worth trying a generic explanation if you would prefer not to delve into an unpleasant situation, but be prepared for more pressing questions.

❻ A direct and simple statement of the problem is better than an emotional diatribe, if you can honestly be that objective.

❼ Honesty and realism are your best defenses in fielding difficult questions.

❽ Understand that unprovable conflicts are best handled by as much calm distancing as you can muster—you can never prove the case, so just tell it your way and rise above the clouded issues.

❾ As you explain the negative past, try to project a positive future.

❿ Make your case without letting the incident brand you as a wrongfully terminated but troubled worker who is risky to hire.

Case History 13—Situation

STANDING YOUR GROUND WHEN YOU HAVE TO

Background

Sam Boyd is the resident manager of a condominium complex and a candidate for a prestigious new project in another part of the country. ❶ He expects tough questioning on his role in converting the last property from a rental into a condominium property. It is the kind of questioning he has faced before, and while his answers are ready, so is his ❷ willingness to defend his position.

Situation

Sam is met by the marketing vice president. She tells him that he is to meet with her and several other senior managers. They arrive at the sales office, ❸ he takes the tour, and the interview begins. They ❹ begin to probe the sensitive area of handling conversions—the slow real estate market is ❺ forcing them to rent many of the units initially and convert them to condos later. "Sam, we know you've been through the conversion wars—❻ you and K-Group got a lot of bad press. Would you do the same thing to us?" one of them asks. ❼ "No one plans to get 'bad press' and, no, I wouldn't want to repeat the experience," Sam responds. ❽ "But that's how you got the job done there, isn't it?" the marketing VP asks. "If you are saying that we won by fighting the battle against rent control, yes," he answers. "No, I read it as more than that—you headed a group that busted the tenant organization at any price in spite of the image loss!" she continues. ❾ "It sounds like you have something more direct to say to me—please just say it and let me respond. I have a well-documented record through a difficult period that I'll be happy to explain and let you verify with third parties," Sam urges, positioning himself to respond objectively and not get into an argument about appearances.

Conclusion

Sam could ❿ continue responding to individual barbs about his controversial role in the conversion project; instead he confronts the veiled hostility and pleads for an objective evaluation of the public record.

Case History 13—Analysis

STANDING YOUR GROUND WHEN YOU HAVE TO

General Strategy

Sam knows innuendo will be part of his interview—the press paints him as a ruthless tenant property manager. He wants to retain the reputation of an effective businessman capable of dealing with tenant/landlord issues but be seen fairly, not as someone who will trash the company's reputation while accomplishing its objectives. He is willing to confront the issue if necessary.

Specific Points

❶ In this case, Sam knows that he is in for tough questioning.

❷ If the questioning gets out of line, Sam plans to control the issue by bringing it into open discussion.

❸ Often the ride in from the airport or the preliminary tour provides clues as to the tone of the interview.

❹ A pet issue will surface that is both of vital interest and troubling to the interviewers.

❺ Economic conditions are forcing this group to consider tactics they had hoped to avoid, and Sam is taking the brunt of their discomfort.

❻ The interview drifts away from the problem and focuses on an incident in Sam's past.

❼ Sam acknowledges the difficulty and tries to let the issue rest.

❽ The interview gets accusatory, and they trade increasingly different perspectives on the issue.

❾ Sam seizes the opportunity to end the drift toward an argumentative interview and gives it a positive spin by suggesting third-party verifications.

❿ An entire interview can be spent dancing around hidden agenda items that should be confronted. The candidate sometimes has more to gain by forcing the issue.

Satisfy the curiosity of your interviewer with as much objective detail as necessary, and then set your focus on the future. If you possibly can, formally make peace with the person who was the problem in your former position and offer him or her as a willing "negative reference"—someone who will say you had your differences but were essentially a competent worker. The best ending for a bad incident in your career is healing the wound and letting the past sleep. Case History 14 illustrates how you might do this.

INTERVIEW PSYCHOLOGY

Psychology is the science of explaining human behavior. Interviewing for a job is an exercise in using your knowledge of human behavior to influence an employer's opinion of you favorably. The employer does the same to sell you on his or her company. Plus the interviewer assesses how you will probably react to various questions and situations to judge what kind of person you are. Your job interview is a two-sided experience in applied psychology. Here are some of the fundamental things you should keep in mind as you become a player in this exchange and measurement of behavior known as the employment interview.

TECHNIQUES USED BY INTERVIEWERS

The kinds of interviews identified in Chapter 10 are showcases for the interviewers' psychological techniques. Most interviews are of the unstructured, informal variety where neither side invokes much in the way of identifiable psychological manipulation. A few techniques, such as the stress interview, are deliberately designed psychological tests of how you behave when forced into certain situations. Most interviewing psychology is less deliberate, and two people test one another for compatibility and likability—shared values that will allow them to work harmoniously together.

You might encounter more formal applications of psychology in the hiring cycle and find the results introduced into the interview. For example, you may have been asked to take a formal test that measures your personality, honesty, or some other attribute relevant to your employment. In some instances, prospective employees are interviewed by a professional psychologist. Chapter 14 discusses the technology used in interviewing and includes a look at psychological testing.

PERSONALITY AND THE JOB INTERVIEW

Since your interview is with another human being, the chances are good that it will be with a personality different from your own. That matters for two reasons:

- You will be interacting with someone who places importance on things differently from how you might.

- Your personality will be, at least informally, typed as suitable or unsuitable for the job offered.

While the literature of popular psychology is filled with schemes for attaching catchy names to the differences in people's personalities, Dr. John Holland of Johns Hopkins University made a science of relating personality types to careers. Here are six personality types, abstracted by the author, which Dr. Holland has observed:

1. *Realistic*—unsociable, emotionally stable, materialistic, genuine, concrete, and oriented to the present.

2. *Intellectual*—analytical, rational, independent, radical, abstract, introverted, cognitive, critical, curious, and perceptive.

3. *Social*—sociable, nurturing, dominant, and psychologically oriented.

4. *Conventional*—well-controlled, neat, sociable, inflexible, conservative, persevering, stereotyped, practical, correct, lacking spontaneity and originality.

5. *Enterprising*—adventurous, dominant, enthusiastic, energetic, impulsive, persuasive, verbal, extroverted, self-accepting, self-confident, orally aggressive, exhibitionist.

6. *Artistic*—complex outlook, independent judgment, introverted, original, subjective, imaginative, expressive, interpretive, fantasy-oriented.

The main relevance of this model to job interviewing is in showing you how very different people are. You can benefit by entering your interview with an appreciation of the breadth of possible values you might encounter. It can help you account for people's motivation. You need to appreciate that we are each a blend of the personality types that Dr. Holland factored into six separate entities for the purpose of studying them. In reality, you are expected to be more than a single type—and those with whom you must deal in the interview (and later the workplace) will be equally complex human beings. All of that is to say, have an appreciation for personality differences but don't allow yourself to be short-circuited for a position that seems right or wrong for you because of a superficial appearance of incompatible personalities. The science is imprecise, and you should view personality as only one more indicator in making your vocational choice.

Case History 14—Situation

DEALING WITH PAST NEGATIVE EXPERIENCES

Background

Connie Williams is an assistant manager in an upscale suburban shopping mall boutique. She is a ❶ candidate for manager at a similar concession in the anchor department store in the same complex. Her interview may reveal that she had a ❷ minor criminal conviction some years ago for being in the wrong place at the wrong time. She plans to explain if asked, but not volunteer the information.

Situation

Connie is met by Ted Jensen, who invites her to be seated for their interview. ❸ The usual questions are asked and everything goes well. She is asked if there are any questions she would like to ask of him and takes the occasion to clarify a few things. ❹ As the interview nears its conclusion, Mr. Jensen asks, ❺ "Connie, is there anything you would like to tell me about yourself that we haven't discussed? Something you'd rather mention now rather than have it come to light at a later time?" Instead of baring her soul, ❻ Connie looks at him and asks if there is something he has in mind. His response is, ❼ "Yes, there is. We do routine background checks on our candidates, and yours showed a conviction." ❽ "Let me tell you about that," she continues. "More than ten years ago I was dating a guy who meant more to me than he should have. I went places with him that I shouldn't have. One night he got arrested for drug possession and I couldn't clear my name—my attorney recommended accepting the misdemeanor and putting it behind me. My life before and after is clear of any wrongdoing." "Why didn't you mention it?" he inquires. ❾ "Because it is a small incident from a long time ago. I was hoping it had passed," she answers.

Conclusion

Connie tries to have her interview on the merits of her present life ❿ but runs into an incident from the past. When confronted she gives a reasonable explanation but feels no obligation to damage her image forever by citing a small negative that has little relevance to what she is today and what she wants to become.

Case History 14—Analysis

DEALING WITH PAST NEGATIVE EXPERIENCES

General Strategy

Connie knows there is a possibility that an employer check will reveal a minor criminal conviction from her past. She decides that there is more to be gained by distancing herself from the incident than by volunteering the information. If confronted, she will give a completely truthful explanation and express the understandable desire to let it fade.

Specific Points

❶ Managing a retail store is the kind of job that logically could produce a criminal-record check.

❷ Since the charge did not involve mishandling money or anything directly relevant to retail management, she decides not to volunteer the information.

❸ A minor conviction like Connie's might be used to eliminate an otherwise undesirable candidate, but her overall record was good.

❹ The timing of such an inquiry could be different, but coming at the end of the interview is common.

❺ "Is there anything you'd like to tell me . . ." can be phrased many ways, but it is an open invitation to tell all that you feel is relevant.

❻ An acceptable and still limited response is to ask the interviewer if there is something he has in mind.

❼ The worst case is that he does have something that you might not have mentioned.

❽ And when that is the case, you are not startled by it but prepared to tell your story.

❾ If pressed, you explain that mentioning the incident is something you just don't do— and surely they can understand why.

❿ Put the entire incident in the context of a total life that is otherwise positive.

HIDDEN AGENDAS

Psychological awareness can help you understand another fundamental of human behavior that will likely be operating during your job interview. People and their questions are not always what they seem to be. Each of us can selectively misrepresent our true intentions to accomplish something else. In job interviewing, the hiring official's hidden agenda while interviewing you might be to find flaws that justify hiring a friend instead. Her or his outward agenda is the objective evaluation of your qualities relative to the position.

All hidden agenda actions are not so sinister. The practice can take the form of seemingly off-the-subject questions that actually form a legitimate evaluation for an important job success criterion. Your task is to recognize what is going on and still make your case as you respond. If you are unaware of the hidden agenda phenomenon, you can be lulled into thinking that your interviewer is wandering off the point when he or she is actually zeroing in quite deliberately on your suitability for the job.

DEALING WITH STRESS

Putting you under deliberate stress has already been mentioned as a specific interview technique. You are more apt to encounter it as a less deliberate adjunct to the interviewing process. Stage performers have long credited nervous anticipation with ultimately energizing their performances. Their secret is in harnessing the energy—acknowledging that it exists and deliberately channeling it toward a useful end. You can do the same thing at your job interview. No one is going to tell you that stressful feelings can be eliminated, but they can be controlled and directed toward supporting your effort instead of detracting from it.

The first thing you can do to reduce the stress of your job interview is to prepare thoroughly. But don't overdo it. Perfection is not your goal, and trying to reach it can be stress-producing in itself. Follow the guidance of Chapters 9, 10, and 11 of this book and you will have anticipated 90 percent of your interview's potential surprises. With those removed, let the remaining 10 percent add spontaneity to your interview. Go in well prepared and be realistic about the fact that there will still be challenges that you will have to respond to on the spot. Not to have such residual unknowns would deny you the opportunity to show off your ability to think on your feet. Welcome the opportunity rather than dread it.

The other things you can do to reduce stress include getting rest, having a positive, realistic attitude about the whole interviewing process, and coming to the session feeling good about your physical condition and appearance. There are both physical and mental exercises that some people find helpful when facing stressful situations. Most of them boil down to giving you an alternative point of concentration—you occupy your mind with calm thoughts of something other than the interview. Some people use their religious faith in this regard. For the more secular there are books and tapes on the subject of managing stressful feelings. If stress is an unusually threatening problem for you, investigate the popular literature at your library or bookstore, or enter the keywords "stress management" in your Internet search engine and examine the options.

BODY LANGUAGE

While you sometimes find more prominence given to the phenomenon of body language than it deserves, there is something to it. The way a person physically postures probably does communicate something that has an impact on others. If you are aware of the potential for sending the right or the wrong message, you can discipline yourself to communicate only the one you intend.

Translating and Controlling Body Language

- Follow your host's lead as you go through the ritual of meeting—accept his or her handshake firmly, but only when offered, or you risk coming across as too aggressive and dominant. Mirror the interviewer's greeting expressions, such as the traditional smile and uplifting of the eyebrows—naturally, of course, not affected.

- Respect personal space—arm's length is comfortable for most people. Crowding your host is uncomfortable and signals an intrusive personality that can be awkward or difficult to deal with on the job. A forward-leaning gesture is positive; a forward move into the personal space is not.

- Being attentive and interested is largely shown with the eyes—"natural" is the key word. Avoid extremes of looking away, staring, blinking or not blinking, or closing your eyes—anything other than what you would do in regular social or business discourse. It shows insecurity and an inability to handle this special situation. The same is true of facial muscle tension as manifested in eyebrow positioning, smiles, tight lip line, etc. Breathe deeply a few times, relax, and be natural. Tell yourself that the interviewer likes you, and picture him or her as a friend—but not an overly familiar one! Be careful how you fix your gaze if the interviewer is an attractive member of the opposite sex—there are all kinds of possibilities for inappropriate communication there.

- Nervous bobbing of the head indicates impatience to get on to the next topic. Slow the same gesture down a bit and you show agreement and interest.

- Gestures should be open and uplifting, whether it is your arms, posture, smile, or other facial feature—up is usually associated with positive and winning, down with defeat and negative things. Crossed or folded arms is a closed gesture and is viewed as protective instead of welcoming. Even crossed legs and ankles are said to connote stubbornness. Showing your palms on occasion as you gesture is a sign of openness, nothing to hide.

- A naturally invoked and periodically used gesture is better than a constant one—a fixed smile appears artificial; a spontaneous one, genuine.

- Nervousness and discomfort show on your face in how you position your mouth, touching it frequently or clearing your throat too often or on cue when you are put on the spot—all come across as insincere and unnatural, the opposite of what the interviewer wants to see.

- Avoid doing nervous things such as tugging at your clothing (tie, collar, etc.) or distracting ones such as fidgeting, tapping your foot, or anything else that breaks the desired image of control and poise you want to convey.

- Smugness is to be avoided, too—overly familiar or relaxed gestures such as crossed hands behind the head, the "wrong" kind of smile, an all-knowing look and demeanor maintained throughout your interview, extended legs crossed at the ankles, and hands on hips and thumbs in belt are all potentially read as inappropriate dominance.

- Slow is better; when in doubt, take your time in deliberately executing any gesture—again, not artificially so, but don't rush and convey nervousness or anxiety.

- Finally, don't become paranoid about the magic of body language. While these points are worth considering, forget about molding them into some contrived pattern of presenting yourself—your own natural state will come across better than stilted conformity to "rules" you read in some book. If you can incorporate them into your routine, do it. If you have to fight to achieve the image you want, forget it and be yourself.

POSITIVE EXPECTATIONS

As you go into your interview, try to keep the whole thing in perspective. It is important, but it is not a life-and-death situation for you. At the very least, this interview will be a learning experience that will put you on a firmer footing for the next one.

You should take a positive view of the situation and expect the best. Your interviewer has a job to do and so do you. She or he has the task of selecting the best-qualified person for the job, and you have an obligation to do your best to meet her or his needs. There are no miracles in job interviewing. You and the competition are what you are—nothing more, nothing less. What you could do to prepare yourself for the opportunity has been done, and now it is time to relax and be a confident participant in the contest.

The chances are minuscule that anything devious is on the interviewer's mind. You are best advised to assume that you are entering a level playing field in which the interviewer honestly wants to see what you have to offer. You should assume that you will be interviewed in good faith, measured fairly, and ultimately judged on the merits.

Let your confidence in the fairness of the process and in your own outstanding qualifications show in your positive expectations as you participate in the interview. End the session thinking the best of everyone involved and mentally getting ready to move on to the next phase—accepting their offer of employment.

SUMMARY CHECKLIST: DURING THE INTERVIEW

- This is the time to impress your interviewer with honesty, job knowledge, a pleasing personality, and a believable, consistent pattern of interviewing behavior.

- Be a tactful but strong advocate of your own qualifications for the job.

- Expect to influence the interview's direction with the way you answer and ask questions.

- Transform yourself from an ink-and-paper resume image into a flesh-and-blood person.

- Understand that background checks are necessary because a significant number of resume claims are exaggerated or untrue.

- Be enthusiastic about the interview and the opportunity.

- Recognize that you can affect your mental attitude, and use that knowledge to maintain a positive view of the interviewing situation.

- Make an effort to like and be liked in the interview process.

- Being courteous throughout the interview process can make you an attractive candidate.

- Expect to adapt to your interviewer's style and energy level.

- Minimize drinking and totally avoid smoking unless it is very clearly shown to be an acceptable practice where you are interviewing.

- Be prepared to accept different kinds of personalities at your interview.

- Use your knowledge of the company sensibly to sell yourself at the interview.

- Make learning more about the job an early priority in your interview so you can focus your presentation correctly.

- Communicate your awareness of workplace technology.

- Identify the decision maker and direct your attention to satisfying his or her priorities.

- Hold discussion of your salary concerns until later, when a strong interest has developed in hiring you.

- Show interest in your interviewer.

- Learn the rules for dealing with interviewer questions, including reading the interview situation as it unfolds rather than concentrating blindly on your own performance.

- Be prepared for "behavioral interviewing," where you are asked to be more expansive in answering questions about your performance.

- Take time to think before you respond.

- Expect the difficult question and be ready for it.

- Recognize the motives behind the questions.

- Avoid negative comments about former employers and colleagues.

- Understand the applied psychology of job interviewing.

- Be alert to the messages sent by body language.

- Have positive expectations about your success during the interview.

Internet Tip

If you want to try a "virtual interview" on the Internet, visit http://interview.monster.com. You can opt for various kinds of employers and explore a wide range of interviewing advice.

13

AFTER THE INTERVIEW

Your interview is just one more step along the way to getting hired—there is more to come. This chapter prepares you for what comes next—skillfully "closing the sale" after you have presented "the product." It covers four phases in the interview cycle: (1) leaving the interview, (2) evaluating the interview, (3) interview follow-up, and (4) concluding the interview process.

Leaving the Interview

You have a right to relax as you leave the interview, but not to stop thinking about or working on getting the job. There are important things still to be accomplished— mistakes to correct, favorable impressions to leave. Look at Figure 5 and orient yourself in the job interview cycle. Review the thumbnail sketch of what you are about to examine in detail and remind yourself of its importance in your goal of getting hired.

LET IT END

Your interview is a two-way street right up to the end. Both you and the interviewer begin to signal when it is time to quit. Sometimes the end is dictated by the clock running out—another appointment is waiting, for example. More often, the two of you have said what there is to say—she or he has asked the questions, you have made your points, and the interview is complete.

GETTING THE INTERVIEW
- Finding a job
- Applying
- Networking
- Getting invited

PREPARING FOR THE INTERVIEW
- Researching the company
- Preparing personally
- Anticipating questions

APPEARING FOR THE INTERVIEW
- Reconnaissance
- Personal readiness
- Timing

DURING THE INTERVIEW
- Names and personalities
- Style and substance
- Satisfying agendas

LEAVING THE INTERVIEW
- Reading your audience
- Positive expectations
- Last impression

EVALUATING YOUR INTERVIEW
- Substantive match
- Personal chemistry
- Judging your chances

FOLLOWING UP AFTER YOUR INTERVIEW
- Thank-yous
- Additional information
- More networking

CONCLUDING THE INTERVIEW PROCESS
- The offer
- Negotiating
- Accepting

You are still being evaluated and making judgments of your own as you leave the interview. As you rise, shake hands, thank your interviewer, and make your way out past the receptionist, subtle judgments continue to be made that could weigh heavily at decision time. This is when you express continuing interest. Leave with the last image being an upbeat, expectant, can-do person—and a firm handshake. Look for the best in your interviewer, but be alert to any signs of wrong or incomplete impressions that a follow-up might correct. Don't overstay your welcome, read the body language, and help your interviewer conclude the session gracefully.

Figure 5. Leaving the Interview.

One way to sour an otherwise good interview is by not knowing when to leave. The body language and verbal cues should signal that—looking at his or her watch, rearranging and closing your file, sitting back from his or her desk, making closing remarks. This is not the time to open new lines of inquiry or offer elaborate clarifications on points already made. Neither should you push for a decision that is not to be made at that point. You need to be ready to accept a gracious "Thanks for stopping by, I'll be getting back to you . . ." if that is how the session ends. All the better if your interviewer is clamoring to schedule you tomorrow with the big boss before someone else can steal you away, but don't rely on such a dramatic outcome. Express your appreciation, offer to cooperate in future efforts to clarify your qualifications, say that your interest in the job continues (if that is the case), and say good-bye.

FINAL BUSINESS

It is perfectly correct to ask what comes next or when a decision might be expected, if that information has not been volunteered. You have probably already been given instructions on reimbursement for your interviewing expenses. If not, take that up with personnel or your clerical point of contact the next day, not with the interviewer as you leave the session. Let the parting be professional.

CHANGE OF HEART

If you learn in the course of the interview that the position is not what you had in mind, you have an obligation to say so graciously as the interview ends. Sometimes the chemistry is wrong or the duties and level of responsibility are not up to your expectations. When that is the case, express your appreciation for the interview and then take yourself and the interviewer off the hook by withdrawing your name from further consideration. You can give it a positive twist by mentioning that you were impressed by the company and its people but that the particular position doesn't sound right for you at this time; if something comes up that the interviewer would consider more appropriate, you would welcome the opportunity to discuss it. That kind of ending leaves everyone feeling satisfied and ready to do business without unnecessary tension should future circumstances call for it.

THE EVALUATION GOES ON

The two-way process of evaluation is anything but over after the final handshake. Everyone involved continues in the evaluation process on some subtle level. The opinion of your interviewer is the most important, but everyone involved matters. When decision time comes, the hiring official looks for consensus. Everyone from his or her number two person to the receptionist will have some degree of influence. Remember that as you make your exit. Polite good-byes, thank-yous, and gently applied personal charm are in your interest as you leave.

The way to handle exit comments and actions varies with individual people. You express your continuing interest and appreciation for professional courtesies to your peers and seniors. Support staff get a heartfelt kind word for their help in making your travel arrangements, taking care of telephone messages, or whatever they did to make your visit a pleasant one. Everyone gets a polite, interested smile and "Thanks. I'll look forward to seeing you again." No one is left with any negative impression—"Where's my cab? I asked you to have one waiting when I came out of there!" You can't afford to have even the lowest-level eyes roll when your name gets mentioned during the decision-making phase.

Remember to say your good-byes in a style that is natural for you. This is no time to come on as a backslapper if you are a reserved type—just let the real you say, "Thanks. You made a difference in my interview day. I appreciate that and look forward to seeing you again." Such thoughtful small extensions of courtesy cost you nothing and can make a difference in the ultimate outcome of your interview.

KEEPING YOUR STORY STRAIGHT

If you are in the midst of a comprehensive job search, you are probably juggling more than one interview and need to keep track of the facts and a multiple cast of characters. Few things are more damaging to your prospects of getting hired than a follow-up call or a thank-you note that confuses the facts. Either one of them betrays what no employer wants to hear—not only did she or he fail to leave an indelible impression on you, you are also talking with a rival firm. It is unforgivable for you to confuse someone with a competitor.

As soon as you clear the interview area—when you get to your car or settle into a cab—make a brief summary of names and events that will jog your memory in the future as the facts begin to fade. While it is possible to take notes during the interview, that can be awkward and distract you when you should be fully alert to what is going on. Save it for when you leave, but don't ignore the task after the high motivation that accompanies the interview session passes. You will need the particulars to impress your interviewers with thorough and accurate recall in your follow-up calls and correspondence.

Leaving Summary

- Avoid the temptation to ask how you did.

- Don't raise questions about salary or benefits.

- Ask what's next in the hiring cycle, suggest scheduling your next interview before leaving, but don't push for a hiring decision.

- Summarize the key requirements and link your attributes to them.

- Get the answers to any remaining questions you might have—briefly.

- Be prepared to accept an offer—contingent on terms to be negotiated later.

- Know who your interviewers were and their correct titles.

- Think and act positively, even if there were rough spots.

- Leave as you entered, with a confident handshake, a smile, and pleasantly enthusiastic about what is to come.

Evaluating Your Interview

You have survived the interview, made your way out of the building, and taken the requisite notes for future reference. Now it is time to evaluate how you did. As you settle into the drive home or get ready for a drink and two bags of airline peanuts, reflect on how it went. Be honest with yourself on these dimensions of your job interview:

- How did you do on the objective matters?
  - ✓ Did you measure up to their expectations?
  - ✓ Did they measure up to your expectations?
- What about subjective details?
  - ✓ Did your personalities mesh well?
  - ✓ Was the corporate culture to your liking?
- What is your gut feeling regarding your prospects?
  - ✓ Did you get the job?
  - ✓ Do you still want the job?

Figure 6 highlights the evaluation stage of job interviewing. Examine it as you prepare to learn more about this crucial step that brings you almost to the decision point in the hiring cycle.

GETTING THE INTERVIEW
- Finding a job
- Applying
- Networking
- Getting invited

PREPARING FOR THE INTERVIEW
- Researching the company
- Preparing personally
- Anticipating questions

APPEARING FOR THE INTERVIEW
- Reconnaissance
- Personal readiness
- Timing

DURING THE INTERVIEW
- Names and personalities
- Style and substance
- Satisfying agendas

LEAVING THE INTERVIEW
- Reading your audience
- Positive expectations
- Last impression

EVALUATING YOUR INTERVIEW
- Substantive match
- Personal chemistry
- Judging your chances

FOLLOWING UP AFTER
YOUR INTERVIEW
- Thank-yous
- Additional information
- More networking

CONCLUDING THE
INTERVIEW PROCESS
- The offer
- Negotiating
- Accepting

You are out of the interview and on your way home. It is time for an honest look at how you did—and what you now think of the opportunity you are seeking. First you examine the substantive things and determine whether you fill the bill and vice versa. Next you make judgments of whether you clicked with the personalities involved, how well the corporate culture seemed to fit your style and values. Being both positive and candid with yourself, assess your chances of getting the job—and whether you still want it.

226

Figure 6. Evaluating Your Interview.

LOOKING AT THE OPPORTUNITY OBJECTIVELY

Now that you have had your interview and discussed what the job consists of with the principals, you are in a better position to judge your fit for it. Look at it carefully from the following two perspectives.

DID YOU MEASURE UP TO THEIR EXPECTATIONS?

Put yourself in the place of the people who interviewed you. The interview has brought you closer to knowing what they really want. What do you think? Would you hire yourself if you were in the interviewers' position? You don't know exactly what they're thinking, but put yourself in their shoes and answer these questions:

- Did you have the qualifications, or was there something seriously missing from your training and experience?

- How was your fit on the seniority dimension? Were you right for this particular job, or would you be coming in either too "light" or too "heavy" to function well in it?

Work with these points as you recall specific questions and comments at the interview. Make a tentative judgment on whether you came out a winner from the employer's point of view. You don't have to force a definitive answer, but sometimes you find yourself clearly positioned at one or the other end of the continuum—a sure winner or a likely loser. Chances are you will rate yourself in the ambiguous middle that says you are still in the running and will just have to wait for the official decision.

DID THEY MEASURE UP TO YOUR EXPECTATIONS?

You have taken the trouble to apply, prepare, and interview. Momentum alone is pushing you to take a favorable view of the opportunity by this point in the hiring cycle. But is it really warranted? How do you feel about the job now? Before you rush headlong into a questionable move, objectively think through these points:

- Will this job challenge your abilities and ambition, or is it more of what you already have? Less than what you want?

- What does it do for your career? Is this position going to place you on the bottom rung of an opportunity ladder with a fast track to the top, or is it just an insignificant step up with nowhere in particular to go next?

You need candid answers to these questions, and you are the only person to provide them. This is no time to become negative about the opportunity, but respect your gut feelings if the job doesn't feel right in the reality of your evaluation.

LOOKING AT THE OPPORTUNITY SUBJECTIVELY

You have now met some of the people you will be working with, and you are in a better position to judge the chemistry. How do you feel about your potential colleagues and working relationships?

WERE THE PERSONALITIES COMPATIBLE?

This is the time for you to be totally honest with yourself. If you were a fish out of water during the interview and plant tour, now is the time to acknowledge it—not six months after taking the job when you find yourself isolated, unhappy, and in the midst of people whose values and work style you do not share. Think about it in the context of these questions:

- How was the chemistry and the comfort level?
- Were you at ease with your interviewers, or were you psychologically out of step all day?
- Was the humor your kind of humor, or was it nonexistent?
- Did they seem like bright, motivated people?
- Did you find a worthy mental sparring partner for the future?
- Were these people interesting?
- Were the energy levels within range of your own?
- Any troubling signs on the basic values? Honesty? Social consciousness? Environmental awareness? Fiscal responsibility? Basic morality?

WHAT ABOUT THE CORPORATE CULTURE?

It matters how you feel about the people you will be working with, but it is also important that you are comfortable with the feel and the style of the organization you are joining. Here are a few things to consider:

- Is this a fitness-oriented group that is not to your taste?
- Is it a highly social group after hours that doesn't suit you?

- Is it a smoking environment?

- Is the form of address too casual between every layer of the organization?

- Is the energy level of the office too frantic for you?

- Do you share the organization's social and ethical values?

- Are you comfortable with the dress code?

- Are you comfortable with formal business hours and time accounting procedures?

- Is the business travel policy something with which you can live?

These are the kinds of corporate culture considerations that you should evaluate as you decide how to proceed. The job can be quite attractive but the atmosphere in which you have to function the opposite. Mismatches of personal and corporate style can affect your happiness and future success in an organization. Without overemphasizing peripheral considerations, don't disregard their importance as you evaluate your prospects and how you will respond when the job offer comes.

You have to use discretion in gathering this kind of information. Do it informally in your research and with the help of people in your network. You don't want to leave a negative impression by asking some of these things directly. Instead, you should look for opportunities to observe and seek subtle clarifications as you deal with the more routine questions of your interview.

FEELINGS ABOUT YOUR PROSPECTS

As you put your objective and subjective impressions about the interview together, you form an impression of what your chances are of getting the job. You can be wrong, but it usually is not hard to separate the two extremes—you ran especially strong, or weak. If your performance is in the middle range, it is difficult to judge. You can explore your prospects on the important dimensions that follow.

Did You Get the Job?

There are times when you leave the interview with the distinct impression that it's all over—something didn't ring true, and you have been given the polite boot out the door, never to return. The opposite outcome is easier to judge and a far more comfortable feeling. Like the insider encouraged with winks and nods, the successful interviewee receives signals—often unmistakable.

Reading the Signs of How Well You Did

- What was the tone as you left the interview—formal and distant? Or relaxed and "familial"?

- Were there anxious questions about your availability? Or best wishes for success in your job search?

- Was it, "I want you to call me tomorrow afternoon about a few things we need to work out" or, "I'll be in touch in a few weeks after the interviews are complete"?

- Were you advised in confidence, "We have a few more people we have to see, but frankly, I'd like you to start tomorrow; call me before you accept anything else" or, "You are one of seven candidates we are considering for the position; the selection committee will advise you of your status in two weeks"?

Many times the cues are less obvious, but they can all tell you a lot that the interviewer would never formally reveal. Listen for indicators as you leave the interview and in the calls and letters that follow. You should not get terribly discouraged if the winks and nods are not thrown your way—many hirings are simply done by the book, with no relief from the "by the numbers" ritual. You can come out of the most uncomfortable interview a winner.

DO YOU STILL WANT THE JOB?

Momentum can be dangerous. It can lead you into a career move you would never make if you considered it calmly. The evaluation stage of the interview cycle is where you owe yourself some honest answers, even if they are disrupting. It is your career, and you are the person who has to function in the job every day. It is time for you to take a mental cold shower and candidly answer some questions.

Is This the Job You Really Want?

- Is it the opportunity you pictured?

- Are they the kind of colleagues you'll thrive working with?

- Is the corporate culture one in which you'll be comfortable?

- Do you still feel confident that you have what it takes to do the job and meet the company's expectations?

- Are things that bad where you are now?

You need to accomplish this personal evaluation of your job interview before you implement the next step: follow-up. After the evaluation phase, you are ready to focus on an effective follow-up that reinforces the interview and sets the stage for hiring. Clear away your doubts and reaffirm your motivation to get the job before you go further; commitment or the lack of it shows, and it can play a significant role in your final rating by those who will make the hiring decision.

Evaluation Summary

- Whom have I met? What do they do? What do I think of them?
- What have I learned about the job that I didn't know before?
- Where would I begin—first projects, principal challenges?
- Can I handle the job?
- Will the job challenge and reward me?
- What were my weak points in the interview? Can I overcome them?
- What can I expect next in the hiring cycle?
- How did interview really end? Positively? Brush-off?
- Do I really want this job?

Interview Follow-up

Now you must strengthen your case for turning the interview into a job offer. You want to say thanks and let the interviewer know that (1) you left the session feeling good about the job, and (2) you still have a strong interest in it. Here are the topics you want to consider in planning your follow-up:

- Reinforce the good impressions you made.
- Perform any necessary damage control.
- Provide additional information that would be helpful.
- Activate your network for both feedback and influence.
- Prepare for any subsequent interviews.

Before going on to the follow-up procedures, look at Figure 7 to get your bearings as you get ready to conclude the interviewing cycle successfully. Scan where you've been and where you still have to go to avoid getting bogged down in already

GETTING THE INTERVIEW
- Finding a job
- Applying
- Networking
- Getting invited

PREPARING FOR THE INTERVIEW
- Researching the company
- Preparing personally
- Anticipating questions

APPEARING FOR THE INTERVIEW
- Reconnaissance
- Personal readiness
- Timing

DURING THE INTERVIEW
- Names and personalities
- Style and substance
- Satisfying agendas

LEAVING THE INTERVIEW
- Reading your audience
- Positive expectations
- Last impression

EVALUATING YOUR INTERVIEW
- Substantive match
- Personal chemistry
- Judging your chances

FOLLOWING UP AFTER
YOUR INTERVIEW
- Thank-yous
- Additional information
- More networking

CONCLUDING THE
INTERVIEW PROCESS
- The offer
- Negotiating
- Accepting

Your interview is history, and you've made your initial judgment on how you did. Now it's time for reinforcing the good impressions you made, damage control (if there were rough spots), filling any information gaps that might make your case stronger, and bringing to bear any influence you might have within the organization. This is a delicate phase where you must avoid pushing too hard or letting the opportunity slip away by doing too little. Use your network to get objective impressions of where you stand and what the best approach would now be. Prepare for any follow-up interviews.

Figure 7. Following Up After Your Interview.

completed tasks or jumping too quickly into things such as salary negotiations that are best left for last. You've come a long way and need to comprehend the efforts that now have you poised on the brink of a successful job offer. Everything is coming together as planned. Finish the process now with an outstanding follow-up effort.

REINFORCING THE GOOD IMPRESSIONS

Let's assume you walked out of the interview a winner. Everyone liked you, and it showed. Just as important, you liked them—now let that show in a tasteful, professional way.

SAYING "THANK YOU"

You have one perfectly good excuse to reestablish contact after your job interview—to express your appreciation. No one can fault you for saying thanks in writing, and it is an opportunity to say much more. E-mail is an ideal medium for the post-interview note of thanks. It is at once appropriately prompt, informal, and businesslike. While you don't want to overdo a good thing, your letter of appreciation for the job interview can also be the occasion you need to make a few points.

Points to Make in Your Letter of Appreciation

- The job was even more exciting than you imagined it would be. Then mention a point or two to validate your statement and keep it from sounding like ingenuous post-interview fluff.

- You felt quite comfortable with the staff and were pleased to learn that you share common professional interests, backgrounds, and aspirations (be careful in spelling out other people's aspirations—you might get someone in trouble).

- You are available for subsequent interviews or inquiries should either become necessary.

- You want the job.

CALLING THE INTERVIEWER

Use your judgment to determine whether an e-mail or a letter of appreciation is sufficient or if a telephone call is also in order. It isn't good to appear overly anxious, and the letter is probably enough, unless you have an existing relationship with the interviewer that eases the way for a more personal expression of gratitude. Another approach is to let some time pass, make a brief call to say thanks, reaffirm interest, and check on the status of the hiring. If your call is not returned, don't push the issue. Understand that formal hiring procedures are being followed and you can expect notification when everyone receives it.

When you have to decide about another job offer, you have nothing to lose by calling, waiting a reasonable amount of time for it to be returned, then calling again, this time leaving the message that you need to know your status in order to make another employment decision. Chances are you will be told that no decision can be reached at that point, but it is worth inquiring just in case they are on the verge of an offer you can't refuse.

DAMAGE CONTROL

You sometimes need to undo a mistaken impression that could not be resolved to your satisfaction during the interview. A deliberately difficult question may have baited you into a response that you still don't feel right about. You have to decide whether it was intended to force the awkward moment you experienced, or something more. If it was the latter, you can't go wrong sending a brief, businesslike letter clarifying your position.

Remember that the "rules of damage control" include a healthy respect for letting sleeping dogs lie. You might be wise not to reopen an awkward moment or amplify genuine differences with the interviewer. Choose your instances for controlling damage carefully, and take initiatives only when you have clearly left behind a situation that can be improved by further attention. When in doubt, leave it alone.

Once you are convinced that the wrong message was conveyed and you have the ability to correct it, set the record straight. Properly done, damage control can turn an interview around for you by clarifying the matter and showing your skill in handling a sensitive situation. It can make you stand out favorably in the crowd and increase your odds of getting the job.

SENDING ADDITIONAL INFORMATION

Your interviewer sometimes reveals a strong interest or discloses a problem that he or she would dearly like to solve. If you have knowledge of the topic, go ahead and share it conversationally during the interview—but you can do more. Perhaps you have seen an article on the subject. When you get home, send a copy to the interviewer with a business card or a short "for your information" note attached. It is a thoughtful, understated way to show interest in a person who can help you. You position yourself as a colleague with this kind of exchange, and it can enhance your image and make you memorable at decision time. Other things being equal, such gestures can make a difference.

Such an approach gives you a chance to provide additional information in the form of straightforward data whose usefulness became apparent to you during the interview. Occasionally after you leave an interview you see something that makes just the point on which you and your interviewer so strongly agreed. Forward it with your card and a brief note resurrecting the moment, saying you enjoyed the exchange of views and wishing him or her success in hiring the right person. It can't hurt and might become the tie-breaking personal touch that gets you the job.

ACTIVATING YOUR NETWORK

After your interview, look for feedback from anyone you know who has an ear to the hiring environment. The more direct the source the better, but don't overlook anyone who can tell you what kind of impression you made. At this point, make the connections and let the information flow from wherever it might. Make the qualitative judgments later. Get as many views from independent sources as you can.

Consistency is one way to confirm the accuracy of what you are being told. Use the information as another source for judging where you stand and what you might do to improve your chances. The quality of this kind of feedback varies widely, so leave room for personal judgment before taking it too seriously. Unless the source is someone you personally know and trust, sift the information carefully, and use it only in combination with other indicators that point to similar conclusions.

A second way for you to use your network following the interview is to bring third-party influence to bear. You have to do this sparingly and with considerable care, but it can be a useful technique. If you know people who are respected by the hiring organization, this is the time for them to check discreetly on your status. Since it is obvious that they want to see you hired, finesse is needed. A skillful politician can give your prospects new life with the right touch; a clumsy one can hurt you. You are the person best able to judge the potential for help or harm—be cautious, but don't hesitate to use networking for influence as well as information when warranted. Here is a final summary of things you want to accomplish in your follow-up phase:

Interview Follow-up Summary

- Show your enthusiasm for the job.
- Demonstrate your understanding of the requirements.
- Summarize your competence for the job.
- Indicate that you want the job.
- Tell how you can contribute—be specific to the first project, if possible.

- Show that you listened by recapping a point the interviewer made (attribute it to him or her—"You suggested that . . . and I believe . . .").

- Be impressed with what you saw and whom you met—mention names.

- Say you're looking forward to whatever comes next—more interviews, an offer.

- Say thanks for the courtesies extended.

- Touch all bases—a letter to the most important managerial interviewer, copies to others with personal notes attached.

- One page is all it should take—be brief.

- Act now—go home and get your letter in the mail in time to affect the hiring process and revive your favorable image as decisions are being made.

- Unless you've been asked to call, wait a week before deciding that a telephone follow-up is necessary.

- Be prepared to exploit any turndown into more job leads.

GETTING READY FOR ANOTHER INTERVIEW

You may have a single interview or a series of them. If the one you just completed is the first of several, you need to go back to the earlier chapters on preparing for, appearing at, and performing during your interview. This is especially true if your subsequent interviews are to be of a different kind. For example, you may have passed an initial screening interview with the human resources officer coordinating the hiring and are about to face a selection interview with the department head who will hire you. You might also be facing a group interview where your ability to function with others is to be tested, or a panel interview in which you will be formally interviewed by several people. Do what you can to determine the nature of your next interview and use the preceding chapters and the information gained in the interview just ended to prepare for the next one.

Concluding the Interview Process

Everything you have done so far was to achieve one thing: an offer of employment. You found the job, applied for it successfully, prepared for the interviews, and passed them with flying colors. Now it is time to wrap it all up with the kind of terms that satisfy both you and your new employer. Here are the final steps in your job search cycle:

- receiving the offer of employment

- deciding whether to pursue the offer

- negotiating salary and terms of employment

- getting the offer in writing

- formally accepting the position

- notifying your present employer

For the last time, see where you stand on the hiring continuum by looking at Figure 8. It shows you ready to conclude the job search in a way that leaves nothing in doubt. Too often in the euphoria of the offer, you let your disciplined approach lapse and settle for exactly what is offered. Sometimes you have no choice if it is a take-it-or-leave-it proposition. Some companies fill standard positions and offer uniform benefits with no room for negotiation, but usually there is something negotiable. While you certainly don't want to torpedo the deal by becoming unreasonable at this late hour in the hiring, there is nothing wrong with pausing to clarify the terms. In the process you can be sure of what you are getting and often improve some aspect of the offer.

THE OFFER OF EMPLOYMENT

Generally you will receive a congratulatory telephone call that constitutes an offer of employment and carries with it a presumption of on-the-spot acceptance. If the offer is to your liking, then by all means accept. You are the person in the best position to judge whether you have any leverage at this point. For example, your network may have informed you that it was a close decision with you getting the nod, but if you hesitate, the number two is a perfectly satisfactory choice. If that is the case, you are in no position to delay—take the job if you want it. On the other hand, your sources may have revealed that you were the only acceptable candidate or the strong first choice. In that situation you can probably accept conditionally using wording like this: "Thank you for the offer, Mr. Jones, everything sounds about right to me. Let's consider it a deal contingent on formally spelling out the fine points. When could we go over the remaining details?" Unless the offer is really out of line or you have totally lost interest in the position, it is worth seeing what can be worked out.

GETTING THE INTERVIEW
- Finding a job
- Applying
- Networking
- Getting invited

PREPARING FOR THE INTERVIEW
- Researching the company
- Preparing personally
- Anticipating questions

APPEARING FOR THE INTERVIEW
- Reconnaissance
- Personal readiness
- Timing

DURING THE INTERVIEW
- Names and personalities
- Style and substance
- Satisfying agendas

LEAVING THE INTERVIEW
- Reading your audience
- Positive expectations
- Last impression

EVALUATING YOUR INTERVIEW
- Substantive match
- Personal chemistry
- Judging your chances

FOLLOWING UP AFTER YOUR INTERVIEW
- Thank-yous
- Additional information
- More networking

CONCLUDING THE INTERVIEW PROCESS
- The offer
- Negotiating
- Accepting

Your follow-up is complete. Everyone with influence in your network has spoken on your behalf and given you his or her impression of where you stand. You've answered all the questions, and an offer has been made. Now is the time to examine the compensation and benefits package in detail and see if it can be improved upon. This is also when your duties, authority, and place in the organization are defined. At this stage you are someone the employer wants and will try to accommodate.

Figure 8. Concluding the Interview Process.

DECIDING ON WHETHER TO PURSUE THE OFFER

You have bought time with your contingency acceptance. Now you have to examine the offer calmly and decide whether it is attractive enough to pursue. The choice before you should not be a surprise, and the main points of comparison among the position offered, your present job, and other realistic opportunities call for little more than an informal review in your own mind. With that concluded, it is time to get on with the negotiations.

NEGOTIATING SALARY AND TERMS OF EMPLOYMENT

Whether you are dealing face-to-face, over the telephone, or through the good offices of a third party such as an executive recruiter, the next phase requires realism and sensitivity. For most people who change jobs, the expected salary increase is 10 to 15 percent. If you are really in demand or grossly underpaid at present, it might be possible to make that 20 to 25 percent. Expect the employer to start with the lower figure. Know your market value and degree of attractiveness to other employers before coming back with your expectations. If you are working with a recruiter, he or she should be able to advise you on the realities of your situation and what the company will probably do. Make your expectations known in a professional way, have some rational basis for them (such as a reasonable increase over current salary plus next expected raise in your present position), and see what happens. You are putting the offer at risk in any negotiating situation. The employer can always take offense and withdraw the offer, but you can usually have a reasonable discussion that leaves room for compromise. Sometimes nonsalary items can sweeten the deal—more paid leave, time off for consulting, a stock option or a company car, a club membership. The possibilities are endless, and the trick to getting what you can is asking and making a plausible case for both the increased value you are placing on yourself and your worth to the company. You have to keep the two in balance to be successful in your negotiations. Here is how you want to go about conducting the negotiations.

Guidelines for Negotiating

- Figure out what you are worth in the marketplace by checking others in similar positions, those above and below you, government statistics, professional publications containing salary surveys, executive recruiters, and the want ads (especially the national ones).

> **Internet Tip**
>
> Salaries can be checked on the Internet. Try sites like http://www.careerjournal.com or enter the keywords "salary information" in a search engine and explore the results for relevance to your situation. You can also review professional association and publication Web pages in your specialty by entering their names in search engines.

- Determine whether you have room to negotiate by finding out (if you can) how badly the company wants you and how many others are waiting to accept if you prove difficult. If you are ever in a position to affect your future earnings, this is it. Find out, and act accordingly.

- Avoid settling for a percentage kicker to your present salary by taking the attitude that your present compensation should not be the sole basis for determining your future salary, be as evasive as you can about disclosing current earnings (make them ask twice, give a range, include the value of your perks and benefits, and say that your salary has increased every year), try to steer the negotiations to what similar positions pay at the new company, but never refuse outright to give a truthful figure if pressed (it can always be verified, and you want to be able to defend your answer).

- Test your expectations by mentioning your desire to work for a company that will pay you what you are worth and not just place you on a salary schedule. Ask if they are in a position to do that, and if they are, suggest that they begin now by establishing your starting salary based on your real value to them, not on your past earnings or some arbitrary scale and step.

- Avoid the "name a figure" trap by recapping the responsibilities you see yourself having in a flattering way, then turn the question back by asking: "What did you expect to pay for someone who could handle all of that as well as I will be able to?" "What range did you have in mind?" "I've assumed from the beginning that you'd make me a fair offer—what do you have in mind?" Keep the focus on the responsibilities and remind them of their conclusion that you have what it takes to meet them.

- Work the "ranges" by defining a new one that is anchored in what they name but exceeds the limit. If they say $62,500 to $67,500, come back with the positive statement that you are both in the same ballpark and express the hope that they have some flexibility on the up side—what you had in mind was a $65,000 to $70,000 range, with a midpoint starting salary. That would put you at the top of the scale they offered and give you growing room.

- Don't bring on a "sorry, but we can't afford you" response by staying away from absolutes. You can always talk in ranges that don't exceed theirs; you can always negotiate down.

- Know what you are going to be worth in the future by being aware of the compensation of people in the next few ranges. It will put you in a good position to respond intelligently to future expectation questions. Show that you are being realistic today, but know the progression expected for successful people in your industry.

- Make one last try by being very professional and businesslike but countering their offer with something like: "We are so close to agreement already, my career plans have projected just a little bit more at this stage—surely we have room for some final adjustments here?" Back off if they effectively say take it or leave it, but it is worth a polite final push.

- If the offer really is too low, stay positive by saying how complimented you are by their interest in you, how impressed you are by the situation and challenges outlined, how confident you are of succeeding and making a contribution—if only their initial offer could be improved. See if that brings a renewed effort to find a solution or a take-it-or-leave-it response.

- Offer some alternatives by suggesting that if you are exceeding the range, perhaps the position could be reclassified and you might be started near the bottom of the next range. Suggest starting where they must classify you, but with a hiring bonus and insured promotion at the end of a given time period if your work is satisfactory. While entry ranges are often sacred, bonus and promotion flexibility can sometimes compensate.

- Price the perks by seeing what might be made available to you in noncash compensation—paid memberships, medical and life insurance, automobile-related expenses, investment options, etc. Salary is not the only way to get paid, and every useful thing that can be provided directly is a dollar of direct compensation not spent. Dental, vision, and legal insurance are add-ons you might consider valuable, as are child care allowances, profit sharing, paid days off for consulting, financial and tax planning assistance, and termination pay.

A WRITTEN OFFER OF EMPLOYMENT

Your next step is another contingency. Shake hands. Do whatever good-faith things are necessary to clinch the deal, and orally summarize your understanding of the terms but ask that they be put in writing before you resign your present position or they announce your acquisition. Just as good fences make good neighbors, so letters of understanding, if not formal employment contracts, make for good workplace relationships. Ask for the terms to be summarized in a letter signed by someone in authority, secure any clarifications and corrections that are necessary, then accept the terms with a letter of your own.

NOTIFYING YOUR PRESENT EMPLOYER

Only after you have a written offer of employment that is satisfactory to you should you prepare your letter of resignation and present it to your current employer. There are many instances where your departure is no surprise and your efforts to grow professionally have been fully and openly supported; that makes it easy. Other situations are less comfortable, and your resignation will be an awkward moment. Decide two things before making your move:

- Your decision is irrevocable—nothing the employer says is going to change your mind.

- You will not be drawn into any rancor or bad feelings—you will leave with positive feelings regardless of the possibility of a negative reaction when you resign.

There were valid career reasons for considering a change when you decided to seek another position, and they are equally true the day you resign. Faced with a valuable person's resignation, some employers will make what is known in recruiting circles as a "counteroffer/buyback." That is, they will offer you a raise that is good enough to keep you from leaving. Don't take it. Research shows that most people who do are not around for the long term. You have compromised your security by threatening to leave once, and they expect you to do it again. The usual objective of the counteroffer is to buy them time to replace you. Every such offer may not be so sinister, but the general truth of the matter is that once you have decided to move on, do it and don't look back.

You do owe your employer reasonable notice and an offer to cooperate in training your replacement, whenever he or she comes on board. It is in everyone's best interest to make your parting a positive experience. Express your gratitude for the opportunities you have enjoyed. Offer to be of any assistance you can be in the transition. Speak well of the company in the future. As you learned earlier in the hiring cycle, there is no room in the employment marketplace for bashing your previous employer.

SUMMARY CHECKLIST: AFTER THE INTERVIEW

- When you leave the interview, take notes and keep track of the facts and personalities involved.

- Realize that your evaluation continues as you leave the interview; continue to leave favorable impressions on your way out.

- Be sensitive to when the interviewer wants to conclude the session, and help him or her reach a gracious ending point.

- Limit your parting questions to a brief expression of continuing interest in what comes next; take care of housekeeping tasks such as travel reimbursements later.

- Bow out graciously and positively if you determine that the position is not for you.

- Be positive but objective in assessing how you did.

- Be candid with yourself about how much you want the job now that you know more about it.

- Realistically try to rate your chances of receiving an offer.

- Be ready to deal with an offer.

- Realize that your compensation package is worth negotiating, and know how to handle the process without turning the employer off.

- Always get the offer in writing before resigning from your present job; accept orally contingent on a written offer.

- Resign with dignity—express your appreciation for the opportunity just passed, give adequate notice, and offer to cooperate in the transition.

PART IV

MORE TIPS AND STRATEGIES

This section consists of a series of brief chapters highlighting things you should know about:

- Technology and the Job Search
- Using the Internet
- Working and the Law
- Sex and the Interview
- Special Situations
- Accommodating Forced Career Changes
- Protecting Your Employee Benefits When You Change Jobs

For each topic you are given an overview of factors that might influence your job search. Where relevant, Internet references are provided for readers wanting additional detail.

14 TECHNOLOGY AND THE JOB SEARCH

You will almost certainly confront technology in the course of your job search. Some of it will be straightforward attempts to make communication with you easier—videoconference interviewing, computers, e-mail, and fax. In another dimension, computers linked to various databases, increasingly via the Internet, may verify the correctness of claims you made on your resume and application. Less likely, but possible, other devices and materials may try to measure everything from how honest you are to how well you might perform certain tasks or get along with people. As debates continue in professional and regulatory circles about the accuracy and fairness of some of these measures, you need to be aware of them and how your hiring might be affected.

Tips for Technology and the Job Search

In addition to the extensive range of technological contributions to the job search process mentioned already, science applies in other areas too:

- Videoconference interviewing is being used by more employers since it is no longer limited to large companies able to afford elaborate equipment. For example, you may be asked to go to a nearby business services retailer's videoconferencing suite for your next out-of-the-region interview. If you are, you will want to become familiar with the setup, which includes such things as voice-activated cameras that follow the action and a special camera for your charts and graphs.

> **Internet Tip**
>
> Visit http://www.kinkos.com and examine the company's videoconferencing services.

- Lie detector testing has been outlawed for applicants for most kinds of jobs.

> **Internet Tip**
>
> The American Polygraph Association provides information on lie dectector testing practices, limitations, and issues at http://www.polygraph.org/, and the Department of Labor describes restrictions on its use at http://www.dol.gov/asp/programs/handbook/eppa.htm.

- Psychological and aptitude tests have many limitations, but you may have to take one, and you will do better by responding from a business rather than a personal behavior frame of reference.

> **Internet Tip**
>
> Visit http://www.computerpsychologist.com/ if you are interested in pursuing personal testing or want to see what services such firms provide employers.

- Physiological testing for drugs and AIDS/HIV is commonplace, and you have to take precautions to keep from having your character damaged by false positives. Here are some specific cautions for taking physiological tests: (1) Get whatever information the company provides on drugs and foodstuffs that might alter the test unfavorably; (2) Scrupulously list all substances that you have been taking that could affect the test; (3) See if you have the option of having the screening done at a private professional clinic or through your personal physician, where your privacy is assured; and (4) Take whatever precautions you can, such as flushing your system with lots of water; test late in the day to avoid an overly concentrated specimen; and nail down every assurance possible that you will be treated professionally should you test as false positive.

15

USING THE INTERNET

Looking for a job today without reasonable awareness of the Internet is like showing up for work not wearing a significant article of clothing. You simply aren't complete without it, and it could prove to be embarrassing.

That varies, of course, with the job you seek and the market in which you are competing. Provincial jobs and companies still exist, but they grow fewer by the day. Web commerce, information, and communications make the Internet relevant to almost everyone, everywhere.

If the Internet is relevant to companies who hire, it is relevant to the people who want to work for them. As a resume writer and job seeker, the Internet can help you:

- Stay current in your field
- Get career advice
- Research career opportunities, salaries, and working conditions
- Train for a new job or specialty
- Learn more about resume and letter writing
- Look up zip codes and telephone numbers
- Present your resume to the world (or selected parts of it) at little or no cost
- Communicate instantly by e-mail with employers and others who can help
- Find employers interested in hiring you
- Learn more about the company to which you are applying

- Examine the cost of living and view homes where you consider moving
- Map your way to an interview and make travel arrangements
- Have an initial interview

At the very least, even if you do not have access to the Internet personally, find an acquaintance who does or go to a library where it is available to familiarize yourself with it. In a short time you can remove the mystery that separates you from those who have experienced the Web.

Looking over someone's shoulder, you can take a tour that leaves you comfortably aware of what a "search engine" is and what it can do, and that is half the battle. Enter a few topics and appreciate the sheer volume of information presented. Click some hyperlinks and see how one thing leads to another on the Internet. Armed with that brief experience you become a different person, better prepared to take your place in the new world of high-tech job hunting and employment.

If the only use you make of even superficial Internet exposure is in an interview saying, yes, you know what it is, your time was well spent. But there is so much more you can do to facilitate your job search.

This chapter is filled with illustrations, but a word of caution before you begin. Internet references are perishable: Internet addresses (URLs or Universal Resource Locators) change. Like telephone numbers and address changes in the noncyber world, forwarding addresses (links, in the case of the Internet) are posted only for a limited time. However, when they expire, you can go to a search engine and enter keywords until you find the new address.

Illustrative Web Sites

What follows is a loose collection of useful information intended as starting points for what will quickly become your own original search. Any one of them will start you on a journey that can easily last for hours, criss-crossing and interlacing the topics listed and unearthing others that may be even more relevant to your particular needs and interests. Should you find a URL expired or need a different emphasis, go to a search engine and begin entering keywords: "maps," "real estate," "travel reservations," "white pages," "yellow pages," "zip codes," or whatever you need—it is probably there for the asking.

If your appetite for job search information is not satisfied by these links, try relevant keywords in search engines and you will find an unending supply of sources to examine.

USEFUL JOB SEARCH INTERNET SITES		
Topic Keywords	**URL**	**Comments**
area codes	http://decoder. americom.com/	Returning a call to an unfamiliar area code? Identify the city by entering the area code at this site.
business newspapers	http://www.bizjournals. com	Examine specialty business papers serving forty leading cities for general information and networking contacts.
career advice	http://www. jobhuntersbible.com/	*What Color Is Your Parachute?* author Richard Nelson Bolles's Web page is filled with recommended links.
	http://jobstar.org/	Resumes and more, including salary surveys.
	http://stats.bls.gov/ ocohome.htm	The Department of Labor's *Occupational Outlook Handbook* online describes nearly every job you can imagine and discusses pay, working conditions, the demand for workers, expected education, where to go for more information, etc.
	http://www. employmentguide.com	Job search, career-management advice, and more.
	http://www.dbm.com/	Click "Site Map" and go to articles and a great guide to Web job hunting.

(cont'd)

Topic Keywords	URL	Comments
careers	http://www.usnews.com/usnews/work/wohome/htm	*U.S. News & World Report's* excellent collection of career articles, advice, hot jobs, and salary information for entry-level candidates.
	http://careers.wsj.com/	Salaries, advice, articles, and more. Also features *Korn/Ferry Futurestep*, an appraisal of your market value by a preeminent search firm.
college job placement	http://www.jobtrak.com/	A site serving prospective college grads and alumni at more than 700 colleges. Professional advice.
company information	http://www.hoovers.com/	Research a company: Free capsule, financials, and news or you can enter the keyword "investing" in a search engine and find sites with links to other company research resources.
company search	http://pic2.infospace.com/_1_244791928_/_info.jbank/bizweb.htm	Find any company's Web page using this site.
dictionary and the-saurus	http://www.m-w.com/	Look it up in this giant online reference.

(cont'd)

Topic Keywords	URL	Comments
employment	http://www.nbew.com/	*National Business Employment Weekly's* Web page includes the expected job search features plus an index of Web job listings.
equal opportunity	http://www.eeoc.gov/	Everything you need to know about EEO rights.
foreign language translator	http://babelfish.altavista.com	Enter a phrase and get a translation.
health care info	http://www.dol.gov/dol/pwba/health.htm	Department of Labor's consumer information on health care rights.
interviewing	http://www.itworld.com/Career/1895/ITW0226essex	"CU-SeeMe" interviewing mainly for technology-related positions.
	www.job-interview.net	Advice on preparing for your interview.
IRS forms and instructions	http://www.irs.gov/	Download tax forms and instructions.

(cont'd)

Topic Keywords	URL	Comments
job listings	http://www.ajb.dni.us/	Department of Labor Public Employment Service job/resume posting site. National and regional job search capabilities—the Web's version of the local employment office.
	www.careerbuilder.com	An advertising-supported Web job and resume posting site.
	http://www.wm.edu/csrv/career/stualum/jregion.html	An example of an alumni-focused job-search site.
	http://www.washington post.com/jobs	An example of a big city newspaper listing with extensive job search resources of its own.
	http://www.jobbankusa.com/	Links to everywhere in the job search universe.
job market	http://stats.bls.gov/	The Bureau of Labor Statistics' latest numbers relating to status and trends in all sectors of the labor market.
	http://www.dol.gov/	Department of Labor laws, regulations, statistics, data, and news.

(cont'd)

Topic Keywords	URL	Comments
job search	http://www.jobweb.com	National Association of Colleges and Employers links to useful job information.
	http://www.career.vt.edu/	Virginia Tech's links to regions and occupational specialties. Other colleges have similar services—try your alma mater.
	http://www.job-hunt.org/	An extensive index of job search Web sites complete with evaluations of usefulness.
letters	http://www.careerlab.com/	General advice and over 200 model letters on nearly every topic.
maps	http://www.mapquest.com/	Maps and directions to your interview.
pension information	http://www.dol.gov/dol/topic/retirement/consumerinfpension.htm	Department of Labor's consumer information on pension rights.
pension guarantees	http://www.pbgc.gov/	Pension Benefit Guarantee Corporation information on pension rights.
polygraph	http://www.dol.gov/dol/asp/programs/handbook/eppa.htm	Employee Polygraph Protection Act—your related rights.

(cont'd)

Topic Keywords	URL	Comments
resume advice	http://provenresumes.com/	Tips for various kinds of resumes including types of occupations and electronic formats.
	http://www.eresumes.com/	Electronic resumes are this page's specialty.
retirement benefits	http://www.dol.gov/asp/programs/handbook/erisa.htm	ERISA and related laws to protect your pension.
salary information	http://www.dbm.com/jobguide/salary.html	Salary surveys, negotiation strategies, and more.
	http://jobstar.org/tools/salary/index.cfm/	Salary surveys by professional category.
search engines	http://www.metacrawler.com	Six search engines in one. Also try *Yahoo! HotBot, Infoseek, Excite, Lycos, Magellan,* etc., and examine their individual career sections that link you to many other sites.
time zones	http://www.timezoneconverter.com	Find the current time in a distant city before you call.
travel information	http://www.biztravel.com	Check flights, make reservations of all kinds, and optimize travel incentive programs.

Limitations

While the Internet is a wonderful source of career information, it has limitations. Use it with the same caution you would apply outside cyberspace:

- If confidentiality is important to you, investigate and understand the safeguards job posting services employ before giving them your resume.

- Be sensible in offering personal information on the Internet. Employment listings are generally legitimate, but be skeptical enough to protect your privacy and personal safety. Verify with whom you are dealing before providing personal information or meeting a stranger for an interview. Don't become paranoid, but use common sense.

- Expect to be spammed (receive unsolicited commercial e–mail) if your e–mail address appears on the Internet. It is, unfortunately, the price you pay for using the Web.

- Understand that Internet job searches work best for hard-to-find technical people. To judge how many responses your Internet resume is apt to attract, ask yourself how many calls you already receive from headhunters. Unless your telephone regularly rings and an executive recruiter is on the other end of the line, posting your credentials on the Internet may be disappointing. Employers seldom pay recruiters or search the Web for vacancies they can fill from traditional sources.

- Anyone can represent him or herself as a career expert on the Internet. Evaluate them as you would any other service before following advice that may lead you where you don't want to go or before buying ineffective goods and services.

With those few words of caution, by all means explore and make the most of the job search riches of the Internet. Remember, there is so much more than resume posting that might prove helpful in your job search.

16

WORKING AND THE LAW

You have rights in the job market, but exercising them can be a delicate proposition; good judgment is required. In this chapter you will learn about the broad legal and regulatory concepts that protect you from unreasonable discrimination and the loss of your employee benefits. You will see that there is legitimate concern behind many "improper" interviewing questions, and you should deal with them positively instead of announcing your right to sue. You will be better able to judge an interviewer's intentions and respond effectively without compromising either your rights or your chances of getting the job. And just in case you do encounter the real thing—blatant, damaging employee selection discrimination—you are told where to go for specific help in fighting back. And the same thing goes for your employee benefits.

While discrimination is the dominant issue, it is not the only area where legal matters can have an impact on your job interviewing and overall workplace success. Topics covered in this chapter include:

- equal employment opportunity
- credit checks
- privacy
- job references
- employee benefits

As you will see, these issues have a tendency to intermingle and overlap. You should be aware of what is right and what is wrong in the employment process, but view them in a practical job hunter's context—not an attorney's. Your objective throughout your search is to get the job you want. The law is there if you really need it, but most employers act in good faith. However, that does not mean you should endure sexual harassment or any other threatening behavior. When interviewing, try to be practical and go with the flow when the intent is not mean-spirited and you can help your cause with a more expansive answer than you might technically have to give.

Equal Employment Opportunity

Employers are not allowed to discriminate against you on the basis of race, color, sex, religion, national origin, or age. The federal agency that administers this policy is the Equal Employment Opportunity Commission (EEOC). It enforces:

- Title VII of the Civil Rights Act of 1964
- The Age Discrimination in Employment Act of 1967
- The Equal Pay Act of 1963
- Section 501 of the Rehabilitation Act of 1973

As the names imply, Title VII ensures your civil rights. The next prevents age discrimination (if you are over forty), the third outlaws unequal pay for men and women doing the same work, and Section 501 represents your interests if you are handicapped. You can obtain detailed information on any of these statutes by contacting your local EEOC agency, by dialing 1-800-USA-EEOC, or by visiting the EEOC on the Web at www.eeoc.gov.

SEXUAL HARASSMENT

You should be aware that it is illegal under federal laws administered by the EEOC to harass people sexually in the workplace. If your fundamental rights to seek employment are interfered with by sexual coercion, you may have the basis for a complaint.

The EEOC issued guidelines in 1980 that make sexual harassment in the workplace illegal. In 1986 the U.S. Supreme Court unanimously affirmed those rights and spelled out the two types of sexual harassment that can be the subject of legal redress:

- *Quid pro quo* is the most blatant form of "environmental" sexual abuse, and it can be verbal and not just physical in form. In this situation you are expected to trade sex for the privilege of obtaining, keeping, or getting promoted in your job.

- *Hostile working environment* is the other, more subjective half of the sexual harassment equation. Here you are placed in a work environment that makes it difficult to do your job. The actions of your coworkers create a hostile or offensive environment and, in effect, deny you the right to go about your business of doing a good job without undue emphasis on your sex.

The reality is that most problems with sexual harassment occur between a female subordinate and a male supervisor. You cannot be overly sensitive to the routine sparks that will always fly between the sexes. The Ninth U.S. Circuit Court in California ruled that judgment is required. Behavior subject to redress under the law would have to be that which would offend a "reasonable woman."

You are left with the day-to-day reality of sex in the workplace. Understanding one another takes effort, good communication, and optimism about the pleasures of working together once we find our way around the obvious obstacles.

Here are a few commonsense guidelines for a less litigious approach to the issue. Without compromising either your rights or your personal safety, you need to treat your interview as what it is: your opportunity to land a job.

Interview Sexuality and Common Sense

You really must have perspective if you are to deal effectively with sexual attraction in the workplace. All the laws and regulations in the world are not going to eliminate the inevitable chemistry between men and women—at work or anywhere else. You are left with the task of sorting it all out case by case.

- Is your interviewer being mean-spirited and planning to cause you continuing problems? Or is the person naïve and unaware of the impact he or she is having on you?

- Is the comment just a clumsy way to get at a valid business concern and, therefore, deserving of a creative answer that will get both of you off the hook? Or are you dealing with a sexist bigot?

- Do you have the gut feeling from the beginning that your professional talents will be dwarfed by the constant need to defend yourself against sexual innuendos and worse?

- Are you the one deliberately bringing the sexual emphasis to the interview, and have you exercised good judgment?

- All manifestations of sexual attraction between an interviewer and applicant don't have to be negative and destructive ones.

- You have a degree of choice as to what role your sexual attractiveness will play in your job interview.

- Perspective and common sense play major roles in judging the proper role of sexual attraction in your job interview.

- Seemingly improper questions can mask legitimate employer concerns, and you might voluntarily and selectively address them without yielding important rights.

DEALING WITH ILLEGAL INQUIRIES

You are only allowed to be asked information that is directly related to your ability to perform the job for which you are applying. Here are some things you probably should not be asked about:

- racial or ethnic background
- religious affiliation, church attended, religious holidays observed
- national origin, where parents, spouse, or relatives are from—native language
- marital status
- number of children

Employers may try to get at this information indirectly by asking about:

- a woman's maiden name
- place of birth
- social clubs
- hobbies
- person to notify in case of emergency
- photographs

Keep in mind that many states have their own lists of questions that can and cannot be asked in preemployment interviews. You should inquire locally if you have a concern about improper questioning in your jurisdiction. Following are guidelines for dealing with sensitive employer questions. The suggested answers show your willingness to address an employer's honest concerns but not to be discriminated against.

HEALTH

Instead of asking you what health-related problems you have, the interviewer can inquire whether you have any condition that would prevent you from doing the job. Rather than refusing to answer the question, your answer can be a straightforward assurance that you have no health conditions that would limit your ability to do the job, should that be the case.

CRIMINAL RECORD

In the case of criminal records, the employer can ask if you have any pending indictments, since that could be relevant to your availability for work. The nature of the crime might make a difference in determining your desirability for the position and is a legitimate question, too. In most states you can be asked if you have been convicted of a crime, but that alone cannot keep you from being hired. Your employer would have to consider the nature and seriousness of the crime and when the crime occurred, and show that it has relevance to the job.

RELIGION

Your interviewers' concern with religion could be a practical one. They want to know whether your faith would keep you from being available for work at important times. While they are prevented from asking about your religion, they are within their rights to inquire about your availability to work on certain days. You can help an interview if such a line of questioning drifts off the mark by responding that your beliefs are a very private matter for you, but you can assure them that they would not interfere with your work schedule or ability to perform your duties.

NATIONAL ORIGIN

You cannot be asked about your ancestry or the status of your family in the immigration and naturalization process, but it is proper to establish whether you are a citizen of the United States. Employers are required to do so. If a job requires knowledge of a foreign language, a direct inquiry about your language skills is proper. If language skill is not a requirement and the inquiry is used to uncover national origin, your interviewer has probably broken the law.

AGE

Your interviewer can establish that you are age eighteen or older, and that is about all. If you encounter the "How old are you?" question, answer it by making your age a strength—couch your response in terms of experience and ability to do the job better.

MARITAL AND FAMILY SITUATION

"Are you married?" and "Do you plan to have children?" questions are illegal, but they often show more ignorance of the law than bad faith. Try assuming that it shows an honest concern about your quitting soon to raise a family. Consider giving the response that the interviewer is looking for without feeling obligated to elaborate. Volunteer that you separate work and family obligations and see no problem meeting the expected work hours or travel obligations. In those rare instances where such a line of questioning persists, politely ask that relevancy be established if you are expected to provide details about your personal life. Only a naïve interviewer would push the issue further, and if you have been careful, no harm was done to your hiring prospects.

Tips for Answering Questions

Your best approach to fending off an improper question is the polite three-step procedure that:

- answers any question that won't do you harm
- makes an inoffensive aside that you had the impression such questions were illegal
- avoids threatening the interviewer or labeling yourself litigious

Correctly done, this procedure clears the air on potentially sensitive issues that could be damaging if left unanswered, lets it be known that you are aware of your rights (and discourages further improper questioning), and keeps the goodwill of your interviewers by giving them an easy way out of something that could have gotten them into trouble.

Credit Checks

The Fair Credit Reporting Act protects you from certain kinds of credit investigations that might be associated with your application for a job. In general, routine credit checks are acceptable, but "investigative consumer reports" that involve interviewing people who know you are not, unless you are notified. Laws vary by state, so check your local situation if you suspect discrimination. When you sign most job applications, you authorize a credit check. It will mention investigative consumer reports if the inquiry is to go beyond the routine report.

Privacy

Your rights to privacy are protected by the Fourth Amendment to the Constitution, and it is the basis for limiting unreasonable preemployment inquiries. A discussion of some of the key privacy issues as they relate to your situation as a job candidate follows. The objective is not to alarm you, but to prepare you for the possibility that you will be confronted with these procedures. For a broader discussion of privacy and psychology as they relate to the interview, refer to Chapter 12.

DRUG TESTING

Following abuse by employers, the courts and states are establishing limits that focus testing on certain professions where public safety is at risk and where there are grounds to suspect drug use. The EEOC does not have specific policies on drug testing, but it will investigate on a case-by-case basis charges alleging that testing procedures adversely and unjustly impact on the hiring of minorities or women.

AIDS/HIV

Job candidates with **AIDS/HIV** may have certain rights under laws that protect the handicapped, and you should check with the EEOC or private advocacy groups for details in this rapidly evolving field.

HONESTY TESTS

The Employee Polygraph Protection Act of 1988 ended routine use of the polygraph except in a limited number of occupations and where there is some basis for suspecting wrongdoing. "Voice stress analyzers" are included in the prohibitions of the polygraph act. Here are the highlights of what you should know about the Employee Polygraph Protection Act:

- It prohibits most private employers from using lie detector tests for pre-employment screening.

- While local laws and collective bargaining agreements can be more restrictive, federal law says that federal, state, and local governments are not affected by the law. It does not apply to tests given by the federal government to private individuals engaged in national security-related activities.

- Polygraph tests can be administered in the private sector to prospective employees of security service firms (armored car, alarm, and guard) and of pharmaceutical manufacturers, distributors, and dispensers.

- Polygraph testing is also allowed when there is reasonable suspicion of private workplace theft, embezzlement, etc.

- If you are examined, you have rights relating to the length of the test, written notice before testing, the right to refuse or discontinue a test, and the right not to have the results disclosed to unauthorized persons.

- For additional information or to file a complaint, look in your local telephone directory under U.S. Government, Department of Labor, Employment Standards Administration, Wage and Hour Division.

Pencil and paper tests are not prohibited, and that includes "graphology" or handwriting analysis. They are still legal, and the EEOC will entertain only case-by-case complaints on tests used in a discriminatory manner.

Internet Tip

The Internet source for polygraph rights information is:
http://www.dol.gov/dol/asp/programs/handbook/eppa.htm.

GENETIC SCREENING

While the practice is not widespread, you can add to your list of concerns the use of new tests to discriminate against job candidates whose genetic traits make them susceptible to certain diseases.

Job References

According to specialists in defending employers against defamation suits, your ex-employer can say anything about you if his facts and records back it up. Poor performance is a legitimate cause for dismissal, and information relating to you can be shared in an objective way. You are never well advised to go looking for unwarranted litigation. What you want to remember about job reference wrongdoing is that you have redress if you find yourself among the few whose careers are unfairly damaged by a malicious reference.

Protecting Your Employee Benefits When You Change Jobs

Unless you are applying for your first job, you are a "job changer" and have important personal interests to protect while finding another job. You need to be aware of your pension and medical coverage continuation rights as you move from one employer to the next. If you are leaving a position in a solvent, well-organized company, you should routinely receive statements describing your pension and medical coverage options. Employers are required by federal regulations to provide this information. But if you are involved in a takeover, merger, pension plan termination, or bankruptcy, or if your former employer fails to comply with the regulations, you need to know how to pursue your rights.

Your Pension Rights

If you work for a private company that "affects commerce"—which almost all of them do—and that company has a pension plan, it is protected by the Employee Retirement Income Security Act of 1974 (ERISA). So unless you work for the government or have an unusual employer like certain international or religious organizations, you are among the 54 million workers covered by ERISA.

WHAT ERISA ENSURES

- Age and service requirements for pension plan participation are reasonable.
- People who work for a specified minimum period under a plan will receive at least some pension at retirement.
- Money will be there to pay pension benefits when they are due.
- Plan funds are handled prudently.
- Employees and their beneficiaries are informed of their rights and entitlements.
- Spouses of pensioners are protected.
- The benefits of certain plans are protected in the event of a plan's termination.

- You can appeal if you are denied benefits.

- You will not be harassed or interfered with for exercising your pension rights.

- You can sue in federal court to recover your benefits.

> **Internet Tip**
>
> Visit http://www.dol.gov/pwba for the Department of Labor's consumer information on pension rights, and http://www.pbgc.gov/ for Pension Benefit Guarantee Corporation information.

Your Health Benefit Rights

In 1985, Congress passed the Consolidated Omnibus Budget Reconciliation Act, known as COBRA. It provides that terminated employees or those who lose group health coverage because of reduced work hours can buy group coverage for themselves and their families for limited periods of time.

WHAT YOU NEED TO KNOW ABOUT HEALTH BENEFIT RIGHTS

- COBRA covers group health plans of employers with twenty or more employees. It applies to plans in the private sector and to those sponsored by state and local governments.

- If you are entitled to COBRA benefits, your health plan has to notify you of your right to continue your benefits at your own expense. Plan administrators have fourteen days after receiving notice of a "qualifying event" to notify employees and family members of their election rights. You then have sixty days to accept the coverage or lose all right to benefits. If the employer paid part of the premium while you are employed, COBRA coverage will probably be more expensive.

- You have rights of appeal if your claim is denied. In most cases you submit your claim in writing to your employer or plan administrator. If it is denied, you have to be told why in writing within ninety days and can then appeal in writing within sixty days and receive a decision within sixty days.

- Private-sector employees can get additional information by writing to Division of Technical Assistance and Inquiries, Room N-5658, Pension and Welfare Benefits Administration, U.S. Department of Labor, 200 Constitution Avenue NW, Washington, DC 20210. State and local government employees write: Grants Policy Branch (COBRA), Room 17A-45, Office of the Assistant Secretary for Health, U.S. Public Health Service, 5600 Fishers Lane, Rockville, MD 20857. Federal employees should contact their agency personnel office.

- "Health Benefits Under the Consolidated Omnibus Budget Reconciliation Act (COBRA)" is an eighteen-page booklet available from the Pension and Welfare Benefits Administration, U.S. Department of Labor, 200 Constitution Avenue NW, Washington, DC 20210, or call 202-219-8776, or contact the Superintendent of Documents, U.S. Government Printing Office, Washington, DC 20402.

Internet Tip

For the latest consumer information on health plans visit http://www.dol.gov/dol/topic/health-plans/consumerinfhealth.htm. Should that URL expire, use your search engine and the keywords "Public Welfare and Benefits Administration."

You have powerful advocates who will try to determine the merits of your case, get the problem solved out of court if possible, and in some cases sue on your behalf if a simpler solution cannot be found. You keep the right to take action privately. For it all to work, you have to meet the deadlines set up in the various statutes. So if you have a serious complaint, establish contact early and determine precisely what you must do and when and act promptly.

Keep in mind that the laws relating to many of these issues are constantly evolving. For areas such as AIDS/HIV and drug testing, you are advised to check the information services of the national advocacy groups that monitor the situation for their constituents and can advise you of the most current conditions.

SUMMARY CHECKLIST: WORKING AND THE LAW

- You have to balance using your legal rights with your objective of getting the job.

- Employees are not allowed to discriminate against you on the basis of race, color, sex, religion, national origin, or age.

- Preemployment questioning risks being illegal unless it relates to your ability to do the job.

- As a practical matter, you should answer any reasonable question that won't harm your chances of being hired.

- Routine credit checks are generally permitted, while "investigative consumer reports" require your consent.

- Most preemployment testing is legal unless it can be shown to discriminate against protected classes such as minorities, women, the handicapped, or people over forty.

- Lie detectors are illegal except for limited special applications.

- Job reference givers can be liable for suits based on defamation and wrongful discharge or termination, but are free to be critical based on documented facts.

- Look for advice on the violation of your preemployment rights at your local equal employment agency, or call

  1-800-USA-EEOC or visit http://www.eeoc.gov/.

- AIDS/HIV, drug abuse testing, and other special-interest concerns are best addressed by national help lines operated for their constituents.

- ERISA exists to protect your pension rights and COBRA your health benefit rights; both are federal laws and the particulars regarding coverage and enforcement are found on their respective Web sites.

17

SPECIAL SITUATIONS

If you find yourself out of step with the traditional career ladder—not clearly pursuing the next logical position in your field—this chapter can help you have a successful job search. There are things you need to know about attitudes you might encounter and proven techniques to help you gain understanding and respect in your circumstances.

A special approach is needed for job seekers who enter the world of work from nontraditional situations. An employer advertising a vacancy usually expects to attract people who are working full time in a job closely aligned with the position being offered. For example, applicants for a senior management position are generally people already working as senior or middle managers in roughly the same kinds of settings as the job for which they are applying.

When you depart from the traditional career ladder, your approach to job hunting has to compensate for your differences from what the employer expects. You try to anticipate the negative things and neutralize them by accentuating your strengths and minimizing your weaknesses. Prepare to do that well, and the very experiences that led you off the yellow brick road can actually make you more attractive than candidates with routine careers.

Among those who will find this chapter particularly useful are people who are:

- returning to the workplace following an absence caused by family obligations, a small business venture, involuntary loss of employment, or full-time study

- applying for a less prestigious job than the one previously held due to organizational downsizing or a reduction in the workforce

- students preparing for a first professional position, including work-study arrangements, as a lead-in to a career position

- establishing a second career following early retirement

- looking for flexibility in hours or overall working arrangements

- coming from another culture and struggling to articulate the value of their work and training in alien settings

Returning to the Workplace

Stepping out of the traditional career path is increasingly common. A free society provides opportunities for uniquely personalized work lives, and many of us exercise those options. Another factor is that our rapidly evolving, competitive economy does not necessarily guarantee job continuity throughout our lifetime.

Here are some reasons why you might find yourself sitting in a job interview explaining why you are coming to the job market with a less than traditional work history:

- a period of unemployment, self-employment, or part-time employment to raise a family

- a small business or consulting venture of your own that is no longer as attractive as a traditional position

- a merger or reorganization that leaves you unemployed

- a period of full-time study that was necessary to change careers or achieve the level of employment you wanted

- ending a relationship in which you served as an executive partner (spouse of an executive) but not an employee

RECOMMENDED APPROACH

In each of these instances your approach to the hiring is one of being positive and objective. You do not attempt to hide your actual situation; neither do you apologize for it. Determine what your marketable strengths are and decide how to bring them to the attention of someone who can use them.

You are what you are—there is no need for, or anything to be gained by, posturing as something else. If you are a homemaker who worked only briefly as a management trainee before spending ten years outside the workplace, then you are an entry-level employee with some experience—plus a great deal of added maturity and motivation to bring to the next phase of your career.

There are ways for you to deal with the apparent negatives of your situation during a job interview. The following table lists a few of the things you might face (openly or beneath the surface) and how you can compensate.

CHALLENGES AND RESPONSES FOR RETURNING WORKERS	
Challenge	**Response**
Your experience is out-of-date.	I have remained active in the marketplace as a consumer of your services and can bring that valued perspective to the job.
You are too old for this level position.	Think, act, and look young—this is usually more a problem of perception than reality. Chronological age has little to do with working age in most contemporary, non-physically-demanding jobs.
Your education is dated.	Take a refresher course or seminar. It will not only bring you up to date on terminology, but you also stand a good chance of networking with people who can help you find employment.

RESUME AND JOB INTERVIEWING TIPS

Since you lack the perfect continuity that looks best in a Work History Resume, opt for the Competency Cluster or Focused Resume that places the emphasis on what you can do, rather than where and for how long you have done it. Market yourself very deliberately. Do your homework on the company and the job being offered. Put yourself in the hiring official's shoes and make a case for why you should be an attractive hire. You should be prepared to respond to the interviewer's questions and make points of your own during the interview that stress your competency and help to dismantle the myth of needing continuity through a series of lesser positions to do well in this one.

Couch your experience in terms and with examples that relate to the proposed work situation. If you are listing experience as a telephone volunteer for your alumni association fund drive or the local public television station, use terms such as "telemarketing"—translate your experience into the buzzwords of the business world so the interviewer doesn't have to. Use the "Overview" part of the resume to portray yourself as someone:

- aware of what the position entails
- qualified to perform the duties
- motivated to assume a realistic role in the company

Before the hiring official begins recounting your precise experience and training, you want to make the point that you know what he or she wants and can provide it.

You need to have a selection of "competency clusters" or qualifications and achievements in mind that substantiate your claim. This is where your homework pays off—by knowing what the job actually entails, you have the advantage of being able to translate your strengths into those valued by the employer. You can describe an experience in general terms or in job-specific terms; the latter focuses employer attention on exactly what you can do for him or her, rather than relying on him or her to reach the same conclusion the hard way—by puzzling over your uninterpreted activities. Make the logical connection that your experience supports the company's needs—in that way you put the burden on the interviewer to refute your claim.

If you are coming to the interview unemployed, from a recently closed consulting practice or small business, or any other circumstance that makes it look like you are off the road to career success, here are the kinds of interviewer questions you can expect to face—and the kinds of answers you should be prepared to give.

These kinds of reactions can build confidence in your interviewer—the stigma of failure is avoided. The employer wants to sense that you understand his or her needs, can meet them, and have the potential to fit in and grow. A traditional work history is not the only way for you to establish such a link with the employer—you might have to work harder at the logic of your presentation if you lack the step-by-step progression of readily understood and expected jobs, but it can be done. Comments can be used as a closing reaffirmation that you understand the realities of the employer's needs and can meet them. You can tersely answer the obvious questions that might be associated with your situation and put them to rest—at least until the interview. Brief comments can become subtle building blocks of confidence between you and the reader of your resume. Throw out as many little lifelines as you can that will give them honest cause to reel you in for a closer look. The employer wants to sense that you understand his needs, can meet them, and have the potential for fitting in and growing. A traditional work history is not the only way to go

QUESTIONS AND ANSWERS FOR THE UNEMPLOYED JOB SEEKER	
Question	**Answer**
Why did you leave your last job?	The company was recently bought by XYZ Corporation, and thirty accounting positions were consolidated into ten at their West Coast offices.
Why did you close your business or consulting practice?	After I spent years of successfully building my company, it was acquired by ABC Company. I am intrigued by the opportunity your vacancy represents.
Coming from your background, what appreciation could you possibly have for our career development expectations?	I am currently enrolled in the CFA study group and plan to take the Series I examination in June.

about establishing such a link between applicant and employer-you just might have to work a little harder at the logic of the presentation if you lack the step-by-step progression of readily understood and expected jobs.

Chapter 1 includes a resume prepared by an executive partner seeking reentry into the workplace after the relationship with her spouse ended. Refer again to the resume of Bernadette J. O'Conner and the point-by-point explanations of how her resume was strengthened by changing it.

Applying for a Less Prestigious Position

American business goes through periods in which management and technical worker ranks are being thinned. For years layoffs affected mainly production workers, and the managers and technical people were spared. That may not be the case now, and you could find yourself out of work with no comparable positions available in the job market. When it happens, you apply for what you can get—and face the added interviewing burden of explaining why you are taking an apparent step down the career ladder.

RECOMMENDED APPROACH

When you approach the job interview as an "overqualified" candidate, you have several obstacles to surmount:

- You don't fit the usual experience pattern.
- You may pose a threat to the people who are hiring you.
- Your salary has been too high.
- You are accustomed to having more responsibility.

Here are some suggestions for dealing with the inevitable questions, whether they are posed directly or are hidden-agenda items that can be just as threatening to your candidacy.

CHALLENGES AND RESPONSES FOR CANDIDATES STEPPING DOWN TO LESSER JOBS	
Challenge	**Response**
You are used to dealing with bigger issues than you'll be facing here and will leave as soon as something more challenging comes along.	This is a permanent career realignment. My professional peers are experiencing the same thing I am. I want an opportunity to take one step back with the prospect of taking many steps forward as I prove myself here.
You won't be earning what you did at XYZ Corporation, and you'll be working just as hard. Will that be a morale problem for you?	I'm sure you'll compensate me fairly, and that's all I can ask. If I'm given the opportunity to show what I can be worth to your organization, the problem will eventually take care of itself.
What do I tell my own people who will view you as a threat?	Tell them you are in business to succeed and that you are hiring the best person for the job. I'm sure I'll have to perform to earn my promotions, not rely on the fact that I've already been to the next plateau.

JOB INTERVIEWING TIPS

When you enter the interview, unless it is apparent that your previous status is not presenting a problem, take the initiative and speak to the obvious. Do it diplomatically—do not say "I know I probably pose a threat to you people, but . . ." Instead, gently, in the course of the interview, let it be known that you are aware of the possible sensitivities that naturally surround the selection of a person who is coming in from a more senior position. Choose your words and timing carefully, then make these points:

- You really do want the job in spite of the fact that it appears to be a step backward on your career ladder.

- You can live with a fair compensation package for the position being offered and recognize the potential differential with what you had been making.

- You expect to prove yourself just like everyone else, and you won't be coming in wearing vestiges of your former "rank" on your sleeve.

You need to portray yourself as a realistic candidate. While there is always the possibility that there is no sensitivity, and you certainly do not want to raise issues that

QUESTIONS AND ANSWERS FOR THE LESSER-POSITION CANDIDATE	
Question	**Answer**
Why would you want to come to work for us after working for the giant ABC Company?	Because there are things I do very well and I need a place in which to keep doing them. You are aware of the effect of mergers on people like us [talking with a peer]. Frankly, I need to get started again, and this looks like a good place to grow in a new career.
Do you realize we do our own correspondence here on personal computers?	No, but what do you think of that resume? I did it on my PC at home. I've always consulted on the side and love formatting my own reports.
How do you feel about reporting to a person who would have been a subordinate in your last position?	I am applying for *this* position and fully expect to fit into *this* organization. No problem.

are not troubling anyone, in most instances you would be safe to take a disarming approach to the situation and make the three points noted. It clears the air and, like affirmative action issues, ranks among the questions that interviewers are uncomfortable asking but may want to know. You can volunteer a well-thought-out story that puts you and your advanced status in both a positive and a nonthreatening light at the same time.

Student Work Experience

When you apply for your first professional position, you can help compensate for not having a working track record by making the most of your part-time experience. There is no better way to get the job you want after college than by having an established working relationship with the company as a highly regarded student-worker. Summer and part-time jobs lead to career positions for thousands of students every year. You can prepare for your interview in such a way as to take advantage of this kind of experience. Whether you are still a student accumulating your part-time experiences or a graduate seeking your first full-time job, the approach is much the same. This section distinguishes between the two and advises you on applying essentially the same logic to the two situations.

RECOMMENDED APPROACH

As a student interviewing for a part-time position with an organization, the best way to make yourself stand out is to show evidence of career thinking. You should be interested in the seasonal position for what it is, but aware of its implications for overall career development as well. If you are applying for your first full-time position, make the connection between your part-time experience and the job for which you are applying. You need to understand the linkage and communicate the value you place on the career-related part-time experience while interviewing in either situation.

This has to be done without overkill. You want to come across as someone aware of your present place in the order of things, but cognizant of its potential contribution to your career. You do that by expressing interest in both the position and the company—your awareness of what the firm does and its position in the marketplace, for example. Taking advantage of your research, you might mention a recent acquisition or new product as a way to show your awareness of the business world in general—and the interviewer's company in particular.

POINTS FOR STUDENTS AND RECENT GRADUATES TO MAKE	
Desired Message	**Method of Relating It***
Part-time: I want this seasonal job—it is important to me for several reasons. *Full-time:* I valued my seasonal jobs—they were important to me for several reasons.	I value the work ethic and financial responsibility—this job will help me gain valuable work experience and avoid building debt as a student.
Part-time: My education can contribute to doing this job well. *Full-time:* My education contributed a lot to doing my part-time jobs well, and you'll benefit as my employer from the experience I've already had in combining classroom and practical experience.	As a student of [engineering, marketing, or whatever], I have seen a lot of theory and case study examples of what you do at XYZ Corporation that would bring me to the job with a lot of orientation already in place, and anxious to apply it as a worker.
Part-time: I can see future possibilities with XYZ Corporation. *Full-time:* As a seasonal student worker I saw where my experience could make me a valuable full-time employee of XYZ Corporation.	I have a lot of respect for the market position of XYZ, have heard positive things about it as a place to build a career, and would welcome the opportunity for us to learn to know each other better in a worker-employer relationship.

*These are stated for the part-time applicant; rephrase them to show the value of *past* part-time experience to *future* full-time employment when interviewing for a career position.

JOB INTERVIEWING TIPS

As a student applying for a part-time position or a former student seeking a first career position, you do not have a track record of previous positions and responsibilities to explain to an interviewer. However, in either case you can use the interview to accomplish these objectives:

- Identify the part-time position you seek, and define the linkage with your studies and career aspirations—or make that connection retroactively if you are using the experience while interviewing for a career position.

- Qualify yourself for performing the required duties in either case—establish that you can do the job.

- Show career motivation as an applicant for part-time employment—or validate career interest as a prospective full-time employee by making the connection with past part-time positions.

Whether you are looking for seasonal or career employment, you need to show that you know what the job entails, can perform the necessary work, and that you see part-time employment, your studies, and your career as part of the same overall experience. This is what you want to communicate in the job interview:

"I am [or was, in the case of a full-time applicant] a third-year electrical engineering student applying for the summer position as Field Engineering Aide III. My studies and prior Army experience qualify me for working in your testing environment, and I consider the seasonal position an exploratory one linked to what I hope will be a long professional affiliation with XYZ Corporation."

Your session might end with the interviewer inviting you to make a concluding comment on your own behalf. This is not the place to restate what has already been

QUESTIONS AND ANSWERS FOR THE SEASONAL-JOB APPLICANT	
Question*	**Answer***
Why are you still a student at age twenty-eight?	Describe your military service as relevant to your career—possibly a year spent touring Europe after leaving the service and prior to returning to college.
Why would a person within a year of being a graduate engineer want a job like this?	Amplify your respect for learning the business from the inside out—this position could give you that perspective before crossing over to the professional level.
What kind of career expectations do you have?	If your awareness is sufficiently specific, briefly conclude with an expression of interest in exploring future employment with them in fiber optics transmission—or whatever.
*Each question and answer would be stated retrospectively in the case of a graduate making reference to past part-time experiences when interviewing for a full-time position.	

said, but it can be useful to focus on the objective and dispel any lingering problems. Here are examples of "problem" thinking that you may have sensed as your interview progressed—and appropriate points to offer in summary.

Establishing Second Careers

Government and industry offer early retirement to reduce their workforce in a nondestructive way. People leave completed careers still vigorous enough to want the continued ritual of the workplace—a reason for getting out of bed in the morning, socialization with coworkers, the satisfaction of accomplishing something, and—last, but not necessarily least—money. Whether you are a service member retired with a substantial pension in your forties, or an older clerical worker retired with a modest income by a large corporation, you could find yourself interviewing for a second career.

ATTITUDES FACED BY AND RESPONSES OF SECOND-CAREER SEEKERS	
Attitude	**Response**
You are "retired." Why would I want to hire you?	In the modern workplace, careers are sometimes incremental—"retirement" is often a misnomer for a person successfully transitioning to another career stage.
Your background is from another environment entirely. How will you adapt to our situation?	Work is far more appropriately categorized by task than by employer. I have successfully managed people and resources for the past [number of] years, and I can do it for you.
What if you are looking to retire on the job?—my job!	The work ethic is very much a habit. My motivation in applying for this position is to continue deriving the satisfaction of a job well done. My references will vouch for my level of energy and commitment.

RECOMMENDED APPROACH

With one career behind you, your objective is to look ahead to the next job as an opportunity to use your past experiences and discover some satisfying new challenges. You are in transition and trying to make the case that you have something to offer the new employer. Here are some of the attitudes you want to anticipate encountering during your interview—and effective rebuttals for each:

JOB INTERVIEWING TIPS

As a second-career person entering a job interview, you are interested in immediately establishing several basics:

- Identify the position or category of position you feel best qualified to handle as a second career.
- Establish your qualifications for the job.
- Express sincere motivation to pursue a second career and not leave your profession at your relatively young age.

QUESTIONS AND ANSWERS FOR SECOND-CAREER CANDIDATES	
Question	**Answer**
How do I as an employer in the X business compare the certification of a specialist who has spent an entire career working in Y?	Professional certification for paraprofessionals in military health care facilities is the same as for those in civilian hospitals.
How will a person accustomed to having military rank and authority function in the less structured civilian environment?	Express your authority and rank functionally with examples of responsibility—rather than power and rank—that will be more readily understood in the civilian sector.
You are in the service; how can I be assured you will be able to report for duty on the date you promise?	Mention that your retirement orders have been issued and that you will be separated from the service on a date comfortably in advance of your reporting date for the new position.

While the points made during your job interview will vary by job and background, here is an example of how you might begin:

> "I am a retired Navy senior enlisted woman with a successful paramedical career, and I'd like to become affiliated with a civilian health management organization. I'm a fully certified professional anxious to continue a rewarding health services career without interruption. I view my 'retirement' as the end of a job, not the end of a career."

When you are given the opportunity during your interview, offer answers to some of the employer's questions that might otherwise have remained unsaid. Take these hidden-agenda doubts on directly rather than risk being hurt by negative conclusions that can come by default. Here are several examples and responses that can be helpful.

Looking for Flexibility

You might find yourself wanting to be employed in the regular workforce, but with less than a full-time schedule and regular hours. You might be surprised to learn that the same requirement often exists on the hiring side of the equation—employers sometimes welcome the idea of having first-rate talent available to them on an "as needed" basis rather than full-time. You start by communicating what you want and what you can deliver while working a nontraditional schedule. Approach the job interview by convincing the employer that you can deliver a lot of service while operating outside the office routine.

RECOMMENDED APPROACH

As a nontraditional worker in a job interview you need to represent yourself as a practicing professional whose only difference is situational. You are fully qualified but do not want to work full-time. There are advantages to the employer as well as the worker in such arrangements, and you want to communicate them during your interview. Here are a few examples of traditional thinking that you might encounter with your interviewer, and suggested responses.

These are representative of the issues that might arise. If you have a particular orientation or want to steer the hiring in a certain direction, things such as the independent contractor versus part-time employee arrangement can be given greater emphasis during your interview.

QUESTIONS FOR AND RESPONSES OF CANDIDATES SEEKING NONTRADITIONAL WORKING ARRANGEMENTS	
Question	**Response**
How could a part-time person possibly plan the annual meeting?	The job is a series of tasks to be accomplished, not hours to be logged. Let's discuss what has to be done, and I'll show you how I can do it.
How will you be able to get the "feel" of our organization if you are here only part-time?	Involvement and perceptiveness are not measured by hours in the presence of others. Has my reading of your requirements so far been accurate?
How will we handle taxes and benefits?	There are several approaches. If you want me to be an employee, then pay the taxes and provide partial benefits. If you prefer, I'll work as an independent contractor, a more arm's-length relationship that can easily be arranged.

Internet Tip

To learn more about independent contractor status, research the term in the self-employment section of http://www.irs.gov/.

JOB INTERVIEWING TIPS

You want to enter your interview as a serious, fully qualified candidate with the additional advantage of bringing flexibility to the employer. You might consider doing it this way:

"I am a paralegal with six years' experience preparing corporate documents for law firms, and I'm looking for part-time employment in that specialty. I'd prefer to operate as an independent contractor and do the work in my home office. You don't have to be concerned about my professionalism and respect for confidentiality. The references I provided will be glad to establish those for you."

In this case you took advantage of the opportunity to introduce yourself at the start of the interview to describe your desired situation and the terms under which the work would be accomplished, and preempted an expected question about professionalism and confidentiality. You have laid the groundwork for responding to the interviewer's questions regarding your educational qualifications, specific abilities, and achievements. If you sense that it would be helpful, volunteer your reason for wanting the flexibility; since equal opportunity regulations keep interviewers from inquiring about family status, a comment like this might clear the air and help your cause.

> "After six years of successful full-time employment in two law firms, I want to continue my professional pursuits privately for several years to give me the flexibility to raise my young children at home."

Another purely functional reason that has nothing to do with affirmative action could be:

> "I'm building a consulting practice with clients that are not at all like yours. So I am in a position to use my talents on your behalf in the hours that I don't have committed and still not compete with you. I think we can help each other."

Coming from Other Countries and Cultures

The United States is still a melting pot for the special talents of people who join its workforce with education and experience from other countries. The challenge for those job seekers is in translating their talents into terms that can be readily understood by U.S. employers. As a foreign worker, your job interview is an opportunity to simplify your situation for the employer—demystify the jumble of different-looking things in your resume and bring your real skills into focus.

RECOMMENDED APPROACH

You begin preparing for the interview by clarifying your own notion of where your experience fits in the American job market. If you need assistance, ask a friend who is familiar with jobs and qualifications in this country to help you translate your background into terms that will be recognized here. You should prepare thoroughly for the interview by doing the research necessary to understand what the company does and where it fits into its industry. Go the extra distance and match your experience to the company's operations—picture how your career would have unfolded in that corporate environment. It will put you in a better position to respond meaningfully during the interview.

JOB INTERVIEWING TIPS

If you are an engineer, you come to the interview with a common technical language that makes communicating with your interviewer easier. As a candidate with less-well-defined skills—a manager, perhaps—you have to make a greater effort to be sure your interviewer comprehends the connection between your background and his or her needs.

You approach the substance of the interview in much the same way as any other candidate—establishing your suitability for the job by describing your background, and making a case for what you have to offer. Where things get different for you as an applicant from another culture is establishing that certain peripheral things will not be a problem. Here are several examples of things you have to be prepared to address in the course of your interview.

INTERVIEWING CONCERNS AND POSSIBLE SOLUTIONS FOR THE FOREIGN CANDIDATE	
Concern	**Possible Solution**
My schooling was not in a system equivalent to American schools and colleges.	Sort your educational experiences into categories that equate to American levels—high school, junior college, trade school, or college. Employers may have to establish that you meet minimum requirements for the job and will need your assistance in making the case.
I will need my employer's support with visa considerations. How do I treat that subject?	Be honest about your immigration status, but do not make an issue of it. Objectively state the category that you hold and that to which you aspire. Leave the details of what that all means until you have an offer, if possible.

(cont'd)

Concern	Possible Solution
I want to establish that I can function in the American culture—language and customs.	Demonstrate what you have done—earned a degree attending an American college, held a job that clearly required English language proficiency, etc.

In the final analysis, the foreign student or worker faces the same problem as any other job candidate—making the point as directly and convincingly as possible that you know what the job entails and that you can do it. Your job interview is your best opportunity to make the case personally.

You will find the English as a Second Language Teacher example in the Resume First Aid section of Chapter 1 helpful in preparing your resume.

SUMMARY CHECKLIST: SPECIAL SITUATIONS

- People in special situations benefit from using special approaches to their job search.

- A properly prepared nontraditional candidate can use his or her special circumstances to make the job application and interview more impressive than traditional career path competitors.

- Unemployment, mergers and reorganizations, self-employment, family obligations, and periods of full-time study can take you temporarily off the traditional career path and require special approaches for returning.

- You can anticipate and prepare yourself for the kinds of questions asked of candidates coming to an interview in these special situations.

18 ACCOMMODATING FORCED CAREER CHANGES

You are doing nothing unusual if you are changing jobs. Americans do it often, according to the Bureau of Labor Statistics. Recent figures show most people worked for their current employer for only about four years. At any given time, about one fourth of wage and salary workers have been with their employers for twelve months or less. (Since these are changing figures, search for current "Job Tenure" articles at http://www.bls.gov/bls/newsrels.htm.)

This suggests that several job and career changes may take place during your working life. It would be unusual for you to retire from the job in which you began your career. And while some job changes are voluntary, as workers move from one opportunity to the next, many people are forced to alter their plans. As technology and a changing global economy reshape the workplace, job changes can mean career changes, too, as specialties lose their attractiveness and lifelong career maps become obsolete. Cradle-to-grave jobs are a thing of the past.

You need a new approach to career planning to take advantage of opportunities in the changing workplace and not become its victim. Understand the trends, anticipate change, and prepare to make the most of it. The dangerous approach is to remain passively in your position, waiting to be uprooted in a predictable cycle of change, and relying on chance for your next job.

In this chapter you will learn to deal with jobs that may not last a lifetime. Specifically you will see: (1) how to deal with getting fired—or otherwise unexpectedly terminated, (2) how to plan your working life to avoid surprises, and (3) how to adjust to an irregular career path that includes reversals.

Worst Case: You're Fired

You may feel it coming, or it can be a surprise. You can have your options ready or be in disarray. You can get the news from a compassionate boss, or it can be a nasty experience. Any way you experience it, being fired is traumatic. But like any social ritual, knowing what is coming helps you protect your interests. Here are tips on what to expect and how to react, according to outplacement experts and professionals who deal with terminated employees (Pollan and Levin, 1992):

- If you sense the ax is about to fall, discreetly verify your suspicion with other employees, your supervisor, or someone in personnel. Once you have confirmed the likelihood of your dismissal and made what preparations you can, consider initiating preemptive negotiations that might result in a more generous severance package.

- Before your access is limited, copy things that could be helpful in your severance negotiations and in finding another job: your address file, parts of the personnel manual, etc.

- Shore up your personal finances: pay off bills, don't buy things that can wait, build a cash reserve, refinance your home, or establish a home equity credit line while you still have a job.

- See if you are protected by antidiscrimination laws—Title VII of the Civil Rights Act of 1964 (race, color, sex, religion, national origin) and the Age Discrimination in Employment Act (forty years and older)—and check your state laws. They probably will not stop your dismissal, but they may provide leverage in your negotiations. Consider retaining an employment lawyer.

- At meetings held to discuss your dismissal: (1) be professional but don't be intimidated; (2) take notes in case you have to prove things in the future; (3) convey awareness of your rights and a subtle willingness to act on them if necessary.

- Do not sign a waiver of your rights to future actions against the company until you have a satisfactory settlement signed and in your possession.

- Try to negotiate for more than the company offers: extended lump-sum severance, outplacement assistance, company-paid health insurance, your computer, continued office and clerical support while job hunting, etc.

- Apply immediately for unemployment benefits.

- Evaluate your situation realistically, and start your job search.

Controlling Future Job Changes

Once you are reinstated (or before you face dismissal), understand that you can control your fate in tomorrow's job market. Here are things you should be doing on your own behalf—before a forced change limits your options.

MANAGING YOUR CAREER

You deal with change better when you anticipate it. The difference between being awkwardly thrown out of work and making a comfortable transition depends on personal initiative. So prepare for orderly change while you have a job, and make the next move on your terms.

You don't have to relocate every few years to revitalize your career. Change can occur in ways that are to your liking and advantage. That could mean anything from advancing in your present position to starting a business or beginning a new career. These are realistic goals if you appraise your situation objectively and prepare.

Managing your career to accommodate the inevitability of change involves different things in different situations: (1) If you have lost your job, you begin by reentering the world of work—preparing a resume, networking widely, identifying available positions, then polishing your job interview skills. (2) If you are working, look ahead to what you would do if your position were eliminated. Don't become negative about your present job, but start planning for personal growth. Network and take the other necessary initiatives to position yourself well whether you choose to capitalize on an opportunity where you are or move elsewhere.

ADAPTING TO REALITY

Perform a reality check as if you were being forced to change jobs. Verify that you can do what is necessary to succeed in the working environment you've chosen. Are you willing and able to adapt to the demands of organizational life? Your plans should reflect an appreciation of several basic realities:

- There are fewer jobs at each step up the career ladder, and most people will reach their plateau short of the top.

- The good guys or gals don't automatically rise on their merits. The dynamics of success usually include more than competence (add "likability," "organizational fit," and other intangibles).

- Organizational gamesmanship is a necessary part of most careers. A good mentor, for example, speaks well of you behind closed doors and eases your entry into necessary professional relationships.

Decide whether you can correct the problem if you plateaued, failed the likability test, or were an unsuccessful gamesman. If not, consider consulting, a business of your own, or a performance-oriented specialty more immune to organizational pressures. If you are an individualist and choose to make it on the inside, select an organization in which you can partake of the necessary relationship building activities.

An attitude and organization mismatch can spell career disaster. Avoid being "selected out" because you don't fit the group dynamic—a common cause of job loss when critical skills are not at stake. As you choose current employment options or plan future career moves, select a comfortable setting. The way you feel about your working environment, your relationships with your colleagues, and the social and professional dynamics of the organization in which you work can affect your ability to succeed.

PURSUING TRAINING

One sure way to prosper in any employment climate is to have skills employers can't do without. Take additional training and become an irresistible candidate; you have to stay on top in your field to remain competitive. Look for training opportunities that set you apart. Training is tangible; it can go on a resume and be discussed at a job interview. Earn your basic credentials; then seek out trade and professional opportunities that focus on skills of the future. You gain more than knowledge attending sessions with a leading-edge orientation; you learn new buzzwords and make contacts that open future career doors. If your request exceeds what is routinely provided, barter with your company. Explain how what you learn will benefit your employer; then volunteer to pay for the course if the firm will allow you time to attend.

By participating in training sessions, you get an opportunity to meet people and hear of career leads you never would have in the formal job market. So whether you are out of work and looking or are comfortably employed and wise enough to know your circumstances could change, use training to enhance your employability. Earning a college degree, taking the right combination of courses, or attending a workshop to acquire special skills can enhance your value and ease your climb to the top.

NETWORKING

Stay connected to sources of influence and career information in your field. Begin networking in your own organization, and then cultivate contacts at other companies with which you do business or have colleague relationships. Use telephone networking to supplement the face-to-face variety, and establish even more professional linkages that can help your career grow. In the modern business environment there is no need to limit your contacts to people you meet. Executive recruiters, who use personal connections to build careers and make a living, meet only a small percentage of the people with whom they interact.

Being known, liked, and respected in your field is no accident. A few people accomplish it by the sheer weight of their talents and personalities, but most cultivate it. Watch your successful colleagues. The very activities they profess to dread—attending meetings, sitting behind closed doors with the boss, being on selection committees—are the ones they want to be part of because they represent vital connections.

That is how business is done, and you should participate in the process unless you consciously choose to spurn the organization and have the talent to succeed on the outside. Networking and mentoring are important in traditional jobs, and you have to initiate the necessary connections if they don't occur naturally. You can choose whether your network leads upward in your own organization or reaches across to another one, but you must network. Even starting your own business means cultivating contacts; the only difference is that you represent yourself.

So whether you are secure in a career or are on the street looking for a way back in, networking is an essential activity. You choose how and with whom to network, but to be effective, your relationships should be mutually advantageous and genuine.

CONTROLLING YOUR PERSONAL FINANCES

If your personal finances are in poor condition at job-changing time, they can limit your flexibility. The balance between your debts and your savings often determines whether you choose a real opportunity or rush into something less desirable. Personal finances also mirror how you manage your life. Credit checks are common in hiring, and a financial statement is sometimes required—always, if you start a business.

Your personal finances can also affect your confidence and poise. Strained personal finances show when you network with friends, interview for a job, or seek financial backing for a business venture. If you find yourself in financial difficulty, make the best of it, correct the problem, and then give personal finances the importance they deserve in your overall career plan.

Personal financial planners advise you to:

- Have at least six months' worth of bill-paying power in liquid assets to deal with the unexpected.

- Keep your credit obligations to a minimum.

- Build investments that can yield income if necessary—a growth mutual fund that you can convert into an income fund, for example.

You can find books, Internet resources, and professional advisers to help you plan a sound personal financial situation. Do what is necessary to make the contingency of disrupted income a part of your lifetime career plan.

Internet Tip

Explore The Motley Fool's financial planning advice at http://www.fool.com/ or enter the keywords "financial planning" in a search engine to find similar sites.

Taking One Step Back

In today's job market you cannot count on moving up (or even sideways) after losing a position. If you do not meet the high demand profile in the current marketplace you may have to adjust your attitude and expectations to realistic levels and be ready for the questions of employers who may view you as overqualified for a one-step-back position. Refer to the section "Applying for a Less Prestigious Position" in Chapter 17 for more information. It is critical that you make three points:

- You really do want the job in spite of the fact that it appears to be a step backward on your career ladder.

- You can live with a fair compensation package for the position being offered and recognize the potential differential with what you had been making.

- You expect to prove yourself just like everyone else, and you won't be coming in wearing vestiges of your former "rank" on your sleeve.

When you exhaust your possibilities for a parallel or better move, you face reality, get back on the career ladder, and start moving up again. If you have prepared for the challenge, you face opportunities for renewal and growth that might never have been yours in a cradle-to-grave job. Your success depends on your being able to consider options ranging from an entrepreneurial solution to taking one step back to make future steps forward. When your employment situation stabilizes, be sure to use the five keys to having the luxury of choice in the future: (1) manage your career, (2) adapt to reality, (3) pursue training, (4) network, and (5) control your personal finances.

PART V

MODEL RESUMES

For an introduction to this section, including an index and suggestions for using the model resumes, please refer to Chapter 3, "Model Resumes."

Administrative Assistant

WORK HISTORY RESUME

General Strategy

Ms. Williams chose the Work History Resume to quickly highlight her two blocks of highly relevant experience:

- four years as a military officer with leadership training, experience, and substantial responsibilities
- current employment in a dynamic business position that shows success in the demanding field of marketing

A brief Overview section says what she has done and what she wants to do. Comments clarify that she wants to apply her skills assisting a senior manager with the clear implication that she views the position as her stepping stone to the executive ranks.

Her resume conveys the message that she has succeeded in two entry-level positions, but doesn't want to pursue either specialty as a career. Rather, she presents herself as a proven performer ready for higher-level, more general management duties. She builds her case on a foundation of clearly stated work experience that would instantly command the respect of a senior person looking for a sharp assistant who has already been in the trenches.

Specific Points

❶ What she has done and what she wants to do.

❷ Evidence of success in being persuasive with professional people.

❸ Proven ability to communicate aggressively.

❹ Industry knowledge that can be valuable assisting a senior executive.

❺ Tangible proof of effectiveness in setting and meeting business objectives.

❻ Relevant, applied leadership training.

❼ Ability to travel and function successfully away from home.

❽ Demonstrated success in taking on responsibility rapidly.

❾ Tangible proof of recognition by her supervisors.

❿ Relevant academic preparation for the role she seeks.

Carol J. Williams
1256 Kolorotura Drive
Washington, DC 20099
202-222-9988 (Office)
202-333-9075 (Residence)
cjwms@att.net

Overview

❶ Strong organizational and people skills. Proven leader with over 6 years of progressively successful experience in personnel, management, and sales. Seek to combine talents at senior management level as administrative assistant with potential for assuming broader responsibilities.

Experience

❷

❸ **June 2000 - Present**: *Account Executive,* Witherspoon & Company Investments, Washington, DC. Twice awarded outstanding salesperson of the quarter as a retail stockbroker catering to professional clients. Organize and conduct ongoing business development activity including extensive telephone contact and mailings. Licensed broker with broad market knowledge in a variety of industries. Generated $2.5 million dollars in new business during the last year including eight employee benefits accounts for professional corporations.

❹ **❺**

❻ **June 1996 - May 2000**: *Administrative Officer,* U.S. Air Force, Ramstein AFB, Germany. Following three months of officer candidate school and four months of administrative officer training, assigned as Assistant Personnel Officer of 287 person reconnaissance squadron. Responsible for pay, benefits, and assignment processing of all new and departing staff. Promoted to Chief Administrative Officer after 13 months, responsible for personnel and operational administrative matters, reporting directly to the commander. Awarded commendation medal for outstanding performance that included exceptional ratings in eight high level operational readiness inspections. Concluded active duty obligation as a Captain. In the active reserve as a Major.

❼ **❽**

❾

July 1992 - May 1996: **Various part-time positions** while attending college including retail sales, secretarial positions in professional offices, and assisting my father in the operation of his consulting firm.

Education **❿**

BS, Business Administration, Northwestern University, 1996

Comments

While I have succeeded in direct selling on the professional level, I prefer to combine that experience with my administrative talents and pursue a career in management. Combined leadership, sales, and administrative perspectives prepare me as a seasoned administrative assistant to a senior manager.

Advertising Account Executive

COMPETENCY CLUSTER RESUME

General Strategy

Mr. Kirk used the Competency Cluster Resume because his strong points center around two things that his potential employers care most about:

- He has managed large advertising accounts successfully and shown that he can generate new business.

- He can relate well to the creative side of the house in the advertising business because he has been there as an award-winning professional.

The college affiliation has been placed prominently because he knows his alma mater has a great reputation in the field and a lot of hiring officials are also graduates.

Work history is solid, but not exceptional. Better to lift the skills and present them as valued competencies than to try to paint a glowing picture within the context of pedestrian jobs. His Overview says as much—nine years of successful experience that covers both the creative and marketing sectors. His strength is in making the clients happy by mustering the best efforts of his former peers in the creative part of the agency.

Specific Points

❶ Overview establishes his dual skills and identifies his industry specialty.

❷ Education is an important identity factor in his industry, so it is stressed.

❸ Quantification of what he does and what it's worth in dollars is important.

❹ Identifies the specific class of clients he is skilled at dealing with.

❺ Proven ability to take over an account and make it grow.

❻ A record for attracting new business that promises significant profits.

❼ Shows he can bridge the gap between clients and creative people.

❽ Experience in dealing successfully with a large, prominent client.

❾ Major regional award from national industry group—worth mentioning.

❿ Employment is self-descriptive to those who would evaluate him.

Hugh M. Kirk

2179 Beach Drive, Apartment 142
Jacksonville, FL
904-222-9988 (Office)
904-333-9075 (Residence)
kirk2179@aol.com

Overview

❶ Advertising manager with nine years of successful experience in both the creative and marketing sectors of consumer electronics. Proven ability to develop existing and new business using thorough industry knowledge and creative persuasion within the firm's specialized divisions and the client's organization.

❷ Education

Bachelor of Science
Marketing Management
North Florida University, 1993

Account Development ❸

❹ Currently overseeing six accounts with annual agency revenues of $250,000 to $1.5 million each. Product families include consumer electronics directed toward the home-based professional and small consulting firms. Assumed management of four **❺** existing accounts each of which have been increased by over 20% in less than 18 months. Added two accounts in the same period, each with the potential for exceeding the annual fee volume of present largest client within two years.

Creative Experience ❻

❼ Acquired present position while serving as an independent consultant to the advertising layout department. Was employed full-time to oversee the artistic **◄❽** development of print media advertising for the largest retail electronics chain in North Florida. Campaign won Southeast Region Style Award from the American Advertisers' Guild in 2000. **❾**

Employment Summary

❿ Wilson & Johnson Agency, 39th Floor, Suite 300, Gulf Life Building, Jacksonville, FL. Account Executive. July 1998 to Present.

Creative Design Consultants, 15 Business Park Circle, Orlando, FL. Artistic Layout Consultant. June 1995 - July 1998.

Daytona Evening Press, 3500 Del Ray Avenue, Daytona Beach, FL. Advertising Department Apprentice. June 1993 - May 1995.

Advertising Copy Writer

FOCUSED RESUME

General Strategy

Ms. Baker is advised to use the Focused Resume because it is an efficient way to present her unique combination of talents, which would not stand out in separate job descriptions. She needs to communicate quickly to the employer—who is known to be in the business of high-fashion sportswear, since she is focusing on that job market—that she:

- grew up in the retail clothing business
- has traveled to where her clients go (can identify with them as she writes copy designed to appeal to them)
- is herself a former fashion model

A few years as a clerk in the family store and a few more as a model turn into an attractive applicant when focused on the specific job she has in mind.

Specific Points

❶ Brief Objective tells the employer she has a special combination of skills for the particular position.

❷ A geographic preference is important to her, so she says so up front.

❸ Worked in the industry already—with a major retailer, even though it was family.

❹ Merger—a logical reason for not continuing in the family business.

❺ Evidence that she knows technological as well as fashion side of sportswear and has hands-on experience using the Internet to market sportswear.

❻ Model background adds both fashion credibility and glamour.

❼ Shows she has lived the lifestyle of those for whom she intends to write.

❽ A highly respected agency, known in the region, endorses her.

❾ Advantage to being in the family—saw all sides—more than a clerk.

❿ Respectable liberal arts degree is fine for what she is trying to achieve.

Kathryn C. Baker
38 Ohio Place, Apartment 403
Rapid City, SD 57709
605-222-9988
kcbak@juno.com

❶
❷ **Objective:** Copy writing position in an established mail order firm in the North Central region. Particularly interested in applying strong sense of style and knowledge of top market sportswear gained working in family retail clothing business and modeling career.

ASSETS

❸ • **Overall perspective** on the national sports clothing market from a lifetime of participation in my family's store which was the 2nd largest retailer of ❹ sportswear in Minnesota prior to its acquisition by a national chain upon by father's retirement.
❺ • **Familiarity with the trends and technological features** associated with contemporary all-weather sports clothing.
• **Internet aware** creator of a personal Web page for direct–marketing several of my own designs. Used Web–authoring tools provided by my Internet service provider.
❻ • **Fashion sensitivity** in the sports garment industry enhanced by over 2 years of successful modeling in Chicago market following college graduation.
• **Extensive travel** throughout the winter sports areas of the United States, Canada, and Europe. ❼

EMPLOYMENT

❽ **The Wood Agency**, 1000 Market Square, Mercantile Center, Chicago, IL. Model specializing in active sportswear. June 2000 - January 2002.

Outdoor Classic Design, Wilmount Mall, Minneapolis, MN. Seasonal sales work in family business from age 16 through college. Observed and ❾ participated in buying and merchandising as well. December 1991 - June 2000.

EDUCATION
❿
Bachelor of Arts
Liberal Arts
National College, 2000

Advertising Sales Manager

COMPETENCY CLUSTER RESUME

General Strategy

Mr. Kearney decided to bracket his employment so boldly that it needed no heading, such as Objective. In six words he makes clear:

- what he wants to do—sell radio advertising
- the level at which he wants to operate—management
- the market for his talents—top-ten radio

With that taken care of, the best way to proceed is with the Competency Cluster Resume where he continues the powerfully simple message he has begun. The headings alone say he is competent in marketing, management, creative, and technical aspects of his specialty. He then goes on to say exactly how under each heading, briefly putting forth a career path that endorses his readiness for sales management, concluding with a pair of degrees that complement what he is trying to do occupationally.

Specific Points

❶ Six introductory words can say a lot about what you want to do.

❷ Sidebar headings themselves serve as an outline of competencies.

❸ Identifies the specific market niche in which he is knowledgeable.

❹ Quantifies sales productivity with dollar figures and percentage of growth.

❺ Shows he can develop other salespersons—a key skill for a sales manager.

❻ Proves he is a creative ad man—major station/regional awards/bonuses which are only paid when efforts generate the profits to pay for them.

❼ Demonstrates early work ethic and shows valuable experience as a DJ.

❽ Even a simple electric typewriter will generally bold and <u>underline,</u> adding interest to the resume and distinguishing between levels of headings.

❾ Career path is shown clearly in this simple listing of positions held.

❿ Degrees listed vouch for general education and specific business preparation relevant to a career in sales management.

Alfred D. Kearney

289 Atlantic Boulevard
Alameda, CA 94502
510-722-9988 (Office)
510-443-9075 (Residence)
kearney289@aol.com

1

Advertising Sales Manager, Top-Ten Radio

2 **Marketing**

3 Successful radio advertising sales experience for major market top-ten station. Established in the college and young adult market segments including physical conditioning, fast food, and sportswear. Servicing **4** 37 accounts with annual ad budgets in the $4,000 to $175,000 range yielding combined yearly revenues of $3.2 million. Increased account dollar value base by average of 30% annually while adding new accounts at a rate of two monthly.

Management

5 Developed a team of six junior sales representatives from point of recruitment through field training and into independent operation. Retained four of the six after two years with two earning individual productivity awards and all substantially exceeding minimum production objectives.

Creative

6 Three years as advertising copywriter for lead station in the Western Radio Group. Twice earned regional awards for creative impact and client retention. Each involved substantial, documented, renewal bonus.

Technical

7 During four years of college, worked average of 20 hours weekly as combination disk jockey and station engineer for mid-size university town AM station serving a comprehensive rural market.

8 ## Employment

WQRA Alameda, Group Advertising Sales Manager. 1996-Present.
WLUX Phoenix, Advertising Copywriter. 1993-96.
WTBP Manhattan, KS, Disk jockey/Engineer. 1991-93. **9**

Education

Associate in Science
General Studies **10**
West Kansas Junior College, 1983

Bachelor of Science
Business Administration
Manhattan College, 1996

Apartment Manager

FOCUSED RESUME

General Strategy

Mr. Blakemore is making an application within a specialized employment field and is advised to use the Focused Resume in order to:

- highlight his professional certification and minimize his lack of a college degree, which is not overly relevant here and easily compensated for
- stress the base of successful experience doing exactly what he is asking to do in yet a larger, higher-paying facility

This resume format is ideal for placing the emphasis on the skills, experience, and training most immediately applicable to the position in question.

Specific Points

❶ Overview is used to categorize immediately the scope of his experience.

❷ It is also the place to establish the existence of his instantly credible professional certification, the Certified Building Manager (CBM) designation.

❸ Tells what kinds of projects he has managed and for how long.

❹ Says what the employer wants to hear—occupancy up, turnover down.

❺ Can supervise the sort of employees known to exist in the new setting.

❻ Experienced in dealing with a union workforce.

❼ Gets along well with the project staff—an essential quality for a manager.

❽ Knows how to deal with tenant organizations.

❾ Has practical experience applying Internet marketing techniques in the rental real estate market.

❿ Work history shows responsible positions logically supporting aspirations.

Wilson W. Blakemore
3179 Clayton Place, NW
Washington, DC 20039
202-821-9988 (Office)
202-538-9075 (Residence)
blkmor@hotmail.com

Overview

1

<u>**Residential property manager**</u> with 16 years of progressively more responsible positions in 250 to 500 unit upscale apartment projects. Certified Building Manager (CBM) with highly successful combined operating and marketing experience.

2

Strengths

3

4

- <u>**Managed two general-population buildings**</u>, each for a period of approximately six years prior to assuming general management of present major senior retirement complex in 1998. Occupancy increased from mid-70% to 95% range in each situation with corresponding reductions in tenant turnover.

5

6

- <u>**Oversaw building engineers, building and grounds maintenance staffs, contract marketing efforts, and lobby personnel**</u> in each facility. Twice in collective bargaining situations. Staff retention raised from average of 8.3 months to over three years in high attrition positions. Executive staff stabilized completely.

7

8

- <u>**Successfully dealt with tenant organizations**</u> in each situation. Established sufficient goodwill to reduce litigation to management companies involved by an average of 30% within one year of assuming duties. Led crucial tenant relations campaign resulting in voluntary condominium conversion of major inner city property following 8 years of costly opposition.

9

- <u>**Collaborated with Web site developer**</u> on the preparation and maintenance of a corporate page displaying available properties.

Employment

10

- Simonton Place Apartments, 487-unit seniors' rental facility, predominantly two-bedroom, top-decile rent category. Washington, DC. General Manager. 1998-Present.
- Wilkins Gardens, 364-unit general population rental complex, mixed one-, two-bedroom, and efficiency building with extensive grounds including golf course. Richmond, VA. Resident Manager. 1992-1998.
- Randal Place Apartments, 295-unit young professional building, 85% efficiencies, remainder one- and two-bedroom, midtown location. Washington, DC. Resident Manager. 1986-1992.

Education

Diploma
Business Management
District Business College, 1993.

Bank Collector

General Strategy

Mr. Rogers has completed a career in the navy with an outstanding record and a lot of highly relevant skills. He needs to showcase those talents without drawing undue attention to the fact that they were gained while working in a military environment and for a single employer. His best approach is to use the Focused Resume, with which he can establish that he:

- welcomes the challenge of public contact and problem solving

- has comparable skills to someone in a personnel career in the civilian sector

- has been successful in positions of considerable responsibility

- possesses the practical training necessary to do the job

Specific Points

❶ An Objective statement makes it clear that he is willing to take on the challenge of solving problems with the general public—a general focus suited to many civilian jobs, including Bank Collector.

❷ Immediate verification of his experience in dealing with people.

❸ Qualification of the scope of his responsibilities and the fact that they dealt with financial matters.

❹ Notes that current technology was available to him in his environment.

❺ Experience in relating to all levels of clients—junior to very senior.

❻ Was an innovator in using the same kinds of technology called for in a bank conducting credit collection efforts over a large region.

❼ Verifiable success in handling sensitive issues to the satisfaction of the customer would be attractive to those reading his resume.

❽ Another specific illustration of initiative and successful results.

❾ A simple statement of work history that speaks for itself.

❿ A brief Comments statement can do a lot to meld experience with objective—bridges the gap between careers in divergent settings.

Charles L. Rogers
9075 Salem Place South
Augusta, GA 30901
706-662-9988
clrogers@copland.net

❶ **Objective**: **To obtain a business position that involves problem solving and public contact.**

Strengths:

❷ • Twenty-year career as a Navy non-commissioned officer in the personnel specialty— customer service and problem solving.

❸ • Managed a nine-person office adjudicating pay and benefits claims for a command (customer base) of 7,000 sailors.

❹ • Conversant in telemarketing techniques and equipment as applied to financial applications.

• Mature, experienced manager accustomed to dealing successfully with diverse clients ranging from new enlistees to senior flag officers.   **❺**

Achievements:

❻ • Established an 800-number service line for Navy pay and personnel problem resolution.

❼ • Increased customer satisfaction rate by 42 percent while reducing staffing and support costs by one half.

• Set record for Navy Fund (United Way-type organization) participation in the Pacific Command by using telephone solicitation techniques.

Work Experience: **❽**

1982-2002: United States Navy ⟵**❾**

Education:

Diploma
Office Management
Wilson Business School, 1982

Comments: Enlisted in the Navy following graduation from business school. During 20 years of service, attended an ongoing series of professional development courses in **❿** the personnel and financial services specialties. While work experience has been limited to military, human relations and financial skills are essentially the same as among civilian clientele.

Bank Officer

WORK HISTORY RESUME

General Strategy

Ms. Anson chose the Work History Resume because she has a straightforward pattern of employment in her professional field. It is effectively described by listing each position in order and detailing her various responsibilities:

- starting with minor experience in the industry as a summer teller
- beginning her professional lending career in the recognized entry-level position of credit analyst
- moving up to Assistant Loan Officer

Her well-ordered, brief resume establishes that she is moving successfully through the progression expected for the next step in her career ladder—a lateral move to a better opportunity or larger institution or a promotion to full fledged Loan Officer status.

Specific Points

❶ The Overview effectively states level of experience in a single sentence.

❷ Continuity is shown by the dates of employment at each institution.

❸ Large employers like these are understood in their industry—no further description of them is necessary.

❹ The position title is sufficient to tell those in the business the kind of work she does— what is needed is enough quantification to describe exactly what level of responsibility she had in the position.

❺ When it can be safely verified by future reference checks, ranked performance is a strong way to demonstrate strength. Knowledge of how to apply Web page technology to a profit center in the industry is an invaluable point to illustrate when possible.

❻ Expected background experience is established by this entry-level position.

❼ Shows rapid, successful assumption of responsibility.

❽ Discreet, matter-of-fact explanation of reason for leaving first position.

❾ Career-oriented degree shows commitment to the profession.

❿ Professional affiliations are enhanced by noting a leadership role.

Sally N. Anson

8567 South Murray Lane
Columbia, SC 29205
803-222-9988 (Office)
803-333-9075 (Residence)
sna292@hotmail.com

❶

OVERVIEW

Commercial lender with four years of successful experience in regional bank lending to middle market accounts as a credit analyst and corporate calling officer.

EXPERIENCE **❸**

June 2000 - Present: *Assistant Loan Officer,* **Southland Banks,** Columbia, SC. Commercial loan officer with extensive business development responsibilities in the Carolinas, Georgia, and North Florida. Manage a $35 million portfolio which includes $27 million outstanding and $8 million committed. Generated $11 million in new deposits and $19 million in new loans in 2.5 years— **❺** number two performer on a staff of 12 regional lenders. Using the text editor BBEdit, developed an on-line loan application section on the bank's Web page that prequalifies candidates and significantly reduces the number of lending officer calls on unqualified prospects. **❹**

❷

❻

June 1998 - May 2000: *Credit Analyst,* **Coastal National Bank,** Sea Pines, GA. Entry position upon college graduation. Credit review and analysis for middle market companies. Rapidly assumed full supporting activities for lenders prior to leaving and assuming an officer position in the interest of professional growth not available at Coastal National. **❽**

❼

July 1994 - May 1998: Various part-time positions while attending college including seasonal retail sales, clerical positions and **summer employment as a bank teller.**

EDUCATION

Bachelor of Business Administration
❾ ➔ Banking and Finance
University of West Georgia, 1998

❿ ## PROFESSIONAL AFFILIATIONS & TRAINING

Professional Member, Robert Morris Associates,
Secretary of Carolinas' Chapter.
Currently pursuing the National Commercial Loan School,
Norman, Oklahoma.

Biological Technician

COMPETENCY CLUSTER RESUME

General Strategy

Mr. Woodward is just completing his college studies and, while he has some valuable experiences, they do not lend themselves to a traditional resume where dates must show continuity, one position follows another, etc. Because his experience is part-time and irregular, but important to potential employers, he was advised to use the Competency Cluster Resume. This allows him to say precisely what he did—and even where and when he did it—but without having to emphasize the mixed nature of his experiences.

With this approach, he can clearly highlight the fact that he:

- has laboratory work experience
- has field experience
- has contributed to formal research
- was educated for this specialty

Specific Points

❶ Combined and categorized, two summer jobs take on greater meaning.

❷ Work ethic demonstrated by evening employment during college.

❸ Classifying his and his supervisor's levels of responsibility defines the magnitude of the work done.

❹ Field experience for a regionally known organization is worth noting.

❺ Establishes a lifelong working knowledge of applied animal biology.

❻ Cites applications that will be valued by the kinds of firms apt to hire him.

❼ Associates himself in an appropriately limited way with known research.

❽ The right degree for his career, earned from a respected local institution.

❾ Notes a nationally recognized association's accreditation of his program.

❿ An entry-level person, in particular, needs strong, relevant references.

Vernon D. Woodward

1279 Creek Valley Avenue
Pittsburgh, PA 15214
412-222-9988 (Office)
412-333-9075 (Residence)
woodward1279@att.net

LABORATORY EXPERIENCE

❶ • Two summers of full-time experience assisting biochemists at University Associates, Inc., in the analysis of test-animal body fluids, drug reactions, and food assimilation studies.

❷ • Evening employment with National Labs in the capacity of a biological ← **❸** technician aide during final academic year. Assisted senior microbiological technician in immunological research.

FIELD EXPERIENCE

❹

• Summer experience with Save the Lake Foundation assisting wildlife biologists in the collection of data on the effects of pollution on the ecosystems of Western Maryland.

❺ • Grew up working on family poultry farm constantly involved in practical application of nutrition and disease management including assisting in **❻** taking blood samples, mass vaccination drives, on-site analysis and data gathering by feed contractor's scientists.

RESEARCH CONTRIBUTIONS

❼

• Acknowledged for supporting efforts in Wilson-Walker study of immunological parasitology in farm/college environments, 2000.

EDUCATION

Associate in Applied Science   **❽**
Laboratory Technology
Allegheny Junior College, 2002

COMMENTS

❾

Formal clinical training in AJC's nationally accredited program in Laboratory Technology supplemented by significant periods of employment in the industry on a part-time basis. Lifelong exposure to applied application of laboratory technology in field settings. High motivation and competency verifiable by references upon request.

❿

Biomedical Engineer

FOCUSED RESUME

General Strategy

Ms. McNair has excellent credentials, but a history of short terms of employment. Her choice of the Focused Resume is a wise one because it tends to showcase her strong abilities and achievements without making the employer search for them in a string of positions that didn't last very long. All of her employers are important names to mention and the dates are not withheld, just not emphasized.

With this approach, the reviewer's attention is focused on:

- six powerful sets of professional skills
- three clearly important professional achievements
- six nationally recognized employers
- the right degrees and affilations

Specific Points

❶ A headline-type Objective classifies the field and level of employment.

❷ Established abilities in the technical specialty.

❸ Indications of ability to lead other scientists and work within standards.

❹ Proof of being able not only to design, but to implement her achievements.

❺ Security clearances may be an attractive asset worth mentioning discreetly.

❻ National professional recognition establishes stature in her field.

❼ By moving the dates of employment to the right of the employer and not making them a separate column, they are deemphasized, but available.

❽ Rapid movement to more important job titles does much to compensate for relatively brief tenure with various employers.

❾ Excellent degrees and universities discreetly noted.

❿ The expected professional affiliations are confirmed.

Edith K. McNair

8236 Thurmont Street
Petersburg, VA 23805
304-333-9075 (Residence)
ediemc@yahoo.com

❶ OBJECTIVE: Biomedical Engineer—Research and Development

ABILITIES:

❷
- Apply computer-aided design to advanced prosthesis testing
- Adapt artificial intelligence to mechanical applications
- Direct design staff integrating digital/mechanical dimensions
❸
- Liaison with civilian and military government scientists
- Conduct feasibility testing within established industry standards
- Coordinate with regulatory boards on operating approvals

ACHIEVEMENTS:

❹
- Designed and implemented advanced aerospace prosthesis applications for unmanned environments
- Applied CAD/CAM principles to previously unapproached design areas within the aeromedical arena (details classified)   ←**❺**
- Woman Engineer of the Year Award winner in 1997 for work in articulating joint modification mechanics in AI theory

❻
WORK HISTORY:

- Woodruff Laboratories, 2001-02   Senior Scientist
- Digital Medical Corporation, 1998-2001   Applications Developer
- Johnston Medical, Inc., 1997-98   Design Engineer
- NASA, 1995-97   **❼** Biomedical Researcher   **❽**
- Johns Hopkins University, 1993-95   Graduate Assistant
- United States Air Force, 1989-93   Engineering Instructor

EDUCATION:

Bachelor of Science   **❾**   Master of Science
Mechanical Engineering   Biomedical Engineering
Virginia Polytechnic Institute, 1986   Johns Hopkins University, 1995

PROFESSIONAL AFFILIATIONS:

- Society of Women Engineers
- Biomedical Engineering Society   **❿**

Bookkeeper

COMPETENCY CLUSTER RESUME

General Strategy

Mr. Joseph has held only one position, but he has the kinds of abilities that would be very attractive to an accounting firm looking for a bookkeeping associate. The best way to display his strengths is with the Competency Cluster Resume. It allows him to relegate his single employer to the bottom of the page and draw attention to his most marketable qualities:

- an associate degree in accounting from a respectable local college
- experience preparing taxes for small business clients
- outstanding applied knowledge of accounting-related computer software
- a willingness and ability to work directly with clients

Specific Points

❶ In the absence of a long work history, the academic credential is important.

❷ Practical, quantified experience with which the employer can identify.

❸ Bread-and-butter business for the kind of firm he seeks to join.

❹ Demonstrates software knowledge and the proper role relative to professional staff—knows how to fit into the team.

❺ Ability to use an important class of software and an indication that he can figure out the use of others by using the manuals provided.

❻ Knowledge of relevant computer hardware and peripheral equipment.

❼ Valuable skills in using computer communications equipment and programs are alluded to in this point.

❽ Level of responsibility indicated by representing the firm to clients directly.

❾ Respect for professional strengths and limitations shown here—i.e., won't be getting the firm into trouble by making decisions better left to the CPAs.

❿ Solid, continuous employment history with an established firm.

Enrique E. Joseph

491 Baldwin Place, Apartment 29
Corpus Christi, TX 78404
512-261-9988 (Office)
512-443-9075 (Residence)
eej491@btc.com

Education

① Associate in Science
Accounting
Bee County Junior College, 1999

SMALL BUSINESS TAXES

② • Maintain ledgers, statements, and running status forms for 36 small business clients.

• Prepare federal and state quarterly withholding forms for clients. **❸**

COMPUTER USE **❹**

• Enter tax data into TaxWise software under the direction of professional staff of CPA firm.

• Data entry and routine analyses using the Primary Spreadsheet software package and related manuals. **❺**

❻ • Data entry and reports generation using the Twin Ledger II system on the ProCal 37 computer and operating system.

• Operate modem data exchanges quarterly with three large client **❼** companies.

CLIENT CONTACT **❽**

• Serve as point of contact for 17 small business owners whose books are maintained by the firm.

• Explain reporting procedures and respond to client assistance requests not involving CPA advisories. **❾**

Employment

❿ 1999 - Present: Bookkeeper
Bell & Weathers, CPAs, PC

Business Machine Service Representative

General Strategy

Ms. DuVall has held two positions that display her talents quite well. For that reason, she has chosen the Work History Resume format. It allows her to show:

- the right kind of formal technical education
- inside technical service employment
- field service employment
- an impressive array of manufacturers' specialized training schools

Specific Points

❶ The applied electronics degree is a valuable asset worth using as a lead item in this resume directed toward technical employment.

❷ Current employment is both verified and described as relevant.

❸ Position title is self-descriptive, but needs further qualification as to whether she was a generalist serving many lines or a specialist limited to one or two categories of equipment.

❹ Competency as confirmed by a competitive award is worthy of mention.

❺ Customer relations is very important in this field and her ability to cite strength in that area adds value to her credentials.

❻ Demonstrated in-house competence speaks well for her ability to coordinate field troubleshooting with the main office staff—speaks their language—has "been there."

❼ Good to specify the kinds of service work done—warranty, preventive maintenance, etc.

❽ Current manufacturer-specific training is invaluable—stress it if you have it.

❾ A subtle expression of willingness to travel and pursue opportunities for technical growth is also conveyed in this list of courses attended.

❿ Progress in achieving formal professional certification should be noted.

Elaine P. DuVall

472 Ross Road NE
Frederick, MD 21702
240-222-9988 (Office)
240-333-9075 (Residence)
elaine21702@msn.com

Education

① Associate in Applied Science
Electronics Technology
Middletown Community College, 1996

Experience

③

June 2000 - Present: **②** Technical Representative, Micro Copiers & Office Electronics, Inc., Frederick, MD. Install and service complete line of office copiers, mail processing, and personal computer equipment on site. Runner-up in Mid-Atlantic Region **④** Xeno Technical Trouble Shooting Contest last year. Customer satisfaction bonus this year. **⑤**

June 1996 - May 2000: **⑥** Bench Technician, Wilmont Office Systems, Rockville, MD. In-house service technician responsible for major repairs to all kinds of office electronics products. Testing, preventive maintenance, and component replacement on top lines under warranty of manufacturers. **⑦** Formally recognized for outstanding performance on six occasions.

⑧ Specialized Manufacturers' Training

- October 1996—two week resident course, Xeno Corporation Training Center, Portside, NC, Copier Repair Courses I & II.

- April 1997—one week resident course, Mika Computers Technical Center, Palo Alto, CA, Office Computer Trouble Shooting Basics.

⑨

- July 1999—ten day seminar, Appricot Service Center, Taos, NM, Upgrading and Maintaining Appricot Computer Systems.

- September 2000-Present—Computer Assisted Instruction courses by the Office Electronics Institute in preparation for certification tests. Passed Series I & II, completion of Series III & IV anticipated in 2003 for designation as a Certified Office Electronics Technician (COET). **⑩**

Chemist

COMPETENCY CLUSTER RESUME

General Strategy

Dr. Hasenworth has outstanding credentials, but her experience does not include full-time employment outside the academic community and related work-study positions. She is advised to stress her excellent abilities and all that she has achieved, without drawing undue attention to the fact that she has never held a job. The Competency Cluster Resume is the best format for accomplishing this. With it she can show that she:

- knows where her training can best be used in industry
- has the industry-related skills and achievements to be attractive
- holds academic credentials appropriate to an advanced research position

Specific Points

❶ In a brief introductory Objective sentence, she establishes that she is pursuing a position in industry, not the academic world.

❷ Practical, industry-related research is noted versus the esoteric, academic variety that might be of less importance to the people who will read her resume.

❸ Computer literacy appropriate to her field is established authoritatively.

❹ Sensitivity to a possible role as an industry spokesperson to environmental and other community groups may make her a more attractive candidate in today's climate, which is filled with such concerns.

❺ Linkage with a respected industry group as credibility by association.

❻ Evidence of working with up-to-the-minute issues and technology.

❼ National stature confirmed by competitive award in her field.

❽ Respect of mentors implied by selection for key studies and publications.

❾ The correct academic credentials are in place for top-level research.

❿ References are key to confirming her qualities and potential in the absence of a traditional employment record.

Jill C. Hasenworth

367 Jamesway Avenue
Overland Park, KS 66211
913-333-9075 (Residence)
jillch@att.net

❶ OBJECTIVE: An advanced research position within the polymer coatings segment of the paint industry.

COMPETENCIES:

❷ • Designed polymer coating testing procedures based on computer modeling and mathematical weather effects simulation.

❸ • Extensive computer programming capabilities in specialized scientific languages and servo linkages among non-complementary systems.

• Outstanding lay communication skills invaluable asset in articulation of scientific needs and achievements to broader scientific and business constituencies. **← ❹**

• Broad industry exposure across the specialized polymer segment gained during work-study and research fellowships supported by the Polymer Council over five years of graduate work-study.

❺

ACHIEVEMENTS:

❻ • Applied attrition analysis assumptions successfully to the oblique abrasion theory permitting breakthrough advances in space age coating durabilities.

❼ • Placed second in national competition sponsored by American Chemical Institute's Polymers Division in new research articulation.

• Selected as one of a team of three doctoral students to continue the grant-based work of Hans Bremmer in polymer isolation.

• Dissertation entitled "Assumptive Bremmerian Polymer Attitudes Beta Testing"
❽ published as a monograph of the ACI Institute, Polymers Division.

EDUCATION

Doctor of Philosophy
❾ Theoretical Polymer Chemistry
University of Chicago, 1992

Master of Science
Chemistry
University of Chicago, 1988

Bachelor of Science
Chemistry
Ottawa University, 1986

COMMENTS

Extensive work-study experience in a variety of industry settings adds practical dimensions to my theoretical training. Upon request, references will be provided to substantiate my performance in those settings.

Child Care Worker

FOCUSED RESUME

General Strategy

Ms. Busch has a specific goal in mind that calls for presenting a rather specific set of strengths—she can do this most effectively by using the Focused Resume since it makes these qualities the central focus of her presentation. With it she is able to:

- show that she is formally trained for the position she seeks
- qualify the level of position and the setting she most values
- enumerate her five greatest strengths unencumbered by spreading them across a series of different positions
- properly establish work experience
- verify important certification and affiliation

Specific Points

❶ Legitimacy and professionalism are conveyed by her formal training at a known institution.

❷ Precisely what she seeks is noted up front—including private-sector setting that will make clear her commitment to business day care.

❸ Institutional experience separates her from home child care applicants.

❹ Directly addresses community concern with health and character.

❺ Demonstrates familiarity with child care in a variety of settings.

❻ References alluded to—essential in such a sensitive position.

❼ Work history is brief, but establishes context for strengths noted above it.

❽ Verification of required licensure.

❾ Certification of personal health and character available.

❿ Member of national association that espouses professionalism and high standards.

Lois M. Busch

672 Pocatello Drive, Apartment 78
Lewiston, ID 83501
208-333-9075 (Residence)
busch78@aol.com

EDUCATION

❶
Certificate
Child Care
Boise Community College, 1996

POSITION DESIRED

❷ Child Care Director — Private Sector

STRENGTHS

- Six years of progressively more responsible experience as a child care
paraprofessional in institutional settings. **❸**

- Established credentials verifying personal health, character, and professional
❹ status.

- Experienced in public education, private non-profit, and industry child care
❺ situations.

- Formal training in a certified public postsecondary institution.

- Proven effectiveness in working with children, parents, educators, and company
management — references available. **❻**

EXPERIENCE

❼ 2000 - Present: Assistant Director of Child Care Program, Amsel Industries,
Wilmington, ID

1998 - 2000: Child Care Aide, Main Street Methodist Church, Kinton, ID

1996 - 98: Teacher's Aide, Johnson Elementary School, Sioux, ID

COMMENTS

❽ Licensed Child Care Worker, Idaho County Board of Commissioners

❾ Health and Personal Background Certified

Member: National Association of Child Care Paraprofessionals

❿

Civil Engineer

WORK HISTORY RESUME

General Strategy

Mr. Choy is an engineer with a substantial list of substantive employment situations that fits the Work History Resume format well. With it he is able to convey that he has:

- a broad base of specific civil engineering experiences
- a long, responsible history of upward movement on a well-defined career ladder
- the appropriate formal education
- an array of career-related short courses that have kept him current

Specific Points

❶ A Summary is appropriate in a long, reasonably detailed work history. It serves to draw out important specifics for preliminary attention.

❷ In a few bulleted statements he sketches the breadth of his experience.

❸ The work history relates an unbroken chain of responsible employment from college through present position.

❹ Quantified technical and supervisory experience lets his importance be adequately appraised.

❺ Mention of successfully dealing with specific environmental problems of his industry marks him as a progressive and sensitive technical manager.

❻ Reporting relationships tend to show relative status and are important in describing your place within an organization.

❼ Being both a competent engineer and a person who can relate to government and community concerns is a plus worth mentioning.

❽ Early experience within a major federal agency vouches for an ability to deal with such institutions successfully.

❾ Verification of holding the basic educational credential of his profession.

❿ Evidence of remaining current in his field by attending specialized training over the course of a long career, offsetting a lack of graduate study.

Winston K. Choy
387 Mililani Street
Honolulu, HI 96813
808-222-9988 (Office)
808-333-9075 (Residence)
winchoy3@yahoo.com

Summary

① Civil Engineer with extensive infrastructure experience, including:

- Liaison with government and private environmental interests
- 26 years of increasingly responsible field experience
- Federal, state, and private workplace exposure
- Professional continuing education
- Significant design innovations
- Major supervisory roles

②

Experience

<u>June 1998 - Present</u>: **Senior Operating Engineer,** Hawaiian Cane Group, Inc., Honolulu, HI. Ranking civil engineer in charge of field irrigation, infrastructure, and fixtures for the number two sugar cane producer in the Islands. Supervise a staff of 129 professionals, technicians, and workers engaged in the design, installation, and maintenance of systems supporting the planting, growing, and harvesting of the crop on three islands. Directly responsible for conversion from immersion to drip irrigation resulting in savings of 32 million gallons of water per year. Developing mechanically induced, high temperature burn-off techniques to comply with EPA air pollution mandates and residential development complaints. **④**

<u>April 1991 - May 1998</u>: **Field Engineer,** Knaurhowser Timber Management Corporation, Pine Coast, NC. Led the engineering team responsible for grading, erosion, and fire control mechanics for a 300,000-acre plot of pulp and timber pines in Coastal North Carolina. Reported to Engineering Group Chief Engineer at Atlanta office. Personally responsible for maintenance and emergency response engineering for the full spectrum of plant maturities. Extensive coordination with local and federal fire resources, EPA regulators, and recreation managers. Successfully settled long-standing controversy regarding All Terrain Vehicle (ATV) use on company properties. Supervised engineering and support staff team of 74, approximately two-thirds of them professionals. **⑤**

③ <u>January 1982 - March 1991</u>: **Staff Engineer,** California Department of Highways, Palo Alto, CA. One of 47 engineers staffing the expansion of the Interstate Highway environmental impact retrofit project. Team effort in developing innovative techniques for correcting undesirable impact of initial engineering on 300 cut and fill sites, 47 bridges, and 3,492 water distribution device faults along the 4,229 coastal highway segments of California Interstate highways. Working level liaison with government and private environmental interests. Led a team of 12 civil engineers and draftsmen. **⑥**

<u>June 1980 - December 1981</u>: **Civil Engineer III,** San Mateo County Maintenance Division. Working civil engineer supporting the parks and lands division of the county property maintenance group. Participated in design and approval of contractor implemented projects involving roads and infrastructure serving the county's 398-acre park system and adjoining properties. **⑦**

<u>June 1976 - May 1980</u>: **Lieutenant, Army Corps of Engineers,** Fort Belvoir, VA. Junior engineering officer participation on coastal wetlands survey group. Ultimately merged with teams responsible for design and placement of beach erosion devices on the Outer Banks. Supervised a civilian contract construction group. **⑧**

Education

Bachelor of Science
⑨ Civil Engineering
University of East Texas, 1976

Comments

Participated in a series of applied career related short courses, including:

- 1978 - Army Corps of Engineers Advanced School for Coastal Problem Resolution, Charleston Regional Office, SC.
- 1981 - Environmental Coalition Associations Symposium, Mare Island, CA
- 1983 - Southwestern Highway Engineers Retrofit Annual, Tucson, AZ
⑩
- 1986 - Major Contractors' Annual Meeting, San Francisco, CA
- 1987 - The Environment and the Civil Engineer, Lake Louise, AL
- 1991 - Timber Management Engineers Regional Conference, Lumberton, NC
- 1998 - Agricultural Civil Engineering in the 1990s, Great Valley, CA

College Professor

FOCUSED RESUME

General Strategy

Ms. Dow is in the process of making the transition to a higher level of functioning in her present specialty—teaching history. The Focused Resume gives her the format to present her admirable work history and associated educational credentials, but, importantly, it also lets her focus on her strongest assets outside the context of the setting she wants to move from.

She focuses on her:

- objective of moving from the high school to the community college-level institution
- ability to teach history to anyone, regardless of level or ability
- scholarly productivity

Specific Points

❶ An Objective statement says in a sentence what she wants to do, at what level, and in what geographic area.

❷ Six years of teaching history are documented.

❸ Successful part-time experience teaching history at the community college level to which she aspires is demonstrated.

❹ Professionalism beyond that expected of a high school history teacher is shown—desirable traits for a college professor and apt to impress those reviewing her resume.

❺ Experience recounted in traditional work history fashion.

❻ Honors as an outstanding teacher validate her competence.

❼ Community outreach project is apt to be a well-regarded initiative at the college level where similar arrangements are valued.

❽ Adjunct position shows ability to function on college level with adults.

❾ Willingness to teach in a nontraditional setting is potentially important.

❿ Being a former community college student looks good for this position.

Cynthia M. Dow
9827 North Millwork Lane
College Park, MD 20740
240-922-9988 (Office)
240-373-9075 (Residence)
cmdow@hotmail.com

❶ Objective: To obtain a tenure-track position teaching U.S. History at the community college level in the Central Atlantic region.

Overview

❷ • Six years of teaching history at a public high school to a cross-section of different ability-level students.

❸ • Three years of teaching history at the community college level on a part-time adjunct faculty basis.

❹ • Secretary-Treasurer of the Maryland History Teachers Association and active in public outreach historical promotions.

• Published articles in *Mid-Atlantic History* in 1998 and 2000.

Experience

❺ **September 1996 - Present**: **Teacher of history,** Prince George High School, Ableville, MD. Teach U.S. History to top three sections of eleventh grade students; World History to two mid-level sections of seniors; and one section of honors students on Contemporary Policy Issues. Voted teacher of the year twice, first runner-up for ←**❻** Maryland Teacher in 1998. Co-founder of Parents, Students and Business Leaders, a community foundation that raises non-public funds to augment the school budget for special equipment and events.

❼

❽ **August 1996 - Present**: Concurrent with full-time position noted above, assumed duties as **U.S. History teacher at Johnson County Community College.** Responsible for an evening class of working young adults at the campus and a study-release class of inmates at the college's outreach campus in Stanboard Correctional Institute.

❾

Education
Master of Arts
History
University of Maryland, 1996

Bachelor of Arts
History
Johns Hopkins University, 1995

Associate in Arts
Liberal Arts
Hagerstown Junior College, 1993

325

Computer Maintenance Specialist

FOCUSED RESUME

General Strategy

Mr. Garrett's IT resume addresses a specific job and specialized kind of work so it is best structured as a Focused Resume, which helps to:

- highlight specific kinds of technical skills
- concentrate on building a logically ordered resume containing appropriate keywords since information technology (IT) resumes are generally sent by e-mail in an unembellished text format
- still create a strong core resume that is easy to adapt should aesthetics become important

Specific Points

❶ The address element includes the most practical ways to contact him. An e-mail address is probably expected, especially in an IT environment.

❷ While it isn't essential, he includes a personal Web page because it tells a more complete story than his resume. See Point **❿** for details.

❸ Immediately relates his technical expertise using keywords recognizable both to programs that evaluate them electronically and to hiring officials.

❹ Conveys both software and hardware familiarity.

❺ Work History substantiates his claims of experience and documents his progress through greater levels of responsibility.

❻ Work History accounts for continuous employment.

❼ Work History communicates the scope of his responsibilities with quantified information.

❽ Relevant part-time student employment.

❾ Professional certification is often on a par with college training in the IT field.

❿ Indicates why his personal Web page is worth examining.

GEORGE C. GARRETT ❶

7341 Vandue Range
Charleston, SC 29401
803-721-9321 • FAX 803-721-1255
GCG294@aol.com
http://14507@collegeplacement.com ❷

OBJECTIVE

Computer Maintenance Specialist working in the installation, maintenance, and support of PC networks.

TECHNICAL EXPERTISE ❸

❹
- Large PC network installation and support
- AS/400 and Novell Network qualified
- PC software integration including Windows 98, AS/400, Microsoft Office and Microsoft Exchange
- Novell experience and certification
- Demonstrated troubleshooting skills

WORK HISTORY ❺

❻ 1999-2002—<u>Computer Maintenance Specialist</u>. Fort Gordon, GA. Served as a civilian maintenance technician for the installation and support of a series of 30-station PC networks for the Army's BNCOC classrooms at a large technical ❼ training facility. Integrated Windows 98, AS/400, and a variety of other off-the-shelf and specialized software packages. Assisted instructors in modifying and operating the system to include extensive troubleshooting activities.

1997-99—<u>Computer Laboratory Assistant</u>. Student assistant working part-time installing and maintaining college instructional and administrative LAN ❽ PC under the direction of instructors and certified maintenance personnel.

EDUCATION AND CERTIFICATION

College of the Low Country, Beaufort, SC
❾ Associate of Science in Computer Studies, 1999
Novell Certified NetWare Engineer (CNE)

COMMENTS

Personal Web page includes links to work samples and links to previous employers. ❿

Computer Operator

FOCUSED RESUME

General Strategy

Ms. Paris has the training and experience to do the job, but she has been out of the workplace for several years. She will use the Focused Resume to place the emphasis on specific, enduring skills lifted from the context of her somewhat dated work history.

With this approach she focuses on her:

- ability to use either of the two best-known families of computers
- familiarity with the kinds of software most likely to be encountered in a new position
- overall quality of being a good worker in a team setting

Specific Points

❶ Since her experience is not current, she begins by documenting her basic formal preparation to do computer work—her education.

❷ Establishes the fact that the most popular computer systems are familiar.

❸ Verifies that she knows the software and can use it in either environment.

❹ Traditionally presented work history showing dates of employment.

❺ Demonstrates that she has continued to be productive using her computer skills even while not employed in a regular position.

❻ Evidence of being able to coordinate her work with those who generate the input for her computerized efforts.

❼ Experience with a larger mainframe computer is mentioned to show versatility.

❽ Ability to work in the absence of immediate on-site supervision.

❾ Demonstrates ability to do more than just operate equipment.

❿ Brief explanation of her absence from the workplace.

Elizabeth R. Paris

856 Lincoln Way, Apartment 102
New Orleans, LA 70119
504-363-9075 (Residence)
pariser@mymail.net

Education

❶

Diploma
Data Processing
Dauphine School of Business, 1993

Strengths **❷**

- Trained in the operation of both IBM and Apple Macintosh families of personal computers and peripherals.
- **❸** Experienced in word processing, desktop publishing, database management, and spreadsheet software for Windows and Macintosh operating systems.
- Task oriented, independently productive worker with the proven ability to cooperate in team efforts.

Experience

June 1996 - 1998: **Data-entry operator** working from my residence as an independent contractor to major publishers. Enter author-prepared text data into book formats using appropriate desktop publishing software on my **❺** Macintosh computer. Produced four books annually for the three year period. Excellent evaluations from authors and editors, with whom I coordinated closely. **❻**

❹ **June 1993 - May 1996**: **Computer Operator,** Middlesex County Library, Suffolk, NY. Responsible for the operation of the library's TI-5000 stand-alone computer system used in catalog maintenance, ordering, lender **❼** record keeping, and payroll. Worked under the supervision of the Data **❽** Systems Manager who oversaw similar operations in three other county office complexes. Instrumental in bringing on line the library's first CD units for user research. Assisted in obtaining a Library of Congress grant for that project.

❾ **Comments:** I left the workplace in order to be in the home during my child's early years and I now want to return to a traditional career path.

❿

Computer Programmer

WORK HISTORY RESUME

General Strategy

Ms. Leone is an entrepreneurial professional with several years of valuable experience that she wants to present to like-minded people. Since her experience is traditional, in good order, and descriptive of her talents, she appropriately elected to use the Work History Resume, although she inserted a Technical Expertise section to highlight her technical skills.

With this presentation she can:

- show what she has to offer and what she aspires to achieve
- show her technical expertise and detailed work history
- comment on her inclination toward participating in a business on a speculative basis

Specific Points

❶ Key to her presentation is the fact that she is prepared technically—has the right degree.

❷ Next she summarizes her dual experience in the manufacturing and user communities.

❸ In the Overview, she addresses her orientation toward taking a participating position in a high-tech start-up—trading talent for future profits.

❹ Highlights her technical expertise in a separate section.

❺ Describes a large applications project that she oversaw that was commercially successful.

❻ Uses quantifiable measures of her success in helping the firm make money by using applied computer capabilities.

❼ Her knowledge made a computer fit the marketplace profitably.

❽ Experience working in the national systems programming community.

❾ Bonus as verification of the value of her contributions.

❿ A brief recap of willingness to take a business risk and what she might contribute to the success of a start-up.

Raye F. Leone
8734 Woodland Avenue
Louisville, KY 40294
502-222-9988 (Office)
502-333-9075 (Residence)
rfleone@worldnet.att.net

Education

①

Bachelor of Science
Computer Science
Kentucky State College, 1991

Overview

② Six years of combined systems and applications programming experience in both the computer manufacturing industry and a major commercial user's organization. Seek stable, entrepreneurial start-up willing to trade ownership participation for exceptional technical contributions. **③**

Technical Expertise ④

- Installed and tested software and provided corrective maintenance
- New software problem diagnosis and resolution
- DBA for Oracle 7.0 on IBM mainframe running MVS/ESA
- Product customization, user support, and tuning
- Experienced in use of IBM SMP/E installation utility

Experience

June 1995 - Present: **Director of Computer Applications,** Seemans Regional Office Supplies, Louisville, KY. Assumed newly created position with major ($437 million annual sales) regional office supply firm. Tasked with computer order placement and remote technical support for a field sales force of 143 professionals covering the Southeastern U.S. Successfully acted as systems analyst, applications programmer, and **⑤** interacted with supplier systems programmers to achieve an industry recognized **⑥** breakthrough system of laptop/modem support sales. Development costs recovered in 16 months. Sales staff turnover reduced 38 percent in last year. Lost sales attributable to support lag reduced to less than 4 percent after 14 months.

June 1991- May 1995: **Systems Programmer,** Comtrack Computer Corporation, Waco, TX. Adapted existing operating systems to fit the unique needs of Comtrack's market **⑦** niche—the traveling technical sales representative. Worked in cooperation with applications programmers in the Seattle and Atlanta software markets supporting conversions of popular products to Comtrack operating systems. Created the conversion and installation systems provided with new Comtrack desktops that strengthened marketing and accounted for a substantial share of the firm's $38 million **⑧** of crossover sales last year. Consistently earned performance bonuses for outstanding contributions. **⑨**

Comments

Offer a solid base of user and manufacturer experience, excellent technical credentials, and a willingness to take reasoned business risks.

⑩

Computer Sales Representative

FOCUSED RESUME

General Strategy

Mr. Winters is just out of college, has all the right training, and some good part-time experience, but lacks a history of full-time employment. In order to show what his strengths are, he has decided to use a Focused Resume.

In this case the focus will be on:

- a college education that directly and practically prepared him for technical sales
- seasonal jobs that have already given him a start in the business
- a technical background sufficient to let him sell authoritatively

Specific Points

1 Specific college training in the technical sales specialty.

2 Identification of the technical sales market segment that he aspires to serve—small-business and personal computers.

3 Demonstrated experience in the business beyond the sales floor.

4 Seasonal sales of relevant software for a nationally franchised outlet.

5 Specific experience dealing with small-computer users as customers.

6 Hands-on technical experience in a laboratory setting—transferable skills include demonstrating computer equipment.

7 Success as a salesperson in the technical market.

8 A practical way to demonstrate link between college activities and potential success as a professional in technical sales.

9 Recognition of the career ladder and a motivation to climb it.

10 An understanding of the compensation system and subtle confidence that he will prosper under it.

Roscoe V. Winters

8037 Mahaney Avenue
Norwich, CT 06360
860-345-9075 (Residence)
rosvwin@bci.net

Education

❶ Associate in Science
Technical Merchandising
Mitchell Community College, 2002

❷ **Objective:** To obtain a technical marketing position with a major retail vendor of personal and small business computers.

Strengths

- Three summers of full-time employment in The Computer Shed, a retail computer outlet of the Systems Computing Corporation of Sunnyvale, CA. Performed **❸** backroom assembly, stock maintenance, and inventory for their line of desktop and laptop computers.
- **❹** Christmas seasonal employment as a floor sales representative at The Software Place, a nationally franchised purveyor of off-the-shelf applications software to **❺** small commercial users and individuals.
- College work-study experience as a computer laboratory assistant to the professor of data processing technology at Mitchell Community College. Spent 15 hours **❻** weekly assisting in the set-up and operation of the lab sessions in which students from non-computer disciplines learned the basics of practical computer use.
- Junior Salesperson of the Year Award 2001, Technical Magazine and Book Direct Sales Organization. Award included a $500 tuition grant and was earned by **❼** leading the Northeast region in subscription sales on behalf of the Campus **❽** Computer Users Club.

Comments

❾ Highly motivated for a career in technical merchandising with aspirations for management after acquiring experience. Planning to pursue continuing education in the related technologies. Receptive to incentive-based compensation.

Computer Systems Analyst

FOCUSED RESUME

General Strategy

Ms. Alamitos has a lot of strengths and she can demonstrate achievement, but it comes across more boldly if extracted from the four relatively brief periods of employment that constitute her work history. Her best bet is to use the Focused Resume in order to concentrate the reviewers' attention on her strong points and not make them dig it out of the several places where she acquired it.

Her correct choice of resume will present her as someone with:

- a strong educational background for being an analyst
- experience that spans several important user-group industries
- valuable familiarity with systems of great commercial potential
- a set of significant achievements as a systems analyst

Specific Points

❶ Her combination of degrees is particularly strong and worth highlighting.

❷ Overview emphasizes ideal preparation and adds her broad, if brief, experience in large-market industries—also names the position she wants in terms readily understood in her specialty.

❸ Specific industry groups and perspectives detailed.

❹ Details her technical expertise in the midst of her overall strengths.

❺ Gives practical application to her dual-track education.

❻ Award indicates success and offsets short tenure in the position.

❼ A specific project with tangible results achieved.

❽ A systems analysis case history in capsule form.

❾ Employment gives a chronology of significant positions.

❿ Summary format provides dates, but after strengths and achievements have already been made clear—instead of along with them as would have been the case in a work history resume, for example.

Louise S. Alamitos

8231 Fairway Drive
Costa Mesa, CA 92628
714-222-9988 (Office) • 714-333-9075 (Residence)
lalamit@westnet.com

Education

❶

Bachelor of Science
Business Administration
California State University, 1990

Associate in Science
Computer Sciences
Palomar Junior College, 1988

❷ **Overview:** Rigorous business training backed by technical credentials in computer sciences. Experienced in major industry segments of business systems analysis including banking, government, and manufacturing. Seek Lead Analyst position with services company catering to a cross-section of such clients.

Strengths

- Broad systems experience across the government, defense contractor, commercial and consumer banking industries.

- Perspectives of government contract review authorities, major industry bidders, and funding sources.

❹
- Installation and administration of OS/2 and UNIX/LANs with IBM architecture using TCP/IP and IPX protocols and RS6000 administration.

- Outstanding ability to extract and relate requirements to non-systems managers and decision makers.

❺
- Knowledge of computer and business fields enhances ability to convey business system requirements to computer programmers.

Achievements

❻
- Commerce Department Junior Analyst of the Year Award, 1991, for contributions to advanced industry sampling model.

❼
- RWC bonus system restructured on the basis of cost-benefit analysis conducted by my project group resulting in reallocation of 73 percent of middle-management bonus dollars.

❽
- Billing errors reduced by 39 percent and customer complaints reduced 78 percent at SuperCard after sampling-based analysis of historical problems data revealed correctable procedural errors.

Employment

❾
Senior Analyst, Card Services Division, SuperCard, Inc., San Francisco, CA, December 1995 - Present.

Systems Analyst, Bank of the West, San Diego, CA, June 1993 - November 1995.

Specifications Analyst, Rocket Weapons Corporation, Reston, VA, July 1992 - May 1993.

Junior Systems Analyst, U.S. Department of Commerce, Washington, DC, June 1990 - June 1992.

❿

Corrections Officer

WORK HISTORY RESUME

General Strategy

Mr. Gregg has a logical progression of jobs in the law enforcement and security areas that are easily described in the traditional Work History Resume format. What he has done relates directly to the particular job and this approach to describing his abilities will:

- show that he is trained for security work
- verify in specific settings that he has gained valuable experience that relates directly to his occupational objective
- convey the unique nature of his circumstances and just what he is trying to achieve

Specific Points

❶ He has formal postsecondary training at the college level in the corrections field that matches his goal directly—a strong point worthy of prominence.

❷ Since he is seeking another federal job, it is relevant to establish that he is already on the register—a part of the federal employment system.

❸ His experience as a security officer—shift supervision in a secure environment—is compatible with the corrections job he seeks.

❹ A responsible position, related to his field and indicative of good character.

❺ Jailhouse supervision is relevant and worth mentioning.

❻ Experience in prison disturbance control is also a strength to note.

❼ Honorable military service is a plus in his line of work.

❽ Guard duty, even in a diplomatic setting, has relevance for the job sought.

❾ Comments is a good place to explain his situation briefly—in case the cover letter gets separated from the resume.

❿ No concern about privacy since a change is mandated, so he correctly asks that his resume be passed along to anyone who might be able to help him.

Thomas G. Gregg
8309 Agassette Circle
Dobbs Ferry, NY 10522
914-222-9988 (Office)
914-333-9075 (Residence)
gregg8309@aol.com

Education

❶ Associate in Science
Corrections
Myrth Valley Community College, 1992

Employment **❷**

<u>June 2000 - Present</u>: Security Officer, Meredith Air Force Base, NY. GS-9
❸ position as an Air Force civilian law enforcement officer charged with
maintaining gate security. Supervise a shift consisting of six USAF enlisted
security police and two civilians.

<u>June 1996 - May 2000</u>: Deputy Sheriff, Grapevine County Sheriff's
Department, NY. Performed general duties in a mid-sized, rural law
enforcement organization. Obligations included serving court papers, crowd
❹ and traffic control, and supervision of the county jail, as one of three officers
on rotation. Augmented prison authorities in controlling major disturbance at **❺**
Northern State Prison in 1998. ← **❻**

<u>July 1992 - May 1996</u>: United States Marine Corps, Quantico, VA. Served as
an enlisted combat Marine. Left active duty as a Corporal selected for
❼ Sergeant, a rank assumed in the Reserve. Experience included two years as
an embassy security guard in Europe. **❽**

Comments: Due to the general reduction of forces occurring internationally,
Meredith AFB is scheduled for deactivation in the spring. I am interested in
❾ transitioning to a law enforcement position within a federal corrections
institution. A completed Form 171 and references are available upon request.
Please feel free to share this resume with other agencies.

❿

337

Credit Manager

WORK HISTORY RESUME

General Strategy

Mr. Masden has an array of work experiences that serve to verify his preparation for the next step on his career ladder. The Work History Resume is ideal for showcasing his steady rise in this conservative line of employment.

His resume will show that he:

- has made the necessary career steps to assume a more responsible position in the same line of work

- has a college degree and has compensated for its nonbusiness nature by taking a number of specialized courses in his occupational field

Specific Points

❶ A terse Summary is all that is needed to set the stage for his presentation, which simply says: "I'm ready for the next step."

❷ The stature of his current employer is established in order to convey his own responsibilities impressively.

❸ It is important to indicate the kinds of client companies that he has experience analyzing.

❹ Implementing systematic procedures was a specific and successful practice that he was responsible for and it is properly mentioned—with results.

❺ Even more dramatic bottom-line savings are shown by this example of his work.

❻ A brief but understandable picture of his credit analysis experience at the bank.

❼ Knowledge gained in this position has obvious value in future credit analysis roles, so that is implied in this entry.

❽ A responsible entry-level position in credit analysis.

❾ A less-than-ideal college degree is noted, but not emphasized.

❿ His strong suit is specialized training courses within the credit industry.

Edmund S. Masden

784 East Main Street
Cheyenne, WY 82009
307-222-9988 (Office)
307-333-9075 (Residence)
masdenes1@aol.com

❶

Summary: Experienced credit manager seeking growth opportunity.

Experience

❷ June 2000 - Present: Credit Manager, Watkins Wholesale Restaurant Supply, Greensboro, WY. Responsible for data collection, interviews, analysis, and credit **❸** approval recommendations for a $4.5 million annual sales wholesaler. Clients include national franchise, small start-up, and established traditional restaurants and institutions. Default rate reduced 39 percent during the second year of implementing **❹** National Credit Rating Standards procedures under my direction. Implemented Quick-Screen, a procedure for preempting poor risks without the inefficiency of **❺** extensive application and credit analysis—resulting in savings averaging $14,000 per quarter for the past 18 months.

❻ June 1996 - May 2000: Credit Analyst, Bank of Northwest Wyoming, Suffolk, WY. Worked as the main officer analyst of small business and consumer credit applications. Maintained a caseload of 45 active files per week, resolving 80 percent within that time frame. Knowledge of credit network protocols and ability to digest **❼** elaborate business plans quickly. Supported the lending efforts of six commercial and nine consumer lenders.

❽ July 1992 - May 1996: Credit Clerk, Wilcoxson Consumer Finance, North Woods, WY. Assisted the local office manager and secretary in the operation of a storefront consumer lending business. Took credit applications from walk-in clients and conducted rapid credit checks to approve high-risk/low-amount unsecured consumer loans.

Formal Education

❾ BA, Art History
Smith University, 1996

Specialized Credit Training

• 1996—Two week training session at the American Consumer Training Academy, Washington, DC, in basic credit analysis.

• 1997–98—Completed the correspondence version of the National Credit **❿** Association's Basic and Intermediate Credit Management Courses and earned their Certified Credit Manager (CCM) designation.

• 2000—Advanced Credit Analysis and Management Course, Wholesale Merchants of America, two weeks of resident and six months of correspondence learning, Chicago, IL.

Customer Service Representative

FOCUSED RESUME

General Strategy

Ms. Falls has been out of the regular workplace for many years and wants to present her assets outside the context of chronologically listed jobs. The best format for her situation is the Focused Resume because it will allow her to:

- make a pointed case for an accumulation of valuable experiences gained outside the traditional workplace
- show that she can demonstrate achievements there that are relevant to potential success in the full-time job she now seeks
- present herself as a worthwhile applicant with the motivation, training, and ability to succeed in a regular position after a long absence

Specific Points

❶ A strong Summary says it all briefly, but convincingly enough to get the reviewer to read on to the specifics of what she has to offer.

❷ Her planned transition is designed to take full advantage of current skills in telephone-based sales and services.

❸ A core of retail merchandising experience is timeless and a valuable base.

❹ Volunteer work on a local telephone hotline is relevant experience.

❺ More valuable is her home-based telemarketing of commercial services.

❻ Productivity vouched for by incentive awards.

❼ Further evidence of initiative and effectiveness as a persuasive telephone personality.

❽ Weak employment history seems less important after the relevant strengths have been extracted and sold in the preceding parts of the resume.

❾ Initiative to get a current education in merchandising is a good endorsement of attitude and potential, plus assurance that she knows the latest trends and terms.

❿ A closing word of explanation that clarifies situation and goal.

Kathleen T. Falls
3179 MacCline Street
Milwaukee, WI 53203
414-333-9075 (Residence)
kfalls3179@aol.com

Summary

(1) Woman with formal training in merchandising returning to workplace after 18 years as full-time housewife. Seeking a telephone customer service/sales representative position with a national retailer to build on base of successful, current, part-time **(2)** telemarketing experience.

Relevant Experience

- Five years as a retail clerk and department head for F. A. Olson Department Stores, **(3)** Milwaukee, WI.
- Suicide Hotline of Montgomery County telephone volunteer for six years. **(4)**
- Home-based telephone marketing person for *SignCard* of Wisconsin for 34 months **(5)** selling credit card registry, buyers club, and private club privileges to gold card holders.

Accomplishments

- Won three incentive trips during as many years in peripheral bank card services **(6)** telemarketing.
- Voted Volunteer of the Quarter for the community hotline dealing with teen suicide **(7)** potentials.

Work History

(8) 1999 - Present: Part-time telemarketing person with *SignCard* of Wisconsin, Wisconsin State Bank, Milwaukee, WI.
1984 - Present: Full-time housewife and mother with heavy involvement in community affairs.
1980 - 1984: Retail sales and department manager, F. A. Olson Department Stores, Milwaukee, WI.

(9) Education

Certificate
Merchandising
Milwaukee Community College, 2002

Comments: Never far removed from the mainstream of commercial and community activity during the raising of my family, I returned to college during the past year to ensure currency in my skills. Highly motivated to build a successful full-time telemerchandising career now that time is available. **(10)**

Database Administrator

FOCUSED RESUME

General Strategy

Ms. Hayle's IT resume addresses a specific job and specialized kind of work so it is best structured as a Focused Resume which helps to:

- highlight specific kinds of technical skills
- concentrate on building a logically ordered resume containing appropriate keywords since information technology (IT) resumes are generally sent by e-mail in an unembellished text format
- still create a strong core resume that is easy to adapt should aesthetics become important

Specific Points

1. Especially in an IT environment, an e-mail address is expected as a practical means of initial contact. It is disclosed automatically when a resume is transmitted by e-mail, but she includes it here for clarity.

2. While not essential, her personal Web page tells a more complete story than her resume and cover letter, so it can be useful to the reviewer.

3. Shows her technical experience using keywords recognizable both to programs that evaluate resumes electronically and to people who read them.

4. Experience presentation is focused on the job announcement and how she meets the employer's requirements.

5. Work History substantiates her claims of experience and documents her progress through greater levels of responsibility.

6. Work History accounts for her continuous employment since college.

7. Work History also communicates the scope of her responsibilities and includes additional keywords that respond to employer requirements.

8. Actual work in her area of professional certification is valuable.

9. Professional certification is often on a par with college training in the IT field.

10. Says why her personal Web page is worth reading.

SHELLY J. HAYLE
4419 North Main Street
Milwaukee, WI
414-484-9876 • FAX 414-484-2541
SJH@att.net
1
http://www.attpwp.13987.net
2

OBJECTIVE

Database Administrator responsibilities that include supervising data modeling and logical and physical database administration.

TECHNICAL EXPERIENCE **3**

4
- Data Warehouse design, development, and support
- Database tuning and troubleshooting
- Leadership of system development projects and LDD translations
- Informix qualified
- Novell and Oracle certification

WORK HISTORY **5**

6 1999 - 2002—<u>Database Administrator</u>. CoMax Computer Support Services, Ltd., Menomonee Falls, WI. Provided SYBASE DVA administrative support for day-to-day operations at the firm's operations center. Responsibilities specifically included passwords, database modifications, storing procedures, writing triggers, keeping error logs, creating a database, and restoring from backup. **7**

1997 - 99—<u>LAN Administrator</u>. Spectrum Services, Inc., Mequon, WI. Worked with NT Server Technology, Windows 98, and MS Office 95 applications software. Provided user support and implemented Novell NetWare and Windows NT network standards in multi-protocol and multi-server environments. **8**

EDUCATION AND CERTIFICATION

9
Marquette University, Milwaukee, WI
Bachelor of Science in Computer Studies, 1997
Novell Certified NetWare Engineer (CNE)
Oracle Certified Database Administrator (DBA)

COMMENTS

See my Web page for links to CoMax and Spectrum, sites that continue to reflect my work. **10**

Dental Assistant and Hygienist

WORK HISTORY RESUME

General Strategy

Ms. Wilkinson is applying for a paraprofessional position within a narrow, well-defined specialty. Her training and experience are nicely conveyed in the traditional Work History Resume even though her employment record is relatively brief.

Her resume will be used to:

- highlight the special educational preparation
- note her professional certification
- show a record of successfully applying her talents and defining a specialty

Specific Points

❶ Seeking quickly frames the limits of what she wants to do and where.

❷ The applied degree in dental assisting from an accredited program is a strong asset worth placing at the top of her list of qualifications.

❸ Professional certification is almost more valuable than a degree in many specialties—it constitutes approval to practice and a valued measure of job competency.

❹ Experience is very specific in this case and lends itself to point-by-point statements.

❺ Portrayal of the size and specialized nature of the practice she supports.

❻ Statement of the kinds of procedures performed is especially necessary, considering her goal.

❼ Describes how she has prepared for the specialty—vendor schools valued.

❽ The extent of her interest in advanced technology use is conveyed by mentioning the latest computer simulation and design procedures.

❾ Specific professional references are essential here and they are listed.

❿ A brief, easily understood reason for leaving is given in closing.

Cher W. Wilkinson
1123 Marshall Avenue
Shepherdstown, WV 25443
304-222-9988 (Office)
304-333-9075 (Residence)
cww1223@yahoo.com

❶ Seeking: Full-time position with an institutional dental plan or health management organization in the greater Washington area having an advanced cosmetic dentistry practice.

Education

Associate in Applied Science
❷ Dental Technology
Huntington Junior College, 1996

ADA Board Certified
❸ Cosmetic Dental Assistant (CDA)
2000

Experience

April 1998 - Present:
- Dental Assistant in a one-doctor family practice. **❺**
- In the past 18 months it grew from 10 percent to 68 percent cosmetic dentistry clients.
- Primarily bleach and bonding, with increasing attention to porcelain caps and **❻** reconstructive alterations.
- Extensive reading and attendance at vendor-sponsored workshops on the latest cosmetic dentistry assisting techniques. **❼**
- Routinely assist in acid-prep cleaning and heat finishing of final applications.
- Trained and experienced in aesthetic approximations technology and related computer modeling where CAD/CAM applications are being used in the preparation of dental prostheses. **❽**

❹

Reference: Ruth A. Flausmun, D.D.S., College Park Professional Center, Suite 305, Shepherdstown, WV 25442, 304-222-9988.

June 1996 - March 1998:
- Traditional dental assisting position in a two-doctor practice.
- Prepare materials for various treatments.
- Take and develop X-rays.
- Chair-side assistance in standard practices.
- Cleaning and scaling.

❾

Reference: William J. Schwartz, D.D.S., Johnson & Schwartz, P.C., 309 Middletown Pike, Hagerstown, MD 22501, 301-743-9099.

Comments: Present employer relocating her practice to California.

 ❿

Editor

WORK HISTORY RESUME

General Strategy

Ms. Jason has a solid record of traditional workplace experience in her profession and it can be well presented in the Work History Resume.

She uses the resume to accomplish:

- an effective Overview of her experience

- a detailed enumeration of duties in various positions

- a suitable college degree

- comments that relate her special orientation and goal

Specific Points

1 The New York address has significance in certain fields—publishing is one.

2 Her work is described sufficiently in the Overview to allow efficient screening by other professionals in her business.

3 Experience in her case is an objective detailing of times, tasks, and firms.

4 Quantification is important even in the arts—it defines level of responsibility and places achievements in a meaningful context.

5 A signal accomplishment is a strong way to end a particular job description.

6 Similarly quantified achievement portrays work in another setting.

7 Showing specific instances of measurable success strengthens credibility.

8 Verification that she performed well at the working level before entering the higher echelons of editorial work.

9 A worthy college background for an editorial career.

10 Comments frame her real objective and distinguish her for those entrepreneurial publishers she has decided to target with her resume.

Christine A. Jason
873 West 49th Street
❶ New York, NY 10019
212-222-9988 (Office)
212-333-9075 (Residence)
chrisj@hotmail.com

Overview

❷ More than a decade of successful editorial experience in trade book divisions of national and regional presses. Outstanding record of productivity in acquisitions, development, and market penetration.

❸ **Experience**

❹ <u>June 2000 - Present</u>: *Executive Editor, Business Books Division, Delconte & Sons, Inc., New York, NY.* Supervise 12 acquisitions and developmental editors and a supporting staff of 18 individuals, nine professional and nine clerical. Responsible for bringing Delconte into the modern era of published how-to-do-it books for the small business market. Increased market share by 47 percent in last 14 months. Products of this division opened airport and mass discount retailers to Delconte books where sales now account for 15 percent of the firm's gross sales. ❺

❻❼ <u>June 1996 - May 2000</u>: *Senior Editor, Bicycle Books, Inc., Irvine, CA.* Managed the acquisitions editing division of this New Age regional press generating an average of 23 new trade titles annually in the career choice and health foods niches that constitute its areas of specialization. Highly successful in efforts to identify fresh ideas among first-time authors and generate successful books using developmental editing techniques. Ratio of break-even titles increased from 2-in-3 to 7-in-8 during my tenure.

❽ <u>July 1992 - May 1996</u>: *Project Managing Editor, Multi-Title Press, Inc., New York, NY.* Worked as a developmental editor in the new author acquisitions department of the paperback trade division of the number three seller of such books nationally. Participated in the successful development of such solid national sellers as J. K. Wilson and Carol Minor Jones.

<u>June 1991 - June 1992</u>: World travel following college graduation.

❾ **Education**

Bachelor of Arts
Liberal Arts
Metropolitan University, NY, 1991

Comments: Primarily interested in acquiring participating status in a contemporary trade start-up or small house with potential for specialized growth in association with aggressive national distributor. Entrepreneurial orientation and financially positioned to consider delayed compensation for the right opportunity.

347

Electronic Engineer

COMPETENCY CLUSTER RESUME

General Strategy

Mr. VanGogh has a powerful combination of operational and research-and-development experiences that are best presented in a Competency Cluster Resume. His particular goal is to make the transition from the military to the civil aviation side of the industry and his most convincing case is made by addressing aggregates of talent valued in both sectors.

His resume is structured to show:

- solid college credentials in his specialized technical field

- specific, successful experience in three major competency areas

- achievements that would be meaningful anywhere in the industry

- a record of continuous employment in the field

- a brief statement reaffirming his objective and why it makes sense

Specific Points

❶ Address has relevance in this case since the civil aviation industry is largely found in the Seattle area—he is available without relocation expenses.

❷ College degrees clearly relate to the professional goal and establish him as a qualified applicant.

❸ Tells how he has implemented successful applications.

❹ Credible as a manager with quantified measures of his experience.

❺ Implications of familiarity with federal regulators and space technology.

❻ Important operational experience adds to technical preparation.

❼ An example of applying military knowledge to a civil aviation application.

❽ Tangible evidence of excellence in his work.

❾ A respectable work history that accounts for all time periods since college.

❿ Comments concludes his personal presentation with the goal statement.

Robert P. VanGogh
284 Chanute Lake Drive
Bellevue, WA 98009
425-222-9988 (Office)
425-333-9075 (Residence)
robvan@att.net

1

Education

Bachelor of Science
Electrical Engineering
University of Seattle, 1993

2

Master of Science
Electronic Systems Engineering
University of Seattle, 1999

Applications Experience

- Used night flying and terrain avoidance radar systems as an operational crew member flying F-15s in all weather simulated combat environments.
- Revised Huguenot calibration procedures for standardization of LanSat-based night navigation equipment on transport aircraft.

3
- Implemented total auto-pilot integration sub-sets for all J-79 systems in use, military and civilian, during the mid-1990s.

Managerial Experience

4
- Led a team of four engineers and five technicians supervising the installation of retrofit SatSys decoders on the commercial passenger fleet of Divided Airlines, Inc., over a period of 17 months.

5
- Quality assurance engineer in charge of 35 technical inspectors in the Final Phase Division of Wilson & Bell Avionics responsible for satisfying FAA mandates on all KeyStat installations.

Research and Development Experience

6
- Flew debugging missions as an EWO in F-15 aircraft for the operational testing and calibration of BV-3 Birdseye radar systems during their first all weather night tests.

7
- Master's thesis focus was an unclassified cross-talk translation of military to civilian night wind shear avoidance systems.
- Developed first solid state blind-flight ergometer with sufficient deviation tolerance to satisfy FAA and military STANBOARDS.

Achievements

8
- Twice received the USAF Commendation medal for contributions to night flying safety, first as an active-duty aviator, then as a contract engineer.
- Reduced material costs 86 percent on EWSD's crossover shear detection night goggles by implementing first industry use of SeepTAC-4 in such applications.
- Secured 14 contracts with a total value of $83 million during six years as a contractor's engineer.

Employment

9
November 2001 - Present: Senior Engineer, Wilson & Bell Avionics Corporation, Bellevue, WA.
June 1999 - October 2001: Project Engineer, Electronic Warfare Systems Division, Elliot Systems, Inc., Los Angeles, CA.
September 1998 - May 1999: Full-time graduate study.
June 1993 - August 1998: Lieutenant, United States Air Force. Electronics Warfare Officer, F-4 Phantom, Tactical Air Command.

Comments: Objective is to make the transition from aerial weapons systems applications to civil aviation. Experience and training in non-visual systems is universal to both sectors.

Emergency Medical Technician

WORK HISTORY RESUME

General Strategy

Ms. Ward is creating her resume to obtain a teaching job in the field in which she is now a practitioner. Since her employment has been in a logical career pattern and it describes her strengths well within the context of the jobs held, she is advised to use the Work History Resume format.

Her resume will feature her:

- education and certification for a specialized service
- six years of experience actually practicing her paramedical skills
- efforts to make the crossover to teaching

Specific Points

❶ The EMT associate degree is the key to her training and is featured prominently.

❷ Overview is used for the dual purpose of noting professional certification and previewing her work history.

❸ Experience accounts for all periods of time and distinguishes full- and part-time positions clearly for the reviewer.

❹ Position and job title describe her duties fully to those who know the field.

❺ Level of responsibilities within that position need further amplification that is given by noting team rank and describing duties beyond the expected.

❻ Position is self-descriptive to those familiar with the region's services.

❼ Amplification includes team size and precise mission, including breaking down categories of response.

❽ Part-time experience especially relevant since it represents the desired crossover.

❾ The award for valor adds stature in this business.

❿ Goal clarification and statement of moral commitment to the helping profession.

Dorothy L. Ward

783 Shoreline Drive
Newport News, VA 23606
757-222-9988 (Office)
757-333-9075 (Residence)
dorwar@hotmail.com

Education

Associate in Applied Science
❶ Emergency Medical Technology
Hampton Area Community College, 1996

❷ Overview

Board certified Emergency Medical Technician with six years of urban mobile trauma unit response experience.

Experience

<u>Full-time:</u>   **❹**

<u>June 2000 - Present</u>: *Emergency Medical Technician, Eastern Beach Community Rescue Team*, Eastern Beach, VA. Response vehicle team captain assigned to street duties similar to those described below, but with   **❺** approximately one-third of time devoted to dispatcher training and assistance in telephone administered trauma management.

<u>June 1996 - May 2000</u>: *Emergency Medical Technician, Woodside Fire and* **❻** **❸** *Rescue Service*, Tidewater, VA. Member of a two-person response team answering calls in a 300 square block segment of Southeast Tidewater. Emergencies attended included 34 percent vehicle accidents, 48 percent **❼** violent crime, 9 percent drug overdoses, and 9 percent routine medical emergencies such as heart attacks and illnesses.

<u>Part-time:</u>   **❽**

<u>October 1998 - Present</u>: *Instructor* of American Red Cross advanced First Aid, Cardio-Pulmonary Resuscitation (CPR), and EMT certification training at Bayside Community College during the fall and spring terms.

Comments

❾ Recipient of the Governor's Award for Lifesaving as a result of 1997 recovery and resuscitation of automobile accident drowning victim.

Reason for Leaving

Seeking a full-time teaching position where my skills and experience can be conveyed to others.

❿

Employment Counselor

COMPETENCY CLUSTER RESUME

General Strategy

Mr. Richards has mixed two types of employment—business and public. He is crafting a resume that will help him take the best of both and gain a position in the private sector that will satisfy both his love of counseling and his desire to profit. In his situation, the Competency Cluster Resume will make the strongest case by presenting his most attractive attributes apart from their somewhat restrictive settings.

His resume will describe:

- his education
- the clusters of business and counseling skills he has acquired
- how he now wants to pull them together as an executive recruiter

Specific Points

❶ The degrees show the counselor side of his assets.

❷ Objective says he is more complex than his education indicates—he has both business and counseling interests and sees how to combine them profitably.

❸ The first competency cluster to establish is business and sales—this will balance any skepticism about his being an academic not hardened to the business world.

❹ Counseling experience is put in the context of the employment marketplace.

❺ Again, a link is established between counseling and job seekers.

❻ Implication that he can bring desirable professionalism to recruiting.

❼ State licensure verified.

❽ Specialized licensure relevant to recruiting is noted.

❾ Both counseling and business experience are established by employment record.

❿ Goal expresses motivation for the change.

Perry L. Richards

891 Triad Square
Montpelier, VA 23192
804-222-9988 (Office)
804-333-9075 (Residence)
perryr891@interland.com

Education

Bachelor of Arts
Psychology
Southern University, 1996

Master of Education
Counseling
Maryland University, 2000

Objective

To apply professional training, licensure, and combined counseling/business experience to a fee-based position in a professional executive recruitment organization.

• **Business Experience**

Four years as a professional marketing representative for a major pharmaceutical firm. Interacted heavily with professional clients and business associates.

• **Counseling Experience**

Two years as a full-time counselor with the Virginia Employment Service. Counseled adults on job opportunities and assisted arranging training, interviews, the preparation of resumes, and good work practices. One of nine counselors in a rapidly expanding urban job market. Most clients were high school graduates with little technical or business training or experience.

• **Training**

Psychology degree augmented by a master's degree in educational counseling with a concentration on employment counseling.

• **Supervision**

Practicum experience in master's program consisted of 600 hours of supervision by fully certified professional counselor in an Employment Service Office. Administered in accordance with the requirements for Virginia licensure.

• **Licensure**

Licensed Professional Counselor, Virginia Board of Professional Counselors, General certification with specialization in Employment Counseling. Initially licensed in May 1998.

Certified Personnel Counselor (CPC), National Association of Personnel Consultants, Alexandria, VA.

Employment

June 2000 - Present: Employment Counselor, Virginia Employment Commission, Mount Scenario, VA.

June 1996 - May 2000: Medical Sales Representative, Lampton & Boxworth Pharmaceuticals, Inc., Baltimore, MD.

June 1996 - May 2000: Full-time graduate study.

Comments: Entrepreneurial inclination and strong interest in the private sector motivate me to adapt my counseling and occupational choice training to a career in executive recruitment. Seek commission-based incentive pay not available in institutional counseling settings.

Environmental Technician

WORK HISTORY RESUME

General Strategy

Mr. Lee has a set of experiences that conform to the positions and time periods in which they were acquired. In the absence of strong assets that would stand out as aggregate qualities, he is advised to present himself in the context of the standard Work History Resume.

His employment history will reveal:

- a candidate looking for an environmental position in the private sector
- a work history that stems from a logical beginning and progresses through contemporary environmental issues
- the basic technical education to support his professional efforts

Specific Points

❶ Introduction serves as a headline stating who he is and what he wants.

❷ Experience relates an unbroken chain of employment dating from college graduation.

❸ Current position is public, but presented in such a manner as to appeal to developers—his target job market.

❹ Specific reference is made to future residential development projects.

❺ More evidence of competency in the region's environmental concerns.

❻ Notes that his efforts have produced profit centers for his employers in the past—the test he developed continues to earn money for the consulting firm.

❼ Shows that he can think like a regulator—he has been one.

❽ Chemistry teaching is a logical springboard for environmental employment.

❾ The right degree is presented—no elaboration needed.

❿ A career value judgment is communicated in his reason-for-leaving statement—he is more comfortable in the private sector and wants to establish himself there.

Winston K. Lee
45 Harriston Boulevard
Ogden, UT 84404
801-222-9988 (Office)
801-333-9075 (Residence)
winklee@mindspring.com

❶

Introduction

Experienced environmental scientist seeking private sector position.

❸

Experience

2000 - Present   <u>Environmentalist III</u>, <u>U. S. Environmental Protection Agency,</u> Ogden Field Office, Ogden, UT. GS-13 scientist participating in an industry/river management project in North Snake Development Region. Major project management responsibilities. Benchmarks being established for luxury recreational development communities. Template analysis initiated at outset under my direction. **❹**

1996 - 2000   **❺** <u>Environmental Consultant</u>, <u>Eco-Systems Consulting Corporation</u>, Denver, CO. Consulting chemist working in conjunction with engineers on the correction of mining-related pollution problems in southern Colorado. Devised tests and neutralization procedures that are now **❻** proprietary and constitute standards in the industry.

1993 - 1996   <u>Staff Environmentalist</u>, <u>Oregon Department of Fish and Wildlife</u>, Portland, OR. One of three scientists monitoring industries for compliance with state regulations regarding the discharge of materials potentially harmful to wildlife. **❼** Visual inspection and chemical testing of suspicious effluents.

1989 - 1993   **❽** <u>Chemistry Teacher</u>, <u>Portland High School</u>, Portland, OR. Instructor of general chemistry.

❷

❾

Education

Bachelor of Science
Chemistry
Utah State University, 1989

Reason for Leaving: Desire to return to private sector employment either in a consulting capacity or as an employee of an environmentally sensitive real estate development firm.

❿

Financial Analyst

WORK HISTORY RESUME

General Strategy

Ms. Robinette has selected the Work History Resume to present her string of responsible positions in the investment management profession. With it she will attempt to convey that she:

- has the right degrees and professional certification
- currently holds one of a series of impressive positions in her field
- knows when it is time to move on

Specific Points

❶ College majors are relevant in a specialized field such as finance.

❷ Professional certification is a benchmark in institutional investment firms.

❸ Experience is presented straightforwardly with connecting dates and a full description of duties related to each position.

❹ Since her job market is national, she describes the dollar size of her present department so those unfamiliar can better judge her status.

❺ Details can be tersely presented and still say a lot within an industry group—types of clients, investment orientation, etc., quickly categorize a financial analyst.

❻ Most organizations value business development (selling) skills, so mention them.

❼ Computer literacy is essential and it is wise to verify it.

❽ Short tenure in this position is explained—references would verify.

❾ Other rather standard duties duly noted on her way up the career ladder.

❿ Comments used to communicate two important points: (1) She is realistic about heading for a more favorable economic climate, and (2) her performance as a money manager will be of interest so it is volunteered.

Darlene W. Robinette
96 Galveston Lane
Houston, TX 77071
281-222-9988 (Office)
281-333-9075 (Residence)
darrob96@overlake.com

Education

①

Bachelor of Science	Master of Business Administration
Business Administration	Finance
Smith University, 1978	University of Texas, 1989

Chartered Financial Analyst (CFA) 1994

②

Experience

④

April 1996 - Present: **Vice President & Trust Investment Officer, National Bank & Trust of Eastern Texas, Houston, TX ($1.5 billion trust department).** Senior portfolio manager in a group of six; managing both fixed and equity in collective and other funds (personal, pension, and endowment). Responsible for all fixed income funds (aprx $300 million personal/$100 million employee benefits); responsible for most equity funds (aprx $400 million personal/$20 million employee benefits); foundations and charities account for an additional $75 million. Involved in business development activities, including presentations to support new business and existing accounts—also cooperative development projects with other elements of the trust department. Handled installation of IBM-AT dedicated to investment function; computer literate and proficient with DOS, LOTUS, asset allocation programs, Microscan, LOTUS Financial, Norton Utilities, communications, and disk maintenance.

⑤

⑥

⑦

June 1995 - March 1996: **Vice President & Trust Investment Officer, United Bankshares Trust, Fort Worth, TX ($580 million trust department).** Chaired the investment committee. Lowered transaction costs 32 percent. Implemented standard investment procedures. Established a research capability and client newsletter. Brief tenure accrues to inability to adapt to the culture and lifestyle of the area.

⑧

July 1992 - May 1995: **Assistant Vice President and Trust Investment Officer, Chicago Retail Trust Bank, Chicago, IL ($250 million trust department).** Senior investment officer responsible for setting overall investment posture; conceived and implemented a new common trust fund, revised others. Organized and conducted investment conference for 200 members of the local professional community. Implemented formal procedures to control commission use and allocation. Established investment management goals, including performance measurement techniques. Wrote monthly economic/investment commentary for distribution to 300 regional bankers, government officials, corporate officers and selected clients.

⑨

Eight previous years: **Retail stockbroker,** Scott & Delmonico, Inc., Milwaukee, WI.

Comments: Reason for leaving relates to the declining economy of the region where oil, gas, and space programs show little promise in the near future. Investment performance for the past five years: 14th percentile equities; 23rd percentile fixed income; 19th percentile combined.

⑩

③

Food Technologist

FOCUSED RESUME

General Strategy

Mr. Boyd has held a series of positions in the food processing industry, but wants to stress his particular strengths rather than just describe each job. The recommended format for this is the Focused Resume.

Using this resume vehicle he will be able to focus on:

- special capabilities that he has developed that would be of value across the industry

- several substantial achievements

- an overall work history into which these highlights logically fit

Specific Points

❶ The ideal degree for his specialty is noted.

❷ Professional certification is valuable—often can offset graduate study.

❸ Overview states what he has to offer—stresses production and R&D.

❹ Capabilities states aggregate skills that might get lost when spread across the several jobs in which they were acquired.

❺ Familiarity and success in dealing with government in this regulated industry.

❻ Language capability important in this business.

❼ Sensitivity to marketing concerns is an asset as he aspires to higher, more general management positions.

❽ Specific evidence of excellence and quantified, verifiable savings are strong points.

❾ Had a team-member role in establishing an industry standard—mention it.

❿ The work history stands alone, now that the strengths have been extracted and presented with emphasis in their own right.

Donald C. Boyd
78 Overton Way
Memphis, TN 38112
901-222-9988 (Office)
901-333-9075 (Residence)
dboyd@erols.com

Education

(1) Bachelor of Science
Food Technology
East Memphis University, 1993

(2) Certified Food Technologist (CFT)
1996

(3) **Overview:** Nine years of progressively more responsible food processing industry positions involving both production and research and development.

(4) Capabilities

(5) • Experienced in FDA-based texture and temperature testing technology as it applies to juice, convenience meals, and bulk vegetable preparation.

(6) • Supervision of processing personnel and team leaders—native language capabilities in Spanish.

(7) • Participation in sales, advertising, and marketing research—included regular consultation with ad agency personnel regarding verifiable claims of nutritional content and taste validity.

Achievements

(8) • Recipient of the 1997 Golden Platter Award from the Convenience Food Marketing Association for excellence in technical support consultation.

• Top bonus award 1994 earned for equipment selection recommendations that resulted in savings of $138,000 over previous year's operations due to 24 percent reduction in contract staff maintenance costs.

(9) • Member of a three-person team credited with the 2001 discovery of the frozen gravy stabilization technique (FGST) now the standard of the convenience food industry.

Employment

November 2000 - Present: Food Chemist, Dinner Time Frozen Foods, Memphis, TN.

January 1996 - October 2000: Production Supervisor, Minuterite Natural Juices, Inc., Ocala, FL.

(10) July 1993 - December 1995: Junior Food Chemist, King of Vegetables Processors, Salinas, CA.

Fund Raiser

FOCUSED RESUME

General Strategy

Mr. Oden is a private fund raiser for private colleges. He uses a resume to make his services known and to present his firm for consideration as the institutions select those who will assist them in the coming year. His employment record is relevant, but this specialized need is best met by the Focused Resume.

The resume will focus attention on:

- his own prestigious college background
- the style of his work, as much as its substance
- respectability by association

Specific Points

❶ The Yale degree constitutes instant endorsement for his work and is featured prominently as is his most appropriate major in marketing.

❷ Summary says what he does, with whom, and for how long.

❸ Dollars and cents results couched in tasteful terms.

❹ The promise of a commercial quality campaign that won't look that way.

❺ Clients identify and classify the practitioner in this business.

❻ Employment history is given a classier name with the implication that he has been more than a mere employee.

❼ His own firm is identified—little description needed here since the whole resume is focused on defining that image.

❽ A campus development (fund raising) position adds to credibility.

❾ Five years in big-time advertising circles brings commercial respectability.

❿ The solicitation itself is tastefully and briefly held for last. Cover letter also amplifies the purpose of this communication—to seek additional clients.

Ronald P. Oden
43 Aiken Avenue
Charleston, SC 29403
803-222-9988 (Office)
803-333-9075 (Residence)
rpoden@mindspring.com

Education

❶ Bachelor of Science
Marketing
Yale University, 1987

❷ Summary: Experienced marketing professional with six years of outstanding performance as an institutional fund raiser in the private college sector.

Performance Characteristics

❸
- Ambitiously realistic goal setting with institutional leaders and mentors.
- Alumni participation rates consistently exceed industry standards by 25 percent or more.
- Noted for tastefully conducted, professional campaign with the impact of a commercial promotion, the feel of a traditional appeal. **❹**
- Goals consistently exceeded by an average of 15 percent.

Current Client List

❺ Alverno College, Texas
Asbury College, Maine
Bard University, New Mexico
Defiant College, Kentucky
Hope University, South Carolina
Rockhurst Academy, Michigan
Sacred Dominican University, Indiana
Whitman College, California

Present and Prior Affiliations

❻ 1996 - Present: President and Chief Executive Officer, Ronald P. Oden and Associates, Ltd., Charleston, SC. **❼**
Consultants to the annual giving and special project financing of private institutions of higher education nationally.

1993 - 1996: Director of Development, Witherspoon College, NH. **❽**

1988 - 1993: Associate, The John Melon Krumpright Agency, New York, NY. **❾**

Comments: Currently accepting invitations for proposals for the 2002–2003 college giving year. I would welcome the opportunity to consider your needs.

❿

Graphic Designer

COMPETENCY CLUSTER RESUME

General Strategy

Ms. Lyle is a graphic artist with a continuous work history, but she is more interested in establishing an array of special competencies. The way to do that is to use the Competency Cluster Resume in which the skills gained in several settings are pulled together and presented as one.

This resume will be directed toward:

- identifying her as a technologically up-to-the-minute artist
- establishing her solid foundation in traditional settings
- pulling it all together around the right awards, credentials, and past affiliations

Specific Points

1 Since she has the equipment and graphic art is her field, a modest amount of style is added to the resume with lines and unusual typefaces.

2 Competencies establishes her three main skill areas.

3 Computer graphics is highlighted, since it is a highly marketable specialty. Demonstrating familiarity with Internet applications is particularly desirable.

4 Enough technical jargon is used to communicate understanding.

5 No computer-capable graphic artist would be complete without desktop publishing credentials, so they are established.

6 Confirmation that all the technology is underwritten by the skills of a basic artist.

7 Awards selected to show across-the-board excellence.

8 Employment history is continuous and correct.

9 Her degree is the right one and from a respected institution.

10 Comments clarifies what she is out to accomplish with her career move.

①

Patricia D. Lyle
51-C Mount Pleasant Drive
Providence, RI 02908
401-222-9988 (Office)
401-333-9075 (Residence)
patlyle@aol.com

②

∘ Competencies ∘

Computer Graphics
③

Color and B&W graphics capabilities using Aldus Freehand on the Power Macintosh G3 computer system. Experienced in using both text and graphic scanners. Preparation of products using PhotoGrade and FinePrint technologies for photorealistic images and text. Expert at trace modification art and logo design. Expert user of Adobe Systems' Page Mill 2.0 HTML editor and associated Web-authoring software. **④**

Desktop Publishing
⑤

Oversized Radius screen used for layout of single illustration and multipage publications with desktop publishing software, principally PageMaker. Experienced in brochure, tabloid, magazine, and newspaper layout—expert integration of graphics, including photography.

Drawing Board Artist
⑥

Nine years of combined college and commercial experience. Began as illustrator and paste-up person for university publications. Followed by three years of newspaper and two years of national magazine advertising and story art.

⑦ ∘ Awards ∘

- *Computer Monthly Magazine,* 2001 First Place Award for Commercial Graphics
- The New England Gazette Syndicate, 1998 Award for Excellence in Advertising Graphics
- Numerous collegiate graphic arts and journalism awards.

∘ Employment ∘

⑧
<u>2000 - Date</u>: Senior Graphic Artist, *Rhode Island Weekends Magazine,* Providence, RI.
<u>1998 - 2000</u>: Paste-up and Insertion Technician, *The Providence Daily,* Providence, RI.
<u>1996 - 1998</u>: Freelance Artist/Photographer

⑨ ∘ Education ∘

Bachelor of Arts
Commercial Design
Rhode Island College of Design, 1996

∘ Comments ∘

⑩ Interested in taking combined artistic, journalistic, and commercial experience and applying it in a computer-equipped graphic arts studio.

Heating, Air Conditioning, and Refrigeration Mechanic

FOCUSED RESUME

General Strategy

Mr. Blackwell is a recent technical graduate who needs to emphasize his strengths independent of a traditional employment listing. His best choice is the Focused Resume, which will allow him to:

- highlight his excellent technical education
- show that he has had significant work experience, if not regular jobs
- indicate that he has excelled in several categories that have relevance for occupational success

Specific Points

❶ The right degree for his specialty from a respected local junior college.

❷ Introduction establishes him as a properly prepared recent graduate with references ready to vouch for his potential.

❸ In the absence of a full-time work history, the resume properly focuses on academic preparation, experience related to training, and evidence of excellence—awards.

❹ In his urban market, the specialized skills can be attractive to a large firm.

❺ Summer work with a respected firm adds credibility and potential references.

❻ Evidence of ability to deal with older equipment as well as the most modern.

❼ Work-study experience provided experience and showed initiative.

❽ Quantification of the situation helps others judge its relevance to them.

❾ Awards provide unbiased endorsement of excellence and promise.

❿ Note shows awareness of the next steps to take professionally and the fact that they are being actively pursued.

Harold S. Blackwell
45 Cheney Creek Road
Philadelphia, PA 19153
215-333-9075
blackwell45@att.net

Education

① Associate in Applied Science
Heating, Air Conditioning, and Refrigeration Technology
Philadelphia Junior College, 2002

② **Introduction:** Recent graduate with up-to-the-minute technical training and work-study experiences with latest commercial and institutional cooling and heating units. Excellent trade and academic references available. Seek growth opportunity in my field.

③

Academic Preparation
- Completed a two-year, 90 quarter hour, Heating & Cooling Institute accredited course of study concentrating on commercial and institutional installations.
- **④** Specializations included plant failure diagnostics, passive heat loss control, and third generation heat pump installation and maintenance.

Work Experience
- **⑤** Two summers of full-time employment with Jones & Whitman Engineering, Inc., installing new heating and air conditioning plants in commercial buildings. Last three weeks of each summer spent servicing, in preparation for the heating season, existing heating systems ranging in age from new to 20 years. **⑥**
- **⑦** 17 hours weekly college work-study experience with the maintenance department of Philadelphia Junior College District. Assisted in the maintenance of four separate heating, air conditioning and refrigeration systems serving the 327,000 square foot facility.

⑧

Awards
- **⑨** Quail Industries Student Trouble-Shooter of the Year Award for 2002, presented at their annual meeting in Washington, DC.
- Honors Graduate, Philadelphia Junior College, Technical Division, 2002

Note: Currently pursuing National Association of Heating, Air Conditioning, and Refrigeration Technicians' professional certification. Anticipate having the Certified NAHACRT designation in minimum time following three years of qualifying full-time work experience and supervision. **⑩**

Hospital Administrator

WORK HISTORY RESUME

General Strategy

Ms. Munford has held only two full-time positions, but they are sufficiently well defined to describe her capabilities and accomplishments. She has selected the Work History Resume in order to show:

- the right degrees for a career in hospital administration
- solid, successful experience in the number-two slot at a major hospital
- prior experience that adds to her credibility in managing resources

Specific Points

❶ The undergraduate degree in business administration would be adequate.

❷ Add a master's degree in hospital administration and you have a combination worthy of leading the resume.

❸ Overview tells the reviewer what is to come and the presenter's objective.

❹ Employment History is brief, but totally relevant—also accounts for all dates.

❺ Position is clarified beyond title to show full responsibilities.

❻ The institution is described to convey the scope of what she manages.

❼ Strength in hospital personnel management is verified.

❽ Familiarity with hospital accreditation is noted.

❾ Since it is highly relevant, military experience is detailed.

❿ Commendation for excellent performance is worth noting.

Dea S. Munford
84 Newburg Avenue
Eugene, OR 97405
541-222-9988 (Office)
541-333-9075 (Residence)
deamun@erols.com

Education

❶
Bachelor of Science
Business Administration
Smithson University, Oregon 1992

❷
Master of Science
Hospital Administration
Oregon State University 1997

❸ **Overview:** Experienced administrative officer with nearly ten years of institutional finance and personnel management experience, five of them in a hospital setting. Desires to assume chief hospital administrator position in a mid-size urban institution.

❹ Employment History

❺ 1997 - Date: *Assistant General Administrator,* Eugene Memorial Hospital, Eugene, OR. • Second ranking administrative officer in a 375-bed, 84-doctor general care facility serving a suburban population of 123,000 residents. **❻** • Manage a budget of $22 million annually. • Responsible for staff liaison **❼** and labor contracting. • Major role in rate negotiations with insurance carriers. • Designated coordinator of combined annual giving and community volunteer program. • Achieved outstanding results in all areas including: 38 percent reduction in nursing staff turnover, contracts maintained within CPI guidelines, and hospital restored to full accreditation after two years of probation.
❽

1996 - 1997: Full-time graduate study.

❾ 1992 - 1996: *Personnel and Finance Officer,* United States Navy, Norfolk and San Diego. • Officer in charge of personnel and financial records management for carrier squadrons nine and 37 out of the ports of Norfolk and San Diego. • Accountable to senior managers and commanders for a biweekly payroll of $678,000. • All personnel records maintained according to Navy regulations. • Navy Commendation Medal awarded upon change of **❿** command and return to inactive reserve status.

Hotel Manager

WORK HISTORY RESUME

General Strategy

Mr. Brown has pursued the expected career ladder and each position provides a forum for his accomplishments at that level. His choice of the Work History Resume is a correct one.

The resume will be structured to show:

- a degree directly related to the job pursued
- a career path that moves logically from entry level to management
- an explanation of why he wants to make a career move now

Specific Points

1 Hotel management degree from Cornell is worth featuring.

2 Introduction notes length and level of service in the industry.

3 Experience is a textbook example of upward mobility in the hospitality industry.

4 Clarification of reporting authority within the organization and the nature of the property managed are both important in establishing his level.

5 Verifiable measure of excellence noted.

6 Quantified depiction of the property and his role in its management are needed.

7 Success in managing a specialized profit center is worthy of note.

8 Valuable to demonstrate success in a turnaround situation—even at this less-than-comprehensive management level.

9 States what it would take to entice him to move on.

10 Shows that he is continuing to build his industry credentials.

Darrell T. Brown
763 Boone Street, NW
Norman, OK 73070
405-222-9988 (Office)
405-333-9075 (Residence)
dtbrown@interland.com

Education

Bachelor of Science
Hotel Management
❶ Cornell University, 1994

❷ Introduction: Nine years of successful experience in positions of growing management responsibility in commercial chain hotels catering to up-scale business travelers in the continental United States.

❸ Experience

2000 - Present **❹** Manager, Hildome Resident Business Suites, Norman, OK. Site Manager responsible to a Regional Manager for the complete operation of a 214-unit suites-only business travel facility near the university research park. Supervise a food and beverage manager and housekeeping manager in addition to contract grounds maintenance services and security. Led the region past three quarters in ratio analysis profitability. **❺**

1997 - 2000 Assistant Manager, Airport Inns of America, O'Hare International Airport, Chicago, IL. Reported to the General Manager while **❻** serving as the second in charge of the total management of this 387-room middle market business traveler's airport hotel. Special **❼** duties included group and convention sales staff supervision. An area in which O'Hare achieved a 500 percent increase in bookings during my tenure.

1994 - 1997 Food and Beverage Manager, Lakeside Inn and Conference Center, Avalon Lake, NY. Assumed management of a failing restaurant, conference, and room service operation in this 277-room **❽** business resort facility and turned it into a profit center in 17 months. Converted kitchen from traditional preparation to local chef's entree supplemented by top quality prepared supporting products. Reduced staff by 65 percent, reinvested proceeds in upgrading chef and investing in state-of-the-art high-intensity cooking facilities.

❾ Comments: Reason for leaving—To pursue multiple unit, regional management responsibilities with a major national business property. Continuing Education— Enrolled in the final section of the Hotel Managers Institute remote learning series leading to designation as a Certified Hotel General Manager (CHGM). Completion expected next summer. **❿**

Insurance Agent

WORK HISTORY RESUME

General Strategy

Mr. McClay has moved successfully and profitably up the insurance sales career ladder. The jobs he has held are perfect devices for displaying his talents and the nature of his accomplishments. He is well advised to present himself on the strength of his professional positions arrayed in a standard Work History Resume.

His resume will be used to:

- show a logical insurance career path
- classify himself as a successful group sales agent
- state his objective of achieving participating status in an agency

Specific Points

❶ Overview is used to identify his segment of the industry.

❷ His objective of becoming a business partner in an agency is also noted up front.

❸ Experience is arrayed to show movement in timely fashion from individual sales to major group sales.

❹ His present position is described in the terms of the industry.

❺ Ability to train and manage other agents is an attractive partner quality.

❻ Results that can be shown in profit-generating numbers are impressive.

❼ Another successful group sales situation is described quantitatively.

❽ Clients and products are described and measures of success noted.

❾ Power as a one-on-one salesman is always worth establishing, as are the basic certifications of the industry and the fact that they have been achieved.

❿ The college degree is a basic credential worth noting—nothing to stress.

Robert J. McClay

12-F Devils Lake Avenue
Columbus, OH 43209
614-222-9988 (Office)
614-333-9075 (Residence)
robmccla@usa.net

❶ Overview: Twelve years of successful group sales with life and health products of a single underwriter in the institutional non-profit segment of the market. Seeking partnership interest in an agency engaged in these aspects of insurance marketing. **❷**

Experience

June 2000 - Present: *Senior Group Sales Agent,* The Haas Agency, **❹**
Suite 300, Embassy Square, Columbus, OH. Manager in charge of four salespersons concentrating on the colleges in North Central Ohio and Western Pennsylvania. Duties include training and motivation for those under **❺** my supervision and sales presentations to principal client institutions. 1998 revenues for my segment exceeded 1997 by 300 percent. New accounts ←**❻** added in 37 colleges and universities previously serviced by national firms.

❸

June 1996 - May 2000: *Group Sales Representative,* Wilcox & Wilson Insurance Agency, Inc., One South River Front Road, Columbus, OH. Lead group sales representative for the number one volume firm for non-profits in Columbus. Served hospitals, professional organizations, and governmental **❼** entities within a 50-mile radius of Columbus with life and health packages. Multi-Million Dollar Roundtable member 1994 through 1997, logging higher combined sales than all but 17 other similarly situated agents in the Eastern **❽** United States.

July 1990 - May 1996: *Agent,* Ohio Life and Casualty, Cleveland, OH. Sale of individual life and casualty products to professional clients in the greater Cleveland market. Exceeded company production records for a new hire **❾** agent in 13 months and opted to enter their group sales division where I remained until 1996, learned the business and earned all relevant professional licenses, certifications, and designations.

Education

❿ Bachelor of Arts
Liberal Arts
Clarkson University, Pennsylvania, 1990

Interior Designer

FOCUSED RESUME

General Strategy

Mr. Gilbert has done some things that make him attractive as a decorator and they are best viewed when pulled together from their separate occupational experience sources. To do this he has correctly selected the Focused Resume format.

His resume will have the objective of focusing the reviewer's attention on those several qualities and experiences that constitute his main assets:

- academic credentials appropriate to his field
- urban experience
- commercially successful accomplishments in various settings

Specific Points

❶ A traditional college program in the arts is offered as a basic credential.

❷ Specialized training in a recognized design institution adds an important dimension.

❸ Strengths all cater to the large urban market to which he again aspires.

❹ Points out the power combination of training he possesses.

❺ Experience is confirmed in accepted settings and situations.

❻ Accomplishments show that he is commercially successful.

❼ Versatility is evidenced in a range of projects that reach from an institutional setting to a piece of commercial equipment to a prestigious home.

❽ Magazine article recognition is important endorsement.

❾ Work chronology is necessary, but requires no elaboration beyond that given above.

❿ Comments describe desire to return to urban market.

Thomas K. Gilbert

32 Bismark Drive, NW
Minot, ND 58701
701-222-9988 (Office)
701-333-9075 (Residence)
thom32@aol.com

Goal: To obtain a decorator's position with an established urban interior design studio.

Education

❶ Bachelor of Arts
Art History
Smith University, 1986

❷ Certificate
Interior Design
New York School of Design, 1990

❸ Strengths

❹
- Educated in the classical art tradition, yet specifically trained in the practical aspects of the contemporary design industry.

- Two years of full-time experience with the commercial design firm of Winston Interiors, Ltd., New York.

❺
- One year of teaching and working as a freelance interior designer with residential clients in an urban setting.

- Three years of part-time commercial design work on referral basis while a full-time student at the New York School of Design.

❻ Accomplishments

- Redesigned the Minot Air Force Base Officers Club which subsequently won the 1992 Air Combat Command Award for Non-Appropriated Funds Facilities Improvement.

❼
- Credited with the selection of colors and textures used in the bulkhead tapestries for the new Trumpet Shuttle 727D airliners while a Winston Associate in 1991.

- Residential design of the William S. Reed apartment in New York, done on a free-lance basis while a student, featured in *NY Apartment Living Magazine,* June 1987.

Chronology ❽

1991 - Present: Self-employed interior designer, Minot, ND.
1990 - 1991: Commercial Design Associate, Winston Interiors, Ltd., New York.
1987 - 1990: Full-time student in interior design, New York.
1986 - 1987: Teacher of Art History, Darien Saints Preparatory School, Darien, CT.

❾

Comments: After returning to small town environment and opening my own studio, am convinced that the best opportunity to reach my potential is in the city.

Internet Security Engineer

FOCUSED RESUME

General Strategy

Mr. Wagoner's IT resume addresses a specific job and specialized kind of work so it is best structured as a Focused Resume which helps to:

- highlight specific kinds of technical skills
- concentrate on building a logically ordered resume containing appropriate keywords since information technology (IT) resumes are generally sent by e-mail in an unembellished text format
- still create a strong core resume that is easy to adapt should aesthetics become important

Specific Points

❶ An e-mail address is expected; a personal Web page is optional. He includes it because it adds to information already available in his resume and cover letter.

❷ Because the position involves managing or interacting with others, he acknowledges nontechnical skills and expectations in his overview.

❸ Shows his technical experience first using keywords recognizable both to programs that will evaluate his resume electronically and to people who will read it.

❹ The experience section focuses on the job announcement and matches his preparation to the employer's requirements.

❺ Work History substantiates claims of his experience and documents his progress through greater levels of responsibility.

❻ Work History accounts for continuous employment from graduation through his current position.

❼ Work History also communicates the scope of his responsibilities and includes additional keywords that respond to employer requirements.

❽ Work experience in your area of professional certification is flagged.

❾ Paints word pictures of his work environments that show the scope of his responsibilities.

❿ Professional certification is on a par with college training in the IT field.

LAWRENCE A. WAGONER
117 Sheridan Drive
Menomonee Falls, WI 53051
414-552-0336 • FAX 414-522-2851
lawagoner@nucleus.com
http://www.conceptlaw@nucleus.net

OBJECTIVE

Internet Security Engineer position with responsibilities for design, consultation, and integration efforts supporting new security capabilities for commercial Internet services.

TECHNICAL EXPERTISE

- Eight years of programming and design experience
- Understanding of security architecture design for the Internet
- Knowledgeable of public key cryptography and infrastructure, digital certificates, single sign on, S/MIME, SSL using mutual authentication and Virtual Private Networks
- Implementation of cryptographic solutions
- Experience with LDAPv3, direct services, SSL hardware, SET, CORBA/IIOP, UNIX, NT, and PKSC.

WORK HISTORY

1998-2002—<u>Internet Security Engineer</u>. GenCo Information Services, Milwaukee, WI. Hands-on management experience with Internet security and IP networks. Managed firewalls, conducted IP network threat analysis and implemented protection strategies. Used DES MD5, IPSEC, TCP/IP Perl and Unix. Extensive familiarity with distributed systems and IP sockets.

1995-98—<u>WebMaster/Web Engineer</u>. Micro Modeling Technologies, Inc., Waukesha, WI. Oversaw technical and maintenance requirements for the company's Web sites. Responsible for the day-to-day operation of the server (MS and Netscape), monitoring performance, usage statistics and log files, adjusting configuration settings, and as-needed backing up the system. Handled Web site security to include permissions. Worked extensively with authoring tools, image editing utilities, templates, style sheets, CGI scripts, and publishing back-end DB information on the Web.

1992-95—<u>Programmer/Analyst</u>. E. F. Thomas, Companies, Ltd., Elkhorn, WI. Hands-on development experience using C, C++, SL, Oracle, UNIX. Internet development experience in a client/server environment. Implemented software development methodologies and relational database concept.

EDUCATION AND CERTIFICATION

- Marquette University, WI: Master of Science, Information Systems, 1992
  Bachelor of Science in Computer Studies, 1990
- Oracle Certified Database Administrator (DBA)
- Novell Certified NetWare Engineer (CNE)

Landscape Architect

WORK HISTORY RESUME

General Strategy

Ms. McGee has a very straightforward presentation to make that involves two periods of employment that directly represent her skills and interests. For that objective, nothing is better suited than the Work History Resume.

She will rely on her resume to:

- communicate her basic education and experience

- recount specific projects that speak to her ability to handle both the technical and public relations work associated with the position she seeks

Specific Points

❶ Landscape architecture is the ideal degree and worthy of prominence in this brief resume.

❷ The Objective is used to identify a specific position for which she is applying.

❸ Experience is brief and pointed since it is directed toward a specific objective.

❹ Present position title endorses her as a player in the local restoration community.

❺ Her public position will not be that different from the proposed foundation position she seeks, so the comparison is appropriate.

❻ Among her present duties are two that will attract attention in the resume screening process: A successful role in articulating a restoration's outcome on the Internet, and the ability to relate to the commercial sector of her nonprofit industry.

❼ Experience obtaining grant money is going to be an attractive quality.

❽ Commercial developers will be involved in the Lowlands project and this shows she is familiar with how they work.

❾ Specific roles in community development will be valuable.

❿ Ability to work with community and government groups will be essential, so it is worth providing evidence that she can do this.

Wanda H. McGee

87 New Bern Road
Greenville, NC 27858
252-222-9988 (Office)
252-333-9075 (Residence)
wanda87@mindspring.com

Education

❶

Bachelor of Science
Landscape Architecture
South Carolina University, 1996

❷ **Objective**: Applying for the position of Landscape Architect II with the Historic Lowlands Foundation, Charleston, SC.

❸ Experience

❺ May 1999 - Present: *Resident Landscape Architect*
Old Town Historical Society, Greenville, SC. **❹**

❻
- Report to the City Manager and responsible for the design and management of public green spaces within Greenville.
- Close working relationship with Park Authority, Department of Highways, and other agencies impacting the green spaces.
- Coordinated park restoration project which involved excavation and reestablishment of a historic garden in downtown district.
- Provided technical and cost estimate support for local resident drive to save the vintage peach trees lining Woodrow Marsh Avenue in suburban Greenville. **❼**
- Secured federal grant for the study of requirements and funding needed for the restoration of Meeting Square Gardens, private residential plots adjoining the town square.
- Coordinated with the city's Web page designer in adding an award-winning historic landscape feature which was hyperlinked by travel agencies and prominent landscape firms serving the restoration industry.

June 1996 - April 1999: *Architectural Design Assistant-Exterior*
Bantum Development Company, Atlanta, GA. **❽**

❾
- Layout and specifications designer for major developer in the greater Atlanta area.
- Reported to the Chief Landscape Architect and responded to requests for assistance with land treatments beyond the walls of project structures.
- Liaison with community and government environmental and preservation groups.

❿

Legal Assistant

COMPETENCY CLUSTER RESUME

General Strategy

Ms. DeMagio has an acceptable, but undistinguished work history. It will make a stronger presentation if her competencies are extracted and showcased instead of her jobs. To do that she will use the Competency Cluster Resume.

In making the most of her skills, she will use her resume to:

- show that she can prepare all sorts of materials for legal cases
- demonstrate that she can prepare individual and corporate legal documents

Specific Points

❶ The starting point for her paralegal resume is an associate degree in the field.

❷ Competencies constitutes a three-item summary with supporting detail.

❸ All of the basic skills of paralegal case preparation are acknowledged here.

❹ Affidavit taking can constitute a specialty in its own right.

❺ Document preparation is a mainstay of the paralegal, so it is supported here.

❻ Depending on the concentration of the hiring firm, it may be more important to have corporate skills, so they are developed separately.

❼ The employment history shows steady, relevant employment.

❽ Both corporate and institutional experience are available, so they are cited.

❾ Private-practice experience still represents a large segment of the potential employers, so it is covered separately.

❿ Professionalism is shown by the appropriate affiliations.

Joanne G. DeMagio
7-B Flushing Drive
Plattsburgh, NY 12903
518-222-9988 (Office)
518-333-9075 (Residence)
jodemagio@aol.com

Education

❶

Associate in Science
Paralegal Technology
Junior College of Staten Island, 1996

Competencies

❷

Case Preparation

❸
- Background work for cases pending before the courts.
- Researched appropriate laws, judicial decisions and drafted written opinions.
- Prepared preliminary arguments and pleadings.
- Obtained affidavits. ← ❹

Document Preparation

❺
- Prepared draft contracts, mortgages, separation agreements, tax returns, estate and trust instruments.

Corporate Support

❻
- Assisted in preparing employment applications, contracts, shareholder agreements, employee benefit plans, loan documents, and annual financial reports.

Employment History

❼

June 2000 - Present: Legal Assistant, The Kilgore Corporation, Plattsburgh, NY. ❽

June 1996 - May 2000: Legal Aide, Trust Company of Northwest New York, Irvington, NY.

May 1996 - December 1997: Legal Technician, Joseph, Joseph, and Wilkins, Attorneys at Law, Ithaca, NY. ❾

Professional Memberships

National Association of Legal Assistants
State Bar Association, Legal Assistants Division

❿

Library Technician

COMPETENCY CLUSTER RESUME

General Strategy

Mr. Warden is a recent liberal arts graduate at the associate degree level. His challenge is to portray himself as what he legitimately is—a rather well-trained library technician. With neither the degree title or full-time work experience to support his claim, he is well advised to present himself in the context of a Competency Cluster Resume that can:

- highlight his various less-than-formal, but valuable library experiences
- explain that his degree is more than it appears to be

Specific Points

❶ With no full-time position, it would be inappropriate to list an office phone.

❷ Experience is arranged in such a manner as to show two strong clusters of highly relevant library experience.

❸ One dimension is the technical services area addressed here.

❹ Specific experience includes the latest technology—CD-ROM disk.

❺ Experienced in the clerical aspects of library work.

❻ Further evidence of involvement with library technology.

❼ The second major cluster is user services, developed here.

❽ Examples include both front desk and telephone work assisting the public.

❾ Degree is noted and clarified effectively with verification offered.

❿ Professional affiliation is useful even at the entry level.

Barry W. Warden

98 Levermour Street
Las Cruces, NM 88004
505-333-9075 (Residence)
barryww@att.net ❶

❷ Experience

TECHNICAL SERVICES ❸

❹ • Assisted faculty and students in the use of the library's newly installed CD-ROM databases for card catalog, periodicals and newspapers.

❺ • Prepared documents for shipment to microfilm copying service.

• Validated information requests for technical research.

❻ • Participated in the conversion of library catalog holdings to electronic media.

USER SERVICES ❼

❽ • Manned New Mexico Library Consortium Hotline as a volunteer responding to statewide inquiries about library use and resources.

• Work-study desk clerk 20 hours per week at the college library for two years of full-time study.

Education

❾ Associate in Arts
Portales Community College, 2002

Comments

Degree in library technology not approved at Portales Community College, but took a concentration of 15 semester hours in related courses. See college transcript for verification and specifics.

❿ Professional Affiliation

Associate Member: American Library Association

Manufacturers' Sales Representative

COMPETENCY CLUSTER RESUME

General Strategy

Ms. Black is an engineer and a salesperson. Her objective is to convey both technical competency and the ability to sell this class of products and services. Since only one of her three positions deals with sales, she has correctly elected to present herself in the framework of the Competency Cluster Resume.

Her use of the resume is to:

- demonstrate field sales competency with technical clients
- show familiarity with the field and manufacturing aspects of her product line
- establish credibility as a serious sales professional

Specific Points

❶ Since she is seeking a sales rep position, her address may have some relevance—in this case it is a good jumping-off point for working her desired territory.

❷ Overview tells the story of her dual experiences and her objective of joining an appropriate manufacturers' rep agency.

❸ Competencies is used as a heading to highlight her three areas of greatest strength.

❹ Technical selling is the lead item since it points directly to what she seeks.

❺ Knowledge of codes, estimating, and field sales support technology are rightly stressed.

❻ This item establishes that she can relate to customers—she's been there.

❼ She knows the product line from the manufacturing perspective—strong selling point in the field.

❽ Employment history covers all that is necessary to say—emphasis has already been placed earlier in the resume.

❾ Appropriate technical degree noted.

❿ Affiliations reflect commitment to professional sales career.

Frances C. Black
2-A Cinnaminson Road
Hackettstown, NJ 07840
908-222-9988 (Office)
❶ 908-333-9075 (Residence)
franblk@att.net

❷ **Overview:** More than six years of combined civil engineering experience in the manufacturer, contractor, and sales representative sectors. Seeking an expanded manufacturers' representative opportunity in association with an established agency.

❸ Competencies

TECHNICAL SALES

❹

- Market a full line of heavy drainage and conduit products to contractors in the New York, New Jersey, and Eastern Pennsylvania region.
- Experienced estimator familiar with various codes and ordinances as well as the product line. **❺**
- Accomplished user of the laptop computer for on-site demonstrations and estimates and remote order placement and field support communications via modem.

FIELD ENGINEER **❻**

- Supervision of survey and design crews in the construction of interstate highway systems.
- Specifications engineer for the district office of a state highway department with field verification responsibilities.

MANUFACTURING

- Design and testing of pre-cast concrete components for highway drainage systems.
❼
- Familiarity with the materials and manufacturing processes involved in producing pre-cast civil engineering components.

Employment History

November 2000 - Present: Manufacturers' Representative, Norton & Associates, Inc., Denville, NJ. One of three independent contractor sales representatives coordinated by the Norton agency.

April 1998 - October 2000: Field Engineer, New Jersey Department of Highways, Dover District Office, Dover, NJ.
❽
August 1996 - March 1998: Staff Civil Engineer, Concrete Castings, Ltd., Edison, NJ. Design and testing for largest manufacturer of pre-cast drainage system components in New Jersey.

Education
❾ Bachelor of Science
Civil Engineering
Fairleigh Dickinson University, 1996

Trade Affiliations
❿ Women in Sales
Manufacturers Agents National Association

Medical Records Technician

FOCUSED RESUME

General Strategy

Mr. Webb has had three jobs, all in his field of medical records technology, but they amount to an unfocused summary of his true capabilities and achievements. When he put it all together in a Focused Resume, here is what he was able to accentuate:

- the right degree and professional certification
- an aggregate of valuable experience and a goal to match
- a clearly presented set of capabilities and achievements

Specific Points

❶ The associate degree in his specialty leads his resume.

❷ Professional certification follows.

❸ Overview provides a focus in summary form and states the occupational objective.

❹ The size facility is important for the position sought, so it is prominently mentioned.

❺ Capabilities are shown in the terms recognized and valued by those who would review his resume.

❻ A mix of technical and supervisory tasks supports aspiration to management. Showing he knows how to apply Internet technology to industry issues is worthwhile.

❼ Achievements are phrased to show bottom-line consciousness.

❽ They demonstrate effectiveness in hospital and HMO environments.

❾ Employment is listed matter-of-factly after emphasis was placed earlier in the resume.

❿ Range of experience from insurance company to hospital and HMO gives widest possible job market potential for his skills.

Kenneth N. Webb
78 Portsmouth Street
Manchester, NH 03103
603-222-9988 (Office)
603-333-9075 (Residence)
kennweb@juno.com

EDUCATION

① → Associate in Applied Science
Medical Records Technology
New Hampshire Community College, 1996

② → Accredited Records Technician (ART)
American Medical Record Association

③ **OVERVIEW:** Six years of increasingly responsible positions in the medical records field with in-depth exposure to hospital, insurance, and health management organization systems. Seek a supervisory medical records administrator position in a 500-bed or larger care facility. **④**

CAPABILITIES

⑤
- Code and record diseases, operations, and therapeutic procedures according to standard classification systems.
- Oversee the accurate transcription of medical records by clerks.
- Conduct analyses of patient medical records for reporting and statistical purposes.
- Quality control of medical records for completeness, consistency, and accuracy.
- Access insurance company Web sites to facilitate the filing of complex medical claims and the interactive resolution of conflicts. **⑥**

ACHIEVEMENTS

⑦
- Completed the conversion of 35 years accumulated insurance medical records to modern computer coding and microform.
- Devised major hospital governmental reporting procedures that satisfied regulatory requirements and reduced staff time involved by 31 percent.
- Implemented a records clerk training program at the HMO that speeded entry by 48 percent and reduced errors by 82 percent. **⑧**

EMPLOYMENT

⑨
June 2000 - Present: Medical Records Technician, Old New Hampshire Life and Casualty Company, Manchester, NH. **⑩**

December 1998 - May 2000: Medical Records Technician, Boston Health Management Organization, Boston, MA.

June 1996 - November 1998: Coding and Recording Technician, Northeastern Community Hospital, Bayside, NH.

Minister

FOCUSED RESUME

General Strategy

Mr. Chapman is a minister and the expectation is that one position will look pretty much like the last. He needs a device for bringing out the special strengths that he has developed in this series of similar positions—the Focused Resume is the preferred format to accomplish his goal.

The minister's resume will assist him in:

- demonstrating such things as his affinity for working with the business community

- showing his expertise in church physical plant management

- making the point that he is effective in setting and achieving major goals

Specific Points

1 Strengths show a series of special skills that might be lost or stated repetitiously in a more traditional resume format.

2 Since businesspeople often sit on church boards and selection committees, mentioning his ability to work with them successfully is germane.

3 An ability to communicate effectively beyond the pulpit is cited here.

4 Achievements as a topic gives him a forum for mentioning goals set and met.

5 The results of his businesslike approach are given in human terms meaningful to the congregation.

6 Leadership and the ability to take initiatives that work and are worthy of replication by others is shown in this point.

7 Specific, tangible achievements are noted.

8 A proper career progression stands alone, with the exceptional aspects already noted.

9 A respectable undergraduate degree is confirmed.

10 Ordination is also shown, since it is the ultimate arbiter of his eligibility.

Harold J. Chapman
89 Atlantic Drive
Omaha, NE 68102
402-222-9988 (Office)
402-333-9075 (Residence)
hjc89@aol.com

Goal: To lead the congregation of a new church in a growing suburban setting.

Strengths

①
- Heavily involved in regional activities with particular attention to involving the secular business community in positive social commitments. ← ②
- Particularly knowledgeable of church physical plant management.
- Committed to staff development, especially involving clergy-in-training and the church youth activities systems.
- Popular articles published in religious and secular journals. ← ③

Achievements

④
- Increased business community giving by 67 percent over a two year period in current assignment.
- Lowered operating costs by 23 percent by implementing a physical plant modernization campaign that involved contributed labor and materials.
- Initiated the House of the Poor Foundation in 1987 that has grown to a system now used throughout the Western Region. ← ⑥
- Encouraged a parishioner-based fund drive that yielded core investment for sanctuary elevator and air conditioning that resulted in improved retention of active elderly members.

⑤

⑦

Experience

⑧
<u>June 2000 - Present</u>: Minister, Main Street Methodist Church, Omaha, NE.

<u>June 1996 - May 2000</u>: Minister, Asbury Methodist Church, Pueblo, CO.

<u>July 1992 - May 1996</u>: Associate Minister, First Street United Methodist Church, Las Vegas, NV.

Education

Bachelor of Arts
English Literature
Nevada University
1990
⑨

Ordination
Methodist Minister
Columbia Southern Seminary
1992
⑩

Network Administrator

FOCUSED RESUME

General Strategy

Ms. McDwyer's IT resume addresses a specific job and specialized kind of work so it is best structured as a Focused Resume, which helps to:

- highlight specific kinds of technical skills
- concentrate on building a logically ordered resume containing appropriate keywords since information technology (IT) resumes are generally sent by e-mail in an unembellished text format
- still create a strong core resume that is easy to adapt should aesthetics become important

Specific Points

❶ If a resume was not sent by e-mail, a printed e-mail address may be key to acknowledging receipt when the resume is scanned into an automated personnel system.

❷ The overview immediately flags her specialization, telecommunications.

❸ Shows her technical experience first, using keywords recognizable to both programs that evaluate resumes electronically and people who read them.

❹ Experience section is focused on the job announcement and how she meets the employer's requirements.

❺ Work History substantiates her claims of experience and documents her progress through greater levels of responsibility.

❻ Work History accounts for continuous employment from graduation through her current position.

❼ Work History also communicates the scope of her responsibilities and is the place to convey additional keywords that respond to employer requirements.

❽ Showing work experience in her area of professional certification is valuable.

❾ Paints a word picture of her work environment to indicate the scope of her responsibilities.

❿ Professional certification is often on a par with college training in the IT field.

KAY MCDWYER
1309 West 22nd Street
Austin, TX 78705
512-744-9955 • FAX 512-744-3457
km@texnet.com

❶

OBJECTIVE

Network Administrator overseeing the operation and maintenance of a sophisticated network telecommunications configuration. **❷**

❸ TECHNICAL EXPERIENCE

❹
- Telecommunications competencies include TCP/IP, Netview, VTAM and WAN connectivity
- Configured and managed connectivity extending devices from mainframes
- MVS/OS390 host experience
- Mainframe SMP/E product installation experience

WORK HISTORY ❺

❻
1999-2002—<u>Information Systems Engineer</u>. Lake Country Systems, Inc., Austin, TX. Installed, maintained, and customized CONTROL-T, CONTROL-M/R, CONTROL-V, and CONTROL-O. Used AMP/E, ISPF, TSO, and JCL. Provided maintenance to products using SMP/E without IOAICE. Troubleshooting with Silo and Magstar Exits, Media DataBase, CTDTREE, Control-D Missions, and New Day Processing. **❼**

1997-99—<u>LAN Administrator</u>. University Associates, Ltd., Denton, TX. Worked with NT Server Technology, Windows 98, and MS Office 95 applications software. Provided user support and implemented Novell NetWare and Windows NT network standards in multi-protocol and multi-server environments. **❾** **❽**

EDUCATION AND CERTIFICATION

University of Texas, Austin, TX
Bachelor of Science in Information Systems, 1997
Novell Certified NetWare Engineer (CNE)

Newspaper Reporter

COMPETENCY CLUSTER RESUME

General Strategy

Ms. O'Hare is in a field that lends itself well to identifying specific, valuable groups of professional skills. While they are not totally lost in a traditional job listing resume, they can be emphasized quite effectively in a Competency Cluster Resume.

Her resume is crafted to show:

- four very specific areas of competency
- enough detail to give them meaning
- confirmation of a suitable career path for the position sought

Specific Points

❶ A journalism degree is central to a reporter's career, so it is the lead item.

❷ Four skill areas form the most obvious heart of her resume and communicate a great deal even without the associated elaboration.

❸ Emphasis is placed on the skill most relevant to her career aspiration.

❹ The numbers show a potential syndicator that she has serious potential.

❺ Nuts and bolts reporting skills are confirmed here.

❻ Evidence of initiative and courage that could spark a winning column.

❼ Four years in the big time add credibility to her desire to address national issues.

❽ Employment record shows a plausible rise through the ranks.

❾ Affiliations add to professional image.

❿ Comments indicate what she seeks—expanded on in her cover letter..

Susan T. O'Hare

5 North Harvey Street
Great Falls, MT 59405
406-232-9988 (Office)
406-323-9075 (Residence)
sue5@hotmail.com

Education

❶ Bachelor of Science
Journalism
Southern Montana University, 1994

Competencies

FEATURE WRITING

❸

❹ Writer of a regionally syndicated feature on environmental and sport fishing concerns. Readership estimated at 350,000; subscribers increasing 22 percent annually.

CITY REPORTING

❷ **❺** Two years as a city desk reporter covering court, jail, and community activities for an urban population of 140,000.

INVESTIGATIVE REPORTING

Developed sources and published stories that led to the indictment of the mayor on **❻** drug charges.

CORRESPONDENT REPORTING

Four years representing second largest paper in the state in Washington, DC. **❼**

Employment

June 2000 - Present: Feature Writer, *Great Falls Courier,* Great Falls, MT.

❽ January 1996 - May 2000: Correspondent, The Minnesota Times Service, Washington, DC.

July 1994 - December 1996: City Reporter, *Minnesota Evening Times,* Duluth, MN.

❾ Professional Affiliations

Women in Communications
North Central Print Journalists' Guild

Comments: Seeking an upper Midwest newspaper affiliation from which to develop
a syndicated column.
❿

Nurse

COMPETENCY CLUSTER RESUME

General Strategy

Ms. Purcell is a nurse with special skills to emphasize. She will use the Competency Cluster Resume in order to make her point.

Her resume is designed in such a manner as to:

- highlight her three strongest areas of competency
- reinforce the skill areas by providing meaningful specifics
- show her educational progression and the goal it is intended to achieve

Specific Points

❶ Overview makes the major point of the resume—experienced associate degree nurse about to become bachelor's degree nurse and assume greater responsibility.

❷ Competencies makes the case for her comprehensive experience—keywords known in the profession take on an almost graphic quality in this format.

❸ Types the hospital and kinds of services in a way that will be understood.

❹ Places herself within a nationally known rating scheme.

❺ Specialized experience is emphasized here.

❻ Supervision experience is noted—relevant to aspirations.

❼ Another care dimension added with part-time experience.

❽ Employment History backs what she has claimed elsewhere in the resume.

❾ Her basic associate degree in nursing is noted.

❿ The expected completion date is listed as a proper qualifier on the bachelor's degree.

Delores K. Purcell, R.N.

3 Cook Avenue, Apartment 172
Columbia, MO 65203
573-222-9988 (Office)
573-333-9075 (Residence)
deloresrn3@msn.com

Overview: Associate degree registered nurse with six years of full-time professional experience nearing completion of bachelor's degree seeking supervisory or nurse practitioner opportunity.

Competencies

- GENERAL NURSING—Floor nurse in two major hospitals (500-bed facilities) with comprehensive care responsibilities including assisting physicians, providing treatment, and the administration of medications, physical examinations, and inoculations. Have attained level four on the five-level career ladder of experienced professional nurses.

- POSTOPERATIVE CARE—Implement physician prescribed treatment regimens for patients recovering from surgery. Special training in resuscitation assistance for cardiac patients. Experienced in the supervision of L.P.N. services in the postoperative-care environment.

- CONVALESCENT CARE—Weekend duty at a convalescent home caring for 274 elderly convalescents provided experience in this sector. Familiar with the treatment regimens and recurring problems found in this population.

Employment History

<u>September 1998 - Present</u>: Postoperative-Care Nurse, Our Lady of Hope Hospital, Columbia, MO.

<u>May 1996 - August 1998</u>: Staff Nurse, Central Memorial Hospital, Springfield, MO.

Education

Associate of Science Nursing Central Community College, MO 1996	Bachelor of Science Clinical Nursing North Central Missouri University (June graduation anticipated)

Personnel Specialist

COMPETENCY CLUSTER RESUME

General Strategy

Ms. Stuart wants to structure her resume in such a way as to place an emphasis on the competencies most highly valued in her profession. She has a long work history that relates well to her career objectives, but the position-by-position style resume tends to obscure the points she wants to make. The solution is the Competency Cluster Resume that will allow her to:

- showcase her special groups of skills
- provide the specifics needed to make them meaningful
- back it all with a logical progression of positions held

Specific Points

❶ With a private office, a discreet call to her business phone presents no problem, so it can be listed along with the home phone.

❷ The outline arrangement of special skills offers an apparent central theme to the resume that makes an introduction or summary less essential.

❸ Recruitment skills are of great importance in a dynamic organization and her background as an executive recruiter is valuable in the several respects mentioned. She can also demonstrate successful use of the Internet for hiring purposes.

❹ Standard employee job training skills are among her talents.

❺ A more specialized training capability that relates to government regulations is also worth stressing.

❻ Ability to function in a collective bargaining environment adds a whole new dimension to her qualifications.

❼ A full range of regulatory compliance work, from planning to court cases to complex reporting, adds to her versatility and attractiveness as a candidate.

❽ Positions Held supplies the specifics expected, but requires no elaboration.

❾ Three working environments and orientations are apparent and valued.

❿ An appropriate degree is listed matter-of-factly.

Rosemary P. Stuart

56 Meridian Avenue
Columbus, MS 39702
601-473-8976 (Office) ◄——❶
601-234-5565 (Residence)
mps@mindspring.com

Specialized Abilities

RECRUITMENT

❸

- Experienced in defining hiring official needs both as an in-house personnel officer and as an executive recruiter.
- Capable of dealing effectively with executive search firms due to prior experience in that sector.
- Successfully exploited both resume and job posting Internet sites to fill key vacancies.

TRAINING

❹

- Conducted new employee orientation and task training in financial, consulting, and retail settings.
- Trained managers on compliance with their obligations under EEO and other regulations affecting their departments. ❺

❷

LABOR RELATIONS

- Company representative during NLRB-conducted vote on union representation for major retail chain. ◄——❻
- Benefits negotiator for bank holding company.

AFFIRMATIVE ACTION

- Designed and implemented EEO/AA programs at two large firms.
- Party to suits at the district court level. ❼
- Coordinated state and federal reporting.

Positions Held

June 2000 - Present: Personnel Officer, Center Bank and Trust Company, New Orleans, LA.

❽   January 1996 - May 2000: Recruiter, Dungill Executive Search, Inc., Marysville, MS.   ❾

July 1993 - December 1996: Training Specialist, Bloomington Department Stores, Ltd., Canton, LA.

Education

Bachelor of Science
Business Administration
Pearl University, Arkansas, 1993

Pharmacist

FOCUSED RESUME

General Strategy

Ms. Brookings has a long history of steady, career-relevant employment, but wants to focus attention on her aggregate capabilities and achievements. This is best done by using the Focused Resume format.

This resume is designed to:

- pinpoint a discrete set of capabilities that she holds within her profession
- show a selected set of achievements that highlight her effectiveness

Specific Points

1 Overview spells out the broad outline of her experience and states a general goal.

2 Capabilities provides a format in which highlighted skills are briefly outlined.

3 Within the profession, this is sufficient to relate the basic competencies.

4 Major retail management experience is unique and warrants mentioning.

5 Computer literacy as applied to the industry and buyer experience are also specialized skills not expected in the average pharmacist.

6 Consulting shows broader role and some authority professionally.

7 Achievements verify in tangible terms how effective she has been.

8 The range of accomplishments would be attractive to a major chain seeking a professional manager.

9 Employment shows the positions in which her achievements were made.

10 The appropriate degree underwrites her professional legitimacy.

Joyce C. Brookings

3098 Birch Lane
Bemidji, MN 56601
218-664-8957 (Office)
218-392-6032 (Residence)
joyce30@att.net

❶ **Overview:** Fourteen-year pharmacist with institutional and retail experience seeks management position in the pharmaceutical industry.

❷ Capabilities

❹

• Licensed, degreed, board certified pharmacist.

• Retail manager with successful supervision of multi-store operation.

❸ • Literate in the application of computers to the pharmaceutical trade.

• Extensive buying experience in both medications and sundries.
❺

• Consultant to hospitals and medical staffs on drug selection.
❻

Achievements

• National Retail Pharmacist of Year runner-up 1990.

❼ • Increased total prescription sales by 200 percent in three years.
❽

• Devised and implemented Cross-Check computerized prescription comparison system credited with identifying dozens of potentially serious medication conflicts monthly.

Employment

<u>March 1998 - Present</u>: Managing Pharmacist, MedPharm Drug Centers, Bemidji, MN.

<u>June 1993 - February 1998</u>: Retail Pharmacist, Start Drugs, Washington, DC.
❾

<u>July 1989 - May 1993</u>: Pharmacy Officer, Army Medical Corps, Devens Army Hospital, MA.

Education

Bachelor of Pharmacy
Brainerd University, MN
 1989

Physician Assistant

WORK HISTORY RESUME

General Strategy

Ms. Reginald has a logical pattern of employment that is uncomplicated and career-supporting. Her choice of the Work History Resume is an appropriate one since it will allow her to:

- present her several credentials in the context of relevant work
- thoroughly describe the duties performed by health provider setting

Specific Points

❶ Overview sets the tone for her work history, which is more PA than RN—an important distinction to establish for her objective.

❷ States her goal of entering a practice where her compensation will be more than a salary.

❸ Education is dual-track—degree plus important certification.

❹ Associate degree nurse status established—basis for achieving RN status.

❺ MEDEX Certificate that qualifies her as a PA needs no further explanation within the community that will examine her credentials—it has the status of an additional degree.

❻ Employment accounts for chronological continuity and describes duties in two settings.

❼ PA and HMO points are made in this job description.

❽ Actual tasks performed as a PA are outlined here.

❾ Accounts for the time period and shows that PA training was full time.

❿ Traditional nursing background is reaffirmed.

Cynthia L. Reginald, RN, PA
8 Rutherford Street
Boston, MA 02129
617-394-0038 (Office)
617-894-2934 (Residence)
cynrn@alpha.com

❶ Overview

Experienced health care professional with formal RN and MEDEX/PA credentials, a year of nursing and four years as a PA. Seeking to enter a private practice situation as a financially participating physician associate. ❷

Education

Associate in Science
Nursing
Greenfield Junior College, 1996

❸

MEDEX Certificate
Physician Assistant
South Boston College, 1999

❹

Employment

❺

June 1999 - Present: Physician Assistant, Boston Area Health Management Association. One of four PAs assigned to Team 1 of the HMO for the purpose of screening patients for primary physician care. Conduct physical examinations and consult on the results ❼ with the patients and, as appropriate, physicians. Other duties include ordering lab tests, diagnosing common maladies, and prescribing routine treatments. ❽

❻

September 1997 - May 1999: Full-time MEDEX/PA training. ❾

July 1996 - August 1997: Hospital Nurse, Greater Boston Presbyterian Hospital. General duty nurse responsible for attending patients on the postoperative care ward. Administered medication and therapeutic regimens prescribed by physicians. Typical shift involved managing the care for approximately 23 patients with the assistance of LPNs, orderlies, and other floor staff. ❿

Private Investigator

COMPETENCY CLUSTER RESUME

General Strategy

Ms. King is a law enforcement professional with several periods of traditional employment, but her most current one is in a self-employed capacity. She is more interested in showing what she can do than explaining why her business is not something she wants to continue. The most desirable way to combine her assets for an employer's evaluation is the Competency Cluster Resume.

The resume will be used primarily to:

- show that she can function as a law enforcement insider
- demonstrate that she can do the things that investigators are paid to do

Specific Points

❶ Overview instantly establishes her as qualified in both public and private sectors.

❷ It also says what situation she seeks and where.

❸ Capabilities highlights the three areas of primary competency.

❹ Ties with the law enforcement establishment are presented here.

❺ Familiarity with the law on a practical level is confirmed.

❻ Evidence that she is capable of gathering information from the standard sources.

❼ Important capabilities in the domestic investigations field are noted.

❽ Ability to use photo and video equipment to document observations for possible use in court or in out-of-court settlements based on convincing evidence.

❾ Employment history verifies claims to various kinds of experience.

❿ An associate degree in criminology adds credibility.

Ida J. King
8 Wilson Lane
Laurel, MD 20707
240-723-8677 (Office)
240-889-2349 (Residence)
idaking8@aol.com

❶

Overview: Experienced law enforcement and security officer with police and licensed private investigator experience seeks affiliation with an established investigative firm in the Baltimore/Washington area. **❷**

Capabilities

❸

INSTITUTIONAL
- Urban police officer in the capacities of patrolman and detective. **❹**
- Knowledge of enforcement and judicial bureaucracies.
- Acquainted with and respected by principals and functionaries throughout the regional law enforcement establishment.
- Working knowledge of civil and criminal statutes. **❺**

RESEARCH
- Government agency files.
- Telephone investigation. **❻**
- Personal interviewing.

SURVEILLANCE
- Domestic evidence gathering. ← **❼**
- Video and photographic techniques.
- Pursuit and documentation of movements.

❽

Experience

June 2000 - Present: Security Consultant, Self-employed.

April 1994 - May 2000: Detective, Baltimore Municipal Police Department, Baltimore, MD.

❾

June 1991 - March 1994: Patrolman, Columbia Police Department, Columbia, MD.

Education

Associate in Applied Science
Criminology
Hamilton Community College, MD, 1991

Product Manager

WORK HISTORY RESUME

General Strategy

Mr. Akrin is using the Work History Resume to portray his series of career-related professional positions. This approach is desirable in his case because the terminology, position titles, company names, etc., are all readily conceptualized by the potential reviewers of his resume.

This resume is designed to:

- state his overall qualifications and next career objective
- demonstrate that he has the academic credentials on which to base his career

Specific Points

❶ Overview briefly states his three areas of specialization and market specialty.

❷ Next, it says that he is after more of the same on a higher level.

❸ Experience is a straightforward listing of career positions held and verifies that employment has been continuous.

❹ A significant position coupled with a successful initiative makes for a powerful introduction to his work history.

❺ Dollar volume is needed to portray the scope of his effort and responsibilities.

❻ Results are clearly demonstrated—verifiable by references.

❼ Position is enhanced by noting the industry position of his company.

❽ Numbers and kinds of people on his staff show the magnitude of the effort.

❾ Served his time on the road selling the products he now manages.

❿ An ideal combination of degrees to back his career.

William K. Akrin
56 Tura Road
Bennington, CT 48009
860-222-9988 (Office)
860-333-9075 (Residence)
wmakrin@mindspring.com

Overview: Seven years of sales, market research, and product management experience in the consumer products retail segment. Seeking expanded opportunities as a product manager in a related industry.

Experience

<u>November 2000 - Present</u>: *Product Manager–Consumer Health Remedies, Milken & Trosper Pharmaceuticals, Inc., Bennington, CT.*
Led Milken back into the forefront of the analgesic market by generating contemporary health benefits strategies for existing products. Directed an $11 million campaign that included the design and implementation of test-marketing procedures, product packaging redesign, direct-mail sample delivery to selected target groups, and national advertising keyed to life-extension health philosophy. Resounding success confirmed by three-fold increase of market share that has been sustained for two years.

<u>May 1997 - October 2000</u>: *Market Research Analyst, Tifton-Williams Company, Trewsberry, CT*
Analyzed the market potential for dozens of retail consumables for the country's third largest producer of personal care items. Directed a team of two statisticians, two clerical, and four area specialists in the evaluation and statistical testing of product receptivity in pre-defined markets. Credited with co-developing the targeted marketing scheme rapidly being viewed as the coming standard of the industry.

<u>July 1995 - April 1997</u>: *Sales Representative, National Home Products, Ltd., Stillwell, CT.*
One of 12 representatives selling consumer home cleaning and personal care products to retail outlets in the Southern New England region. In 18 months rose to the second highest volume in the region and received the Outstanding New Salesman Award for 1997 for the Eastern Division.

Education

Bachelor of Science
Marketing
Smith University, 1993

Master of Business Administration
Marketing Concentration
Drexton University, 1995

Public Relations Specialist

FOCUSED RESUME

General Strategy

Mr. Bellman can do the job of a public relations person and he has the job success to prove it. What he wants to do is avoid repeating essentially the same job description three times in a standard resume. The answer to his dilemma is the Focused Resume. Using its format, he will be able to:

- graphically list the skills he has
- back them with solid accomplishments that demonstrate their application
- underwrite it all with the right work history and college degree

Specific Points

1 He opens the resume by targeting the precise position and level of authority he seeks.

2 Next the institution is classified as one that will provide a growth environment in which he can ply his trade.

3 Skills are those expected for the position and they are put forward without unnecessary elaboration—leave that for the interview.

4 Accomplishments are general as well, but do focus on things with which a college president—the person hiring him—will easily identify.

5 He can keep the alumni happy and contributing.

6 Was the best in the state at conceiving an effective promotion for his college.

7 Knows how to get the president visibility in popular academic media.

8 Employment shows continuity and progression.

9 The position he is coming from is a logical stepping stone to the kind for which he is making application.

10 An acceptable undergraduate degree is in evidence.

Rodney H. Bellman

98 Fairway Circle
Presque Isle, ME 04769
207-564-2323 (Office)
207-895-0267 (Residence)
rodbell@msn.com

Target Position

❶ Managing the public relations staff of a major university with full decision making responsibility. Institution should be rapidly growing or already established as a leader **❷** in its sector.

Skills

❸

- Speech preparation
- News release writing
- Media event coordination
- Publications creation
- Articulation of institutional image

Accomplishments

❹

❺
- Increased alumni participation by 23 percent during two year directorship.
- Won the State Education Associations' Promotion of the Year Award for 1995. **❻**
- Collection of President's speeches drafted by me
❼ published as a nationally distributed monograph.

Employment **❾**

❽ <u>June 2000 - Present</u>: Public Relations Officer, Montpelier University.

<u>February 1997 - May 2000</u>: Director of Public Information, New England Association of Colleges and Schools, Freeburg, ME.

<u>September 1995 - January 1997:</u> Alumni Director, Lourdsburg College, Lourdsburg, ME.

Education

Bachelor of Science
Journalism
Smith University, 1995

❿

Purchasing Agent

COMPETENCY CLUSTER RESUME

General Strategy

Ms. Johns has held two professional positions since graduating from college, but neither was for a very long period of time. She has good references, has learned important job-related skills, and wants to move on again. What is needed is the format of the Competency Cluster Resume, which can draw the reviewer's attention first to what she has to offer and, secondarily, to the brief tenure in her jobs.

The objective of this resume is to:

- present a capable person who knows what she wants and can demonstrate her ability to handle the task

- graphically dominate the resume with desirable skills, highlighted and backed immediately with limited, supporting facts

- confirm work experience, proper college degree, and positions held

Specific Points

❶ Position Sought says what she is after—including level of authority.

❷ Desired characteristics of the company are also noted.

❸ Competencies form the heart of the resume—no need to hunt for them from within several job descriptions.

❹ Knows how to deal with suppliers in two primary situations.

❺ Level of responsibility best shown by dollar value of transactions managed.

❻ Important evidence that she can bargain and achieve savings.

❼ Without great detail, this says she can buy for heavy industry—details can be provided upon request and would be the subject of discussion anyway.

❽ Positions held tend to type her as what she claims to be.

❾ Degree held is appropriate and also needs to be mentioned.

❿ Key affiliation is an expectation in her field.

Mary Elizabeth Johns
42 Woodyard Drive
New Orleans, LA 70186
504-843-7886 (Office)
504-763-2133 (Residence)
maryelizj@mindspring.com

❶

Position Sought: Group Purchasing Manager for commodities group in manufacturing environment with supervisory and purchase authorization responsibilities. Company should be currently profitable and growing.

❷

Competencies

<u>Supplier Relations</u>

- Attend national trade shows to develop contacts and current market knowledge. **❹**
- Receive visiting sales representatives and evaluate offerings.

<u>Bid Acquisition</u>

- Prepared $300,000 to $2 million commodity bidding events and managed the outcomes. **❺**

❸

<u>Negotiation</u>

- Achieved savings averaging 18 percent over industry tender prices for three commodity groups, 13 percent overall. **❻**

<u>Commodities</u>

- Active in raw materials acquisition for heavy industrial components.

❼

Experience

❽

<u>June 2000 - Present</u>: General Purchasing Agent, Jones and Likeland Fabricators, Ltd., Gulf Coast City, LA.

<u>July 1999 - May 2000</u>: Commodities Buyer, Witson Manufacturing Company, Inc., New Carrolton, LA.

Education

❾

Bachelor of Science
Business Administration
Holy Saints University, 1999

Professional Affiliations

Member: National Association of Purchasing Managers

❿

Real Estate Broker

FOCUSED RESUME

General Strategy

Ms. Garrett is in a very performance-oriented field—real estate sales. Less emphasis will be placed on a perfect chain of positions held and degrees earned than on what she has done and how well. The correct vehicle for highlighting her strengths as a sales person and sales manager is the Focused Resume.

This resume will accomplish the following:

- demonstrate in not too many words the fact that she is a sales producer
- show that she has the professional licenses, affiliations, and experience needed to do her job

Specific Points

❶ Overview is used to headline what she is, has done, and is after.

❷ The position sought is qualified—has to be a national franchise affiliate.

❸ Capabilities bullets her functional areas of expertise in the industry.

❹ In a few phrases she ticks off the essentials for the position to which she aspires—elaboration will be left for the interview.

❺ Achievements show how her basic skills have been applied successfully.

❻ Lead item is personal productivity as a salesperson—over time, not just one good year.

❼ Respectability, stature, and character reflected by state board appointment.

❽ Quantified success in performance that relates directly to the task proposed.

❾ Experience backs her claim to such levels of functioning in the business.

❿ Mention of a degree cannot hurt, even if unrelated and nonessential.

Joan F. Garrett

21 Pine Lane
Bowling Green, KY 42101
502-834-9879 (Office)
502-547-8210 (Residence)
joanfg21@att.net

①

Overview: Proven residential real estate sales producer and manager with eleven years of combined sales and brokerage experience seeks affiliation with major national franchise in a senior sales management capacity.

②

Capabilities

③

- Licensed Real Estate Broker
- Eleven years of successful, full-time, residential real estate sales **④**
- Certified real estate appraiser
- Rental management experience
- Training of sales personnel

Achievements

⑥

⑤

- Annual sales in excess of $1.5 million for the past five years
- Elected professional representative to Kentucky Board of Realtors **⑦**
- Managed nationally franchised office that led Central Region in sales volume growth in 1998. **⑧**
- Sponsored and trained 94 of the Million Dollar Residential Round Table salesmen recognized in the Central Region in the last year.

Experience

⑨

June 1998 - Present: Residential Broker, Stallings Better Homes and Farms Realty, Inc., Bowling Green, KY.

June 1991 - May 1998: Real Estate Agent, Norwood Realty, Staunton, KY.

July 1987 - May 1991: English Teacher, Lexington Junior College, KY.

Education

Bachelor of Arts **⑩**
English Literature
Western Kentucky University, 1987

Receptionist

COMPETENCY CLUSTER RESUME

General Strategy

Ms. Kyle is returning home with valuable experiences learned while spending a few years working in a large city. Neither her education nor job descriptions are anything noteworthy, so she wisely opts to feature her strengths in a Competency Cluster Resume.

The object of her resume is to:

- show that she can handle receptionist duties in a demanding setting
- affirm that she has already done so successfully and developed supporting skills in the course of gaining that experience

Specific Points

1 Since she has already left her last position, she lists only her home telephone number.

2 Overview tells her situation and leads into her qualifications.

3 Competencies highlight the kinds of things for which the employer will be looking.

4 Telephone skills are absolutely essential—she establishes both technical competency and a measure of how trusted she has been (initial point of contact).

5 Without saying more than would be proper, she volunteers that she is indeed attractive and good with people—something the employer would want to know, but could otherwise not determine until the interview.

6 The ability to do more than answer phones is noted.

7 Some of these skills could promise upward mobility from the receptionist position.

8 Experience gives chronology and the employers suggest quality situations.

9 References could be noted, but she elects to hold them until interviewed.

10 Diploma is a desirable credential and subtle verification of regional linkage—they're not dealing with an uncomfortable outsider.

Carol H. Kyle

422 Haverhill Drive
Hutchinson, KS 67501
316-767-2843 (Residence)
carolk422@yahoo.com ← ❶

❷ **Overview**: Organizational receptionist returning to Kansas after five years of work experience in Washington seeks opportunity to apply skills locally.

Competencies

❸ TELEPHONE SKILLS ❹

Five years of PBX and key system experience in professional organizations of more than 50 people. Answered and referred calls as the initial point of contact.

PERSONAL QUALITIES

Well-groomed, attractive woman with an excellent professional manner and an interest in people. ❺

CLERICAL SKILLS ❻

Type 60 WPM on conventional or word processing equipment. Filing, basic bookkeeping, and other general office skills. ❼

Experience

❽ May 2000 - October 2002: Receptionist, American Association of Insurance Adjusters, Washington, DC.

April 1998 - May 2000: Receptionist, Criminal Investigations Division, U.S. Department of Justice, Washington, DC. ❾

Education

Diploma
Office Management
Fort Hays Business School, 1998

❿

Retail Buyer

FOCUSED RESUME

General Strategy

Ms. Napier is an accomplished buyer who is seeking another position because a merger is about to eliminate hers. She has spent her entire career with two firms and she would like to distance herself from that limited background. The best approach is for her to relegate the job history to the end of her resume and amplify her special abilities and accomplishments directly and early in a Focused Resume.

Her resume will achieve:

- an honest statement of her situation and desire to continue in her career elsewhere
- a clear demonstration that she has the skills needed to do the job
- evidence that she can apply her talents successfully and profitably

Specific Points

❶ Office phone listing is fine since her employer is assisting in her effort to relocate.

❷ Overview says what she seeks and what motivates her to change positions.

❸ Capabilities make clear the fact that she has specific skills to offer.

❹ Dollar values make it possible for a reviewer to place her on a scale of responsibility held.

❺ Implications of national networking serve her purpose of breaking local image.

❻ Foundation of retail experience is established.

❼ Achievements show she is a nationally rated performer in her class store.

❽ Regional recognition and successful major deal add to her stature.

❾ Experience shows a chronology of work that backs her prior claims.

❿ Marketing degree further confirms the appropriateness of her career preparation.

Janice W. Napier
398 South Akin Boulevard
Cedar Rapids, IA 52407
319-823-7690 (Office) ← ❶
319-334-3254 (Residence)
jannap@msn.com

❷ **Overview:** Experienced retail department store clothing and accessories buyer seeks comparable position. Current firm recently acquired in national merger resulting in staff consolidations.

❸ **Capabilities**

- Clothing and accessories buying experience for a three-store, family-owned department store chain with annual sales of $20 million. ❹
❺ - Experienced participant in major trade shows presenting goods for the industry.
- Budget management for the $12 million clothing segment of the firm's annual sales.
- Proven observer of consumer buying trends.
- Extensive national contacts in the industry.
❻ - Ten years of retail sales and sales management experience before becoming a buyer.

Achievements

❼ - Top quartile performance in acquisitions/returns ratios for buyers in the $5-25 million departmental budget category nationally.
- Responsible for firm's successful adaptation to outlet pricing standards in the coat and outerwear garments segment.
❽ - Twice selected Retail Buyer of the Year by the Iowa Retail Merchants' Association.
- Acquired price commitments on the Potter-Green jeans line before it achieved national status with resultant savings of $2.3 million.

Experience

June 1997 - Date: Clothing Buyer, Miller & Leget Department Stores, Cedar Rapids, IA.
June 1996 - May 1997: Clothing Sales Manager, Miller & Leget Department Stores, Cedar Rapids, IA.
❾
July 1987 - May 1996: Women's Department Manager, Neeman's Fashions, Des Moines, IA

Education

Bachelor of Science (BS) ❿
Business Administration (Marketing)
Des Moines University, 1987

Retail Salesperson

COMPETENCY CLUSTER RESUME

General Strategy

Ms. St. Clair is a top-level retail salesperson whose productivity would be over-shadowed by an ordinary resume. It is important for her to distinguish herself from the image of a passive retail clerk and establish herself as an effective sales professional with her own particular strengths and methods. She is advised to do this in the format of the Competency Cluster Resume since it allows her to:

- graphically portray herself as someone special in retail selling
- note the special situation to which she aspires
- drop the shop names necessary to affirm her elegant image

Specific Points

❶ Overview says precisely what she is and what she wants to become.

❷ Particular Abilities was chosen to complement the phrasing popular in the advertising images of the kinds of places she works—and to which her resume is appealing.

❸ Marketing shows that she knows how to develop clients actively in the expensive goods segment.

❹ Volume demonstrates that she can become a one-person profit center.

❺ Presentation indicates basic retail skills cast in a special light.

❻ Individualized marketing is again stressed.

❼ Present position establishes the level of her sales practice.

❽ Respectable tenure shows reliability in this less-than-stable class of worker.

❾ Major national department store background provided excellent entry-level experience.

❿ Formal training at a respected institution adds to professional image.

Ruth V. St. Clair

875 Washington Avenue
Muncie, IN 47305
765-585-9367 (Office)
765-585-7657 (Residence)
rvsc@mindspring.com

❶

Overview: Top retail saleswoman specializing in exclusive women's wear seeks participating interest in established boutique in winter resort area.

❷ Particular Abilities

MARKETING

❸
- Client base of 587 in exclusive women's store located in suburban mall.
- Developed by direct mail and personal contact.
- Files maintained on tastes, interests, sizes, etc.

VOLUME

❹
- Average annual sales of $367,000 over the past five years.
- Client pattern established at tri-seasonal average of approximately $2,500 each.

PRESENTATION

❺
- Experienced in window and store presentation of elegant merchandise.
- Specialty is individual presentation to top clients on an appointment basis.

❻

❼ Experience

<u>June 2000 - Present</u>: Senior Sales Associate, Elegant Shops, Ltd., Muncie, IN.

<u>June 1996 - May 2000</u>: Retail Sales Consultant, Exclusive Clothing Boutique, Chicago, IL.

❽

<u>December 1992 - May 1996</u>: Retail Clerk, Women's Fashions, Bloomingdales Department Store, Washington, DC.

❾

❿ Education

Certificate
Merchandising
Indiana Fashion Institute, 1992

Robotic Engineer

WORK HISTORY RESUME

General Strategy

Mr. Wright has followed the expected career ladder within his profession and it is proper and effective for him to rely on the Work History Resume to display his abilities and accomplishments.

His resume is designed specifically to:

- show a chain of responsible employment in his technical specialty
- indicate the caliber of companies with which he has been associated
- highlight his special skills and contributions

Specific Points

❶ Overview authoritatively states his position in the industry and the fact that he is looking for an opportunity.

❷ Experience is formatted to emphasize the position held, employer, and duties.

❸ Level of responsibility is made clear with title and place in organization.

❹ Measures are given of how well his efforts have served the company.

❺ Scope of effort and responsibility are again shown with specific examples and numbers.

❻ Cites a key talent—ability to gain government contracts.

❼ Quantifies the magnitude of business generated so it can be easily appreciated.

❽ Makes the link to his junior officer days that laid the groundwork for present-day understanding of the industry and business processes.

❾ Specific value of time spent on the approval side of bid process is illustrated.

❿ Powerful combination of technical degrees is self-explanatory.

Ned V. Wright
387 Streamside Lane
Twin Falls, ID 83303
208-977-6634 (Office)
208-788-3844 (Residence)
nedvw@hotmail.com

①

Overview: Defense industry automation engineer with successful government and private sector experience in aviation-related robotics seeks growth opportunity in the applications area.

② **Experience**

<u>June 2000 - Present</u>: *Robotic Applications Engineer, Huge Aerospace,* Idaho City, ID

③
Chief engineering interface between the production and computer programming segments of the fixed wing avionics robotic production division. Responsible for coordinating and directing the resolution of technical challenges inherent in **④** adapting production line electronics to automated control. Achieved successful implementation on 37 percent of the line within two years. Production increased 23 percent and defects dropped 74 percent during the final quarter of evaluation.

<u>June 1996 - May 2000</u>: *Mechanical Automation Engineer, Nanonectics, Ltd.,* Valley of the Angeles Industrial Complex, Los Angeles, CA.

⑤
Project leader for a five-member team consisting of two engineers, one technician, and two clerical assistants tasked with preparing bids for federal government requests for proposals. Team generated and managed an average of 14 major **⑥** proposals annually, assisted production department with staffing for contracts acquired, and served as project monitor in-house. Yielded an average of five **⑦** successful bids annually resulting in aggregate contracts of $45 million dollars per year.

<u>July 1992 - May 1996</u>: *Engineering Officer, United States Air Force Systems Command,* Andrews Air Force Base, MD.

⑧
Staff technical expert leading a team of six engineering evaluators appraising the potential of automated weapons systems proposed for USAF consideration. Served as intermediate screening authority after conceptual interest had been **⑨** established by senior managers. Feasibility of robotic applications to USAF mission requirements was the focus of the effort that yielded a 19 percent development approval rate over the three year life of the project.

Education

Associate in Science (AS)
Computer Science
Boise Junior College, ID, 1989

⑩

Bachelor of Science (BS)
Industrial Engineering
Idaho State College, ID, 1992

417

School Administrator

COMPETENCY CLUSTER RESUME

General Strategy

Mr. Varney has held a series of jobs as an educator that have prepared him for a senior administrative position. Rather than list the jobs and duties, he prefers to pull together what it all means in terms of being able to handle the job he is pursuing. His choice to do this is the Competency Cluster Resume.

The objective of his resume is to:

- telegraph the fact that he has the specific skills necessary—without the detail that might obscure their collective importance

- back his claim with enough brief specifics to illustrate that he can make his case

Specific Points

❶ Executive Summary is used to say: "I have what you need—here it is point by point."

❷ He uses its headline format to convey both longevity and specific skills.

❸ Competencies outlines the very things that concern the people who will evaluate him for the position—shows he knows what their priorities are.

❹ Each point is made as a topic and then by specific, quantified example.

❺ Both business and educational skills are addressed in a result-oriented format.

❻ Awareness and involvement in the operational use of technology in learning is established.

❼ Underlying teaching skills are reaffirmed—did his time in the classroom.

❽ Respect for the importance of community relations and the ability to exploit cutting-edge technology are illustrated.

❾ Collective bargaining experience may well be essential and a basis for eliminating unsuccessful candidates early in the screening process—make the point, however briefly.

❿ Experience and degrees are essential, but matter-of-fact.

Dennis S. Varney
795 Carlyle Street
Kewanee, IL 61443
309-499-0988 (Office)
309-877-2132 (Residence)
dvarney@msn.com

1

Executive Summary

2

- Public school administrator with ten years of administrative and five years of teaching experience.
- Significant budget, community relations, and unionized teacher management experience.

Competencies

3

ADMINISTRATION

- Principal of a 2000-student, 100-faculty public secondary school in a suburban environment.
- Vice Principal of a 1500-student, 70-faculty rural intermediate school.

BUDGET

- Responsible for the preparation and management of a $5 million school budget.
- Planned and implemented a $1.7 million school renovation.
- Fiscal oversight for community generated non-taxpayer $980 million fund for school improvements.

5

CURRICULUM

- Implemented computer-assisted math and reading instruction in a 500 teacher urban system.

6

TEACHING

- High school mathematics teacher in urban and suburban settings for five years before entering administration.

7

COMMUNITY RELATIONS

- Used a popular Internet Web page to ensure a successful bond drive by illustrating desirable outcomes and providing e-mail links stimulating community feedback.

8

LABOR RELATIONS

- Senior district representative for two suburban systems with successful no-strike negotiations concluded in both instances.

9

4

Experience

10

September 1998 - Present: Principal, Suburban High School, Canton, IL.
June 1993 - August 1998: Vice Principal, Macon County Intermediate School, New Bedford, IL.
June 1992 - May 1993: Consulting Curriculum Leader, Intercity School System, Wilmington, IL.
June 1991 - May 1992: Mathematics Teacher, Millmount High School, East Millmount, IL.
August 1988 - May 1991: Mathematics Teacher, Southside Intermediate School, Westwood, IL.

Education

Bachelor of Science (BS)
Math Education
Central Illinois University, 1988

Master of Science (MS)
Public School Administration
Central Illinois University, 2001

School Guidance Counselor

FOCUSED RESUME

General Strategy

Mr. Sandsome wants to present his credentials as an established educator with a clear focus on his guidance counselor attributes. Rather than list jobs and follow with the usual paragraph of duties, he has selected the Focused Resume as the vehicle for communicating a more directed message.

The goal of this resume is to:

- focus the reviewer's attention on the specific qualities associated with the counselor's role in a school
- substantiate claims to effectiveness with examples of specific achievements
- underline the presentation with solid experience and training credentials

Specific Points

❶ A specific position is being sought, so it is designated at the head of the resume.

❷ Abilities is used to tick off the expected and insert some special talents related to the job in question.

❸ Substance abuse in schools is a major concern, and he has experience dealing with it.

❹ Initiative shown in going beyond government sources of financial aid.

❺ Practical outreach to the community is a valuable asset.

❻ Results are available to back claims of effectiveness in all areas.

❼ Ideas have been good enough to institutionalize—projects he started now have a life of their own and reach beyond his area of influence.

❽ Evidence of stature given by involvement with a national organization.

❾ The right working experiences for the role he seeks.

❿ Degrees appropriate to his aspirations.

Wadsworth T. Sandsome
35 North Island Drive
Haleiwa, HI 96740
808-675-8345 (Office)
808-776-9078 (Residence)
wadsworth2@aol.com

Position Sought

Director of Counseling Services

Abilities

- State Certified School Guidance Counselor.
- Specialized training in the recognition and treatment of adolescent substance abuse.
- In-depth familiarity with the use of computer databases designed to aid students in the selection of appropriate colleges and majors.
- Experienced group counseling leader.
- Knowledge of private as well as public sources of college bound student financial aid.
- Extensive work with private sector community work-study arrangements.

Achievements

- 80 percent of counselees admitted to college of their choice for the past five years.
- Awarded Parents' Club Award for Excellence 2001 in appreciation for efforts to establish private sector linkage between North Shore School and the burgeoning hospitality industry.
- Founder of Island Helpers Teen Substance Abuse Hotline that serves 3500 callers weekly.
- Summer Consulting Fellow to College Boardroom, a non-profit organization that designs career planning software for students.

Experience

<u>June 2000 - Present</u>: Guidance Counselor, North Shore High School, Kawela Bay, HI.

<u>June 1996 - May 2000</u>: Counselor, Kanehoe Intermediate School, Kanehoe, HI.

<u>July 1992 - May 1996</u>: History Teacher, Pearl Harbor High, Pearl City, HI.

Education

Bachelor of Science (BS)
Social Studies Education
University of Maryland, 1990

Master of Education (MEd)
Guidance and Counseling
University of Hawaii, 1996

Secretary

COMPETENCY CLUSTER RESUME

General Strategy

Ms. Andersen's two periods of employment have given her more than a simple listing of duties and dates would indicate. When combined with her education, they provide the basis for describing a very attractive array of skills. In order to bring this to the immediate attention of potential employers, she has selected the Competency Cluster Resume to showcase her assets.

Her resume is specifically designed to:

- portray the professionalism with which she views herself
- list the specific skills and traits that give her claim substance
- define the career path she hopes to pursue

Specific Points

1 Overview and Objective set her resume above the average for such applicants by classifying her interests as professional and executive—only appropriate because she can substantiate the claim.

2 Clear implication that she is looking for an opportunity to do more than be a secretary—administrative management is her goal and that will appeal to an employer seeking to develop such a person.

3 Her degree is specific and valuable—it gets prominent placement.

4 Professional Skills is the wording chosen to highlight her talents and cast them in a more important light.

5 The outline of skill topics tells a potential employer that she has the kind of comprehensive talent that can be considered for serious responsibility.

6 It is made clear that she is in command of modern office technology.

7 Knowledge of hiring procedures and regulatory requirements are apt to be valued by the executive she would support.

8 Ability to make business arrangements is a vital skill worth featuring.

9 Experience shows continuity of employment.

10 Current position verifies executive secretary stature.

Lynn J. Andersen
973 Albacort Circle
Savannah, GA 31407
912-929-6479 (Office)
912-938-7783 (Residence)
lynnja@msn.com

❶ Overview and Objective

Professional Secretary with six years of advanced office services experience seeks Executive Secretary position with potential for assuming an administrative management role. **❷**

Education

❸ Associate in Science (AS)
Secretarial Science
Metropolitan Community College, GA, 1996

Professional Skills

OFFICE MANAGEMENT	• Coordination of office clerical routine. • Schedule management. • Vendor liaison with suppliers of services.
DOCUMENT PREPARATION	• 60 WPM using electric typewriter or word processing equipment. • Advanced user of principal word processing software packages.
EQUIPMENT OPERATION	• Personal computers and associated peripheral equipment. • Fax and modems. **❻**
DICTATION/TRANSCRIPTION	• 60 WPM vocal dictation. • Accomplished transcriber.
PERSONNEL	• Preparation and placement of advertising. **❼** • Applicant response, appointment arrangements, EEO record keeping.
EXECUTIVE ASSISTING	• Planning of meetings and conferences, locally and at remote sites. **❽** • Arranging business travel. • Screening and appointment management.

❺

Experience **❿**

<u>November 2000 - Present</u>: Secretary to the Director of Marketing, Rockaway Manufacturing Company, Ltd., Savannah, GA.

❾ <u>May 1996 - October 2000</u>: Secretary, Jensen & Jensen Management Consultants, Tyron, GA.

Securities Broker

COMPETENCY CLUSTER RESUME

General Strategy

Ms. Proper has an employment history that shows only one relevant position, although her skills are really very well developed. She has decided that a Competency Cluster Resume will do a far more graphic job of displaying her strengths than would a bland position listing and description.

Her resume is intended to:

- show that she is an established and successful salesperson in the financial products field

- prove that she has the professional attributes to practice her trade

- show that she has obtained the education to support her career change

Specific Points

❶ Executive Summary establishes what she has done and in what market segment.

❷ It further states her goal to become a partner in a securities firm.

❸ Professional certification is immediately verified—no one needs to train her.

❹ She brings with her a specialty in the broad field of investment products.

❺ A base of buying clients is already established and likely to follow.

❻ She can demonstrate serious levels of productivity.

❼ Proof is offered that she can generate new business as well.

❽ Brokerage experience is anchored in a respected firm.

❾ Prior teaching experience is noted matter-of-factly.

❿ Education shows commitment to the business career.

Sandra K. Proper
1987 Clearpond Way
Miami Shores, FL 33138
305-966-0980 (Office)
305-877-2167 (Residence)
sanprop@hotmail.com

❶ Executive Summary

Proven exceptional productivity in the retail marketing of investment products to young professionals with performance sustained over a six year period. Objective is to attain participating partner status in a compatible firm. ❷

Professional Abilities

LICENSURE ❸ • Securities and Exchange Commission licensed retail broker

PRODUCT SPECIALIZATION • No Load Mutual Funds ❹
• Emerging Growth Stocks
• College Tuition Fund Plans

CLIENTS ❺ • Young professionals

PRODUCTION ❻ • Achieved $2 million in annual sales in third year; sustained through sixth year.
❼ • Business development activities yielded 54 purchasing clients last quarter.

Experience

❽ <u>June 1996 - Present</u>: Retail Stock Broker, Blackmund Investing Associates, Ltd., Miami, FL.

❾ <u>August 1994 - May 1997</u>: Teacher, Kevinville Schools, Kevinville, CA.

Education

Bachelor of Arts (BA)   Master of Science (MS) ❿
Art History   Business Administration
Smith University, AL 1994   University of West Florida, 2001

Security Manager

FOCUSED RESUME

General Strategy

Mr. Cooper has had a long and complete work history, but he feels his attributes will be better shown if pulled from the individual job descriptions where they are to be found. He selected the Focused Resume because it lets him place the attention wanted on certain skills and traits that are the selling points of his profession.

This resume is designed to:

- paint an overall picture of an experienced professional whose talents stem from a number of work experiences
- show achievements that demonstrate excellence in his field
- back it with responsible experience and relevant educational achievement

Specific Points

❶ Overview sketches the experienced security practitioner and the goal he seeks.

❷ Capabilities lists specific assets that should be valued by private security firms.

❸ Basic qualifying items are affirmed.

❹ Special skills are identified.

❺ Public relations and management experience is noted.

❻ Achievements are the kind apt to be appreciated in his trade.

❼ Character reference items are also included.

❽ Ability to generate business is important to note.

❾ Experience validates claims made earlier in resume.

❿ Education is a nice concluding touch of professionalism—not a mandatory degree.

John V. Cooper

3976 98th Street SW
Washington, DC 20098
202-992-7845 (Office)
202-765-2116 (Residence)
jvc39776@mymail.com

❶ Overview

Successful security officer and manager with experience in military, municipal, and private security settings seeks senior management position with private firm.

❷ Capabilities

❸
- Licensed private investigator
- Military security police training and experience
- Advanced martial arts training ← **❹**
- Five years experience as a municipal police officer
- Six years as a private investigator
- Expert firearms instructor ←
❺ - Experienced speaker before community groups
- Proven security organization manager

Achievements

❻
- Regional NRA pistol champion
- Appointed to state licensing board for private investigators
- Deacon of the Midlands Methodist Church **❼**
- Four-time regional Karate champion
- Security consultant to industry and government
- Increased account dollar volume 45 percent in current position ← **❽**

Experience

❾ <u>June 2000 - Present</u>: Director of Domestic Investigations, Blue Diamond Detective Agency, Inc., Washington, DC.

<u>June 1996 - May 2000</u>: Self-Employed Private Investigator, Bethesda, MD.

<u>July 1991 - May 1996</u>: Patrolman, Alexandria Police Department, Alexandria, VA.

<u>May 1988 - June 1991</u>: Army Military Police, California and Germany.

Education

Associate in Applied Science (AAS)
Law Enforcement Technology
Washington Area Technical College, DC, 1997

Supervisory Systems Analyst

FOCUSED RESUME

General Strategy

Ms. Goodwin's IT resume addresses a specific job and specialized kind of work, so it is best structured as a Focused Resume which helps to:

- highlight specific kinds of technical skills
- concentrate on building a logically ordered resume containing appropriate keywords since information technology (IT) resumes are generally sent by e-mail in an unembellished text format
- still create a strong core resume that is easy to adapt should aesthetics become important

Specific Points

❶ If a resume was not sent by e-mail, a printed e-mail address may be key to receiving acknowledgment after a resume is scanned into an automated personnel system.

❷ The overview quickly indicates the level of responsibility she seeks; supervisory, in this instance.

❸ Information technology resumes show technical experience first using keywords recognizable both to programs that evaluate resumes electronically and to people who read them.

❹ Experience section is focused on the job announcement and how she meets the employer's requirements.

❺ Work History substantiates her claims of experience and documents her progress through greater levels of responsibility.

❻ Work History accounts for her continuous employment from graduation through your current position.

❼ Work History also communicates the scope of her responsibilities and includes additional keywords that respond to employer requirements.

❽ A mix of public and private sector employment is desirable in some positions.

❾ Shows that she has occupied the kinds of positions she will be supervising.

❿ Professional certification is often on a par with college training in the IT field.

THERESA P. GOODWIN

4303 Fernlake Drive
Carrolton, TX 75006
972-562-6403 • FAX 972-835-9027
tgoodwin@compuserv.com

OBJECTIVE

A Supervisory Systems Analyst position in which to take a leading role in the design and development of custom applications.

TECHNICAL STRENGTHS

Possess extensive knowledge and experience in managing systems analysis, design, construction, and implementation projects to include:

- Development of shared applications
- GUI and CASE technology
- Implementation using Mainframe, Client/Server, and LAN configurations
- Knowledgeable of UNIX, NetWare, TCP/IP, and Windows 98
- Database competencies include DB2, Oracle, Paradox, and Powerbuilder
- Background in recovery/restart, input/output control, and file backup
- SDLC documentation

WORK HISTORY

2000-02—<u>Lead System Analyst</u>. Healthcare Cooperative Corporation, Lucerne, PA. Managed all aspects of systems design and development of custom applications. Supervised six programmer analysts using UNIX, Netware, TCP/IP, and Windows 98 technologies. Multiple database competencies used on Mainframe, Client/Server, and LAN configurations.

1997-00—<u>Programmer Analyst</u>. Co-Orbital Systems, Duke Research Park, SC. Worked on Year 2000 tasks for data collection systems using COBOL, IDMS, and JCL. ADS/O implementation and system enhancement.

1993-97—<u>Computer Systems Analyst I</u>. Clark County Government Center, Wilburn, NC. Provided technical and operational support to users countywide. Assisted in developing and distributing system and user documentation. Assisted in PC installation, maintenance, and troubleshooting.

1991-93—<u>JCL programmer</u>. Valley Healthcare Systems, Los Angeles, CA. Setting up systems to run and recover batch processing.

EDUCATION AND CERTIFICATION

- Austin Peay University, TN—Bachelor of Science in Computer Studies, 1991
- Oracle Certified Database Administrator (DBA)
- Microsoft Certified Systems Engineer (MCSE)

Teacher Aide

COMPETENCY CLUSTER RESUME

General Strategy

Ms. Sherington is a teacher aide without a particularly impressive list of jobs held. What she does have is a composite set of experiences that will be viewed with respect by someone looking for a competent assistant in the classroom. To present her skills more attractively, she has decided to use the Competency Cluster Resume.

The tasks to be accomplished by this resume are to:

- show a combination of life experiences and training that qualify her to serve as a paraprofessional teacher
- back the claims with character, educational, and working experiences that will give her claims substance

Specific Points

❶ Present position is part-time and rather informal so she elects to be called at home, rather than at an office where the response might be uncertain.

❷ Summary and Objective states what she wants to do and qualifications.

❸ Skills are grouped in such a manner as to address the main concerns of the potential hiring official.

❹ Where possible, institutional experience is shown first and then further supported by less formal, in-the-home experience.

❺ Specific classroom assisting tasks are listed and can be verified.

❻ Classroom management assistance is probably what is needed most in the setting to which she aspires.

❼ Supporting skills: first aid and awareness of childhood health concerns.

❽ Personal character is important and must be established.

❾ Experience frames the chronology of her adult life and lists relevant, if less than full-time experience.

❿ The college certificate will strengthen her claim to competency and appeal to those who work in a highly credential-oriented field like teaching.

Helen M. Sherington

104 Sandstone Road
Wilmington, DE 19802
302-977-9887 (Residence)
helen104@aol.com ← **①**

② Summary and Objective

Experienced, formally-trained paraprofessional with young children in preschool educational settings seeks full-time public school position as a teacher's aide at the kindergarten or grades 1–3 level.

Relevant Skills

③

CHILD CARE **④**
- Assisted in the operation of a 23-child church day-care center for two years
- Privately cared for four preschool children at my residence for three years

CLASSROOM MANAGEMENT **⑤**
- Prepared art project materials
- Assisted with math and reading drills
- Arranged rest areas
- Led game activities
- Typed and reproduced materials

⑥

HEALTH CARE **⑦**
- Certified in Red Cross First Aid
- Trained in early childhood health

PERSONAL CHARACTER **⑧**
- Married mother of two teenagers
- Ten-year resident of this community
- Active in community affairs
- Extensive references available

Experience

⑨

<u>June 2000 - Present</u>: Day care center assistant, United Lutheran Church, Beltsville, DE.

<u>June 1998 - May 2000</u>: Private day care provider at my residence.

<u>July 1988 - May 1998</u>: Housewife and mother.

Education

Certificate
Child Care
Beacon Junior College, DE, 1996

⑩

Technical Writer

WORK HISTORY RESUME

General Strategy

Mr. Akrin has several positions that constitute the sum total of his working experience and they are the context of his achievements. He decided that the best approach for him was to present a simple, but thorough, Work History Resume that would do a good job of:

- showing that he is a competent technical writer with the background to function at a computer user-oriented magazine

- detailing the kinds of training and experience that show technical preparation for this kind of writing

Specific Points

❶ Overview frames the experience, training, and aspirations of the applicant.

❷ Experience is arrayed in such a manner as to break out the two positions, separate them by full-time study, and provide continuity to the brief section.

❸ The Brainware position establishes him as a technical writer in the industry.

❹ It also notes experience that would parallel the kinds of areas covered by a user-magazine writer—national workshops, instructions for laymen, etc.

❺ The study break should be shown—keeps the chronology unbroken.

❻ The Matson position shows that he has the technical expertise for his writing.

❼ Worked directly with users—indicative of sensitivity to their interests.

❽ User magazines really serve as a link between users and manufacturers, so these experiences are probably going to be attractive to the person hiring.

❾ The technical expertise is well addressed educationally by his associate degree.

❿ The bachelor's degree in technical writing completes the ideal credentials.

William K. Akrin
56 Tura Road
Bennington, CT 48009
860-222-9988 (Office)
860-333-9075 (Residence)
wmakrin@att.net

❶ **Overview**

Technical Writer with formal training and experience in computer technology and technical writing seeks editorial opportunity with mass market user's magazine.

❷ **Experience**

January 1998 - Present: Technical Writer
Brainware Computer Products, Inc., Bennington, CT.

❸ Assist in the preparation of technical manuals that support the use of software products created at Brainware. Experience includes interviewing programmers and systems engineers to identify program features. Convey features and step-by-step instructions for use in lay language. Attend national workshops to receive feedback on manuals and products. Full range of mass market software including desktop publishing, graphic arts, and business packages featuring word processing, databases, spreadsheets, etc. **❹**

❺ September 1995 - December 1998
Full-time study for Bachelor's degree.

❻ June 1993 - August 1995: Customer Service Technician
Matson Software, Ltd., Norwich, CT.

❼ Telephone contact for users of Matson Software products including their complete line of word processing, spreadsheet, graphic presentation, and database programs. Assisted users in isolating their problems and guiding them to solutions. Maintained records on nature of questions addressed and assisted technical writing staff in the revision of manuals. **❽**

Education

Associate in Arts (AA)
Computer Studies
Asnuntuck Junior College, CT, 1993
❾

Bachelor of Technology (BT)
Technical Writing
West Connecticut College, CT, 2000

Telecommunications Specialist

COMPETENCY CLUSTER RESUME

General Strategy

Mr. Goodwell feels that his worth exceeds the sum total of the two job descriptions that he would be presenting with a standard resume. With his technical orientation and the specific nature of his services, he chose to portray himself in the aggregate using a Competency Cluster Resume.

The objective of his resume is to:

- place in bold relief the several highly marketable things that he can do
- back them up with job settings and strong educational credentials that imply that he has the substance to deliver

Specific Points

❶ Overview is used to sketch experience, indicate goal, and show confidence in his ability to thrive in a performance-based pay environment.

❷ Areas of Competency as a topic group draws the reviewer immediately to the productive substance of what he can do, not a mere job description.

❸ Examples briefly show levels of technology and markets where they are used.

❹ Not tied to a single vendor—broader, more independent status established.

❺ Demonstrates hands-on field service experience useful in his proposed role.

❻ Ability to implement and manage user services is evidenced here.

❼ Consulting experience is verified.

❽ Sales experience is noted as well as implied knowledge of the major provider's products and operation.

❾ An applied associate degree is presented.

❿ A specialized technical bachelor's degree caps his formal credentials.

Bernard K. Goodwell
76 La Junta Drive
Colorado Springs, CO 80908
719-332-0983 (Office)
719-776-8955 (Residence)
berngood@erols.com

❶ **Overview:** Six years of designing and marketing commercial telecommunications services. Seeking growth opportunity in the western United States. Receptive to performance-based compensation arrangement in consulting or end-user applications.

Areas of Competency

❷

NEEDS EVALUATION

- Assessment of voice, fax, data, and video requirements in banking, insurance, manufacturing and government environments. **❸**
- Appraisal of volume, costs, and best use of technology.

EQUIPMENT SELECTION

- Independent perspective based on solid technical education and international industry familiarity.
- Established contacts with major vendors. **❹**

SERVICES SELECTION

- Knowledgeable in the available contractible services sectors, both majors and independents.

INSTALLATION **❺**

- Supervised the installation of 25 to 500 set, multifunction telecommunications systems.

OPERATION **❻**

- Managed the user training programs of all installations sold.

Experience

❼ June 2000 - Present: Telecommunications Consultant, Buena Vista Technical Consulting, Ltd., Boulder, CO.

❽ July 1996 - May 2000: Commercial Services Sales Representative, Mountain States Telephone, Denver, CO.

Education

Associate in Science (AS)
Digital Electronics
Mead Community College, AZ 1993
❾

Bachelor of Science (BS)
Telecommunications
State University of Colorado 1996
❿

Television Support Technician

FOCUSED RESUME

General Strategy

Ms. Arnold is seeking recognition in a combination technical and artistic specialty where specific abilities and experience are more important than job listings and duties performed. In order to make the most of her attributes, she has elected to present her record in the Focused Resume format.

The tasks to be accomplished by the resume are to:

- show an aggregate of skills gained in several settings that, together, have a greater value than their individual parts
- provide the concrete employment and training structure to show that she has been consistently productive within the industry

Specific Points

❶ Overview begins with award-winning status and moves on to touch segments of the industry worked.

❷ Her objective is also presented in the opening statement.

❸ Professional Abilities outlines the categories of technical and artistic skill that the reviewer would be laboring to pick from a less pointed resume.

❹ The kinds of productions supported must be made clear.

❺ Status on the production team speaks to authority and role.

❻ Industry-recognized awards cast their glow on those who worked on their more mundane production aspects as well as the stars and producers—claim credit when due.

❼ Achievements is the section that tangibly confirms excellence.

❽ Union cards are so important that they legitimately constitute an achievement.

❾ A team player on award-winning productions.

❿ Employment record and the education credential round out her picture of overall competence.

Margaret A. Arnold
89 University Drive
Santa Marina, CA 93455
310-886-1903 (Office)
310-876-3921 (Residence)
magarn@mindspring.com

❶ Overview

Award-winning Television Support Technician with national experience in multiple aspects of professional news, talk show, and drama productions seeks network or national cable opportunity. **❷**

Professional Abilities

❸
- SET MANAGEMENT — six years of experience in the management of set activities supporting news, talk show, and dramatic television productions. ◄ **❹**
- LIGHTING — four years as associate lighting director for a producer of nationally syndicated television musical productions. Accomplished user of Kludge and special effects lighting in television applications. ◄ **❺**
- SET DESIGN — three years professional and five years amateur set design. Professional years included assistant background construction director for the Emmy Award winning docudrama *War and Space.* **❻**

❼ Achievements

❽
- Union cards held in the areas of television stage management, lighting, and set design.

❾
- On the staff of seven production companies that received national industry recognition for excellence during my tenure.
- 1991 Audience Appreciation Award winner for set design in the live audience participation *Minnie Walker Talk Show* series.

Experience

<u>June 1996 - Present</u>: Set Manager, Gordon Boxwood Studios, Hollywood, CA.
<u>June 1995 - May 1996</u>: Set Design Specialist, KNBB, Santa Clarita, CA.
<u>July 1992 - May 1995</u>: Lighting Technician, Samuel Whitworth Production Company, Los Angeles, CA.
❿

Education

Associate in Science (AS)
Electronics Technology
Allan Whetstone Junior College, CA 1992

Training and Development Specialist

WORK HISTORY RESUME

General Strategy

Dr. Burnside has a unique situation that can be strongly presented in a traditional format—his special talent has been the direct outgrowth of a specific series of occupational experiences that describe him well. He has chosen the Work History Resume to paint a well-ordered picture of his somewhat unusual situation.

The objective of his resume is to establish that:

- he has a successful consulting practice that would be an attractive affiliation for an established training organization
- it all stems from a totally verifiable and respectable rise through traditional professional positions

Specific Points

❶ Affirms his status, specialty, and what he is seeking in a brief Overview.

❷ Experience section is used to show how he put his consulting practice together while pursuing a traditional career.

❸ It begins with a description of his current practice.

❹ Evidence is presented of the growing demand and established reputation. His attractiveness is enhanced by illustrating the successful use of a personally created Web page to expand his business.

❺ Shows how he remained in the mainstream while completing his doctorate and establishing a consulting business.

❻ A solid base of traditional experience and the source of inspiration for his consulting orientation.

❼ His publications would be important to those considering adding him to their stable of authoritative presenters.

❽ His basic degrees are now important background for his consulting field.

❾ The doctor's degree lends authority to his presentations and writing.

❿ Comments explain that he is offering a share of his proven product if an established organization will free him to pursue his specialty.

Robert J. Burnside, Ph.D.

233 Eastwood Street
Beebe, AR 72012
501-883-7913 (Office)
501-989-2244 (Residence)
rob233@westlink.com

① **Overview:** Established national sales and motivation trainer seeks affiliation with a major consulting firm based in the Southeastern United States.

② **Experience**

③ June 2000 - Present: **Independent Training Consultant, Robert J. Burnside, Ph.D., Inc.,** Beebe, AR. Published *The Burnside System for Sales and Motivation* and toured nationally promoting its use in the selling industry. A two-day seminar was structured and presented at 62 companies and six national sales meetings during the past two years. Future schedule includes 37 commitments with deposits. Strong interest expressed in follow-on presentations **④** at advanced level. Used Claris Home Page software to create a personal business Web page that attracts inquiries from markets not previously reached.

June 1992 - November 2000: **Adjunct Faculty Member, Beebe Area Community College.** Taught adult evening courses in career decision making and small business start-up skills **⑤** while completing dissertation, writing, and establishing independent consulting firm in industrial training.

July 1983 - May 1992: **Industrial Arts Teacher, Thurmont High School,** Casey, AR. Taught shop courses to high school students seeking positions in industry. Earned master's degree **⑥** part-time during this period, then began evening employment as a trainer in local industries. Developed insights regarding motivation and success and began doctoral studies in counseling.

⑦ **National Publications**

The Burnside System, 2000
Selling in the Professional Market, 2001

Education

Bachelor of Arts (B.A.) Teacher Education Smith University, TX, 1983	**⑧**	Master of Education (M.Ed.) Industrial Arts Arkansas State University, 1986

Doctor of Philosophy (Ph.D.)
⑨ Counseling
Florida University, 1993

Comments

⑩ The reason for seeking affiliation is that the growth in demand for my services precludes the timely development of follow-on products that have great potential. Willing to exchange partial rights for business management of my seminar business.

Travel Agent

FOCUSED RESUME

General Strategy

Ms. Winters is a very productive travel agent with a special set of skills that she wants to present very clearly. The prospect of listing jobs and duties is not appealing and would not do her justice. She is advised to use a Focused Resume to make the most of her brief but appealing presentation.

The objective of her resume is to:

- describe a geographic travel specialty that she has developed into an attractive and profitable niche

- verify that her claim is substantive—complete with productivity figures

Specific Points

❶ Her Objective states what she is trying to achieve in terms interesting to the potential recipients of her resume.

❷ It also identifies the specialty that she is promoting—Alaskan group travel.

❸ Capabilities tells just exactly what she can deliver—and does so briefly.

❹ Ability to take her presentations to her potential customers is noted.

❺ Experienced tour leader adds to the appeal.

❻ Willing and able to handle the essential routine.

❼ Experienced in coordinating with other travel professionals using the cutting-edge technology of the Internet.

❽ Accomplishments proves she can deliver—meaningful specifics given.

❾ Yeoman experience in the industry is a matter of verifiable record.

❿ Possesses some formal training in the business.

Suzanne V. Winters
4111 Providence Avenue
Fairbanks, AK 99702
907-747-9002 (Office)
907-776-7566 (Residence)
suzwin@msn.com

❶

Objective — Affiliation with a major mainland chain or franchise as a specialist in the promotion of Alaskan group travel. **❷**

Capabilities

- Lower-48-states sales presentations to promote Alaska agency sponsored activities **❹**

- Group presentations to civic and business groups

❸ - Group tour leadership **❺**

- Associated travel office routine and clerical responsibilities **❻**

- Liaison with specialized agencies and tour providers internationally using the Internet. Skilled in using search engine capabilities to research client special requests. **❼**

Accomplishments

- Personally responsible for the sale of $278,000 in group travel from mainland and Hawaii affiliates in 2001.

❽ - Initiated program of cooperative promotion with State Tourism Agency that has yielded 1,823 referrals in the first eight months of operation.

- Designed custom tour for environmental groups following oil spill that attracted an aggregate of 483 travelers in a six-month period.

Experience

June 2000 - Present: *Travel Consultant,* Ask Mr. Williams Agency, Fairbanks, AK.

❾ June 1996 - May 2000: *Travel Agent,* Express Independent Travel, Ltd., Anchorage, AK.

Education

Certificate in Travel and Tourism
Anchorage Business College, AK 1996

❿

Veterinary Technician

COMPETENCY CLUSTER RESUME

General Strategy

Mr. Kline is a specialized animal health paraprofessional whose talents lend themselves well to presentation under the format of the Competency Cluster Resume. While his attributes would be there to find in a more traditional resume, this approach brings them together for greater impact.

His resume is crafted specifically to:

- show a large-animal veterinarian that he has the groups of skills that can form clear profit centers in his practice
- substantiate the claim with specific examples, impressive experience, and legitimate professional credentials

Specific Points

❶ Overview and Objective classify the candidate and say what he wants to do and where.

❷ AVMA certification of his program makes him instantly credible.

❸ Routine vet paraprofessional skills are recounted.

❹ Specialized skills like AI are added attractions.

❺ Emergency field treatment qualifications will appeal to his market—the large-animal vet.

❻ Working experience as a staff vet on a major ranch is of substantial value.

❼ Previous experience in private practice is desirable.

❽ Student experience was with the industry.

❾ The associate degree qualifies him for his specialty.

❿ The special quality of his degree is its AVMA certification—a point worth highlighting both here and under Professional Abilities.

Cary J. Kline, Jr.
788 Overpass Drive
Glendale, AZ 85301
602-345-9878 (Office)
602-667-6483 (Residence)
caryj@hotmail.com

❶ Overview and Objective

Large animal veterinary technician with over six years' experience in the treatment of commercial beef cattle seeks private practice affiliation in the Southwestern United States.

Professional Abilities ❷

❸
- Graduate of American Veterinary Medical Association (AVMA) program
- Trained in large animal care
- Experienced in the administration of medication and vaccinations
- Artificial insemination specialist ← **❹**
- Surgical assisting
- Emergency field treatment of farm animals **❺**
- X-ray and laboratory procedures

❻
Experience

June 2000 - Present: *Veterinary Technician,* Queen Ranch, Glendale, AZ.

June 1996 - May 2000: *Veterinary Technician,* Davidson Large Animal Clinic, Glendale, AZ. **❼**

July 1994 - May 1996: *Seasonal employment* in the commercial cattle
❽ finishing industry of Northern Arizona as a work-study student in veterinary technology.

Education

❾ Associate in Applied Science (AAS)
Veterinary Technology
An AVMA Approved Program of Study
Community College of Tucson, 1996
❿

Web Developer

FOCUSED RESUME

General Strategy

Mr. Wohler's IT resume addresses a specific job and specialized kind of work so it is best structured as a Focused Resume, which helps to:

- highlight specific kinds of technical skills
- concentrate on building a logically ordered resume containing appropriate keywords since information technology (IT) resumes are generally sent by e-mail in an unembellished text format
- still create a strong core resume that is easy to adapt should aesthetics become important

Specific Points

❶ A complete address element for an IT resume should include e-mail. Use an office address if you are satisfied with the privacy aspect; when in doubt use private e-mail.

❷ The overview signals his area of specialization, financial in this case.

❸ Information technology resumes show technical experience first using keywords recognizable both to programs that evaluate them electronically and to people who read them.

❹ Experience section focuses on the job announcement and how he meets the employer's requirements.

❺ Work History substantiates claims of experience and documents progress through greater levels of responsibility.

❻ Work History accounts for continuous employment from college graduation through his current position.

❼ Work History also communicates the scope of his responsibilities and is the place to convey additional keywords that respond to employer requirements.

❽ Notes work experience in his area of professional certification.

❾ Paints a word picture of his work environment that communicates the scope of his responsibilities.

❿ Professional certification is often on a par with college training in the IT field.

MUIR L. WOHLER
130 Matheson Street
Tucson, AZ 85732
520-397-8888 • FAX 520-397-8648
wohlerm@backroadsaz.com

OBJECTIVE

Web Developer position providing support for both intra- and extranet servers in a financial environment.

TECHNICAL EXPERIENCE

- Three years full-time line experience as a Web developer
- Development support expertise for both intra- (IIS) and extranet (TBD) servers
- 4D and SQL Server relational database experience
- Extensive use of HTML in Web page design
- Other programming and applications experience includes: MS Access, VB5, CGI, Cpp, ActiveX, and ASP

WORK HISTORY

1999-2002—<u>Manager of Online Services.</u> ABC Lending Technologies, Inc., Phoenix, AZ. Managed all aspects of identifying, implementing, and maintaining online services provided through the firm's site on the Internet. Used the Web site development and technologies described above to present online features to serve current and potential customer groups.

1996-99—<u>Applications Engineer.</u> Dingwel Investment Information, Inc., Flagstaff, AZ. Oracle Server 7 and MS SQL 6.5 server database administrator designing and implementing Internet strategies. Experience included Windows NT Server 4.0, MS Exchange Server 5.5, DNS, IIS 3.0, Proxy Server 2.0 and Sequel Technology, Inc. Net Access Manager 2.0. Responsible for second-level support enterprise applications and information production software.

EDUCATION AND CERTIFICATION

University of Arizona
Bachelor of Science in Computer Studies, 1996
Microsoft Certified Systems Engineer (MCSE), 1998

Word-Processing Operator

COMPETENCY CLUSTER RESUME

General Strategy

Ms. McDaniel has a narrow specialty and a specific goal in mind. Her strongest presentation format is the Competency Cluster Resume because it will allow her to:

- separate herself from the secretarial stereotype by graphically featuring her very specialized talents

- package herself in such a manner as to convey both special skills and traditional preparation, including clerical experience and formal training

Specific Points

❶ Overview tells the reviewer that a very specific situation is being sought.

❷ The specialization involves both the word-processing product and the fact that the applicant aspires to a training role.

❸ Identifies the product and systems in order to allow effective employer screening and save the inconvenience of an interview by an inappropriate employer.

❹ Mentions the mail-merge and other tasks that can be efficiently done.

❺ Associate the capability with the most modern office technology—that based on telecommunications by fax and modem.

❻ Mentions the ability to support tabular and graphics applications.

❼ Speed in entering data remains an important attribute.

❽ Supporting software that enhances the final product is valuable to cite.

❾ Experience in the clerical environment is established.

❿ Formal training underwrites her practical skills.

Anna P. McDaniel
2909 Phoenix Avenue
Montgomery, AL 36196
334-727-5990 (Office)
334-884-1243 (Residence)
annamc@juno.com

❶ Overview

Single product word-processing specialist with in-depth capabilities in the production and handling of business correspondence and documents in all formats. Seeking large office environment where production activities can be supplemented by the training and supervision of others. **❷**

Word-Processing Capabilities

❸ • Expert user of Microsoft Word on Macintosh and IBM systems.

❹ • Mail-merge specialist experienced in the custom mailing of personalized correspondence.

❺ • Highly competent in the sending, receipt, and reformatting of electronically transmitted documents.

• Accomplished in the integration of tabular data and graphics into word-processing documents. **❻**

❼ • 80 WPM for text entry.

• Thorough familiarity with the use of spell-check and other supporting software.

❽ • Extensive laser printer experience as well as tractor-fed forms and label printers.

Experience

<u>June 2000 - Present</u>: <u>Word-Processing Specialist</u>
Alabama Northern Electrical Cooperative, Enterprise, AL.

<u>June 1996 - May 2000</u>: <u>Secretary</u>
❾ Alabama Association of Real Estate Appraisers, Montgomery, AL.

Education

Diploma in Secretarial Science
Enterprise Community College, AL 1996 **❿**

BIBLIOGRAPHY

"Application of the Employee Polygraph Protection Act of 1988; Final Rule." *Federal Register*, March 4, 1991.

Bacas, Harry. "Hiring the Best." *Nation's Business*, October 1987, pp. 68–71.

Beardsley, Tim. "Mind Reader: Do Personality Tests Pick Out Bad Apples?" *Scientific American*, April 1991, pp. 154–56.

Bolles, Richard N. *What Color Is Your Parachute?* Berkeley, Calif.: Ten Speed Press, 32nd edition, 2002.

Braham, James. "Hiring Mr. Wrong." *Industry Week*, March 7, 1988, pp. 31–34.

Brown, Paul B. "Every Picture Tells a Story." *INC.*, August 1987, pp. 18–21.

Byrne, John. "All the Right Moves for Interviewers." *Business Week*, September 17, 1990, p. 156.

"Charges: Filing a Charge." Washington, DC: U.S. Equal Employment Opportunity Commission, November 1988.

"The Charging Party: Your Rights and Responsibilities." Washington, DC: U.S. Equal Employment Opportunity Commission, February 1990.

"Check It Out." *INC.*, November 1988, p. 148.

Dumaine, Brian. "The New Art of Hiring Smart." *Fortune*, August 17, 1987, pp. 78–81.

"Foolish Interviews." *USAir Magazine*, April 1991, p. 11.

"Get the Bad News, Too." *INC.*, January 1989, p. 107.

"Health Benefits Under the Consolidated Omnibus Budget Reconciliation Act." Washington, DC: Pension and Welfare Benefits Administration, U.S. Department of Labor, 1990.

"How to File a Claim for Your Benefits." Washington, DC: Pension and Welfare Benefits Administration, U.S. Department of Labor, 1991.

How to Obtain Employee Benefit Documents from the Labor Department. Washington: Pension and Welfare Benefits Administration, U.S. Department of Labor, February 1990.

Holland, John L. *The Psychology of Vocational Choice*. Waltham, Mass.: Blaisdell Publishing Company, 1966.

"Julia Roberts: 20 Questions." *Playboy*, November 1991, pp. 151–57.

"Information, Please." *INC.*, June 1989, pp. 135–39.

Mannix, Margaret, Diane Duke, and Marc Silver. "What References?" *U.S. News & World Report*, April 15, 1991, p. 74.

Moreau, Dan. "Answers That Get You Hired." *Changing Times*, April 1989, pp. 53–55.

"NOTICE: Employee Polygraph Protection Act (WH Publication 1462)." Washington, DC: U.S. Department of Labor, September 1988.

"Part 1607—Uniform Guidelines on Employee Selection Procedures (1978)." 29 CFR Chap. XIV (July 1, 1990 edition). Washington, DC: U.S. Equal Employment Opportunity Commission, July 1990.

Pension and Annuity Income, Publication 575. Washington: Internal Revenue Service, 1991.

Pollan, Stephen M., and Mark Levin. "How to Survive Getting Fired." *New York*, September 7, 1992, pp. 26–35.

Posner, Bruce G. "Hiring the Best." *INC.*, April 1989, pp. 169–70.

Richardson, Douglas B. "The Confessions of a Skeptical Resume Reader: What Happens When Your Resume Is 1 of 400." Dow Jones, *National Business Employment Weekly* reprint (undated).

Rohan, Thomas M. "New Tips on Screening Employees." *Industry Week*, January 4, 1988, pp. 33–35.

Schabacker, Kirsten. "Candid Candidates: New and Revealing Interview Tactics." *Working Woman*, September 1990, pp. 62–63.

Statement on pre-employment tests (untitled two-page handout). Washington, DC: U.S. Equal Employment Opportunity Commission (undated).

"Unemployment Strategies." *Harper's*, December 1989, p. 20.

"User's Companion to *Poor's Register*": A Primer of 89 Proven Methods for Effectively Using *Standard & Poor's Register of Corporations*, "Directors and Executives." New York: Standard & Poor's Corporation, 1983.

Welter, Therese R. "Interviewing for a Job—by Satellite." *Industry Week*, May 18, 1987, p. 94.

What You Should Know About the Pension Law. Washington: Pension and Welfare Benefits Administration, U.S. Department of Labor, May 1988.

"Your Pension: Things You Should Know About Your Pension Plan." Washington, DC: Pension Benefit Guaranty Corporation, undated.

INDEX